ALSO BY MICHAEL DOBBS

Down with Big Brother:
The Fall of the Soviet Empire

MADELEINE
ALBRIGHT

MADELEINE ALBRIGHT

A Twentieth-Century Odyssey

Michael Dobbs

An Owl Book
HENRY HOLT AND COMPANY | NEW YORK

Henry Holt and Company, LLC
Publishers since 1866
115 West 18th Street
New York, New York 10011

Henry Holt® is a registered trademark
of Henry Holt and Company, LLC.

Published in Canada by Fitzhenry & Whiteside Ltd.,
195 Allstate Parkway, Markham, Ontario L3R 4T8.
Frontispiece photo credit: *The Washington Post*

Library of Congress Cataloging-in-Publication Data
Dobbs, Michael, date.
Madeleine Albright: a twentieth-century odyssey / Michael Dobbs.
p. cm.
Includes bibliographical references and index.
ISBN 0-8050-5660-2
1. Albright, Madeleine, Korbel. 2. Women cabinet officers—United
States—Biography. 3. Cabinet officers—United States—Biography.
4. United Nations—Officials and employees—Biography.
5. Ambassadors—United States—Biography.   I. Title.
E840.8.A37D63   1999   98-53592
327.73'0092—dc21   CIP
[b]

Henry Holt books are available for special promotions and
premiums. For details contact: Director, Special Markets.

First published in hardcover in 1999 by
Henry Holt and Company

First Owl Books Edition 2000

DESIGNED BY KELLY SOONG TOO

Family tree lettering and design by Jackie Aher

Printed in the United States of America
1   3   5   7   9   10   8   6   4   2

For my parents

CONTENTS

So we beat on, boats against the current,
borne back ceaselessly into the past.

—F. Scott Fitzgerald,
The Great Gatsby

Auguste Körbel (1) died in 1929.

Her oldest son, Arnošt (2), was killed in the Holocaust, together with his wife, Olga (3). Their descendants now live in the United States, England, and Czechoslovakia. Their granddaughter, Madeleine Korbel Albright, became U.S. secretary of state in 1997.

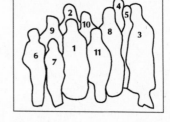

Another son, Karel (4), was killed in the Holocaust with his wife, Grete (5), and oldest son, Gert (6). Their younger son Chaim (7) escaped to Israel.

The oldest daughter of Auguste Körbel, Marta Mahler (8), was killed in the Holocaust. Some of her descendants survived and now live in Brazil.

Another daughter, Emma Altbach (9), survived the Holocaust, together with her children, Mimi and Trude (10) and (11). Their descendants live in Argentina.

Courtesy of Chaim Körbel.

A holiday snapshot taken in the summer of 1927. Three generations of a Czech Jewish family are gathered around a seventy-five-year-old matriarch. The expressions on their faces are happy, even serene. Fortune has smiled on this family. Thanks to new economic opportunities and their own restless energy, they have burst out of the medieval ghetto in which their people had been confined for many centuries. They live in a peaceful, democratic country in the heart of Europe.

By the time the small boy in this picture reaches adulthood, he will lose his father, mother, and brother to the most horrific violence the world has ever seen. More than half the relatives beside him will be killed in the Holocaust, their ashes resting in places like Auschwitz, Treblinka, and Terezín. The others will be scattered across the globe, like leaves before a tornado.

The survivors will rebuild their shattered lives with the same boldness and resilience that enabled their ancestors to escape the ghetto. Determined to overcome past tragedy, some will reject their Jewish origins; others will embrace Judaism all the more. The boy with the cheeky grin will become a Zionist, settle in Israel, and found a kibbutz. Several of his cousins will convert to Christianity. Various family members will build skyscrapers, write books, create profitable businesses, become teachers. By the end of the century, the family diaspora will stretch from Prague to São Paulo, from Tel Aviv to Los Angeles, from London to Buenos Aires.

The old lady in the snapshot is Auguste Körbel. One of her great-grandchildren will become America's first woman secretary of state. This is her story. But it is also the story of a family whose suffering and determination made her ascent possible.

FAMILY OF MANDULA SPIEGEL

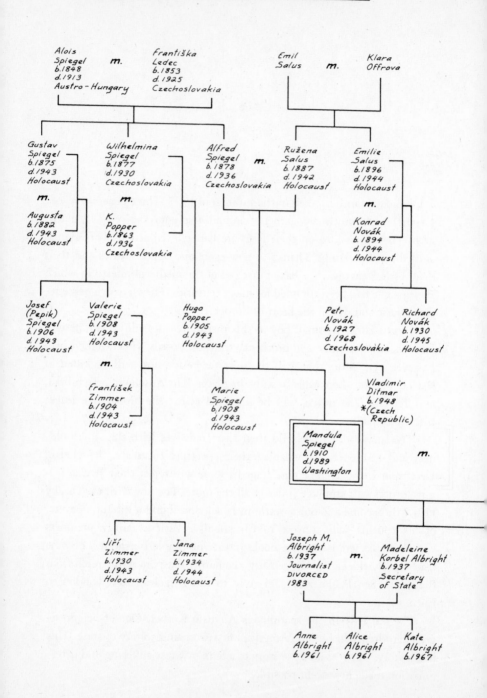

FAMILY OF JOSEF KORBEL

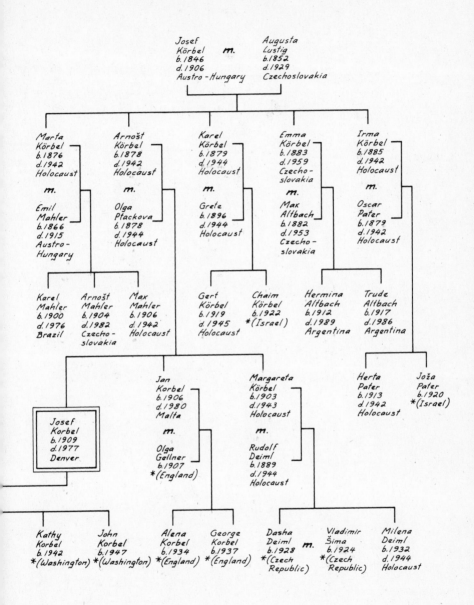

* Residence as of December 1998

MADELEINE
ALBRIGHT

Introduction

The first time I met Madeleine Albright was at a reception for diplomatic reporters in a glittering banquet hall on the eighth floor of the State Department. President Clinton had sworn her in as America's sixty-fourth secretary of state the previous week, and she was still basking in the euphoria of becoming the first woman to be appointed to a job once held by Thomas Jefferson. It was a happy occasion, and Madeleine was at her charming, effervescent best. She worked the room like a seasoned politician, taking time to talk to everybody individually and telling amusing stories about her life as the daughter of a distinguished Czechoslovak diplomat.

"You know the picture of the little girl in the national costume presenting flowers to visiting dignitaries at the airport?" she told a group of us, as a waiter filled our glasses with champagne. "Well, that was me, growing up. I used to do that for a living."

That first, brief encounter helped me understand one of the main reasons for an extraordinary American success story. It is difficult not to like Madeleine Albright. She has a genuinely engaging personality. She is warm, intelligent, and fun to be around. Unlike many public figures, she does not take herself too seriously. She seems humbled by her own achievements. Her enthusiasm is infectious, even touching, as is her gratitude to America for allowing her and her family to live out the classic immigrant's dream. She can use her sharp tongue to devastating effect but has a knack for softening the blow with a smile or a quip. There is a self-deprecating quality to her humor. For all her worldly success, she still conveys an aura of innocence and vulnerability that makes people want to root for her.

But there is another side to Madeleine Albright's character that is equally important in understanding her remarkable ascent. Beneath an attractive, easygoing exterior, she has a tough interior. Without a steely resolve and an ability to pursue a goal single-mindedly, she would never have reached the pinnacle of American political life. It is this relentless determination that, ultimately, sets her apart from thousands of equally talented colleagues languishing in obscure corners of the U.S. bureaucracy or academia. She seems to organize her life into neat compartments, shutting out unwelcome information. When challenged on matters involving her identity or self-image, she can be combative and inflexible. It was this aspect of her personality that struck me most at our second meeting, which took place the day after the formal State Department reception.

As a diplomatic reporter for *The Washington Post*, I had been researching an article for our Sunday magazine about her family background. My interest had been piqued by her moving description of how her family had built a new life for themselves in America after escaping the horrors of Nazism and communism. As she once remarked, her view of the world was molded not by "Vietnam," like most of her contemporaries, but by "Munich." "Vietnam" was political shorthand for the international quagmire that America got itself into in the sixties and seventies, "Munich" for the disastrous policy of appeasement pursued by Britain and France that paved the way for Hitler's aggression against Madeleine's native Czechoslovakia. I thought I could explain a lot about the foreign policy philosophy of the new secretary of state by tracing her journey from Prague to Washington.

By talking to old friends of the family and a cousin stranded in Czechoslovakia after the Communist takeover in 1948, I stumbled across an extraordinary story. It turned out that many members of Madeleine's extended family, including three grandparents and a first cousin, had been killed in the Holocaust as Jews. In an attempt to protect their family from a revival of anti-Semitism after the war, Madeleine's parents had converted to Roman Catholicism. The fate of their relatives became a closely guarded family secret. Madeleine, who was only seven when the war ended, insisted she was told nothing about the family's Jewish origins and the connection to the Holocaust.

We met in the secretary's private office on the seventh floor of the State Department, just off a corridor lined with portraits of her predecessors, from Jefferson to George C. Marshall. It was the first interview that she had granted in her new position, and both of us were a little on edge. I had given her aides a broad outline of my discoveries nearly two weeks in advance of our meeting, so she knew roughly what was coming. Even so, as I presented her with documents showing that her relatives had died in places like Terezín and Auschwitz, I felt as if I were somehow challenging a carefully constructed family myth. The revelations must have been painful to her, but she kept her emotions under tight control.

One of the documents in my possession was a photo of Madeleine, aged one, playing happily in Prague with her cousins, Dasha and Milena, aged ten and six (page 30). Four years after the photo was taken, Milena was gassed at Auschwitz. Her sister Dasha spent the war years in London with Madeleine's family, returning home in 1945 only to discover that her own parents and sister had been killed in the Holocaust. She was the long-lost cousin I had been to see in Prague.

Before our meeting, I had debated with myself over whether to show Madeleine this heartrending picture. It would probably have been more tactful just to give her the photo in an envelope, so she could look at it privately. In the end, my journalistic instincts got the better of me. It seemed to me that the picture of these three innocent young girls told the family story better than I could possibly express in words. Had Madeleine's parents not spirited her out of Czechoslovakia days after the Nazi invasion in March 1939, she would almost certainly have shared Milena's fate. Had they stayed in Czechoslovakia in February 1948 after the Communist coup, she might have ended up like Dasha. A potential secretary of state would have been left to rot in the soul-destroying atmosphere of a totalitarian regime. I thought that the sight of her two cousins might prompt her to contrast her own good fortune with the tragedy that had befallen so many of her relatives.

As I handed the picture to her, I asked if she recognized any of the people in it.

"Well, I recognize everybody," she replied.

I was amazed.

"You do?"

"Yes, this is me." She pointed at Milena.

"This is Dasha." She pointed at Dasha.

"This is my sister." She pointed at herself.

I explained that she was mistaken. The picture was taken in 1938: Her sister Kathy was not born until 1942. The girl she identified as herself was in fact her cousin Milena. "We all kind of look similar," she said. I began to say that Milena was taken to Auschwitz on the same transport as her grandmother, but she turned away before I could finish the story. Her face assumed a steely look. An aide interrupted to say that the interview would be over in ten minutes.

"Is this the only part of the story that interests you?" Madeleine asked, closing the door to any further discussion of Milena.

I tried, somewhat clumsily, to reach out to her as a human being, telling her there was nothing shameful about her family history. Perhaps inevitably, however, we settled into the roles of journalist and politician. Even though I tried to be as gentle as possible on the sensitive issue of when she had begun to learn about her Jewish roots and why her parents had felt it necessary to conceal their past, apparently I did not succeed. Later, Madeleine told a friend that she felt "shaken and somehow violated" by my questions. I, in turn, thought she was unnecessarily defensive.

It is now clear that Madeleine's parents viewed their Jewishness as an encumbrance that made it more difficult, if not impossible, to be accepted by the majority society. They converted to Catholicism, in large measure to relieve their children of the terrible burden of history. They escaped the past by making a myth out of it and focused relentlessly on creating a brighter future for themselves and their children. Aged eleven when she arrived in America, Madeleine spent much of her life transforming herself into a model American. She succeeded so well that she rose to the highest position in the U.S. government attainable by a first-generation immigrant. It seems ironic that she should have been brought face-to-face with her family's tragic past at the very moment that she achieved everything that could possibly be expected of her.

On the other hand, perhaps it is not so strange. It was easy to keep such secrets as long as the world was divided into opposite ideological camps. As the Iron Curtain began to crumble, and information began to flow freely between East and West, many mysteries have been resolved. Family sagas similar to that of Madeleine Albright come to light every day. Her newfound prominence merely accelerated the process of uncovering the truth and made it painfully public.

Why should anyone want to read a biography of Madeleine Albright? The answer, I think, is that she is emblematic of the people who made America what it is today. It is a cliché to say that America is a nation of immigrants, but there is an important difference between the people who came here and the people who were born here. Like many first-generation immigrants, Madeleine and her parents were survivors. They possessed, in highly distilled form, the qualities that turned the United States into a superpower: unquenchable optimism, a burning desire to succeed and prove themselves, an enormous appetite for hard work. Their contribution to America was overwhelmingly positive, but there is a flip side to their story that is reflected in Madeleine's own life. In order to succeed in America, the immigrants had to reinvent themselves, a process that sometimes involved screening out inconvenient memories from the past.

On another level, Madeleine's story can be read as a personalized version of the story of the twentieth century. Her family was formed and buffeted by the great events of the century: the industrial revolution, the collapse of the Austro-Hungarian empire, the rise and fall of Nazism and communism, the Holocaust, World War II, America's ascent to superpower status. Later, in her progress from Georgetown housewife to secretary of state, Madeleine would become a symbol of the women's movement in America and the struggle for full equality with men. Like Katharine Graham and Pamela Harriman, to name two of her Georgetown neighbors, she found a way to succeed in a predominantly male world. The techniques were different, but the result was the same.

For her family, Madeleine Albright's appointment as secretary of state was the culminating point of a long upward odyssey. One of her great-grandfathers worked his way out of a Polish ghetto to become a stationmaster in an obscure Bohemian village. Another great-grandfather owned a pub. Madeleine's paternal grandfather established a small store selling building materials and rose to become the director of a large company. Her father, Josef Korbel, was a brilliant diplomat who might well have become foreign minister of Czechoslovakia one day had it not been for the Communist takeover in 1948.

As I researched this book, I was struck by the parallels between Madeleine's career and that of her father. Born in the old Austro-Hungarian empire, her father identified with the Czechoslovak state created in the aftermath of World War I. Like many Jews, Josef expressed his gratitude toward a country that was ready to treat him as a full citizen by becoming a super Czechoslovak patriot. When he came to America, he and his family transferred their allegiance to a new promised land. They became super-patriotic Americans.

The struggle for acceptance and assimilation is a recurring theme in this story. It is interspersed with setbacks, the most catastrophic of which was the Holocaust. After each crisis, the surviving family members found a way of picking themselves up and beginning the struggle all over again. What strikes one most about this family is its resilience: It never accepted defeat.

The seemingly contradictory strands in Madeleine's personality—an intense desire to please combined with a steely determination to get her own way—can be explained by this continual quest for acceptance. In order to be accepted by the majority society, the Korbels felt a need to constantly prove their loyalty. They had to work hard at being pleasant, even ingratiating. But they also developed a tough inner core to cope with the inevitable setbacks and humiliations. The crises served to make them stronger and more resilient, just as iron is tempered by a furnace.

The personality traits inherited from her ancestors have contributed to Madeleine's own success in America. Just as her great-grandfather escaped from the physical ghetto in which European Jews had been confined for centuries, so too did Madeleine escape from a metaphorical female ghetto. In the fifties, as Madeleine was growing up, the position of American women was not so dissimilar from that of European Jews in the nineteenth century. Their lives were bound by tradition and convention. Entire professions were virtually closed to them. Despite a nominal equality with men, they had to overcome huge hurdles before they could realize their full potential.

Madeleine reached the top of America's male-dominated society not by rebelling against that society, but by a determined drive for integration and assimilation, the very same tactic employed by her Jewish forebears in Gentile-dominated Central Europe. Her marriage into one of America's wealthiest and most prominent WASP families opened social doors that would otherwise have been closed to her. She found ways of making herself useful and indispensable to a series of male patrons, notably Edmund Muskie and Zbigniew Brzezinski. But it was not until a shattering and unexpected setback—her divorce in 1983—that her career really took off. The divorce provided both the motivation and the opportunity for a successful assault on the summit.

When my story about Madeleine's family background appeared in *The Washington Post* magazine in February 1997, it caused a minor furor. People asked how it was possible for a former professor of international relations to be ignorant of her own background. The controversy seemed to strike a nerve among many American Jews seeking to reassert their own identity after what one columnist called the "heavy-duty assimilation" of the 1950s.

What struck me most in the days immediately following publication of my article was not how unusual Madeleine's story was, but how common it was. That, indeed, is what made the reaction fascinating. There were stories of Holocaust survivors keeping quiet about their past because they feared a resurgence of anti-Semitism. From Poland came news of a special telephone hot line that had been installed to help the offspring of converted Jews sort out their identity problems. I learned that numerous books had been written devoted to the phenomenon of "hidden children," children who were brought up as Christians in an effort to save them from the vengeful fury of the Nazis.

The most frequent question asked of me, particularly by Jews, was "Did she know?" Everybody seemed to have an opinion on that subject, whether or not they had evidence to support their conclusion. For a long time, I avoided a direct answer to the question. It seemed to me that the solution to the mystery lay in the sphere of intimate family relationships that are likely to remain hidden from outsiders. I thought it possible that the truth could lie somewhere between a definite "Yes" and an equally definite "No." In many families, there are taboos: topics that by tacit consent no one ever talks about. It is clear that Madeleine adored her parents, particularly her father. These were the people who had saved her—first from Nazism, then from communism—and brought her to America. She may have suspected that there was something strangely selective about their reminiscences of the past. But for her to challenge their story would be to challenge them, and this was something she was not prepared to do.

As I completed the research for this book, I came to the conclusion that Madeleine learned the essential details of her family's past long before February 1997. It is quite probable that her parents kept her and her siblings in the dark about their origins for many years. But too many people, both in America and in Europe, knew what had happened for the secret to be kept forever from such an intelligent, inquiring woman. As I explain in the course of this book, there are simply too many contradictions and inconsistencies in her story for it to be believable.

How does all this affect our judgment of America's first woman secretary of state? At one level, scarcely at all. Many of us have told white lies, only to find ourselves drawn deeper and deeper into an intricate web of deception. Had Madeleine not risen to her present position, few people would care about her religious beliefs or family background. Her conversion, first to Roman Catholicism and then to Episcopalianism, is a personal matter. Her failure to disclose her family's true origins is hardly a barrier to high office.

On another level, however, Madeleine's hidden past is a vital biographical fact. Without it, it is difficult to gain a full appreciation of what has motivated her and how far she and her family have come. The key influence in her life is the father on whom she modeled herself. In order to understand her, you must first understand him. And in order to understand him, you have to go back to the rolling hills of northern Bohemia, where he was born, and the ghetto existence that he and his ancestors were so determined to escape.

This is the story of a woman who had the drive and good fortune to realize her full potential. It is also the story of those who did not make it.

After all, for every person who comes to America, dozens more are left behind. In human life, as in nature, it is not always the best people who survive and prosper, but the fittest and most adaptable. The struggle for survival was seen most clearly in the gas chambers of Hitler's death camps where people, quite literally, climbed on top of one another in a desperate attempt to gasp for air. That is the extreme. But there is some kind of drama at every stage in the quest for fulfillment.

When we are young, we rely on our parents to protect us from the brutal world around us. Like most parents, Josef and Mandula Korbel wanted to give their children the best possible chance in life, which is why they rejected their Jewish origins. Just as they reinvented themselves, so too would Madeleine reinvent herself. During the course of her life, she went through several transformations: from refugee child to all-American student; from student to housewife; from housewife to academic; from academic to world leader. These metamorphoses did not just happen. They were the result of hard work, loyalty, adaptability, determination, and a lot of luck.

Luck is not the least of Madeleine's blessings. While writing this book, I had a mental image of her cousin and grandmother standing on the ramp of Auschwitz-Birkenau. In front of Milena Deiml and Olga Körbel stands the infamous Nazi doctor Josef Mengele, pointing left or right with his baton. One way leads to a labor camp, the other to the gas chambers. Prior to being sent to Auschwitz, Milena had spent three years in a concentration camp at Terezín. We know, from the pictures she drew there, that she spent a lot of time dreaming of the happy family life that had been ripped away from her. Madeleine would live out Milena's dream.

Before the war, Milena's family tried desperately to find a safe haven from the coming storm in the United States, Canada, or Britain. Their requests for refugee visas were turned down. Madeleine, by contrast, had the good fortune to escape to Britain with her parents. When the Communists came to power in Czechoslovakia after the war, Madeleine's family was granted asylum in America.

It could so easily have been the other way around.

Arnošt Körbel and his two sons, Josef (Madeleine's father), left, and Jan, right. Jan followed his father into the building business; Josef became a diplomat. *Courtesy of Dagmar Šima.*

Escape from the Ghetto

Unlike the well-tended Christian cemetery next door, the "new" Jewish cemetery in the little Bohemian town of Nový Bydžov is a picture of neglect and ruin. The gate is usually locked and, in the absence of a caretaker, the only way in is over an eight-foot wall. The two hundred graves are covered with an undergrowth of brush so dense that many of them are inaccessible.

The gravestone of Josef and Auguste Körbel—Madeleine Albright's great-grandparents—has fallen off its pedestal. It lies, forgotten and partially obscured, beneath a thicket of thorns. The inscription carved into the black marble slab is in Hebrew and German:

Senior Inspector
JOSEF KÖRBEL
Stationmaster
Austrian Northwest Railway Company
Passed Away in Litoměřice
On 15 November 1906
In His 61st Year.

AUGUSTE KÖRBEL
Born Lustig.
Passed Away on 24 February 1929
In Her 77th Year.

A few feet away from the fallen tombstone stands a matching marble base. Inscribed in small letters on the top right-hand corner of the pedestal is the name of Madeleine's paternal grandfather: ARNOŠT.

In the absence of family records, most of which were lost during the Holocaust, attempts to unravel the ancestry of America's first woman secretary of state must begin with this gravestone. Every word etched into the marble contains a clue to her ancestral roots. Pieced together, these clues tell the story of a typical Central European Jewish family: escape from the ghetto, the grasping of new economic opportunities, migration, linguistic and cultural assimilation. And all around, in the fallen tombstones and overgrown weeds, are signs of the unspeakable tragedy that befell a once-thriving Jewish community.

A century ago, there were nearly one thousand Jews in Nový Bydžov, around 15 percent of the total population. The town boasts two Jewish cemeteries, the oldest dating to 1520. The cemetery in which Josef Körbel is buried was consecrated in 1885. Today, not a single Jew lives in Nový Bydžov, and the synagogue and Jewish Quarter have long since burned to the ground.

Josef Körbel spelled his family name with an umlaut over the first syllable, as recorded on his gravestone. After World War II, and his conversion to Roman Catholicism, Madeleine's father officially changed the name to Korbel without the umlaut, a small but significant modification. With the umlaut, the name Körbel rhymes with "burble" and has a distinctly German-Jewish sound to it. Without the umlaut, it rhymes with "doorbell" and sounds much more Czech. "Korbel" is, in fact, an old Czech word denoting a wooden pitcher used for drinking.

Unlike the Czech Korbels, the Körbel family arrived on the territory of what is now the Czech Republic comparatively late. According to family tradition, supported by fragmentary genealogical records, Josef Körbel was born across the border in Galicia, in what is now southern

Poland. At that time, Galicia, like the historic Czech provinces of Bohemia and Moravia, was part of the Hapsburg empire, having been annexed to Austria-Hungary in 1772. Galician Jews were considered more bound by tradition and religion than their Bohemian or Moravian counterparts.

For the Körbels, like hundreds of thousands of other Central European Jews, the nineteenth century was a time of freedom and rapid economic progress. In 1781, the emperor, Joseph II, had issued edicts describing the Jewish people as "almost equal" to Christians. He offered the Jews a Faustian bargain. In return for giving up many of their ancient customs, and the Yiddish and Hebrew languages, they would be encouraged to acquire a German education and wear "Christian costumes." They would also be permitted to trade, set up factories, and invest in real estate. Jews without surnames—the vast majority—were obliged to adopt German ones.

Jewish emancipation was taken a step further after the revolution of 1848. Restrictions on domicile were lifted, paving the way for huge population shifts within the empire as newly liberated Jewish families sought economic opportunity. The hated *Familiantengesetz* legislation, which prevented all but the oldest son of each Jewish family from marrying legally, was abolished.

Lifting all these restrictions was like lifting the lid on a pressure cooker. After being bottled up in the ghetto for hundreds of years, living under archaic laws enforced by both Jewish rabbis and the Christian majority, a hugely talented people was suddenly free to realize its potential. The result was an explosion of energy and creativity. The Jewish nation, which had produced scarcely anyone of international reknown in the nineteen centuries since the birth of Jesus of Nazareth, suddenly spawned a string of world-class geniuses. Hapsburg Jewry alone produced the philosopher Ludwig Wittgenstein, the musician Gustav Mahler, the writer Franz Kafka, and the father of modern psychoanalysis, Sigmund Freud. In many cases, the motivating force behind all this creative energy was the yearning for assimilation in majority "Christian" society. It is characteristic that Wittgenstein, Mahler, Kafka, and Freud all turned their backs on the religion of their forefathers.

Central European Jews were both the agents and beneficiaries of economic progress. The factories, banks, and railroads built by Jewish entrepreneurs were the means by which poorer Jews clawed their way out of the ghetto. The railroad system of the Hapsburg empire was largely financed by Jewish bankers such as the Rothschilds and the Pereires. They were among the few private investors willing to risk their own capital in the pioneer stage of railroad construction.

For the Körbel family, the railroads were a symbol of freedom and economic opportunity. Thanks to the patronage of his fellow Jews, Madeleine's great-grandfather was able to get a job with the imperial railroad soon after he became an adult. The family followed the railroad as it expanded through the rolling countryside of northern Bohemia in the 1870s and 1880s. The Austrian North-Western Railroad Company was like an employment and marriage agency for Josef's children. His sons got jobs with the railroads. His daughters married railroad employees.

Josef's choice of occupation suggests that he was not particularly religious. Many of the villages and towns in which he lived did not even have a synagogue. On the other hand, Madeleine's great-grandfather observed basic rituals and made no effort to hide his origins. He had his sons circumcised. Like many Austrian Jews, the Körbels probably went to synagogue three or four times a year for the main Jewish festivals.

Jewish migrants like Josef Körbel were caught between conflicting loyalties. The German-speaking administrators of the Hapsburg empire expected the Jews to do their bidding. At the same time, the Jews also sought to remain on good terms with their predominantly Czech neighbors in the towns and villages of northern Bohemia, who were mistrustful of anyone who did not share their aspirations for political independence.

The resulting psychological conflicts were well described by Theodor Herzl, a Viennese Jew remembered as the father of modern Zionism. "Poor Jews," he wrote in 1896. "Some tried to become Czech, so they got into trouble with the Germans. Some tried to become Germans, so they were attacked by the Czechs as well as the Germans. It's enough to make one lose one's sanity—or find it at last. . . ." He went on to tell a joke about two coach-drivers who meet on a narrow country road:

Neither of the drivers will give way. There is a Jew in each of the coaches. Thereupon each driver cracks his whip at the passenger in the other coach, "You beat my Jew and I'll beat yours!" But in Bohemia they add, "and mine too," so that the Bohemian Jew gets a double beating for his journey.

For Herzl, the obvious solution to this dilemma was for Jews to assert a distinctly Jewish identity. But that seemed a risky proposition to most of his coreligionists, who feared losing everything unless they assimilated into one of the dominant cultures.

Frequently, the choice of culture depended on matters like geographical location. Madeleine's grandfather, Arnošt, settled in a Czech-speaking part of the country and opted to bring his children up as Czechs while also speaking fluent German. Several of his brothers and sisters ended up in German-speaking regions and spoke German with their children. German remained the lingua franca of the Körbel family. "Arnošt really wanted to be Czech and spoke Czech more than the others," recalls his niece, Joža Gruber, who now lives in Israel. "I was born near the border with Austria, so we spoke German at home. We also spoke German with Arnošt."

It is possible to plot the movements of Josef Sr. and his family around northern Bohemia against the opening of new railroad lines. The oldest daughter, Marta, was born in the town of Litomyšl in 1876. Shortly afterward, the family moved some ten miles to the north, to Ústí nad Orlicí, where Josef was appointed the town's first stationmaster. Their first son, Rihard, died of scarlet fever in Ústí before reaching his first birthday. Four days after Rihard's death, Arnošt was born. Three sons and two more daughters followed at regular two-year intervals.

Josef Körbel ended his career as the official in charge of the movement of trains in and out of Litoměřice, an important railway junction at the foot of the Sudetenland mountains. It was here that he died in 1906, aged sixty-one. There were few Jews in Litoměřice, and no Jewish cemetery. As the oldest surviving son, Arnošt had the filial duty of organizing the funeral service. At the time, he was working on the railroad at Nový Bydžov, the site of a well-established Jewish community. He brought his father's body back to the Jewish cemetery at Nový Bydžov to be buried.

Madeleine's grandfather, Arnošt Körbel, was a classic example of a self-made man. Uneducated in any formal sense, he began his career as a railroad clerk in a remote corner of Bohemia far from the big cities, and ended up as the owner of a very successful building materials business in Prague. His energy, drive, and native intelligence propelled him inexorably upward, to the point where he was able to send his second son Josef to Paris for an education. (Madeleine's father was named after his grandfather.) It was thanks to Arnošt that the once penniless Körbel family entered the ranks of the bourgeoisie.

Like Josef and Madeleine after him, Arnošt seems to have owed much of his success to a mixture of sociability and ambition. In the little Bohemian town of Letohrad, where he first began to make money, he is still remembered as a progressive and charismatic businessman who provided his coachman with cooked lunches. A natural salesman, Arnošt had "a talent for getting on with other people," said Vera Ruprechtova, granddaughter of his first business partner, Jan Reinelt. "He was a humanitarian."

Although he did his duty by his father and buried him according to Jewish tradition, Arnošt refused to have anything to do with Judaism himself. He forbade his wife Olga and their three children from attending synagogue. Olga, who was conventionally religious, would occasionally go to the synagogue in secret. The only time the children ever went to a synagogue was when they were with Olga on holiday in the spa town of Karlsbad, away from their father's surveillance.

The drive for assimilation may have been particularly pronounced in Arnošt's case because he was trying to make his career in the building trade, which was difficult for Jews to enter. But his anti-religious attitude was not at all unusual for Czech Jews, who wanted nothing more than to be accepted by their Christian neighbors. In 1899, when Arnošt was twenty-one, the entire Jewish community of Polná, just fifty miles from where he was living, was accused of "ritual murder" following the unexplained killing of a Christian seamstress. A Jewish shoemaker, Leopold Hilsner, was sentenced to death for the murder, and anti-Jewish pogroms broke out across the country, causing many Bohemian Jews to flee to the big cities. The Hilsner case tapped into one of the oldest anti-Semitic myths: that Jews use the blood of Christians to make Passover bread.

The drift away from religion has been well described by numerous other Hapsburg Jews, notably the writer Franz Kafka. The Körbel family sounds very much like the Kafka family, as depicted in this 1911 letter from Franz to his father:

> What kind of Judaism did I get from you? . . . When I was young, I could not understand how, with the insignificant scrap of Judaism you yourself possessed, you could reproach me for not making the effort to live with a similar nothing. . . . On four days in the year you went to the synagogue, where you were (to say the least) closer to the indifferent ones than to those who took religion seriously, you patiently went through the prayers in a purely formal manner. . . . That was how it was in the synagogue; and at home, if possible, it was even more pitiful, being confined to the first Seder evening, which increasingly developed into a farce with fits of hysterical laughter. . . . That was the religious material handed on to me. . . . How one could do anything better with this material than get rid of it as fast as possible was something I could not understand.

It is not difficult to imagine Madeleine's grandfather expressing the same anti-religious sentiment to his father Josef.

Members of the Körbel family recall Arnošt as a stern but loving parent who was able to look at life with a sense of bemused detachment. After his children grew up, and the family moved to Prague, he became inordinately fond of a little wire-haired terrier called Drollo, or Drollik. "It was the dog that attracted me to Arnošt," said his niece, Joža. "Arnošt was very warm. You could see that from the twinkle in his eye. But he was usually very busy and was not at home all that often. He was very energetic. He built himself up from nothing to be a rich man."

Woe betide any child who treated Drollo with less than full respect. Arnošt's granddaughter, Dasha, recalls an incident in Prague in the late 1930s when she was six or seven. She wanted to read and the dog was irritating her, so she tied it to a door handle. "Grandfather was very cross. He took a piece of string and tied my leg to the table. I remained tied up there until Grandmother came and let me go." Arnošt's oldest son, Jan, told his children the story of how he had received a severe beating from his father as punishment for painting the dog. Madeleine's father, Josef, also had vivid memories of the dog. When he got his own dog later in life, he insisted on naming it Drollik, in honor of his father's dog.

Animals and small children seemed to fare better with Arnošt than older children. "He could be a bit of a bully," said Alena Korbel, Madeleine's first cousin. "He loved children until they started saying 'No' and arguing with him."

If Arnošt was the disciplinarian in the family, Olga was remembered for her gentleness and kindness. An excellent cook, she played with the children and protected them from their father's flashes of temper. Alena Korbel remembers her as "nice, but from my point of view not very exciting. . . . She would say all these conventional things like how wonderful everything was." Although Olga may have struck a five-year-old as unexciting, it was she who did most to keep the family together during the Nazi terror. Her unselfish generosity shines through in letters that she wrote to her relatives after Hitler's troops occupied Czechoslovakia in 1939.

Many years later, in written reminiscences to her children, Madeleine's mother, Mandula, described the different personality traits that her husband had inherited from Arnošt and Olga. She wrote that Arnošt's most remarkable feature was his "perseverance": "From a little shopkeeper, he became a shareholder and director of a big building company." Olga, by contrast, was responsible for endowing Josef with what Mandula described as his "good heart, gentleness, unselfishness, and loyalty to his family."

Arnošt appears to have met his future wife while working for the railroad in Nový Bydžov. Olga's father operated the pub at the station in the nearby village of Ostroměř. Running a pub was a typically Jewish occupation in nineteenth-century Bohemia. Catholics steered clear of the distribution of alcohol, which was organized through a lease-holding system. In Czech literature, the Jewish innkeeper is almost as ubiquitous as the Jewish peddler or moneylender. The portrayal was frequently negative. In the words of an American writer, the Jewish-run tavern was "a place of weddings and other celebrations but also of shady deals, the only venue in which a Gentile, a Jew, a count, and a criminal might meet."

Several years after their marriage, Arnošt and Olga moved from Nový Bydžov to the town of Letohrad (then called Kysperk), in northeastern Bohemia, near the border with Galicia. Situated on a hillside, Letohrad is built around a dilapidated castle and a square with a baroque Catholic Church in the middle. It was here that Madeleine's father, Josef, was born, on September 20, 1909. He was the youngest of three children. (His sister Grete was born in 1903; his brother Jan in 1906.) Josef's birth certificate, issued by a Jewish registrar in a neighboring town, describes him as "Jewish and legitimate." There was no synagogue in Letohrad, and the Jewish community was very small—just half a dozen families—another sign of Arnošt's indifference to religion.

The Körbels lived in a modest two-story row house opposite the train station. Arnošt used the ground floor of the house—now a bicycle store—as an office for his building materials business. He also helped set up the local match factory, the first of its kind in the country, turning what had previously been a cottage industry into the most profitable business in town. It was Arnošt's job to supply the wood for the factory. He transported fifteen-foot logs into town on the railroad and then used his own coach and horses to get the logs to the match factory.

The horses were stabled at the back of the Körbel house, in the courtyard. The coachman and his family lived in a small room on top of the stable. Jan Koloc, who was born the year after Josef, remembers playing hide-and-seek among the logs in the station yard with the Körbel children and the coachman's children. When they tired of this game, they would play marbles on the street.

The most momentous event of Josef's childhood was the end of World War I and the collapse of the Hapsburg empire. After three centuries of Austrian rule, the Czechs and Slovaks were finally free to set up their own state. News of the end of the war arrived by telegraph at the railway station shortly after midnight on October 28, 1918, touching off wild celebrations. According to Koloc, "municipal employees went around with accordions, waking up everybody, telling them, 'Don't sleep. We have won our freedom, come celebrate.'" By morning, all the Austrian eagles had been replaced by the double-tailed lion, symbol of the Czech lands.

Czech-speaking Jews like Arnošt and Josef immediately identified with the new state. While never entirely eliminated, anti-Semitism was more muted in Czechoslovakia than anywhere else in Central Europe. There were some 350,000 Jews in the new republic, out of a total population of thirteen million. In some ways, the Jews were the only real Czechoslovaks in a multiethnic country, most of whose citizens regarded themselves as primarily Czech, Slovak, German, or Hungarian. Even after emigrating with his family to America, Josef was always very insistent on this point. "I was brought up as a Czechoslovak," Madeleine would recall after her appointment as secretary of state. "That was the big deal. . . . When I asked my parents, 'Are we Czech or are we Slovak?', they would always say, 'You are a Czechoslovak.' "

Czechoslovakia's first president, Tomáš Masaryk, was a humanist committed to full equality between the country's ethnic groups. His staunch resistance to anti-Semitism made him particularly popular among Jews. He had made his reputation defending Leopold Hilsner, the Jewish shoemaker accused of "ritual murder" in 1899. When Masaryk wrote a series of articles demolishing the case against Hilsner, he was attacked by the Catholic Church for "selling his soul to the Jews."

Josef would always revere Masaryk. In his book, *Twentieth Century Czechoslovakia*, he describes the philosopher-president as "an intellectual and ethical giant" who "fought anti-Semitism all his long life." Without Masaryk, he wrote, "there would have been no Czechoslovakia."

There was no high school in Letohrad so, at the age of twelve, Josef was sent by his parents to the nearby town of Kostelec. He stayed with a family that made a living renting rooms to students. It was here he met his future wife, Madeleine's mother. As Mandula later recalled in notes to her family, "we met and fell in love" in the high school in Kostelec.

With some ten thousand inhabitants, and closer to the plains, Kostelec was twice the size of Letohrad and a generally more prosperous place. Mandula's family, the Spiegels, were one of the wealthiest families in town. Mandula's maternal grandfather, Alois, had founded a profitable wholesale business that serviced stores throughout the region. Among other items, the Spiegel family was renowned for producing its own sweet liqueur, which it marketed under the name "Asko" (short for Alois Spiegel Kostelec). They also roasted their own coffee.

After Alois' death in 1913, the business was taken over by his two sons, Gustav and Alfred, Mandula's father. Of the two brothers, Gustav seems to have been the more dynamic. "He was the brains behind the business," recalled Zdeněk Beneš, a family friend still living in Kostelec. "Alfred was diligent and a hard worker, but not particularly intelligent." Gustav and his family lived above the warehouse. A picture from the early 1920s shows Gustav and his son Pepik, both of whom would be killed in Hitler's concentration camps, standing proudly in front of one of the first cars in Kostelec. They are both dressed in flashy pinstripe suits and white socks and look the very image of rich Jewish merchants. Both brothers had the reputation for being ladies' men and telling risqué jokes. Gustav kept a mistress, who lived several blocks away from the family warehouse. By 1921, when Josef arrived in Kostelec, the family employed thirty or so clerks and workers.

Avigdor Dagan, who knew Josef and Mandula in London in World War II as an official with the Czechoslovak government-in-exile, visited Kostelec as a traveling salesman in the early 1930s. He was struck by the similarities between Alfred Spiegel and his daughter Mandula. "The Spiegels sold anything to do with food: tea, coffee, margarine, all kinds of spices. I remember [Alfred] Spiegel and his wife. They were both very small people. Mrs. Spiegel was a very quiet woman. She would sit at the cash register. I don't think I ever heard more than two words from her. Mr. Spiegel, on the other hand, was a very lively man. He would run around the shop, talking all the time, telling typical Jewish jokes, and asking me to tell jokes. [Mandula] was very much like her father. She had the same kind of wit."

The Spiegels appear to have been a little more observant than the Körbels. It is likely that they went to synagogue once or twice a year, for the main Jewish festivals. "There weren't very many pious Jews in Bohemia," says Dagan, who later edited the standard work on Czech Jewry. "Most Jews in Bohemia limited their Jewishness to taking part in high holidays and going to synagogue occasionally. It was something they just did because it was expected of them. Jewishness with [the Spiegels] was certainly not something very deep, but everybody knew they were

Jews and society forced them to observe a certain limited number of things."

Intellectually, Madeleine would model herself on her father Josef. But she seems to have inherited her sharp tongue and ready repartee from her mother's side of the family. Physically, too, she is a Spiegel. "She looks very much like her maternal grandfather," says Dagan, who emigrated to Israel after the war and became a prominent writer and diplomat. "If I look at her face and take off the hair, it is to a large extent the face of [Alfred] Spiegel."

Nearly half a century later, in a letter sent to his classmates, Josef reminisced fondly about his time in Kostelec. He recalled dances at a nearby baroque castle, walks in the surrounding hills, and the trouble he got into for shooting someone's hat with an air gun. "I can imagine all of you before my eyes as if it was today," he wrote. "I see before me the school with Rabstein and Rabišak [school friends], Havlíčkov street and the gray house number 510 [where the Spiegels lived], the charming river Orlici and the little trails on the hills, the square full of flowers, and the Spiegel store."

Another friend, Josef Marek, remembers spending New Year's Eve in the company of Josef Körbel and Pepik Spiegel. Together with other high school students, they dressed up in costume and paraded around town. More than seventy years later, he can still recall the song they used to sing:

> Kostelec is a town known all over the world,
> Everybody must be envious of our Kostelec,
> Whoever sees Kostelec will become mute,
> Kostelec is the only place on earth.

Josef stood out from the other students because of his determination and ambition. "Already at an early age, he knew exactly what he would like to be, and was trying to plan his education accordingly," Mandula wrote later. "He wanted to be a diplomat, newspaperman, or politician. There were so many possibilities in the new Czechoslovakia for talented young people who wanted to [take part] in building a real democracy under the leadership of T.G.M[asaryk]. . . . Joe wanted very much to be one of them."

In order to prepare for his future career, Josef knew he would have to learn foreign languages and acquire political connections. His family hired a tutor to teach him German, and he lived for a while in the German-speaking region of Czechoslovakia. He became a firm supporter of the National Socialist Party founded by Eduard Beneš, Masaryk's successor as president of Czechoslovakia. (The Czechoslovak National Socialist Party was social democratic in orientation, not to be confused with the German Nazi Party.)

Josef spent the academic year 1928–29 in Paris, studying French and acquiring the social graces of a man of the world. He was quick-witted and opinionated. Once in Paris, he happened to overhear two Czech students, neither of whom he knew, conducting a heated philosophical debate on the street. "Excuse me, but I couldn't help hearing what you were saying," he interrupted in Czech. "Allow me to introduce myself. My name is Josef Körbel, and I disagree with absolutely everything you said."

There would later be some confusion about exactly where in Paris Madeleine's father studied. He said the Sorbonne, but his friend Josef Marek insists he attended a slightly less celebrated school known as Science-Po.

As the daughter of one of the richest men in Kostelec, Mandula also received part of her education abroad. Her parents sent her to a private school in Switzerland. Pretty and vivacious, she was a good catch for Josef. It was he who coined the nickname "Mandula." Her real name was Anna, but Josef started calling her "Ma Andula" (My little Anna) as a term of affection. The name was soon contracted to Mandula, which stuck with her for the rest of her life.

Josef had asked Mandula to marry him in 1928, shortly after leaving high school. She agreed, but their families felt they were too young. The marriage would have to wait until April 1935, after Josef had received a doctorate in law at Charles University in Prague and embarked on a diplomatic career. In her notes to her family, Mandula gives only a hint of the frustration she must have felt over this seven-year engagement. "Joe was certainly a man worth waiting for . . . but it was not always easy." A picture taken on their wedding day outside the registry office shows Mandula, pert and happy as a bird, clutching her husband proudly by the arm. A fur is slung around her neck. Her hat is slanted rakishly over her forehead. A head taller than Mandula, Josef is doing up his coat and moving briskly on with his life.

By the mid-twenties, the descendants of Josef and Auguste Körbel were scattered all over Czechoslovakia. Work with the railroads had taken them from Bohemia in the west to Slovakia in the east. But every summer the family made a big effort to get together again. They rented a cottage in the Bohemian village of Choceň, in the same part of the country where they had been raised.

Since Josef Sr. was long dead, it was left to Auguste to preside over these annual gatherings. By this time, the family matriarch was living with her youngest son Max, a bachelor who later died in a car accident. She had a difficult personality. "Auguste was a very capricious woman," recalls her granddaughter Joža. "She was very good to us grandchildren, but would change her mind about everything all the time. Max, who was the manager of a bank, had a beautiful, comfortable apartment, but nothing was ever right for Auguste. She was always finding fault with something, always making allegations."

Even though they went their separate ways and would eventually end up all over the world, the Körbels retained some distinctive family traits. The most striking of these characteristics are meticulousness and persistence. It is tempting to trace the penchant for order—exemplified in later life by Madeleine's incredibly neat handwriting and her habit of using different-colored pens to take notes—back to the experience of so many family members on the railroads. This was a family that liked to have the trains run on time.

"As a family, we are calm, well-organized," says Chaim Körbel, another grandchild of Josef and Auguste who emigrated to Israel in 1939 and founded a kibbutz. "Because my father worked for the railroads, we could travel very cheaply. Even before we left, my father would have everything planned. Nothing was allowed to interfere with the plan." The love of order, Chaim adds, is accompanied by a certain stubbornness, even obduracy. "I am very persistent. I keep going, I never quit. My father was the same way."

While the Körbels clearly had a lot in common, they differed sharply in the way they reacted to persecution. Even though Czechoslovakia had a well-deserved reputation for being a haven from anti-Semitism in the twenties and thirties, it could not entirely insulate itself from the winds of hatred blowing from neighboring Austria and Germany. Hitler's screed *Mein Kampf*, "My Struggle," first appeared in 1925, denouncing the Jews as "traitors" and "Satans" and calling for the creation of an ethnically pure state. In 1933, the year Hitler came to power in Germany, the German Nazi Party formed a Czech offshoot under Konrad Henlein.

There were essentially two ways for Czech Jews to react to these gathering storm clouds: to become more Jewish or to become less Jewish. Each solution carried certain advantages and certain risks. The Zionists felt that the only way to withstand persecution and discrimination was to combat it openly and support the idea of an independent Jewish state. The Assimilationists believed that such action would only play into the hands of the anti-Semites. They reacted to anti-Semitism by redoubling their efforts to demonstrate their loyalty to the democratic Czechoslovak state founded by Masaryk.

Sometimes, the same individuals reacted in different ways at different times. There are numerous cases of Czech Jews being baptized as children or young adults and then rediscovering their Judaism later in life. It was not at all infrequent for the religious schism to go down the middle of a family, separating children from parents and brothers from sisters. Much depended on an individual's formative experiences, the part of the country he grew up in, and whether his first language was German or Czech. German-speaking Jews tended to hold themselves more aloof from the young Czechoslovak democracy than Czech-speaking Jews.

Chaim Körbel says that his father, Karel, was "not particularly religious." (Karel was the younger brother of Arnošt, Madeleine's grandfather.) "We only went to synagogue on Rosh Hashanah [the Jewish New Year]," he recalls. But the views of this branch of the Körbel family began to change in the thirties, after the Nazis came to power in Germany. Chaim attended a German-speaking school in Brno, the second-largest Czech city after Prague. He left after some of his fellow students showed up at school in white socks, the symbol of Henlein's extreme nationalist party, and began taunting the Jewish children.

Chaim and his older brother Gert both responded to the rise of Hitler by joining the youth wing of the Zionist movement. So did their cousin Joža, who grew up in Slovakia, where anti-Semitism was more pronounced than in the Czech lands. On the other hand, Joža's older sister, Herta, wanted nothing to do with Zionism. (Such distinctions made absolutely no difference to the Nazis. They would kill Herta anyway, together with her parents.)

Chaim, who was fourteen years old when he became a Zionist, thinks that age had a lot to do with his decision. "We were younger, and more aware of these new organizations popping up around us," he says.

By contrast, Zionism was never a real option for Chaim's cousin Josef. By the time Hitler came to power, Madeleine's father was twenty-three and eager to make a diplomatic career for himself. It was hard enough for an assimilated Jew to get into the Czechoslovak Foreign Ministry; for a Zionist it would have been impossible. From this time on, whenever he was asked to state his religion on a form, Josef replied simply: "Without confession."

"Körbel was one of the very, very few Jews who succeeded in getting into the Foreign Ministry before the war. He did so by not giving any signs of his Jewishness," says Dagan, his Foreign Ministry colleague later in London. Dagan speculates that Josef was helped in his chosen career by his connections with the National Socialist Party. "They probably arranged things for him. Without that kind of patronage, it was very difficult."

So determined was Josef to be a Czech that he never publicly explained his decision to repudiate his Jewishness. His voluminous writings as a leading American expert on Eastern Europe contain only fleeting references to Jews. It seems likely that he simply absorbed the stridently secular views of his father, Arnošt, and took them one stage further. None of Arnošt's three children showed the slightest interest in Judaism. After Hitler unleashed his genocidal policies, they and their children were all baptized. In the words of Madeleine's cousin, Dasha Šima, "The only sense in which we were Jews was under the definition of the Nuremberg laws, Hitler and the Nazis."

But even as he rejected his Jewishness, Josef remained influenced by it. Indeed, the quest for acceptance and assimilation is the most striking theme in his life, and by extension the life of his daughter. Fear can be as powerful a stimulus as religion or ideology. The words of the Czech Jewish writer Oskar Baum seem to apply to Josef:

The secret of Jewish energy is the knowledge of near destruction. For two thousand years the nation has constantly stood at the edge of annihilation. Once the sardine can—as a joker called the ghetto—has been broken open, it is free, exposed to all dangers. . . . The danger of destruction, which is now hardly avoidable and which everyone carries around deep in his unconscious, spurs us on.

One-year-old Madeleine, holding doll carriage with her two cousins, Dasha and Milena, in Czechoslovakia in 1938. Milena, right, died in the Holocaust. *Courtesy of Dasha Šima.*

"A Faraway Country"

Mandula and Josef had been married for just over two years when they had their first child. Madeleine Korbel Albright was born in Prague on May 15, 1937, as Marie Jana Körbelova. Her birth name requires some explanation. In the Czech language, surnames are declined: Körbelova is the feminine form of Körbel. Marie Jana was her given name, but it sounded a little prim and formal. The year after Madeleine's birth, a popular movie came out in Czechoslovakia called *Madla from the Brick Factory*. The family liked the heroine of the movie so much that they started calling their daughter Madla, or its diminutive, Madlenka. Madeleine is the closest English equivalent.

From almost the very start, Madeleine was a precocious child with a clear idea of what she wanted out of life. A picture of her as a toddler shows a self-possessed little girl with rosy cheeks and chubby legs taking firm control of a doll carriage. Her cousins, Dasha and Milena, look at her with some amusement, as though they are used to Madlenka getting her own way. "Madeleine is a born leader," Dasha later recalled. "She was very bright, very bossy. There was nine years' difference between us, so I didn't mind it when she bossed me around. It was fun."

Later, Mandula looked back on the years before World War II as an almost idyllic period. After two years' compulsory military service, plus a stint with a law firm, Josef had finally achieved his ambition of being accepted into the Foreign Ministry. In early 1937, he received his first foreign assignment: press attaché at the Czechoslovak embassy in Belgrade. "Because we were young and happy, we both sometimes ignored the dark clouds which were forming on the political sky around us. We were all well aware of it, but were hoping that it would somehow pass without catastrophe," Mandula wrote. "[We] were even planning our new family. Madeleine . . . was certainly the biggest addition to our happiness not only for us, but for our parents."

The year of Madeleine's birth, 1937, saw a lull in the European crisis created by the Nazi election triumph in Germany. Hitler had spent the last four years building up his political power and testing the will of the Western democracies. He had purged the Nazi Party of dissenters, real and potential. He had promulgated laws stripping German Jews of their citizenship and property, forcing tens of thousands of them to flee the country. He had overturned key provisions of the Versailles treaty that codified Germany's defeat in World War I and had sent his troops into the Rhineland, a supposedly demilitarized area. He had embarked on a crash program of remilitarization with an army of half a million men. Now the Führer needed time to consolidate his gains and complete his preparations for war.

The Balkans proved a useful vantage point for observing the gathering storm. Like Czechoslovakia, Yugoslavia was a multiethnic state, created out of the rubble of the Austro-Hungarian empire. By the late thirties, the country was precariously balanced between democracy and dictatorship. Traditionally, it had been allied with France and was also part of a "Little Entente" with Czechoslovakia and Romania. But the regent, Prince Paul, was hedging his bets. Influenced by the authoritarian ideas coming from Germany, he and his government were trying to keep a lid on the pro-Western sentiments of much of the population.

In his book *Tito's Communism*, Josef recalled an incident in December 1937, when the French foreign minister visited Belgrade. Opposition supporters took advantage of the visit to take to the streets with banners like "Long live Democracy" and "Down with the government of Fascists." Josef went out on the balcony of the embassy to see what was going on and was greeted by hundreds of chanting demonstrators. He was in a quandary. If he returned their greetings, he would offend his host government. If he turned his back on them, he would offend his friends. So instead, he wrote later, "I stood like a statue for several minutes. Suddenly, a truck packed with police rushed to the place and opened fire against the demonstrators. I saw someone drop like a log. The crowd dispersed, but the tension continued to mount and remain high."

Naturally inquisitive and gregarious, Josef thrived in the fevered, conspiratorial world of Balkan politics. He spent much of his time in the company of journalists, exchanging information. Favorite places for swapping gossip about the latest political scandal or Germany's intentions included the Jockey Club (now known as the Writers' Club) and the offices of the French news agency Havas. Josef and Mandula cultivated a wide circle of artists, musicians, and writers. Several of these people remained friends for life.

Yugoslavia was a much more rural, backward country than Czechoslovakia, with a high level of illiteracy. But it also possessed a small upper-class elite that felt at home in the great capitals of Europe. In some ways, despite the political turmoil all around, the interwar period was the city's golden age. "Belgrade was like a village in those days. Everybody knew everybody else. The Körbels' house was always open, our house too," says Jara Ribnikar, the Czech-born wife of the owner of *Politika*, Serbia's leading newspaper. "Körbel had a way of encouraging talented people. There were always interesting people at his house. He was not an artist, but he attracted artists to him."

As she talks about Madeleine's father, the grande dame of what is left of Belgrade society closes her eyes and allows herself to dream for a moment. "Most diplomats you forget as soon as they leave. It's impossible to see their faces anymore. It's like an old, forgotten film. But Körbel, I have thought about many times. I can see him exactly now: how he used to come to me, how he sat down, how he talked. For me he was a very interesting personality. He was fascinated with Belgrade."

A great beauty in her youth, Ribnikar says she was attracted to Josef, although their relationship remained "platonic." "It was the kind of attraction we never spoke about, neither him nor me. . . . My husband, I think, was a little jealous. In general, I don't like to dance, but with Körbel I was able to dance. When we met at parties, we would always dance a slow waltz. . . . My husband would say, 'You don't dance with me, but with Körbel you dance very well.' "

. . .

While Josef and Mandula were enjoying the artificial calm of Belgrade, and raising their young daughter, Hitler was pushing ahead with preparations for war. The destruction of Czechoslovakia was part of his plans from a very early date. The country's democratic form of government and multiethnic character—the Czech Sudetenland was home to three million Germans—were a personal affront to him. Its strategic location, sandwiched between Germany, Poland, Hungary, and Austria, whetted his appetite.

On November 5, 1937, at a top-secret meeting with his generals, Hitler announced that the long-term object of German policy was the acquisition of *Lebensraum*, living space. He outlined a plan for lightning strikes against Austria and Czechoslovakia known as "Operation Green." If the two countries could be incorporated into the German Reich through threats and diplomacy, so much the better. If not, Germany would go to war. Hitler had only contempt for the leaders of England and France and did not think they would intervene to rob him of his prize.

Austria, with its entirely German-speaking population, was the easier target. It was incorporated into the Third Reich on March 11, 1938, following street demonstrations by Austrian Nazis and a campaign of military intimidation by Germany. Soon after Austria fell, Hitler finalized his plans for the annihilation of Czechoslovakia. "It is my unshakable will that Czechoslovakia be wiped off the map," he told his generals on May 28. He even set a deadline for this goal to be achieved: October 1, 1938.

Although Madeleine was just one year old when Hitler set about destroying her homeland, the events of the next few months shaped her foreign policy thinking for the rest of her life. Memories of Czechoslovakia's dismemberment by the Nazis and its betrayal by its Western allies would be passed down from one generation of Czechs to another, Madeleine's family included. More than half a century later, the future secretary of state would describe the West's appeasement of Hitler in 1938 as the decisive influence on her foreign policy philosophy. "My mind-set is Munich; most of my generation's is Vietnam," she told *The New York Times* in 1996. "I saw what happened when a dictator was allowed to take over a piece of a country and the country went down the tubes. And I saw the opposite during the war when America joined the fight."

Despite its small size and complex ethnic makeup, Czechoslovakia had some significant strategic advantages. It had a modern, well-trained army that could be expanded to a million men during periods of mobilization. It boasted a system of formidable defenses in the Sudetenland region along the German border known as the "little Maginot line." Finally, the country was part of a Europe-wide system of alliances that was much stronger than the German-led Axis. France had promised to come to Czechoslovakia's aid in the event of external aggression. A French declaration of war against Germany would in turn trigger intervention by Russia and Britain. Senior German generals had warned the Führer that Germany was bound to lose a general European war.

In the event, none of these considerations mattered very much, because the West lacked the will to fight while Hitler had no compunction about plunging the continent into war. In the high-stakes political poker game that followed the German demand that Czechoslovakia surrender the Sudetenland, Hitler held the trump cards. Britain and France signaled their willingness to appease Germany well in advance of the crisis. In a private talk with American journalists in May, which was promptly reported back to Hitler, the British prime minister, Neville Chamberlain, predicted that neither Britain nor France nor Russia would come to Czechoslovakia's aid in the event of a German attack.

The war of nerves began with a campaign to whip up nationalist sentiment among the German population in the Sudetenland. The local Nazi leader, Henlein, was instructed by Berlin to make a series of escalating demands of the central government in Prague. These demands eventually included the transfer of the entire region, with its system of defenses, to Germany. When the Beneš government tried to negotiate, Hitler flew into a rage.

The final act in the tragedy came at a series of meetings between Hitler and Chamberlain, culminating in the Munich conference of September 29–30. At one point, it seemed that the Führer was so intent on humiliating Czechoslovakia that he would not take yes for an answer. On September 22, Chamberlain flew to the little town of Godesberg on the Rhine to inform Hitler that the Czechs had agreed to surrender the Sudetenland. Only the details remained to be worked out. "I am terribly sorry," Hitler replied. "This plan is no longer of any use." The British "compromise" had not set a firm date for the transfer of territory. Hitler insisted that German troops occupy the Sudetenland by October 1 at the latest. Furthermore, departing Czech farmers would not be permitted to take any livestock with them.

For a few days, it seemed that Hitler might have overreached himself. Chamberlain informed Beneš that he could not in good conscience stand in the way of a general Czech mobilization. Over the next few hours, 800,000 Czech reservists were called up, including Madeleine's father. There was widespread popular support for the mobilization decree. Unlike some of their leaders, ordinary Czechs were ready to fight to save their country.

"On the evening of Wednesday [September 21] and again on Thursday [September 22], crowds filled the streets and marched to the castle shouting 'We are not Austrians' and 'Give us weapons, we paid for them,' " reported a Prague eyewitness. "Friday the 23rd was the most nerve-wracking night. The message came through that negotiations at Godesberg had broken down, that Chamberlain was returning to England, and that anything might happen that night. We hurried home across Prague, watches were put before all the houses, the antiaircraft defense patrolled the streets, and planes droned in the sky. Prague was blacked out several times during the night. Gas masks are in readiness, also cases packed with necessities for leaving in a hurry. First aid stations are opened all over town."

France began to mobilize in support of its ally. Morale was high. As the American journalist William L. Shirer noted, "Together the Czechs and the French outnumbered the Germans more than two to one."

Chamberlain, however, was not done with his peacemaking efforts. As Londoners prepared for possible German air raids, the prime minister mused on the horrors of war in a broadcast to the nation. "How horrible, fantastic, incredible it is that we should be digging trenches and trying on gas masks here because of a quarrel in a faraway country between people of whom we know nothing. . . . War is a fearful thing, and we must be very clear before we embark on it that it is really the great issues that are at stake."

Encouraged by a conciliatory-sounding letter from Hitler, Chamberlain set out for Munich on September 29 in one last attempt to prevent war. He left London with cries of "Good old Neville" and "Thank God for the prime minister" ringing in his ears. "When I was a little boy," he told reporters exuberantly, "I used to repeat, 'If at first you don't succeed, try, try, try again.' That is what I am doing." He was joined in the Bavarian capital by Hitler, French prime minister Edouard Daladier, and Italian dictator Benito Mussolini. Two representatives of Czechoslovakia were told to await the outcome of their deliberations in an adjoining room.

The Munich talks took place in what Hitler's interpreter, Dr. Paul Schmidt, later described as "an atmosphere of general good will." Neither Chamberlain nor Daladier put up any serious resistance to the German demands. When Chamberlain pleaded with Hitler to allow Czech farmers evacuating the Sudetenland to take their livestock with them, the Führer exploded: "Our time is too valuable to be wasted on such trivialities." The conference ended with an agreement that the German army would begin moving into the Sudetenland on October 1—Hitler's original target date—and would complete the occupation by October 10. In return, Germany joined Britain and France in "guaranteeing" the security of what remained of Czechoslovakia. Chamberlain also got Hitler to sign a declaration saying that their two nations should never again go to war. It was this piece of paper that the British prime minister flourished upon his return to London, boasting that he had negotiated "peace with honor . . . peace in our time." With the exception of Winston Churchill, who described the Munich agreement as "a total, unmitigated defeat," most British politicians applauded Chamberlain for saving Europe from a terrible conflict.

The Munich pact confronted the Czech government with a huge dilemma. Abandoned by his allies, President Beneš now had to decide whether his country would stand up to Hitler alone. The pressure was almost unbearable. Some of his senior generals and advisers were calling on him to fight, arguing that "death is better than slavery." Beneš, however, was convinced that war would mean "the extinction of the whole nation." "We are alone and encircled on all sides," he told a delegation of Czechoslovak politicians. "It was not Hitler that defeated us, but our friends."

Finally, at 12:50 P.M. on September 30, the Beneš government accepted the Munich ultimatum. The news was broadcast over loudspeakers to weeping crowds in Prague's Wenceslas Square. Standing in the square was an American diplomat, George Kennan, who had just been assigned to the U.S. legation in what remained of Czechoslovakia. He later wrote in his diary:

Prague could never have been more beautiful than during those recent September days when its security hung by so slender a thread. Baroque towers—themselves unreal and ethereal—floated peacefully against skies in which the bright blue of autumn made way frequently for iso-lated, drifting clouds. . . . Rarely, if ever, has the quaint garb of this old city seemed more museum-like, more detached from the realities of the moment, than it did during these strange days. The world had taken final farewell, it seemed, of nearly everything that these monu-ments represented. . . . A remarkable little people, whose virtues and whose failings are alike the products of adversity, found themselves standing out in lonely bitterness against what they felt to be an unjust and unsympathetic Europe.

The Munich agreement destroyed Czechoslovakia's political, military, and economic viability. Its losses were staggering. In addition to giving up its military defenses, the republic lost 29 percent of its territory and 34 percent of its population, including 800,000 Czechs and 3.2 million Germans. The dismemberment of the country deprived Czechoslovakia of 66 percent of its coal, 86 percent of its chemicals, 70 percent of its iron and steel, and 70 percent of its electric power. Its transport and communi-cation system was completely disrupted. In the words of Madeleine's father, Josef, "[In 1918] Czechoslovakia gained independence without fir-ing a shot; twenty years later, the nation lost it without firing a shot."

In a book published in 1977 on the eve of his death, Josef put most of the blame for Munich onto the British and French. But he was also criti-cal of Beneš, his political idol along with Tomáš Masaryk. He depicted the Czechoslovak president as a "mathematician of politics," a man of great analytical powers but utterly lacking in personal charisma. "A leader, a real leader, would have taken the risk [of fighting and provoking a wider European war]. He would have perceived that the valor of Czecho-slovakia could be a catalyst to unite the frightened and diffused elements of the West. But in her hour of supreme crisis, Czechoslovakia had as her president not a leader, but a negotiator."

The Munich agreement dealt a fatal blow to the faith of ordinary Czechs and Slovaks in the country's once admired democratic institutions. The sense of betrayal was overwhelming. "At the time of the mobilization, we weren't scared. We were ready to die for the country," said Jiři Weiss, a

Czech film director, who knew the Körbels in London. "But afterwards, we all ceased to believe in the West. Josef Körbel also. The treason of the Western democracies left an indelible stain in the heart of the Czechs."

In a letter to a friend, George Kennan wondered "whether it is possible for anyone who has not been here to conceive of the chaos which the Munich catastrophe created in political life and political thought in Czechoslovakia. . . . Nothing was left in the popular mind but bitterness, bewilderment, and skepticism. Every feature of liberalism and democracy, in particular, was hopelessly and irretrievably discredited."

If the Munich agreement was a disaster for Czechoslovakia, it was an even greater disaster for the country's 350,000 Jews. Particularly in the western part of the country, the historic Czech provinces of Bohemia and Moravia, the Jews were extremely well assimilated. Nearly one in three Czech Jews married Gentiles. As they watched the alarming rise of Nazi-sponsored anti-Semitism in neighboring countries, many Czech Jews had comforted themselves with the thought that "it can't happen here."

After Munich, this self-confidence vanished overnight. Beneš resigned the presidency five days after German troops began occupying the Sudetenland. The new government, headed by an elderly supreme court judge named Emil Hácha, was almost totally dependent on Germany. There was an upsurge in anti-Jewish publications and demonstrations. The rate of suicides among Jews and conversions to Catholicism also increased sharply. A campaign got under way to purge the government bureaucracy of the relatively small number of Jewish officials.

According to Dagan, the Czechs "were in a state of hysteria after Munich. Even people who were not themselves anti-Semitic thought that it was not healthy to try to help the Jews. Suddenly it became very easy for the real anti-Semites to push their own ideas because the others were afraid. There were very few people left who thought that defending the Jews was something worthwhile."

The Körbels felt the effects of this poisonous new atmosphere immediately. The crisis was over so quickly that Josef did not have time to respond to his mobilization order, according to Lidia Stefan Novaček, daughter of a Czechoslovak embassy colleague, Alois Stefan. "Both my father and [Josef] were ready to report to their regiments, but then they scrapped the mobilization. They were completely dejected. They were crying."

As a Jew, Josef found his position in the embassy had suddenly become very precarious. Mandula, always the outspoken one in the family, had gotten into trouble by criticizing the army's failure to defend the country. On October 14, the Ministry of Defense wrote to the Foreign Ministry demanding Josef's dismissal on the grounds that Mandula had said "in the presence of officers of the Czechoslovak army that she would rather marry a street sweeper than an army officer." This, however, was only a pretext. The army's real complaint against Josef and Mandula was hidden in the last sentence of the letter: "Dr. Körbel and his wife are Jews."

After the war, and his emigration to America, Josef went to some lengths to hide the real reasons for his dismissal from the Czechoslovak foreign service in 1938. In a 1951 book, *Tito's Communism*, he wrote that he was withdrawn from Belgrade at the request of the Yugoslav government, which "did not like my contacts with the democratic leaders of the opposition." He added that the government in Prague was only "too happy to agree with this request" since it had received orders from Berlin to dismiss all "Benešites" from the diplomatic service. In his official biography for the University of Denver, he gave another explanation for his dismissal: Fascist newspapers in Prague had attacked him as "a man of Beneš." He was silent about both his Jewishness and the Defense Ministry complaint.

The family returned to Prague just before Christmas. On December 20, Josef registered himself, Mandula, and Madeleine at the city's main police station. Under the heading "religious confession," he again wrote "None."

Josef's ouster from the Czechoslovak foreign service must have been a terrible psychological blow. Everything he and his family had accomplished over the past half-century was being destroyed. He had set his heart on a diplomatic career. In order to achieve his ambition, he had had to overcome all kinds of obstacles, including tight restrictions on the recruitment of Jews. But now he was being punished in large measure because of a religious background that scarcely meant anything to him. He didn't feel Jewish; he felt Czech. It was as if the Körbels were being thrust back into the medieval ghetto that Josef's father and grandfather had struggled so hard to escape.

In later life, both Josef and his daughter would look at the world through the prism of the Munich disaster. When the debate raged in the United States about whether or not to provide military assistance to

South Vietnam, Josef remembered the West's abandonment of his native Czechoslovakia. America, he believed, had a duty to stand up to aggression. And when Serbian leader Slobodan Milošević began whipping his people up into a nationalist frenzy in 1991, unleashing a murderous spate of "ethnic cleansing" in Bosnia, Madeleine drew analogies with events in Central Europe in 1938.

The final act in the Czechoslovak tragedy took place in March 1939. Just as he had used the German minority to dismember the Czechoslovakia of Masaryk and Beneš, Hitler now used the Slovak minority to destroy what remained of the country. At his insistence, Slovak nationalists proclaimed an independent Slovak state on March 14 under the "protection" of the Third Reich. The German propaganda machine under Dr. Goebbels cranked out yet more stories about alleged Czech "terror" against the German minority.

That evening, a confused and almost senile Czech president, Dr. Hácha, traveled to Berlin for an audience with Hitler. The Führer kept him waiting until he had finished watching a romantic movie called *Ein Hoffnungsloser Fall (A Hopeless Case)*. Then, at 1:15 A.M., he summoned Hácha to the Chancellery to inform him that German troops would begin occupying the rump Czechoslovakia at six A.M. The hapless Czech leader was given a brutal choice. If the Czechs resisted the invading army, their country would be destroyed. If they allowed the occupation to take place peacefully, they would be permitted a measure of autonomy.

Hácha was sent into an anteroom with the commander of the German air force, Hermann Göring, and the foreign minister, Joachim von Ribbentrop, to think the ultimatum over. At one point, the German ministers chased him around a table, demanding that he sign an act of surrender. He refused. They warned that the Luftwaffe was ready to reduce the beautiful Czech capital to a pile of ruins. The president fainted and had to be revived with injections of dextrose by Hitler's personal physician. Finally, at 3:55 A.M., he signed a document "placing the fate of the Czech people and country in the hands of the Führer of the German Reich." He informed his colleagues in Prague that he had been obliged to "sacrifice the state in order to save the nation."

Hitler graciously accepted Hácha's declaration. "Czechoslovakia has ceased to exist," he exulted. "This is the greatest day of my life. I shall go down in history as the greatest German!"

German troops began crossing the border at dawn, as Hitler had planned all along. By ten A.M., they had taken over Prague Castle, the residence of the president and symbol of Czechoslovak sovereignty. "A full blizzard was blowing," reported George Kennan, describing how he encountered a German armored car that had evidently lost its way while trying to find the German embassy. "A crowd of embittered Czechs looked on in silence. The soldier in the turret huddled up against the driving snow, nervously fingering the trigger of his machine gun as he faced the crowd. . . . For the rest of the day, the motorized units pounded and roared over the cobblestone streets: hundreds and hundreds of vehicles plastered with snow, the faces of their occupants red with what some thought was shame but what I fear was in most cases merely the cold. By evening the occupation was complete."

That night, Hitler made a triumphant entrance into Prague, sleeping in Hradčany castle, high above the Vltava River, where both Masaryk and Beneš had worked. The Führer arrived at the castle before Hácha, who was returning to Prague by train. When the nominal president of the new German Protectorate of Bohemia and Moravia arrived at his residence, he was ordered to use the servants' entrance.

The German occupation was a shock to all Czechs, but particularly traumatic for Czech Jews. During "the night of broken glass" (*Kristallnacht*) in Germany the previous November, hundreds of synagogues were burned to the ground and Jewish properties destroyed. Czech Jews had every reason to fear that it was now their turn.

In his diary, Kennan recalls the panic that seized the Prague Jewish community on the day of the invasion. Asylum-seekers "dazed with terror" flocked to the American embassy, only to be turned away. One Jewish refugee showed up at Kennan's home. "For twenty-four hours he haunted the house, a pitiful figure of horror and despair, moving uneasily around the drawing room, smoking one cigarette after another, too unstrung to eat or think of anything but his plight. His brother and sister-in-law had committed suicide together after Munich, and he had a strong inclination to follow suit."

The reaction of other Czech Jews frequently depended on their age and how Jewish they felt. Irena Kirkland, who became part of the Washington social scene as the wife of American labor leader Lane Kirkland, says that before March 15 she did not even know she was Jewish. She was fourteen at the time. "When the Germans marched in, my mother called my sister and me into our bedroom, and told us we were Jewish. She warned that it could have bad consequences." At lunch that day, after school, her mother served apricot dumplings, her favorite meal. "That stays in my mind. I thought it was strange that the world was coming to an end, and we have such a wonderful lunch."

Eva Beckmann was seventeen in 1939. She recalls being woken up at 5:30 in the morning. A friend of her father, a refugee from Germany, was at the door shaking with fear. "The minute the Germans marched in, my overwhelming impression is fear, constant fear. We had a pretty good idea what the Germans were like. We knew what they had done to the Jews when they had marched into Vienna, picking them up off the streets. We were well aware that we were Jewish and were going to get it. We tried to stay off the streets, to be inconspicuous, not to be seen too much."

Five years later, both Irena Kirkland and Eva Beckmann would be transported to Auschwitz on the same train as Olga Körbel, Madeleine's grandmother.

The Körbel family was swept along by the general panic. A few weeks earlier, Josef had gone to Paris to try to make contact with Beneš and other Czechoslovak exiles. According to Mandula, he was already hatching an escape plan. "With his contacts in Yugoslavia and his knowledge of the Serbian language, Joe had an idea that maybe he could be a reporter for some Yugoslav paper from London." It would be easier to get an exit visa for his family as a journalist than as a former Czech diplomat.

By sheer coincidence, Josef returned to Prague two days before the Nazi invasion to pick up Mandula and baby Madeleine. The arrival of the Germans threw his plans into confusion. "To leave Czechoslovakia was technically impossible," Mandula wrote later. "There was complete chaos in Prague. Communications were stopped a little while, banks were closed, friends were arrested. We learned from competent sources that Joe's name is also on some list of people who should be arrested."

In common with many other Czech Jewish families, the Körbels were now not merely struggling for their self-respect. They were fighting for their survival.

Josef Körbel, Madeleine's father, as a young lawyer in Prague. *Courtesy of Alena Korbel.*

"Where Is My Home?"

The Germans plastered Prague with red-bordered posters adorned with the eagle and swastika, announcing the transfer of power. An eight P.M. curfew was introduced. German sentries with fixed bayonets were stationed at strategic points in the Old Town, outside the office buildings around Wenceslas Square, and at either end of the Charles Bridge with its baroque sculptures and breathtaking view of Hradčany castle. Apart from the odd snowball hurled at a German armored car, there were few outward signs of resistance to Nazi rule. The Gestapo established its headquarters at the Palace Hotel. The Czech police cooperated with their new masters, helping German soldiers find their way through the twisting alleyways of medieval Prague and arresting leading Jews and supporters of the old regime.

Determined to evade arrest, Josef and Mandula decided to leave their apartment. "We slept each night with [different] friends and spent the days on Prague streets and in restaurants," Mandula recalled later. "It was mostly during the night when the Gestapo arrested people." In order not to be encumbered with a two-year-old child, they sent Madeleine to stay for a few days with Mandula's mother, Ružena Spiegel, in the countryside.

Although the Germans had arrived in Prague with long lists of names and addresses of potential troublemakers, there was a good deal of confusion in those early days after the invasion. The lists were incomplete and included the names of activists who had long since fled the country. The Nazis failed to live up to their reputation for efficiency. There was a lack of clear instructions. Despite the panic caused by the invasion, the Germans did not introduce terror overnight. The Czechs soon learned to distinguish between the regular Czech police, the security police, and the Gestapo and to find ways of dealing with them. "In the first few weeks of the Protectorate, life continued almost as usual, except for the overnight change in road traffic from right to left," wrote Ruth Bondy, a survivor of Terezín and Auschwitz. "To their great surprise, the Czechs discovered that even [officials] in German uniform could be bribed, especially the lower ranks. . . . Bribery became almost a national duty."

At this time the main emphasis of German policy toward Jews was to encourage them to leave the Protectorate. As far as the new rulers were concerned, the fewer Jews the better. The principal obstacle to Jewish emigration from Nazi-controlled Europe was not the difficulty of getting exit permits, but of finding places of refuge. Britain, France, the United States, and the other Western democracies all had strict quotas for Jewish asylum-seekers. Total Jewish immigration to Palestine, then a British mandate under the League of Nations, was restricted to ten thousand people annually.

Fortunately for the Körbels, Josef had excellent connections with Yugoslav editors and was able to get letters of accreditation as a foreign correspondent from two Belgrade newspapers, *Obzor* and *Jutro*. As he wrote in his 1951 book, *Tito's Communism*, "When my country was occupied by the Germans, my first thought for safety went to Yugoslavia." He submitted the accreditation letters to the German authorities in Prague. After a nerve-racking wait, he was finally granted exit visas for the whole family ten days after the invasion. Mandula later told friends in Denver that when Josef went for his interview with the Gestapo, she and Madeleine were waiting in a coffee shop around the corner.

As Mandula later recalled, "With the help of some good friends and lots of luck and a little bribery, the last plan worked, and we managed to get the necessary Gestapo permission to leave the country. This happened about five in the evening and by eleven the same night, we all three were on the train to Belgrade with two small suitcases which we were able to pack in a hurry. That was the last time we saw our parents alive."

The Körbels spent about two weeks in Belgrade. According to Mandula, Josef had to arrange "a lot of practical things," including the transfer of money to England. Even in Yugoslavia, however, the family was not safe. The government was becoming increasingly pro-German, and former Czechoslovak officials were viewed with suspicion. Josef spent much of his time looking up journalist contacts, including his old friends the Ribnikars. Jara Ribnikar says that her publisher husband Vlado helped the Körbels get to Greece. "It was dangerous. There was a feeling that all diplomats were spies. But Vlado knew everybody in town and had friends in the government. He was able to help them get out."

It was not until the beginning of May that the Körbel family finally got to England, via a circuitous route that took them around the Mediterranean. Josef's older brother, Jan, was already in England, having fled Czechoslovakia the previous year. "My father sensed that a terrible time was coming in Europe," said Jan's daughter, Alena. "He had lived in the United States during the Depression and had seen police attacking peaceful crowds with weapons. When things started falling apart in Europe, he sensed the climate." Before leaving Czechoslovakia, Jan had sold his share in the building business that he operated with his father, Arnošt. According to his niece, Dasha, the money from the building business would be used to keep the family afloat in England and send the children to private schools.

Jan's family arrived in London at about the same time as Josef and his family. Alena, who was two years older than Madeleine, has vivid memories of saying good-bye to her grandmother at the Prague train station. Her mother had told her that they were just going for a "holiday," but Alena found that difficult to believe, seeing the tears of grief falling down her grandmother's face. "My grandmother had never cried like that before when we went away." She also could not understand why she was forbidden to walk about on the platform when the train stopped at a station in Germany. Eventually, Alena's parents told her that the reason was that Uncle Josef was a politician and "we could all have got into trouble with the Germans because of him."

There was an element of truth in this story. Josef Körbel was a convinced Benešite and had been included on a list, drawn up by Beneš supporters, of more than fifty prominent Czechoslovaks believed to be in danger from the Nazis. But an equally, if not more, important reason for the family's hurried departure from Czechoslovakia was kept secret from the children. By the definition of the Nuremberg laws, they were Jews. Josef would later give his own children a similarly misleading explanation for their flight.

Josef and Mandula's first impressions of England were deeply demoralizing. Leading Czech exiles such as Beneš were still in France, and there was little for Josef to do. When they got to London, the only place they could find to stay was a depressing little boardinghouse. The welcome was as damp and miserable as the gloomy English weather. London was full of refugees from Central Europe, many of them Jews, who had fled in horror from Hitler. The Körbels' shock over their first immersion in the English way of life was shared by many Central European refugees. George Weidenfeld, an Austrian Jew who went on to found a successful publishing company, can still remember the "alien smell of cold bacon, lard, kidneys, and rancid butter" that greeted him on his arrival in a humble London boardinghouse.

For most refugees, England was merely a stop on the way to somewhere else. Prior to the outbreak of war, the government did not permit refugees to stay permanently in Britain without a guarantee of financial assistance. The Körbels joined the refugee treadmill, trudging between government offices and embassies and philanthropic organizations like the Czechoslovak Refugee Trust. The big hotels served as clearinghouses for information and gossip. "There was a bustle and a wave of excitement when one discovered a new arrival and heard the latest news from Vienna, Frankfurt, or Berlin," Weidenfeld wrote in his memoirs. "Central European refugees were recognizable by their clothes—overcoats a trifle too long, hats too large and too jauntily set, ties a little too bright and too large, a peculiar type of blazer of artificial wool in gray, blue or black, the waistline taken in at the back with elastic."

While Josef sought out other Czech exiles in the hope of finding full-time employment, Mandula tried to amuse Madeleine by taking her to public parks. She spoke practically no English, so contact with the locals was minimal. As Mandula later wrote, "It took me a long time before I could understand the [English] way of life and feel comfortable in their midst. Just as we were waiting to be able to return home, they were waiting for the time when all the foreigners [would] leave them."

Life began to improve in the summer when Jan Masaryk, a former

Czechoslovak ambassador to London and the son of Tomáš Masaryk, opened a small office. A close ally of former president Beneš, Masaryk recruited Josef and several other exiled foreign ministry employees to run the office, which functioned as a kind of public relations department. Josef had the job of facilitating Masaryk's contacts with British journalists and getting as much news as possible about the German occupation of Czechoslovakia into the British press. The job was also a passport to staying in Britain.

Josef, Mandula, and Madeleine were finally able to leave the boarding-house for more comfortable accommodation in Walton-on-Thames, a lit-tle town forty minutes by train from the center of London. One of the few contacts that the Körbels had in London prior to their arrival was one of Mandula's former teachers in Switzerland. The family became paying guests at her country house.

The Nazi invasion of the rump Czechoslovakia touched off a scramble by other members of the Körbel clan to get out of the country. In March 1939, when the Germans marched into Prague, five children of Josef and Auguste Körbel were still living. Each branch of the family would find a way to get at least some of its members to safety. The survivors from Marta's family would end up in Brazil; Arnošt's two sons would settle in England and America; four generations of Karel's descendants are now living in Israel, along with three generations of Irma's descen-dants; Argentina would become home to Emma's two daughters and their children.

Of all the members of the extended Körbel family, perhaps the best prepared for the Nazi takeover of Czechoslovakia was Karel's second son, Chaim. (Chaim was first cousin to Madeleine's father, Josef.) Now seventeen, he had been a committed Zionist since the age of twelve, planning and training for the day when he could emigrate to Palestine. Over the past year, he had attended courses of the Youth-Aliyah organiza-tion, which prepared Jewish students for agricultural work in Palestine. (*Aliyah* is a Hebrew term for emigration to Palestine.) Chaim had done well in his studies and was chosen as one of 150 Youth-Aliyah youngsters to be given emigration certificates for Palestine in March 1939.

The youngsters were told to gather in Prague on March 15. Chaim

Körbel arrived in the Czech capital from Brno as German tanks were rumbling through the city. Youth-Aliyah had rented a hall on the northern outskirts of Prague where the students could stay until their departure, which was planned for March 20. As luck would have it, the invading army established its headquarters just a few hundred yards away. "It was frightening," Chaim recalled. "We saw a bit of the Germans. They used to come to drink beer in a restaurant near us, and we had to keep quiet so that they would not know we were there."

Chaim and the other students scrounged straw from a local farmer for bedding. Once during the week, they were allowed into Prague to take a shower in a public bathhouse. Finally, after protracted negotiations between Youth-Aliyah and the Gestapo, they received permission to leave the country. They were the first organized group of Jews to be allowed out of Czechoslovakia following the invasion. "At that time, the Germans were just interested in getting rid of the Jews," said Chaim. "The British were stricter about illegal aliens." The circuitous escape route took the students via Germany, France, and Egypt. Once in Palestine, Chaim was sent to work on a kibbutz near Tel Aviv.

His older brother, Gert, was not so lucky. Like Chaim, Gert was a committed Zionist who planned to make his life in Palestine. He had a right to an emigration certificate, but Youth-Aliyah needed instructors to stay behind in Czechoslovakia to train other youngsters. A lottery was held to decide who would stay and who would go. Gert drew one of the instructor lots. When Chaim reached Tel Aviv, he bought an emigration certificate for Gert in exchange for a gold watch given to him by his father. "I sent the certificate to my brother, but it reached him too late," Chaim recalled later.

For a time, Chaim was able to exchange letters with his brother and parents via Hungary. Sometimes written in private code to avoid censorship, the letters reveal some of the agonies and humiliations experienced by Jews in Nazi-controlled Europe. There are references to Gert's hopes of joining Chaim in Palestine, the expulsion of Jews from their homes, the establishment of Jewish ghettos, and finally the family's transportation to an internment camp for Jews at Terezín. Soon, Chaim became an expert at reading between the lines. When his mother Grete wrote that she had heard from her brothers Franz and Fritz, he understood that they had made it safely to Chile. When she wrote that her sister Marianne and her husband had "unfortunately been unable to join" Franz and Fritz, he understood that they were dead, probably murdered by the Nazis.

On June 6, 1940, Grete wrote to say that she and Karel were "finally over the trouble of moving." This meant that they had been forced out of their home by the Nazis and compelled to live in a communal apartment in a much less desirable part of town. Rereading his mother's letter nearly sixty years later, Chaim cannot help crying. "Except for a few small items, everything is OK now. I am always thinking about the fact that your birthday is getting closer. I only hope this letter arrives on time. I would like to have sent you a present. I would like to have at least sent you a pen because I heard that you have lost yours [a hint that they have not been receiving letters from Chaim]. Maybe you will have a chance to send a picture."

Finally, Chaim received a postcard from his brother Gert dated August 11, 1942:

> My dear Heinz [Chaim's name in Czechoslovakia], I am going after the parents and all the other relatives [meaning that Gert too was being transported to Terezín]. All of them are already there, except for Aunt Marianne [Grete's sister, who had already been murdered by the Nazis as a Communist]. Regards from all the friends. Best wishes. May you stay healthy. Your Gert.

It was the last letter he would ever receive from his family.

Next to leave Nazi-occupied Czechoslovakia were the children and grandchildren of Marta Mahler, the oldest daughter of Josef and Auguste. Marta's two oldest sons, Karel and Arnošt, ran a big travel agency in Prague. Soon after the invasion, they decided to take advantage of their contacts in the travel business and move to Western Europe. Since the Gestapo refused to issue exit permits for families traveling together, they had to leave separately.

Karel Mahler sent his wife Grete and nine-year-old son Petr by train to Italy, ostensibly "for the weekend," with their belongings crammed into two small suitcases. Now a civil engineer living in São Paulo, Brazil, Pedro [Petr] Mahler remembers the journey well. It was dangerous to stay in Mussolini's Italy, which was allied with Germany. Pedro and his mother did not have permission to enter France. Karel had made arrangements for them to be picked up by a "ship" in Ventimiglia and taken to Nice. Instead of the ship they had been promised, they found themselves in a small motorboat packed with twenty other illegal emigrants, mainly Jews. On their arrival in France, they were promptly arrested by gendarmes.

Grete and Pedro managed to talk themselves out of prison by telling the French police the story of how they had fled Prague after the Nazi invasion. Eventually, they were joined in Nice by Karel, who had escaped to France via Holland. "We lived in a room next to the train station, with scarcely any money," Pedro recalled. "My mother made leather flowers, which she tried to sell to stores in Nice. I worked at the beach putting out deck chairs for the tourists."

When war broke out in September, Karel Mahler joined a Czech army unit that was formed in France, together with his brother Arnošt, who had also managed to get out of Czechoslovakia. Family friends in Brazil sent travel papers for Grete and Pedro, and they left for South America by steamship. There was one slight hitch, however. In order to get entry visas to Brazil, they were required to prove that they were not Jews. Catholic priests in Nice issued them documents describing the family as Christian, a fiction that they abandoned after reaching Brazil.

After the fall of France in May 1940, Karel and Arnošt Mahler were evacuated to England via Dunkirk. They served in Czech armed forces in exile, along with many other Czech Jews. Their younger brother, Max, was not so fortunate. Having spurned their advice to flee Czechoslovakia while it was still possible, he would be killed in the Holocaust, together with his mother, Marta.

Another escape route was the so-called *kindertransporte*, or children's transports, that were organized throughout Nazi-controlled Europe. Some ten thousand Jewish children were saved in this way, including nearly seven hundred from Czechoslovakia. Madeleine's first cousin, Dasha, was one of them.

The organizing force behind the Prague *kindertransport* was a deter-mined young Englishman named Nicholas Winton. A stockbroker by profession, Winton had gone to Prague shortly before the Nazi take-over to investigate conditions in refugee camps. The scale of the refugee problem overwhelmed him. In Prague alone, at least five separate refugee committees had been set up, each looking after a specific category of asylum seekers, such as Communists, writers, or Jews. Getting the rival committees to work together and produce a combined list of endangered people was very difficult. After he got home to Britain, Winton decided that the most useful contribution he could make would be to organize special transports for the children. He purchased a rubber stamp and some stationery and set up his own subcommittee—British Committee for Refugees from Czechoslovakia, Children's Section—with himself as "Honorary Secretary."

The first obstacle to be overcome was government bureaucracy. Under pressure from refugee organizations, the British government agreed to relax immigration quotas for children. Children were permitted to enter the country on two conditions: finding a foster family to look after them until they reached the age of eighteen, and payment of a fifty-pound (about $2,500 by current prices) deposit against their reemigration. Other governments were not so liberal. When Winton tried to persuade the U.S. government to accept refugee children from Czechoslovakia, he received a series of polite brush-offs. Proposed legislation that would have permitted refugee children into the United States died in Congress shortly before the outbreak of war.

Some of the organizations that accepted Czech Jewish children did so for essentially evangelical reasons. One such organization was the Barbican Mission, whose primary purpose was to convert Jews to Christianity. There were many complaints from Jewish groups. Winton, however, took the view that any sponsor was better than none at all. "It was very difficult to find families to take the children," he recalled. "The fact that there were so many parents [in Czechoslovakia] desperate to get rid of their children made me think they really must be in danger." When a delegation of Orthodox Jews came to Winton to complain about the activities of the Barbican Mission, he sent them away with the comment: "If you prefer dead Jews to Jews who become Christians, that is your business, not mine."

The most fortunate children were those—like Dasha—who had relatives already in England. Josef and Jan agreed to act as sponsors for their niece, which made the whole procedure much simpler. Even so, Dasha's parents took the precaution of having her baptized before leaving the country.

Arrangements were made for the eleven-year-old Dasha to join a group of 241 children leaving Prague on June 30. It was the largest single transport organized by Winton before the gates slammed shut with the outbreak of war on September 1. Her six-year-old sister, Milena, had initially also been on the list of children to be sent to England. But she broke her leg a few days before the scheduled departure and failed to join the group. It is still unclear to Dasha whether her sister remained behind because of her broken leg or because her parents could not bear to part with their youngest child.

Grete and Rudolf Deiml traveled to Prague from their hometown of Strakonice in southern Bohemia to see their oldest daughter off. There were heartbreaking scenes at the railroad station as parents agonized over whether or not they were doing the right thing. Later, one of the other girls on the train would remember how her mother suddenly changed her mind and pulled her out through the window. The mother put the daughter back on the train and pulled her off two more times before finally letting her go, a decision that almost certainly saved her life. Dasha sat by herself in a corner, trying her best to put on a brave face in front of her parents. "Mummy wouldn't like to see me crying," she kept on repeating to herself.

When the train reached the German border, another hitch arose. One of the chaperones had left a suitcase containing the children's passports and visas back in Prague. Eventually, the suitcase was found, but the train was delayed for several hours while a car was dispatched from Prague with the precious documents. The carriages were sealed for the trip across Nazi Germany to prevent anyone getting on or off. On their arrival in Holland, the children received sweets and drinks from the Dutch Red Cross, a gesture that many of them still remember. At the Hook of Holland, they were put on board a ferry for a nighttime journey across the North Sea to England. One of Dasha's companions remembers being lulled to sleep by the "slow, doleful melody of the Czech national anthem" from somewhere in the bowels of the ship. *"Kde domov můj? Kde domov můj?"* the children were singing. "Where is my home? Where is my home?"

There was more chaos at Liverpool Street station when the train finally reached London. Winton's formidable mother presided over a vast pile of suitcases that all had to be sorted and distributed. Still wearing name tags around their necks, the children were formed into lines. A reporter for the *New Statesman* described the scene. "Policemen kept a gangway for the [children who were] led off to a gymnasium . . . curtained down the middle. Children sat on benches on one side of the curtain, the stepparents were on the other. As each name was called out, the child went through an opening in the curtain and was welcomed by its new parents on the other."

Josef and Jan had decided that Dasha would attend a boarding school in Walton-on-Thames after resting a few days with Josef's family. The following evening, she wrote to her parents to describe the journey and give them her first impressions of England. "I was feeling bad on the train. A man gave me some liquor and I felt even worse. On the ship, we all had our own bunks, and I slept all the time. In London, my uncles were waiting for me at the train station. I am now in Walton. . . . Madlenka [Madeleine] is lovely. I like it here very much, although I can't get used to the food. The local bread is white and strange. We have a beautiful garden and are outside all the time."

Madeleine's parents added their own notes to Dasha's letter. "Dashenka is like a giant, a bit bigger than myself," marveled Mandula. "She is very sensible, and you don't have to worry about her at all." In his note, Josef said he was "taking care" of the "other things," meaning that he was attempting to get emigration visas for the rest of the family. But he added a note of caution. "It is harder now because you didn't send Milena [Dasha's six-year-old sister]. Don't give yourself any illusions about Canada. Many kisses."

After an uphill battle with American bureaucrats, Dasha's parents and sister would eventually receive entry permits to the United States. By then, however, it would be impossible for them to leave Czechoslovakia.

On September 1, the Nazis invaded Poland. Two days later, Britain and France both declared war on Germany, in fulfillment of their treaty obligations to Poland. Chamberlain and Daladier had done their best to appease Hitler, but there were limits even to their gullibility. Europe was once again at war.

The outbreak of war did not immediately stop all Jewish emigration from Czechoslovakia, although it severely disrupted it. The price of transportation and transit visas spiraled out of reach of many Czech Jews. With bribes, ingenuity, and a good deal of luck, however, it was still possible to get to Palestine. All emigration was tightly controlled by the Nazis. Shortly before the outbreak of war, an SS officer named Adolf Eichmann had established a central office for Jewish emigration in Prague. In the future, all requests for passports and exit visas would have to go through him.

One of the last people to benefit from this remaining trickle of emigration was Joža Pater, the younger daughter of Irma and Oscar Pater and another first cousin of Madeleine's father. Her father, like most of the sons and sons-in-law of Josef and Auguste, worked on the railroads. Before the war, the family lived in the Slovak capital Bratislava, where anti-Semitism was much more acute than in Prague and the Czech provinces. Bratislava was just a tram ride from Vienna, and when the Nazis took over Austria in 1938, the Slovak authorities began a campaign of harassment against the Jews. The Pater family moved to Prague.

"I remember the day the German army marched into Prague," said Joža, who was nineteen at the time. "We were living in a neighborhood where there were a lot of Germans. I woke up on the morning of the invasion, and saw flags with Nazi swastikas all over the streets. The Germans were all for the occupation. The rest of us sat at home. We did not know what to expect."

The experience of anti-Semitism in Slovakia and the Nazi occupation of Prague strengthened Joža's determination to emigrate to Palestine. Like her cousin Chaim, she had been taking courses from the Youth-Aliyah movement. Since official emigration certificates issued by the British mandate were so scarce, illegal emigration was the only option. After months of waiting, Youth-Aliyah got her a transit visa to Haiti, a fake destination. She was summoned to the SS emigration office to complete the paperwork. Eichmann, who would later be tried and hanged in Israel for crimes against humanity, handed her the passport himself.

It took Joža four months to reach Palestine via a roundabout route. During a stopover in Turkey in early 1940, she received a letter from her parents saying that they had been told to move to a segregated Jewish neighborhood. Joža's older sister, Herta, who did not share her Zionist convictions, had remained behind in Prague with their parents, Irma and Oscar.

"My mother told me in her letter that she wished Herta could be with me," Joža recalled. "From this I understood that life must be really bad."

Rudolf and Grete Deiml with their youngest daughter, Milena, in 1941, prior to being sent to Terezín. Milena is wearing the yellow star that the Nazis insisted Jews wear on their clothing. *Courtesy of Dagmar Šima.*

"We Will Meet Again"

Of all the questions raised by the Holocaust, one of the most perplexing is this: Why did the Jews cooperate in their own destruction? Willingly or unwillingly, consciously or unconsciously, Jews assisted the Nazis at every stage of their own persecution. They handed over detailed lists of everybody of Jewish origin; they selected people to go on the transports and issued the necessary summonses; they were largely responsible for the internal administration of transit camps like Terezín, enforcing German regulations and punishing those who attempted to escape. In death camps like Auschwitz, Jews were pushed into the gas chambers by Jewish *kapos*. Out of the estimated six million Jews murdered in the Holocaust, the vast majority went to their deaths meekly and without protest. With rare exceptions, such as the uprising of the Warsaw Ghetto in April 1943, there were few open rebellions against Nazi genocide.

One explanation for Jewish passivity lies in the nature of Hitler's repressive techniques, which were carefully calculated to reduce resistance to a minimum. The Führer had spent many years refining his techniques of intimidation. At each stage in the process, the victim was alternatively beaten down with terror and pacified with false hopes. He was led to believe that the worst was over, and resistance would only result in even more draconian reprisals. At the same time, the ultimate goal of

Nazi policy was kept secret. Just as Western politicians like Chamberlain wanted to believe Hitler's promises about his latest conquest being his last, so too were Jewish leaders reluctant to give credence to the horrifying rumors of gas chambers and crematoria that swirled around Europe during the war.

The Nazi terror was like a noose, loose at first but gradually becoming tighter. If the victim jerked against the noose, it would tighten suddenly, perhaps fatally. If he decided not to struggle, he would be left at least some room to breathe. By the time he understood what was happening, it was already too late.

Had the Nazis started deporting Jews en masse to concentration camps when they seized control over the rump Czechoslovakia in March 1939, they might well have provoked an uprising. They were sophisticated enough, however, to proceed in stages. The goal of the first stage was to create a climate of prejudice in which Jews would be perceived as somehow subhuman and therefore not worth defending. The next stage was segregation: forcing Jews to live in specific areas of Prague and other big cities. Segregation was followed by deportation to camps like Terezín, which was itself a prelude to physical annihilation. In hindsight, it can be seen that each stage led naturally to the next, but that was not evident to the victims of Nazi persecution at the time.

For the Körbel relatives left behind in the Protectorate, the situation took a turn for the worse in June when the Germans issued decrees forcing Jews to sell their business assets to "Aryans." Anti-Semitic newspapers began to appear on the streets, including a special Czech edition of Julius Streicher's hate-filled *Der Stürmer*. A Gestapo-sponsored exhibition entitled "The Jews as the Enemy of Humanity" opened in Prague, full of claims about supposed ritual murders. At the same time, Czech Jews began to be subjected to a series of petty humiliations, including a ban on entering public swimming pools and baths and all but a few restaurants and hotels. In 1940, more prohibitions and restrictions were introduced. Jews were restricted to the back of the second car of streetcars and excluded from theaters and movie houses. The number of prohibitions was bewildering. That summer, a Prague Jew named Jiří Orten amused himself by making a list of all the prohibitions he could remember. In addition to those already mentioned, they included the following:

I am prohibited from leaving the house after eight o'clock in the evening.

I am prohibited from renting an apartment for myself.

I am prohibited from going to parks and gardens.

I am prohibited from going to the municipal woods.

I am prohibited from traveling outside the Prague city limits . . .

I am prohibited from shopping in any stores except between eleven A.M. and one P.M. and between three P.M. and five P.M.

I am prohibited from acting in a play or taking part in any other public activity.

I am prohibited from belonging to any associations.

I am prohibited from going to any school.

I am prohibited from having any social contact with [ordinary Czechs] and they are prohibited from associating with me. They may not greet me nor stop to talk to me except about essential matters (e.g., while shopping, etc.).

The machinery of repression moved into higher gear in September 1941 with a decree ordering all Jews over the age of six to wear the yellow Star of David with the lettering *Jude* [Jew] in black. The badge, which was roughly the size of a human palm, had to be sewn into the left side of all outer garments, above the heart. September also saw the appointment of a new *Reichsprotektor*, or Nazi viceroy. Reinhard Heydrich, the former head of the Nazi security police, arrived in Prague from the Soviet Union, where he had been responsible for the mass slaughter of Russian Jews. Shortly afterward, he held a secret meeting with Eichmann and other specialists in the "Jewish question" at which he announced plans for purging the Protectorate of its remaining 88,000 Jews.

After scouring the country for suitable transit camps, the Germans finally settled on Terezín, an Austrian military garrison built in the eighteenth century under the reign of Maria Theresa. Terezín, or Theresienstadt in German, was an ideal location for what the Nazis had in mind. Built in the shape of a huge twelve-pointed star, it was surrounded by thick walls and moats. The town was close to the German border, with convenient railroad connections to both Prague and the death camps that were being established in Poland. The cells of the Small Fortress at Terezín had once held Gavril Princip, the Bosnian Serb whose assassination of Archduke Franz Ferdinand in Sarajevo in 1914 had served as the detonator for World War I. Before 1941, Terezín was home to 3,500 soldiers and a civilian population of about 3,700. The regular inhabitants would be evicted to make way for up to 60,000 Jews.

The Germans required all Jews to register with the *Zentralstelle*, the central office for Jewish "emigration." After 1941, when emigration ground to a halt, the office was renamed the "Central Office for the Solution of the Jewish Problem." The *Zentralstelle* gave copies of these lists to the Jewish community in Prague, along with general guidelines about the numbers and age groups of people who should be put in each transport. The transports were marked by letters: A through Z, Aa through Az, Ba through Bz, and so on. Germans did not themselves select people to fill the transports. This task was left to the Jewish leaders.

Madeleine's paternal grandparents, Arnošt and Olga Körbel, spent the first half of 1942 hoping to avoid the inevitable. The wait to be summoned to the transports was agonizing. Every week came news of some friend or relative who had been sent to Terezín or, even worse, farther east.

As with many elderly couples, Olga seemed to bear up better under the strain than her husband. At least she was kept busy with practical matters such as cooking, looking after the apartment, and maintaining some semblance of family life. Arnošt had watched his world fall apart. In material terms, he had probably achieved more than any of the other children of Josef and Auguste, transforming himself from a humble railroad clerk to a respected Prague businessman. His building materials company, Orlid, had been involved in some of the biggest construction projects in the city during the thirties, such as Prague's Jirásek Bridge. Like his children, Arnošt regarded himself not as a Jew, but as a Czechoslovak patriot. Now, at the age of sixty-six, he was on the point of being forcefully thrust back into a ghetto.

To comply with the anti-Semitic legislation introduced by the Nazis, Arnošt and Olga had already given up most of their property. In early 1942, they moved out of their spacious apartment on Kladska Street in the fashionable Prague district of Vinohrady to a communal apartment on the edge of the city. Their two sons, Jan and Josef, had escaped abroad at the beginning of the war. That left their daughter Grete, Madeleine's aunt. Grete was married to a doctor, Rudolf, and lived in the town of

Strakonice in southern Bohemia. As they waited for the transports, Olga and Grete kept up a steady correspondence. Arnošt busied himself by collecting the vast mound of bureaucratic documents demanded by the Germans, from birth certificates to school reports.

Summonses to the transports were usually delivered at weekends, on little slips of paper from the Prague Jewish community. Even if they avoided the transport for another week, there was usually some fresh indignity or prohibition, which Olga relayed to Grete and Rudolf in sometimes daily letters. In July came news that Jews could no longer own pets. Arnošt would have to part with his beloved fox terrier, Drollo. "We received an order yesterday that on the twenty-third we will have to give up the dog," Olga wrote Grete. "It will be very hard on father. He hopes that, when they see that the dog is fifteen years old and half-blind and half-dead, they will let us keep it." In the same letter, Olga wrote that Arnošt had been sick, but "feels a little better."

They managed to avoid the next transport, but the reprieve was short-lived. On July 22, they received a summons for a transport leaving the following week for Terezín. "My dear children," Olga wrote Grete and Rudolf in a hastily scribbled postcard. "I have to tell you that unfortunately we are in a transport. . . . Please don't be upset. It won't help. I will pack tomorrow. . . . Passionate kisses, Mummy." That afternoon, Olga wrote Dasha's parents a longer letter:

It was exactly 9:45 A.M. when they brought us the summons. I don't think I will be able to do much today. First of all, I have to get used to the thought that we are actually leaving. I am going to wash my hair, I am going to do some shopping, and I am going to clean the house. In the evening, I will prepare dough for the challah bread from 1.5 kilos of flour. I will bake the bread in the morning. . . . I hope that once I get [to Terezín], I will calm down. I am not calm right now. In fact, I haven't been calm for a long time. Especially yesterday. I learned the news that Anka Weilova has committed suicide. I feel sorry for her parents . . . I would like to ask you, my dear Gretichka, not to waste your strength worrying about us. You will need it for yourself. I promise that I have a very strong will to survive. Somewhere, in some foreign land, we will meet again. I hope that God will help us, and I beg Him to take you under His wing.

Father must take [Drollo] to the pound, where they are collecting the dogs of the Jews. I know that he will feel awful, but I also feel sorry for the dog. That is all for today. God bless you. Kisses, your Mummy.

For the rest of the week, Olga's thoughts focused on practical matters, like what to pack and what she would do in Terezín. She told Grete that she wanted to "work with children, even if only as one of the baby-sitters." The following day, she wrote to say that she was baking more bread and cake for the journey and was packing as many clothes as possible into a holdall made out of the bedcovers. "Everybody here is doing the same thing. They warned us that we can only take two pieces of luggage with us each." Over the next few days, Olga had to deal with a constant stream of people coming to say good-bye. "Because of the visitors, I am very much behind [in the packing]. . . . Some visitors came to dinner. It is crazy. What were they thinking?" Finally, the last letter before setting off for the reception point, written in pencil on a folded sheet of paper:

We have had visitors all day long. It is now 10:30 in the evening. There is chaos in the apartment. I have taken care of everything. Yenik, Ludar, and Lotte are going to write to you, just remind them. Gretichka, my only daughter, keep healthy. I bless you, my dear Rudolf and Milena. Remember, my first and last thoughts will be with you, my children. I am strong. I think we will see each other somewhere on the other shore. I kiss you with passion, your Mummy.

The following morning, just as she and Arnošt were about to leave for the reception center, Olga added a postscript. "Now we are leaving the house. Good-bye. My kisses. My kisses."

The assembly point for Terezín was on the grounds of the Prague Trade Fair where, before the war, the Czechs had celebrated their industrial and technological achievements. A hangar-like hall surrounded by barbed wire had been set aside to accommodate Jews reporting for the transports.

It was here that the dehumanizing process began of turning people into numbers.

The sight of so many people crammed into a small space conjured up images of the Old Testament. "This was a reenactment of the Flood, the sea disappearing under the multitude of drowning bodies, except that here the human mass was floating on top of thousands of mattresses and suitcases," wrote Helen Lewis, who reported for a transport a few days after the Körbels. "Our senses were overcome by the sight of so many bodies in perpetual motion, and by the eerie and yet all too human sounds that filled the air. But there was no time for reflection, we had to find a space for ourselves, impossible as that seemed to be. When we did find it, we disappeared into an anonymous mass that opened for a moment and then swallowed us up."

Along with the thousand other Jews who had been assigned to transport "AAv," Arnošt and Olga spent two days and nights on straw mattresses. They had to fill out numerous forms, but mostly they just waited. Eventually they were assigned numbers on pieces of cardboard, which they were told to wear around their necks. Olga became "AAv 451," Arnošt "AAv 452."

Finally, early in the morning on July 30, the order came to leave for the train station. The Germans did not want Prague residents to see columns of deported Jews trudging through the streets, so they insisted that all transports leave before dawn. Czech policemen lined the deportees up in columns of five and escorted them six blocks to the Prague-Bubny suburban train station.

For the Körbel family, in particular, there was a terrible irony to the journey they were about to undertake. Once the symbol of their emancipation, the railroad had become the means of their enslavement. The train that took the Körbels out of the ghetto was now returning them to the ghetto, a ghetto far more terrifying than the one that Josef Körbel had escaped in the nineteenth century.

By rounding up European Jews and sending them to concentration camps, Hitler was using modern techniques to reverse the course of history. At one level, the Final Solution can be understood as a terrifying reaction against modernization. As long as the Jews were confined to their ghettos, they were safe from persecution. Once they moved into the mainstream of society and started to fill jobs previously held only by Christians, they became much more of a threat. The Nazis played on the fears of the underprivileged and dispossessed who needed someone to blame for the humiliations that had been piled on Germany after World War I. The newly emancipated Jews were the perfect scapegoat for all the ills, real and imagined, experienced by the Christian majority.

It took roughly two hours for the train to reach the village of Bohušovice. Later on, the railroad line would be extended to Terezín, so that transports could go direct from there to the east. But in the summer of 1942, deportees still had to walk the two miles between Bohušovice and the ghetto, carrying their luggage with them and wearing as many clothes as possible, even under the scorching sun. It was an arduous march, particularly for the elderly and sick. Some of the horror of the ordeal was captured in a drawing by the artist Ferdinand Bloch, who was sent to Terezín on the same transport as Olga and Arnošt. It shows a column of exhausted marchers with name tags around their necks and yellow stars affixed to their left breasts, slumped forward, their eyes grimly gazing at the road in front of them. By the time they reached Terezín, many of the marchers had collapsed under the strain and had to be carried into the ghetto on filthy stretchers.

Once they got to the ghetto, there was more waiting, as the deportees were registered and assigned accommodation. Men and women were separated. "Finding a place for the new arrivals is like a game of chess," Gonda Redlich, the Terezín youth leader, wrote in his diary on July 17.

Based on his date of arrival in Terezín, it is likely that Arnošt was sent to one of the former military barracks where men were accommodated in three-tier wooden bunks rising to the ceiling. Olga probably spent some time initially in a female barracks, but camp records show she was soon transferred to a two-story row house in a back street. At this time, the streets, like the prisoners, were known by numbers. Built in grid-like fashion around a central square, the longer streets were numbered L1 through L6, while the intercepting streets were numbered Q1 through Q9. Olga was assigned to house number L304, i.e., the fourth house in street L3. It was located opposite the Hamburg barracks, a huge women's dormitory that later became the site of the so-called *schleuse* (sluice), where people were processed for transports to Auschwitz. Between eight and thirty people slept in each room of L304, separated by no more than an inch or two of space. At least they did not sleep one on top of each other in bunks. "We slept on the floor, on straw," recalls another inmate of L304, Věra Hájkova. "It was a little more human than in the barracks." The rooms were stifling in the summer, freezing in winter.

It was a communal life, with no privacy at all. Nerves were constantly frayed. "We would argue over minor things, like who moved someone else's saucepan," said Hájkova. Meals were served in the courtyard behind the house from large vats. Breakfast consisted of a murky brown liquid, a kind of ersatz coffee, with bread and margarine. Lunch might be a ladle full of boiled barley, and dinner of soup with scraps of meat floating about in it. The Jewish elders who administered Terezín had a policy of giving slightly bigger rations to children and heavy manual laborers. This meant that the elderly and infirm were on a starvation diet. Frequently, old people could be seen digging for food in rotting garbage heaps.

When Madeleine's grandparents reached Terezín, the ghetto was already desperately overcrowded. The population density was twenty to thirty times that of a normal town. "People arrive by the thousands, the aged do not have the strength to get food. Fifty die daily," noted Redlich on August 1.

Amid the squalid surroundings, the town was also a place of high culture. Some of the brightest and most talented people in Czechoslovakia had been deported to Terezín, including a disproportionate number of academicians, writers, musicians, and scientists. The Jewish leaders of the community devoted a great deal of attention to intellectual and cultural life. Under the circumstances, preserving a sense of intellectual self-respect was the only feasible form of resistance. There were lecture courses by eminent professors, concerts, plays, even the occasional opera. "God, what a life!" Redlich wrote on July 18. "So many contrasts in life here. In the yard, a cabaret with singers, and in the house, the old and sick are dying."

Already ill when he was taken to Terezín, Arnošt got steadily worse. Weak and hungry, he was unable to resist the diseases that spread in direct proportion to the crowded conditions. Between July and September, the population of the ghetto rose from 21,000 to more than 58,000.

That fall, a typhoid epidemic broke out in Terezín, spread through contaminated water and food. Arnošt was one of the first to succumb. News of the rising mortality rate was greeted with satisfaction by the Germans. "The clock ticks well" was the laconic comment of the SS officer in charge of Terezín, Major Siegfried Seidl.

There were so many deaths that the Germans stopped recording the names of the dead in the *Daily Orders*, the nearest equivalent to a ghetto newspaper. Since gravediggers could not keep pace with the number of deaths, a crematorium was built outside the town. On September 18, the ghetto recorded both its highest-ever number of prisoners (58,491) and its highest number of deaths in a single day (156).

Among the dead that day was Arnošt Körbel.

After Arnošt and Olga left for Terezín, Dasha's parents knew that it was only a matter of time before they experienced a similar fate. All their efforts to leave Czechoslovakia with their youngest daughter, Milena, had been frustrated. Rudolf Deiml was one of the best-known doctors in Strakonice, a town of some 10,000 people in southern Bohemia. The Jewish community numbered around one hundred families, of which the Deimls were one of the wealthiest. Everybody knew that they had two maids.

"Dr. Deiml was small and plump, a typical family doctor. He was very friendly, down-to-earth. He spoke with everyone," recalled Hana Malka, another Czech Jew from Strakonice. "His wife Grete was more reserved. She was slim, a little taller than her husband. People knew her as a lady who kept up a certain style of life and did not need to work very much."

In November, the order came for all the Jews in Strakonice and the surrounding countryside to assemble at a reception point in the nearby town of Klatovy. As in Prague, the deportees slept on the floor on mattresses. Most had rucksacks and hand luggage made out of rolled duvets. On November 26, they were ordered to walk to the train station. "It was snowing heavily and it was bitterly cold," remembered Malka. "Most people could not carry their packages and left them, one on top of the other, on the side of the road. The whole road was lined with snow-covered baggage."

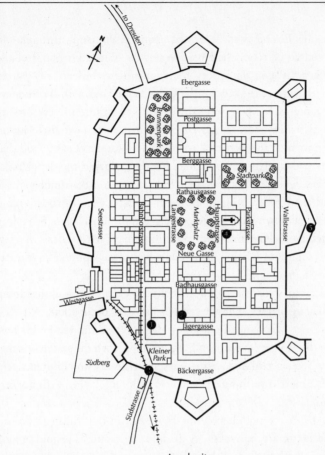

Auschwitz

1. Hamburg barracks. Young girls' dormitory. Milena Deiml was put in room 104. Her mother, Grete, supervised the girls in room 104 and 105 and herself died from a typhus epidemic, which broke out in the dormitory. Later, the Hamburg barracks became the site of the *schleuse*, or sluice gate, where Olga Körbel, Milena Deiml, and other deportees were processed for Auschwitz.

2. L 304. Olga Körbel was assigned to this house soon after her arrival in the ghetto. The street names were changed in July 1943. L3 became Langestrasse.

3. The railway spur leading to Bohušovice and Auschwitz built in June 1943. Prior to this date, the prisoners entering and leaving the ghetto had to walk two miles to Bohusovice.

4. L410. Home for girls. Milena Deiml moved from the Hamburg barracks to L410. Together with other girls aged eight to sixteen, she was taught painting and other subjects.

5. The *schleuse*, or sluice gate, in 1942. When Arnošt and Olga Körbel arrived in Terezín in July 1942, they probably spent their first night in this barracks.

The Terezín Ghetto, 1941–1945

In Terezín, Rudolf was separated from Grete and nine-year-old Milena. A couple of rooms had been set aside on the first floor of the Hamburg barracks as a dormitory for young girls. Milena was put in room 104 with some of the older girls. Grete helped out with the younger children in room 105. There were thirty to forty children in each room, sleeping in two-story bunks. All the girls had their own little locker on the wall, in which they kept a favorite doll or a scrap of extra food that their parents had managed to scrounge for them during the day. Unlike the grown-ups, who lined up for their food in the courtyard outside, the children had their meals brought to them in large vats. In the evening, they were washed down with a sponge from a communal basin. Schooling was forbidden by the Germans, but the adults managed to sneak in a few lessons in reading and writing. A lookout was always posted to warn of approaching SS men.

Other activities for the children included going for walks, singing songs, or playing games. Drawing was a favorite occupation. A pencil drawing made by Milena while in room 104 survived the war and is now preserved at the Jewish Museum in Prague, along with thousands of other drawings by Terezín children. It includes sketches of two children sleeping in a bed, a mother pushing a pram, and children playing with buckets in a sandbox.

In early 1943, a typhoid epidemic broke out in the children's dormitories of the Hamburg barracks. "A dreadful epidemic. Typhoid among children," noted Redlich on February 4. "Generally, typhoid isn't harsh among children, but here it is very severe. There is great excitement among the parents." Over the next few days, as children began to die, there was growing panic over the bacteria-borne disease. Terezín artists were commissioned to draw signs warning the ghetto population to "guard against typhoid" by "washing your hands after going to the latrine and before eating."

More extracts from Redlich's diary show the terrifying progress of the epidemic:

[February 5] Discussions, consultations, how to protect oneself against typhoid. Everyone expresses his opinion, suggests, writes memos. Everyone wants to supervise. [February 6] Parents are frightened, they are looking for guilty parties. Everyone blames the other. Today a meeting took place without a concrete program. [February 8] Some children have died. I fear the disease will not pass. . . . The dying children, the future of the people—even if the end comes, they will not survive. [February 10] They are looking for the center of the contamination. They thought the focus might be in the children's kitchen. But a strange fact—no kitchen attendant is sick. Only two helpers who handle the food. Perhaps the utensils and pots were contaminated. Who knows?

As it turned out, the typhoid epidemic spared Milena, although ghetto records show that she later contracted tuberculosis. Her mother was not so fortunate. Grete appears to have been one of the two adult "helpers" mentioned by Redlich in his February 10 diary entry. Ghetto records show that she died of typhoid on February 15. Six months later, Redlich sent a note to the Jewish leadership of the ghetto asking that Rudolf Deiml be exempted from a transport. "He is a widower with a child who is sick with TB [tuberculosis]. His wife died of typhoid while working for [the youth service]. She contracted the disease while looking after children who were suffering from typhoid."

Some time after her mother's death, ten-year-old Milena Deiml moved out of the Hamburg barracks to a girl's home on Terezín's central square. The three-story building, known as L410, was home to some five hundred girls, only a handful of whom would survive the war. There were separate dormitories for each age group under an adult supervisor, who acted as a kind of den mother. Between twenty and thirty girls lived in each room, in three-layer wooden bunks.

The adults did their best to make life more bearable for the children and encourage them not to give way to despair. Half a century later, former inmates of L410 would recall the nightly battle against the lice and bedbugs that hid in the cracks of the wooden bunks, frequently making it impossible for the girls to sleep. "Often we would wake up in the morning with faces sore and swollen from insect bites," wrote Jana Friesová. "It was terrible, but we could not help laughing when we looked at each other, because our faces were caricatures of our normal selves. We even had insect-catching contests. The one who caught the most got a prize."

Painting was another form of therapy. The drawing teacher, Friedl Dicker-Brandeis, who had studied at the Bauhaus in Germany, helped the girls of L410 escape into a fantasy world far from the grim realities of Terezín. Many years later, their paintings and drawings would go on permanent display at the Jewish Museum in Prague in an exhibit entitled "I have not seen a butterfly around here." The collection includes a dozen works by Milena Deiml in pencil, crayon, and watercolor, reflecting her naturally happy disposition. Milena's drawings range from butterflies flitting about in the tall grass—a favorite Brandeis subject—to two little girls playing in a garden in front of a house. Since the location is clearly not Terezín, it is possible that Milena was inspired by memories of life in Strakonice before the war. One of the girls could be Milena herself, the other her sister Dasha.

Like many of her companions, Milena tended to avoid realistic themes in her painting. Only one of her paintings depicts life in the ghetto. It shows three girls sitting on the top of a three-tiered bunk. The room is decorated with a menorah and flowers (page 92).

Despite attempts by their teachers to shield the children from Nazi persecution, the girls of L410 sensed what was going on as their numbers were decimated by transport after transport. One of Milena's contemporaries, Eva Picková, expressed the feelings of dread in a poem called "Fear":

> My heart still beats inside my breast
> While friends depart for other worlds.
> Perhaps it's better—who can say?—
> Than watching this, to die today?
> No, no, my God, we want to live!
> Not watch our numbers melt away.
> We want to have a better world,
> We want to work—we must not die!

Getting out of the transports became a major preoccupation of both children and adults. Most people were reluctant to believe the rumors of gas chambers that had begun to circulate in the ghetto. At the same time, it was obvious that whatever life awaited Jews "in the east" would be significantly worse than life in Terezín, which was bad enough. As soon as a new transport was announced, the ghetto administration was besieged by appeals for exemptions. Milena's father, Rudolf Deiml, managed to get out of a transport in the summer of 1943 after the youth leader, Gonda Redlich, intervened on his behalf. Milena's grandmother, Olga Körbel, was exempted from a transport in December 1943, after Dr. Deiml wrote a note for her. Like all official ghetto documents, it was written in German. "Frau Körbel has lost her husband. Her only daughter, my wife, has also died. She left behind a ten-year-old girl [Milena]. Frau Körbel is the only one who can look after the sick child. I respectfully ask you to consider this case."

For those who survived the early transports and the deadly epidemics that spread through the ghetto, life in Terezín was a mixture of terror and boredom. Conditions changed from one day to the next, depending on the latest twists and turns in Nazi policy. There appeared to be little rationale behind who was selected for the transports to the east. At times, able-bodied young people were more or less exempt from the transports, which were filled with sick and elderly. At other times, it was the reverse.

While conditions in the ghetto were appalling, they were nevertheless much better than in the Polish death camps. In German propaganda, Terezín was depicted as a model Jewish community. In addition to the Czech Jews, the ghetto also became home for other "privileged" groups, such as Danish Jews and German Jews who had fought in World War I or had otherwise distinguished themselves. When the Nazis needed Terezín as a showcase, they took steps to camouflage the real purpose of the ghetto, which was to serve as an intermediary step toward the "Final Solution." In July 1943, for example, the streets were all given real names. L3, where Olga lived, became Langestrasse or Long Street. The next street, L2, became Bahnhofstrasse, or Station Street. Bahnhofstrasse was the terminus of a railway spur constructed by Terezín residents that enabled the Germans to transport them directly to the death camps.

In November, a bizarre event took place in Terezín after the Germans discovered that fifty prisoners were missing. The commandant responded by ordering a daylong census. Some forty thousand prisoners, including the ill and young children, were made to stand all day in a muddy field outside the ghetto. Planes circled overhead, and there were rumors that everyone would be killed. Instead, the SS guards counted heads over and over again. The numbers never added up as they should. By evening, the field was littered with corpses as the sick and old keeled over. It was well after midnight when the rest of the prisoners were finally permitted to stagger back to Terezín.

The following summer witnessed the even more bizarre "beautification" campaign. The Nazis decided to invite a Red Cross delegation to Terezín and make a film to be titled "The Führer presents the Jews with a city." The purpose of the campaign was to show the world how well the Jews were being treated and counter ugly rumors of genocide. Before the foreign visitors could be summoned, the population of the ghetto had to be thinned out. This was done by sending an additional thirteen thousand Terezín inhabitants "to the east." No effort was spared to spruce the town up. Flower beds and concrete benches appeared in the town square, with a pavilion for a municipal orchestra. The three-tier bunks were removed from the dormitories. Shops were stocked with high-quality goods (none of them for sale). A children's playground appeared overnight. The Elder of the Jews was provided with a car, with an SS man in plainclothes as his chauffeur. After years of being told to salute any German they encountered, Jewish prisoners were now instructed never to salute.

"The Germans are going to make a film here, so they are up to all sorts of tricks. It's really funny," fourteen-year-old Charlotte Verešová confided to her diary. "The sidewalks are being scrubbed and wherever there is even a tiny bit of earth they plant flowers. They carried earth to the main square and have made a park, but no one is allowed to go into it."

When the great day arrived, everything went according to script. The Red Cross visitors were taken on a pre-approved route. They were not permitted to see sick or malnourished people, the cartons containing ashes, or the packed dormitories where most inmates lived. Instead they were presented with a fake facade of smiling faces and well-fed bodies. They "chanced" upon impromptu scenes of Jewish well-being: a fat banker puffing at a (banned) cigar, fit young men playing soccer, girls singing happily as they marched off to tend their allotments, white-gloved bakers unloading fresh bread, children riding a merry-go-round. They dropped in on performances of Verdi's *Requiem* and the children's opera *Brundibar*. The Swiss chairman of the commission, Dr. Rossel, was favorably impressed. He later reported that living conditions were "comfortable," the supply of meat "corresponds to the needs of a normal town," and the "woollen blankets are of excellent quality." The visitors told their SS hosts that what most "astonished" them was that it had been so difficult to get permission to visit such an obviously well-run town.

The transports to the East resumed two months after the visit by the Red Cross. Getting exemptions now became virtually impossible. The demand for new deportees was just too great. Sensing they were losing the war, the Germans now insisted that all categories of prisoner be included in the transports. The children's homes were emptied out, as were the hospitals. A total of eighteen thousand Terezín prisoners were sent to Auschwitz in September and October, reducing the population of the ghetto to just over eleven thousand.

It seems incredible that the Nazis should have devoted so much energy and resources to exterminating Jews at a time when they were fighting to defend their own homeland from an allied assault from both west and east. By October, General Eisenhower's armies were already at the gates of the Third Reich, while the Russians had invaded eastern Poland. The transports of Jews and operations of the death camps put an unnecessary extra strain on Germany's already ravaged economy. But Hitler was so consumed by hatred of the Jews that he had long since ceased to think or act rationally.

Among the final deportees to Auschwitz were Madeleine's grand-mother and cousin, Olga Körbel and Milena Deiml. Their story, however, would become known only much, much later.

The Körbel families in England, around 1943. Back row, left to right: Jan's wife, Olga, Dasha, Mandula, Josef. Front row: George (Jan's son), Alena, and Madeleine. (Jan Körbel is missing from the picture.) *Courtesy of the Albright family.*

London Calling

While Milena was drawing butterflies in Terezín and dreaming of the family life that had been torn away from her, her sister and cousin were transforming themselves into model little English schoolgirls. For Dasha and Madeleine, the war years in London were a mixture of innocence and fear. Half a century later, Madeleine would still remember sitting for hours in air-raid shelters, listening to the sounds of bombs falling on London and singing endless choruses of "Ten Green Bottles Hanging on the Wall."

Dasha, Milena's older sister, was sent away to a boarding school soon after arriving in London. She spent her vacations alternately with the families of her uncles, Jan and Josef. At first, her English was almost nonexistent, but it improved rapidly. "You don't have to worry about her at all," Mandula wrote her sister-in-law Grete in the fall of 1939. "The teachers [at the boarding school] are very strict. They make sure that the girls brush their teeth twice a day, and take a bath every day, and wash their hair every fourteen days. They trim their fingernails once a week. Dasha has to go to bed at seven P.M. every evening. I think Dasha really likes that, and she fits into the regime." In the same letter, Mandula gave a hint of her own frustrations over refugee life in England. "We have a lot of problems and not much joy. Our only joy is the joy that Madlenka [Madeleine] brings us."

Aged two when she first arrived in London, Madeleine was a precocious child who adapted rapidly to her new surroundings. She was a constant source of amusement to Dasha, nine years her senior. "Madlenka is very cute," Dasha wrote her parents in January 1940, after spending Christmas with Josef's family in Walton-on-Thames. "She prays to God every night. One night, she thought she could pray with her little feet [instead of her hands]. She is talking a lot now."

The Körbels moved around a lot during the war. As Mandula wrote later, "We were living in other people's furniture, and moved from one place to another, for many different reasons. Sometimes for financial reasons, or for safety reasons, or for more comfort. We were living a short time in London, but had to be evacuated because of the bombing . . . [We] soon found out that there was no safe place anywhere in England." Dasha believes that they lived for a brief time in the London suburb of Putney, just south of the river Thames. She remembers going for a walk with the Körbels on Putney Bridge and meeting President Beneš, who had become head of the Czechoslovak government-in-exile.

By the time Hitler launched his bombing "blitz" against London in September 1940, the Körbels had moved to Notting Hill Gate, near the center of London. They lived on the third floor of a modern, solidly constructed, brick-and-concrete building on Kensington Park Road. Their neighbors were an eclectic mix of nationalities, including a Polish military attaché, a dashing Spanish colonel, and a beautiful Canadian woman on the seventh floor who jumped out the window during the bombing because she could not take it anymore. Another Czech official, Prokop Drtina, lived on the first floor and saw a lot of the Körbels. In his memoirs, he wrote fondly of "the charming four-year-old Madlenka Körbelova" who entertained all the grown-ups in the building. When the air-raid sirens sounded, everybody moved down to the shelter in the basement, which was filled with gas and hot water pipes. "I remember sleeping in a bunk and going down there practically every night," says Madeleine. Occasionally, the shelter would shake violently from the blasts of bombs falling on the streets around them. Morale rose sharply when they heard over the radio that a German plane had been brought down.

"When the number of destroyed German airplanes reached 180, we celebrated with a big party," recalled Drtina.

The family had at least one close escape. By this time, Josef Körbel was head of the broadcasting department of the Czechoslovak government-in-exile. He and Drtina were working on a radio script when the air-raid alert sounded. Believing that the German planes were headed for a different part of London, they decided to continue working in the apartment, while sending their families down to the basement. Minutes later, the building shook to violent explosions. "We instinctively threw ourselves down and Dr. Körbel darted for the table," wrote Drtina. "The bomb was so loud that it almost deafened us. Our house swung from side to side, like a ship rocking about on the waves." They went down to the basement, which was full of "so much dust and sand that it looked like everything was in a thick fog." They emerged from the basement after the air raid was over to discover that the house across the street had completely disappeared, together with a small pub, killing everybody inside. "There was just a big hole in the ground where the house used to be."

At some point, when the bombing became unbearable, Mandula and Madeleine were evacuated to a seaside resort on the south coast of England. They then went to stay with the family of Josef's brother Jan in an old farmhouse in the town of Berkhamsted in Hampshire. It was not an entirely amicable arrangement. A successful businessman, Jan was much better off than Josef and had different priorities in life, according to Madeleine. "My uncle and father did not get on well. It was not a good relationship at all. . . . They were totally different people. My father didn't have a lot of use for business people who were making money and my uncle didn't have much use for somebody as philosophical and theoretical as my father."

Josef commuted back and forth from London. In October, bombs fell on the Czechoslovak government offices in Park Street in Mayfair, totally gutting the building. Fortunately, the attack took place in the middle of the night when few people were around. By the summer of 1941, the worst of the air raids were over. Madeleine and her family moved back to Notting Hill Gate, living at 35 Princes House on Kensington Park Road. Their two-room apartment became even more crowded the following summer after the birth of Madeleine's younger sister, Kathy, in October 1942. "The beds were kept in cupboards and let down for the night," Dasha recalls. "Madeleine and I slept in one room. Kathy slept with her parents in the other room."

Now fourteen, Dasha helped look after Madeleine and Kathy. She escorted Madeleine to Ealing film studios, where a Czech director, Jiří Weiss, was making a film about Czech refugees. For her first-ever performance in public, Madeleine was given the part of lead refugee child. "I remember thinking that I was a movie star," said Madeleine, half a century later. "My payment for the movie was a pink rabbit with long ears." The fluffy rabbit became one of her favorite toys.

Another of Madeleine's early memories is of accompanying her father to a military parade by the Czech army-in-exile. After the parade, one of the soldiers picked her up and held her in his arms. The next day there was a picture in the newspaper with the cutline "A Father Says Good-bye to His Daughter." This became a running joke in the Körbel family. "I would always ask my father, who is this second father I had," said Madeleine. "It made my father mad."

After three demoralizing years, things were looking up for Britain by the end of 1942. America had entered the war. Montgomery had defeated Rommel at El Alamein. The Russians were beating the Germans back at Stalingrad. The bombing raids on London had tapered off. But there were still some scary moments. The Germans had invented a new type of incendiary bomb. "The barrage was again terrific," reported one of the Körbels' Notting Hill Gate neighbors in January 1943. "I had visions of incendiaries falling through [the skylight]. . . . We did not realize the devils had done such awful damage until later in the day, when rumors began to trickle through that a school had been hit, and there was great loss of life among children and staff."

In the fall of 1942, at the age of five and a half, Madeleine began attending kindergarten. Her first school was the Kensington High School for girls, a private school ten minutes' walk from the Körbels apartment. The dress code was strict: "gray winter coat, cherry red school blazer, cherry beret, gray tunic, pleated skirt." Madeleine's first school report recorded that she "took some time to settle down" but was "making very good progress. Her written work is extremely neat and careful," her

teacher added, suggesting that Madeleine was already establishing a reputation for meticulousness.

In May 1943, the family moved back to Walton-on-Thames, the quintes-
sence of middle-class English suburbia, with finely pruned lawns, musty
tearooms, and walks along the river. Madeleine was sent to the Ingomar
school, the best private school in the area, which was run by two elderly
English spinsters, Miss Dunham and Miss Laity. The school motto was
"Play the game." The children, who wore brown blazers and brown
Panama hats, were required to carry gas masks in tins painted with the
school colors and learn typically English songs such as "The Lass of
Richmond Hill." At the end of the summer term of 1943, Miss Dunham
described her new charge as "a quick and lively member of her class . . .
who learns easily and remembers well." Madeleine's English was "steadily
improving." She did less well at arithmetic ("many careless slips") and
geography, on which she scored a D-minus.

Josef walked Madeleine to school every day. He then walked to the
train station for the forty-minute commute into the center of London,
surrounded by platoons of men in bowler hats with rolled-up umbrellas
and copies of *The Times* under their arms. In the evenings, he was required
to do his bit for the war effort by serving as an air-raid warden, making
sure that everyone was observing the blackout. The blackout made it difficult to find his way home. One night, he walked into a brick pillar and
shattered his glasses. When he got home, Mandula had to help him pick
the glass out of his eyes.

The Körbels shared the house in Walton—a two-story cottage with a
large garden and a gorgeous chestnut tree out back—with another refugee
family. Eduard Goldstücker, a philosophy professor who later became one
of the intellectual forces behind the 1968 Prague Spring, was working in
the education department of the Czechoslovak government-in-exile. "One
day, Josef phoned me to say he had found a beautiful house big enough for
two families, and asked whether I would rent it with him half and half."
For the next fifteen months, the Körbels and the Goldstückers lived in
adjoining bedrooms, sharing each other's jokes and intimate moments.
Goldstücker remembers running into Josef one evening, as he emerged

from his wife's bedroom. Mandula was ill with the flu, but Josef was laughing uproariously. "What are you laughing at?" Goldstücker asked him. "I have to laugh," his friend replied. "Mandula is convinced she is going to die, and has been trying to persuade me who I should marry after her death."

For protection against air raids, the two families invested in a so-called Morrison shelter, a huge steel table with sides of wire mesh. In theory, the shelter was meant to accommodate no more than four people, but four adults and three children were living at 22 Stompond Lane. When alerts were sounded, the Körbels and the Goldstückers would huddle under the table in the living room, trying to get some sleep as bombs exploded around them. Hiding with her parents under the Morrison shelter would remain one of Madeleine's most vivid childhood memories. "They had just invented some kind of steel table. They said if your house was bombed and you were under the table, you would survive," she told a journalist in 1997. "We had this table, and we ate on the table and we slept under the table, and we played around the table." Even more than other children, Madeleine associated her parents with security and protection.

The Körbels were especially grateful for their new shelter in June 1944, when the Germans unleashed their "secret weapon," the V-1 bomb, in retaliation for the allied invasion of Normandy. Popularly known as "doodlebugs," the V-1s were tiny pilotless planes loaded with explosives, an early version of the cruise missile. They moved through the air with a buzzing sound until running out of fuel, at which point they would fall almost vertically out of the sky. As a rule, if you could hear the continuing drone of a doodlebug, you were safe; if it cut out, you had to run for cover. Although the V-1s were aimed at central London, many fell short of their target. Walton-on-Thames was directly beneath the V-1 flight path. A total of eighteen V-1s fell on the Walton area. In the first three days of the new bombing campaign, three people were killed and more than fifty injured.

A rudimentary civil defense system was provided by Canadian troops who had been stationed in Walton since the early part of the war. When the V-1s came over, the lightly armed Canadians attempted to shoot them down with Bren submachine guns. While such efforts helped boost morale, they probably did as much harm as good. Shortly after midnight, on June 19, a V-1 crashed into the center of Walton after being shot at by the Canadians. It exploded on Bridge Street, just a few blocks from Stompond Lane, where the Körbels were huddled under their steel table. Rather than live through the nightly terror of the V-1s, Josef and Mandula decided to spend the next few weeks with Jan's family in Buckinghamshire.

As head of the broadcasting department, Josef occupied a key position in the Czechoslovak government-in-exile. Broadcasts back to Czechoslovakia were among the few tools available to the Beneš government in the struggle to regain control of the country. But the broadcasts also had to reflect the policies and priorities of the British government, which permitted the Czechs to use the facilities of the British Broadcasting Corporation. Josef was at the center of long negotiations between Beneš and the British Foreign Office over what could and could not be said on the air. Under wartime censorship regulations, each script had to be marked with a red stamp ("Passed for Policy"), a blue stamp ("Passed for Security"), and a green stamp ("Passed for Translation"). Josef also had to deal with internal rivalries within the Czechoslovak government-in-exile, which included conservatives, social democrats, Slovak nationalists, and Communists.

The job brought Josef into close contact with the two leading personalities in the government-in-exile: Beneš and Masaryk. The two men could not have been more different in personality and temperament, even though they shared similar political views. Beneš was cold and distant. Masaryk, the son of Czechoslovakia's first president and a high-strung American mother, was almost excessively emotional. Beneš was an uninspiring public speaker, who had to be gently persuaded to be less longwinded in his broadcasts. Masaryk had a natural, homespun manner that went down well with his listeners back home. While Masaryk had many friends, Beneš preferred to keep his own counsel. "I have known Dr. Beneš more intimately than any other British subject," wrote the British diplomat Robert Bruce Lockhart. "Yet the intimacy is cold. He is a curious lonely figure without a real friend in the world, and in his presence even the exuberance of Mr. Masaryk is subdued."

By all accounts, Josef was very successful in his job. He was exceptionally hardworking and efficient, taking instructions from the Czechoslovak Foreign Ministry at Fursecroft on George Street to the BBC studios at Bush House in the Strand. He was trusted by both Beneš and Masaryk and also got on well with the Communists. He was responsible for four broadcasts a day, including one at 11:15 in the evening that featured commentaries by leading Czech politicians. Josef "had good journalistic instincts, even though he was not a journalist by profession. He knew everyone who was worth knowing," said Ota Ornešt, one of the editors on the Czech-language service. "He supervised every broadcast, evaluated it, told us what was good and what was bad." Ornešt credits Josef with coming up with the idea of urging listeners to boycott the official Nazi press in September 1941. Beneš supporters in Czechoslovakia reported that the weeklong campaign was "an outstanding success," with newspapers piling up unsold at kiosks.

Most of the broadcasters were Czech Jewish refugees, like Josef. This is scarcely surprising, since it was the Czech Jews who had most to fear from Hitler and who fled to England in greatest numbers after the Nazi takeover of Czechoslovakia. "The ambiance in the office was unspoken Jewish," said Pavel Tigrid, another broadcaster who became minister of culture in the first post-Communist government in 1989. "No one doubted that Körbel was Jewish. It was well-known. We were all Jewish. We told Jewish jokes, and understood them as Jews." On the other hand, they were not particularly eager to draw attention to their Jewishness. None of the journalists used their real names in the broadcasts for fear of exposing their relatives back home to German reprisals. Instead, they chose Christian-sounding pseudonyms, which some of them kept after the war. (Tigrid's original name was Schönfeld; Ornešt is a Czech version of Ornstein.) It was believed that having too many Jewish-sounding broadcasters would only play into the hands of the Nazi propaganda.

During the first years of the war, Josef broadcast two or three times a week to Czechoslovakia under an assumed name. (Madeleine remembers listening to the broadcasts at home in London and trying to figure out how her father had got inside the radio.) Josef's broadcasts to Czechoslovakia became much less frequent after 1942, as his supervisory duties became more onerous. After doing several broadcasts without remuneration, he asked somewhat "diffidently" if he could be paid for the extra work. After some discussion, the BBC agreed to pay him between six and eight pounds (around $300 at current prices) for each five-minute talk, a useful supplement to his modest salary from the Czech government. The topics ranged from comments on the war from the perspective of the "man in the street" in London to denunciations of Nazi brutality. Josef steered clear of Jewish themes. In May 1942, for example, he denounced the "terror" in Nazi concentration camps. "Never in history has a nation committed such a heap of crimes as the German nation," he said. He described how patriotic Czechs were being killed at Auschwitz but made no mention of the way Czech Jews were being singled out for special persecution. Within a few weeks of this broadcast, Josef's own parents would be deported to Terezín.

Even compared to his well-assimilated colleagues, most of whom did not practice Judaism but made no particular effort to hide it, Josef seemed more than usually sensitive about his origins. "It was like a red flag to him," said Avigdor Dagan, a Czechoslovak Foreign Ministry official during the war and a committed Zionist. "He did everything possible to hide his Jewishness." Dagan, who later emigrated to Israel, said he admired Madeleine's father for his intellect and management skills, but "the Jewish thing was always a wall between us." Josef would clam up whenever Dagan raised a Jewish subject. Once during a car ride Dagan mentioned his dream of an independent Jewish state. Josef made clear that he disapproved. According to Dagan, Josef's reaction was on the lines of "one day someone will beat you up." Dagan believes that Josef's rejection of his Jewish origins involved more than a simple striving for assimilation. "He was a very ambitious man. His ambition was obvious to everybody. I think he felt that being Jewish somehow stood in the way of realizing his ambitions."

Several years after arriving in London, Josef took the extra step of formally converting to Roman Catholicism. A key influence on him at this time was Jaroslav Stránský, the minister of justice in the government-in-exile. Stránský was the son of a Czech Jew who had converted to Catholicism in order to serve in the parliament of the Austro-Hungarian empire in the 1890s. The conversion had not prevented Stránský from being thrown out of the university because of his Jewish origins at the time of the Munich crisis. "I felt sorry for Stránský," wrote a close colleague. "Ever since his childhood, he carried in himself an inferiority complex because of his Jewish origin. . . . This is the whole problem of his life." In the Stránský family, there was a tradition that the parents addressed the children with the polite *vous* form, while the children replied in the familiar *tu* or *thou* form. When asked the reason for this inversion of normal European practice, Stránský replied by citing a saying of his father Adolf, who had originally converted the family to Christianity. "I am just a poor old Jew, but my children are rich Catholics. How could I dare address these people as 'thou'?" Jaroslav Stránský was married to a very devout Catholic named Milada. According to Goldstücker, who later lived with the Körbels in Walton, it was Milada Stránský who persuaded Josef to convert. "She considered it her duty before God to bring lost souls to the flock," he says.

The baptism took place on May 31, 1941, at a ceremony in the Sacred Heart Church of Berkhamsted, where Josef's family was living with the family of his brother Jan. Josef, Mandula, Madeleine, and Jan were all baptized at the same time. (Jan's wife and two children had already been baptized as a precaution before leaving Czechoslovakia, following the Nazi invasion of March 1939.) Jaroslav Stránský served as godfather for both Josef and Jan. Milada's sister, Antonia Císař, acted as godmother for Mandula and Madeleine. The Körbels had partied with the Stránskýs and the Císařs the night before the baptism, celebrating with a couple of bottles of wine. Madeleine says she has no memory of the ceremony. Later on, however, she loved to dress up as a priest and act out the sacraments in front of a make-believe altar.

Josef and Mandula rarely spoke about their decision to become Roman Catholics. When they did, they emphasized the utilitarian aspect of the decision, rather than any religious conviction. Josef told Goldstücker he converted to Christianity for the sake of his children. "He wanted to get away from the complications of a Jewish existence," says Goldstücker. "He did not want his children to be burdened with that horrible inheritance." After the war, Mandula gave a similar explanation to Josef Marek, a family friend from Kostelec. "To be a Jew is to be constantly threatened by some kind of danger. That is our history." The Catholic Marek would serve as godfather to the Körbels' third son, John.

The Körbels do not appear to have been much more serious about their Catholicism than they were about their Judaism. They celebrated Christmas with their children, but many Czech Jews did the same. ("Some Jewish friends of mine used to say that Christmas is the greatest

Jewish holiday," quipped Goldstücker.) Later on, Madeleine would experience a religious phase, as would Mandula. Josef, by contrast, remained indifferent to organized religion to the end of his life. At a memorial service for him in July 1977, one of his closest friends remarked on "the contradiction" in his spiritual life: "Though a baptized Christian, he was not a churchgoer."

Despite their efforts, Josef and Mandula felt they were never really accepted by the English. The neighbors were "not always very friendly," Mandula later wrote. In later life, Josef would contrast the English reserve toward foreigners with the openness of American society. There was an ingrained snobbishness toward the Czechs on the part of senior British officials. The Poles and the French had entrée to aristocratic society and were invited to the country for hunting and shooting parties. The Czechs, by contrast, were viewed as irredeemably bourgeois and middle class. "Our social life was only [with other] Czechs," Mandula wrote. "We could only observe the English people and their reactions to difficult situations from a distance, more as observers than as good friends."

Josef's political views were left-progressive. By temperament a social democrat, he was no Communist, but no anti-Communist either. Like Beneš, he believed that an alliance with the Soviet Union would be vital to postwar Czechoslovakia. After all, it had been the West—not Russia—that had betrayed Czechoslovakia at Munich. Josef worked hard to maintain good relations with the Communist members of the government-in-exile, inviting them to spend weekends in Walton. He was on particularly good terms with Vladimir Clementis, who became foreign minister after the Communist coup in Prague in 1948. In London, Clementis worked under Josef as one of his deputies in the broadcast department. "The Communists had a high opinion of Körbel," recalls Tigrid. "They thought of him as a good, decent, objective bureaucrat."

"The Czechs had a terrible fear of being surrounded by the Germans again and always tried to create a good atmosphere with the Russians. It was pathetic really," recalled the publisher George Weidenfeld, who worked at the BBC during the war. "Körbel shared that [illusion about the Russians]. I never heard him make a disloyal remark."

Josef's pro-Russia stance got him briefly in trouble with the British authorities at the end of the war. He used a broadcast to Czechoslovakia to lash out at British members of Parliament who had denounced the Yalta agreement as a sellout of Poland. He accused the rebels of seeking to undermine "trust in the Soviet Union and British-Soviet collaboration" and insinuated that they were German sympathizers. When one of the MPs complained to the Ministry of Information, Josef first insisted that his words had been mistranslated back into English. But he changed his tune after the ministry threatened to withdraw broadcasting facilities. "Dr. Körbel . . . was most contrite and expressed deep regret that he had caused trouble by his recent broadcast," a senior BBC official reported. "He frankly admitted that the offending passage should have been more accurately and carefully worded."

Any lingering ill feeling over this episode was soon swept away by the euphoria at the crushing victories over Nazi Germany. By May 6, the Czech service was reporting that "American troops are sweeping through Czechoslovakia in the direction of Prague against decreasing German resistance." In the event, the army of General George Patton stopped on the outskirts of the capital. Most of Czechoslovakia, including Prague, was liberated from the East, by the Red Army. "Prague, the last European capital to be liberated, is free this morning," the BBC Czech service reported on the morning of May 8, V-E Day. The report proved a little premature. Renegade German units were conducting a desperate rear-guard action, and fighting was still going on. It was not until May 10 that the Czech service finally reported that the blue, white, and red Czech flag had been hoisted over Hradčany castle.

"The smell of powder is still in the air, pavements are being torn up. We see buildings destroyed or damaged by shellfire," a Czech journalist reported from Prague. "While proceeding through the streets behind Red Army tanks, we can hear people shouting 'Glory to victory, Glory to the Red army.' "

Now that the war was over, many of the Czech broadcasters felt that they should use their real names on the air, rather than pseudonyms. There was a problem, however: the real names were all Jewish names. Tigrid recalls being summoned for a meeting with the Czech government minister in charge of the broadcasts, Hubert Ripka, who tried to discourage them from revealing their true identities. "You know me, I am your friend, a friend of the Jews," said Ripka, addressing the broadcasters as "my Jewish boys." "I have nothing against you revealing your identities, but is it really necessary? Won't it be counterproductive? We will have enemies in the new Republic, and it will be obvious that the Czechoslovak government broadcasts were run by Jews."

Tigrid and the other "Jewish boys" decided to go ahead and announce their real names. As far as Tigrid can recall, Josef did not intervene directly in the dispute but almost certainly shared Ripka's unease.

While many reports reached London about Nazi atrocities against Jews during the war, the extent of the genocide was beyond the imagination of most Jews and non-Jews alike. "These were years of hope and mainly we were young and the horrible news about suffering of so many people in Czechoslovakia reached us much, much later," Mandula would later tell her children. Josef and Mandula almost certainly knew that their parents and many of their relatives had been rounded up and taken to Terezín, but they did not know what happened to them afterward. The stream of anti-Jewish decrees in the Protectorate was public knowledge. Until 1942, when their parents were sent to Terezín, it was possible to exchange carefully worded letters between London and Prague through neutral countries like Switzerland. The horrible reality that Terezín was just a stop on a journey to the gas chambers was beyond comprehension, however.

The first rumors of mass annihilation of Jews reached London in the middle of 1942. On June 25, the *Daily Telegraph* published a report about German gas chambers near Lublin, in eastern Poland. (By coincidence, the story appeared at the same time Madeleine's maternal grandmother, Ružena Spiegel, was transported to a death camp in the same area.) Based on information from Polish exiles, the *Telegraph* report said that 700,000 Jews had already been gassed. Five days later, the Jewish representative in the Czechoslovak government-in-exile, Ernest Frischer, reported that "it appears that Hitler is deporting the remainder of Central European Jews into the Polish camps." Many Czech officials took the view that such reports were alarmist. In November, President Beneš told the World Jewish Congress that he doubted the existence of a German plan "for a wholesale extermination of all the Jews." Foreign Minister Masaryk, who had many Jewish friends, took the reports more seriously. "Hitler's anti-Jewish madness grows in proportion to the imminence of his defeat. I have reliable reports of frightful massacres," he said in a broadcast in December 1942. "It seems that millions of Jews will be slaughtered."

More information about conditions in the Polish camps began to surface the following year. In July 1943, a member of the Polish underground, Jan Karski, traveled to Europe and the United States to give Western governments an eyewitness report of Nazi persecution of the Jews. Before leaving Poland, he had smuggled himself into a transit camp near Lublin, disguised as a Ukrainian guard. He had watched guards shooting and bayoneting Jews at random as they loaded them into boxcars. The floors of the boxcars were covered with quicklime, which ate into the moist flesh of the victims. When he retold these stories in Washington, the reaction was great skepticism. Felix Frankfurter, a Supreme Court Justice and leader of the American Jewish community, told Karski bluntly, "I am unable to believe you." After the war, Karski became a very popular professor of political science at Georgetown University in Washington. He retired in 1984—and was replaced by Madeleine Albright.

The most concrete information about Auschwitz came from four former inmates, who succeeded in escaping from the camp in April and May. Rudolf Vrba and Alfred Wetzler provided Slovak resistance leaders with a detailed report of the gassing of four thousand members of the Czech "family camp" in March, and warned that three thousand more Czechoslovak Jews were in danger of being gassed. (Among the members of the original "family camp" were Madeleine's aunt and great-aunt.) The other report, by Arnošt Rosin and Czeslaw Mordowicz, estimated that 1.5 million Jews had already been gassed. The reports reached London in June by way of a Czech diplomat in Switzerland. On June 19, the Czech service of the BBC broadcast a denunciation of the reported mass execution at Auschwitz. "This new crime of the Nazis is incredible in its inhumane horror," declared an official Czechoslovak statement. "Those who took part in carrying out such bestialities will not escape justice."

The resistance leaders who smuggled the escapees' reports to London called on Western governments to respond to the atrocities by bombing the railway lines leading to Auschwitz and the crematoria. But their appeal was rejected in London and Washington. A British Foreign Office official complained to his superiors that "a disproportionate amount of time" was being wasted "dealing with these wailing Jews." In Washington, the War Department argued that bombing Auschwitz would only divert airpower away from more important industrial targets. Any chance of saving Körbel relatives who went on the last transports to Auschwitz was lost.

As head of the Czechoslovak broadcasting service, Josef was almost certainly aware of the Vrba-Wetzler and Rosin-Mordowicz reports. Like many others, however, he may have believed that they were unreliable or exaggerated. "We were all worried about the fate of our relatives, but we had no idea things were as bad as they were. We could not imagine the Holocaust," said Goldstücker, who lived with the Körbels in Walton.

In Josef's case, his conversion to Catholicism may have inhibited him from expressing his fears in public. "I never heard him express concern about the safety of his relatives," said Dagan, his Foreign Ministry colleague and committed Zionist. "The reason, perhaps, is that he did not want to answer the question 'Why are you concerned?' He would have had to say, 'They are Jews,' and that he was not prepared to say."

Prior to her deportation to Auschwitz in October 1944, Madeleine's cousin, Milena Deiml, drew this picture of her room in the Terezín ghetto. The drawing was later placed on public display at the Jewish Museum in Prague. *Jewish Museum, Prague.*

The Living and the Dead

Toward the very end of the war, news from the concentration camps began to trickle through to London. After the liberation of Terezín by the Russians in May 1945, the Red Cross published lists of people who had died in the ghetto. This is how Madeleine's cousin, Dasha, learned that she no longer had a mother. It is likely that Josef learned of his father's death in Terezín from one of these Red Cross lists. But the information was fragmentary, particularly concerning the fate of Jews who had been transported to camps in Poland and farther east. Even after the war, conditions were chaotic. It took a long time for survivors from the concentration camps to reconnect with relatives returning from abroad. In the absence of written documentation, there was always a chance that a loved one might somehow have survived.

It was not until they returned to Prague that Josef and Mandula discovered the full horror of the tragedy that had befallen their family. Josef was the first to go back, accompanying the first planeload of Czech government officials from London, a week after the end of the war. Mandula followed two months later with Madeleine, Kathy, and Dasha, on a converted Royal Air Force bomber. "It was very rough, the first time I had been in an airplane," recalled Madeleine, who sat huddled together with other passengers in the bomb bay. People were throwing up all around her. Dasha remembers being invited into the cockpit by the pilot and swooping down through the clouds to take a look at Dresden, which had been destroyed almost totally in February 1945 by British and American bombers. All that remained was a carpet of ruined buildings. By comparison, Prague seemed surprisingly intact.

Tracing relatives was a painfully slow ordeal. Every day, thousands of people gathered at the old Customs House in Prague to exchange information about former camp inmates and read the messages pinned to the walls. There were rumors that some survivors had been deported to Russia. "I knew that my mother had died at Terezín because she was on a Red Cross list, but I did not know what had happened to my father," Dasha recalled. "For a long time, I hoped he would come back."

Dasha finally found out what had happened to her father when she received a letter via the Red Cross from a man named Jiří Barbier. Barbier and Dasha's father, Rudolf Deiml, had been taken to Auschwitz on the same transport in September 1944. During the journey, they made a pact: If one of them was killed, the other would find his relatives after the war and tell them what had happened. When they reached Auschwitz, Deiml was sent to the gas chambers and Barbier was "selected" for slave labor.

Josef and Mandula learned the fate of their families in a similar way. Their discoveries were horrifying. All three of their parents still alive at the beginning of the war had been killed by the Nazis, along with more than two dozen other close relatives. Madeleine's parents had each lost an older sister. The only close relatives of Josef to remain in Czechoslovakia and survive the Holocaust were the family of his aunt, Emma Altbach. Together with her husband and children, Emma had bought false papers identifying them as Christians. For a time, they had lived in the forest in Slovakia, hiding under haystacks when German or Slovak patrols appeared in the vicinity. At the end of the war, they were captured and taken to Terezín, but by then the Germans were no longer sending Jews to the gas chambers. On Mandula's side of the family, the closest relative to survive the camps was a cousin, Petr Novák, who came to stay with the Körbels in Prague.

On this and other occasions, Josef and Mandula succeeded in creating a sense of normality for their own children, despite the chaos and turmoil all around them. Replying to questions from their children about their grandparents, they simply said that they had died in the course of war. It was an explanation that seemed quite reasonable to an eight-year-old like Madeleine. Her cousin, Alena, who was ten when the war ended, assumed that the grandparents "died through a combination of old age and the hardships of war. . . . I thought that they probably did not get enough food and they were very old." Dasha, who was seventeen and living with Madeleine's family in Prague, obviously knew the truth but says she would not have discussed such matters with her younger cousins. Alena remembers being struck by horrific photographs of concentration camps in *Life* magazine but not connecting these images with her own family. "What could these pictures of Hell have to do with my kind grandparents," she reasoned to herself.

The full story of what happened to the Körbel family during the war would take many years to piece together.

The first Körbel relatives to be taken from Terezín "to the east" were the family of Madeleine's great-aunt Irma, whose daughter Joža had escaped to Palestine at the end of 1939. Ghetto records showed that Irma was transported from Terezín to Riga on January 15, 1942, together with her husband Oscar Pater and their oldest daughter, Herta. When the train arrived in Latvia, they and 921 other deportees were taken off and shot in a forest. Other early victims of the Nazis included the family of Marta Mahler, the oldest child of Josef and Auguste Körbel, Madeleine's great-grandparents. (Some of Marta's descendants escaped to Brazil.)

The pace of transports to the east grew more frenetic in June 1942 following the assassination in Prague of the *Reichsprotektor*, Reinhard Heydrich, by Czech resistance fighters. To avenge Heydrich's killing, the Nazis went on a murderous rampage, killing more than 23,000 people in direct acts of retaliation. A few days after Heydrich succumbed to his wounds, Madeleine's maternal grandmother, Ružena Spiegel, was ordered to report for a transport to Terezín. She spent just three days in Terezín before being selected for another transport, this time to Poland.

There were no survivors from transport "AAk," so it is difficult to reconstruct precisely what happened to Ružena and the one thousand other prisoners. According to Jakov Tsur, a Holocaust survivor and Israeli historian who has researched the fate of this transport, most of the women were taken to a new camp at Sobibor, on a bend in the Bug River. A handful of the younger, more physically fit women from transport "AAk" were "selected" for work in the camp: Several of these women were seen alive at Sobibor almost a year later. Those not selected for work were gassed. Since Ruzena was fifty-five at the time, this would almost certainly have been her fate.

In June 1942, a very primitive gassing mechanism was in use at Sobibor, one of the first Nazi "death camps." The gas chambers were located in wooden huts made to look like bathhouses. There were false showerheads in the ceiling fitted with rubber pipes leading to the diesel engine of an old Russian tank. Soon after their arrival in Sobibor, the prisoners were told to undress and take a shower. An SS officer known as "the Preacher" assured them that there was nothing to worry about: After the disinfecting process, they would be sent to work in Ukraine. Once the "bathhouse" was full, an SS guard started the motor, sending the diesel exhaust into the gas chamber. It took roughly thirty minutes for the last of the prisoners to stop moving.

If possible, the Spiegel side of Madeleine's family fared even worse under the Nazis than the Körbel side. Fewer managed to escape before the war. At the end of 1942, three generations of Spiegels were taken from northern Bohemia to Terezín on the same transport. They were led by Gustav Spiegel, Madeleine's great-uncle, who had run the wholesale business in Kostelec with his younger brother Alfred, Madeleine's grandfather. (Alfred died before the war of natural causes.) Included in transport "Ci" along with Gustav were his wife Auguste; his son Pepik; his daughter Valerie and her husband František; their children Jana and Jiří; and finally Gustav's nephew, Hugo.

Pepik, Valerie, František, Jana, Jiří, and Hugo were sent to Auschwitz together on transport "Cr" a month after arriving in Terezín. Gustav died in Terezín in February 1943. Auguste remained in the ghetto until September 1943, when she was taken to the "Czech family camp" at Auschwitz. Prisoners were kept alive in the "family camp" for six months before being gassed, another attempt by the Nazis to conceal their true intentions from an incredulous outside world. Marie Spiegel—the sister of Madeleine's mother—also perished in the "family camp."

• • •

Olga Körbel and Milena Deiml—Madeleine's grandmother and first cousin—received notification that they were being included on transport "Et" two days before its departure for Auschwitz. The transports from Terezín "to the east" had resumed in the fall of 1944, after being suspended for the Red Cross visit. The summons came in the form of a flimsy strip of paper, half an inch deep and eight inches wide, containing the name, number, birth date, and address of each deportee. Attached to this piece of paper was a set of cyclostyled instructions.

"On Sunday, October 22, another transport is being prepared for people aged up to sixty-five years," the summons began. Since Olga was sixty-six, above the theoretical age limit for the transport, it seems likely that she volunteered for deportation in order to accompany her eleven-year-old granddaughter. The summons instructed deportees to report to the *schleuse* in the Hamburg barracks by ten A.M. on Sunday. The sick would be carried in on a stretcher, and appeals for exclusion from the transport on medical grounds would be heard only in the *schleuse* itself. (In practice, all appeals were rejected.) The ghetto police would hunt down anyone who failed to report.

Each deportee was permitted to take thirty kilos of heavy luggage and two handbags. The heavy luggage had to be deposited at the *schleuse* on Saturday and would be sent separately to the destination. There was an ominous-sounding sentence—"Tools, washbowls, and buckets may not be taken"—suggesting that the destination was something other than the promised labor camp. "People arriving in the *schleuse* may take only hand luggage. The carrying of heavy luggage onto the transport is forbidden," the instructions continued.

Whatever Olga and Milena had experienced before did not prepare them for their final horrifying journey. For those who survived the journey, Terezín would indeed seem like the "paradise ghetto" of German propaganda. The nightmare began in the *schleuse*, a hall on the ground floor of the Hamburg barracks. A drawing by the artist Bedřich Fritta shows haggard-looking people crammed into a dark, cavern-like hall, slumped over their luggage, each labeled with a large number. In the corner, beneath a bare lightbulb, an official is registering people for the transport. There was a "transport service," made up of young people, to help the sick and elderly onto the transport. One of its members, Alisah Shek, kept a diary:

October 22, 1944. The schleuse. There are big groups of six-to-seven-year-old children who are alone in the transport. Retarded children. [An orphanage was emptied to fill the transport.] Professor Lieben with open tuberculosis. Hans Steckelmacher, a total cripple. It is too terrible. It is hopeless.

October 23, 1944. Night in the schleuse. At 9:30 [A.M.], we began to put people in the wagons. [The train drew up directly in front of the Hamburg barracks.] Sick, sick, sick people. Stretchers without end. Forty people with white caps [the transport service] have to cope with all this, including the loading of the luggage. Luggage. Luggage in front of the schleuse, on the ramp, in the wagons. Even so, people have ridiculously few things, and even that will be taken away from them. Such heaps of futile energy. The last little bit of energy.

I came back into the room. Little children between three and four, screaming. Everybody with his little rucksack, wide-open eyes, some of them have a frighteningly adult expression. They will probably get their luggage back, but their childhood never. They are all alone. Their parents have mostly been murdered in the concentration camps. Babies. A woman is going into labor. The Germans are convinced it is a hoax. People standing in long lines, drag themselves forward, put their luggage down, and then drag themselves forward again. They go, and are courageous, terribly courageous. There is nobody here whose history is not a tragedy. Everybody has felt the terror—left by parents, brothers, sisters, and loved ones. Now they go without any hope of seeing each other again. One looks with wonder on someone who is crying. They are all courageous. They swallow their tears. In the end, they left the [heavy] luggage behind.

In addition to the two thousand people designated for the transport, there was always a "reserve" of several hundred replacements, in case any deportees failed to show up. On this occasion, the entire reserve was pushed into the cattle cars. Supervising the last-minute preparations for the departure of the transport was an SS guard named Rudolf Haindl, a former electrician from Vienna, who had a reputation for brutality even by Nazi standards. According to Zdenek Lederer, a historian of Terezín, Haindl "often snatched a walking-stick from some aged or infirm deportee and, raving like a madman, beat the deportees. . . . On such occasions it was dangerous to be seen by him; anybody who had come to say goodbye to any of the deportees was liable to be beaten and pushed into the train by the enraged Haindl."

Shek's diary entry continued:

Haindl comes. Everybody is quiet, they step back, a path opens up. He goes back through all the rooms, finds four women. A sixty-year-old comes down the steps, blood streaming from her head and face. It is clear to everybody [that Haindl has beaten her]. She is white as chalk, blood is seeping through the dressing. She goes into the wagon. We are all in a trap. There are no windows, no way out. There are [Czech] gendarmes, SS all around us. We [the members of the transport service] thought we would all go with them. All of a sudden, it is over. The train includes two empty wagons.

Although the deportees had no clear idea where they were going, they viewed the journey with dread. "I remember climbing into the cattle car with tears streaming down my cheeks and being overpowered by fear when the doors closed with a clang as the latches locked us in," wrote Eva Benda, who was part of the reserve for transport "Et." "Above eye level, there were two small windows with iron bars and barbed wire strung between the bars. We had one empty bucket for toilet needs and one bucket with drinking water." Fifty or so people were crammed into each cattle car.

The hand luggage was thrown into the wagons on top of the people, so there was scarcely any room to move around. Using the bucket involved climbing over slumbering bodies. "The refuse pail was in the middle of the wagon," recalled another deportee, Eva Beckmann. "I was fortunate because I was shoved on top of the bedrolls near a window. It was a good spot because I could lean against the end of the wagon. I remember taking out a pot, relieving myself in that, and dumping it out of the window." Wrote Benda: "I shall never forget two small children, a six-year-old boy and a girl about four. The children were completely quiet, neither of them cried or complained once throughout this night-marish journey. To this day, I can hear one of the men coaching the little boy, who needed to use the bucket: 'Aim well, my son.' There was also a mother with an infant. She was very concerned because she was running out of diapers. How innocent we all were!"

The train moved excruciatingly slowly, sometimes standing for hours in sidings, waiting for higher-priority military transports to pass by. The route went north via the German city of Dresden, then east through the industrial region of Upper Silesia. The deportees could see the glow of blast furnaces through the high windows of the wagons. On the evening of the second day, well after dark, the train finally rumbled to a halt. The night seemed eerily quiet and still. The only clue to its location was the harsh glare of powerful searchlights penetrating the cracks of the cattle cars.

Olga and Milena had arrived at Auschwitz-Birkenau.

After another long wait, the stillness of the night was suddenly inter-rupted by the yelling of commands and the barking of dogs. The doors of the car were torn open to reveal an electrified barbed-wire fence, banks of floodlights, and four-cornered watchtowers, about forty-five feet high. Prisoners in striped pajama-like uniforms with armbands with the word "KAPO" jumped into the cattle cars. *"Alles raus! Schnell!"* they yelled, pushing people out the door and beating them over the head. "Every-body out! Quick! Leave all your things in the car." SS officers stood on the platform. To the terrified prisoners, they seemed like giants, members of Hitler's "master race." "They may have been small and dark for all I know, but to us they all looked tall, blond, and clean," said Irena Kirkland.

Shoved and beaten by *kapos* and SS men alike, the prisoners were made to form up into two lines, one for men, another for women and chil-dren. "It was mayhem, complete mayhem," recalled Eva Beckmann. "There was a lot of screaming, ordering, threatening. The whole thing was done under such pressure. It was intentional, I am sure. They wanted to scare us." At one point, Beckmann had the temerity to ask one of the Polish *kapos* what would happen to the luggage. He replied with a sneer in Yiddish, an idiomatic version of German, *"Gepeck ist gewesen."* Translated literally, the phrase means "The luggage was," a brusque way of saying "The luggage no longer exists."

At the head of the ramp stood an elegant SS officer in a resplendent uniform with a baton under his arm, identified by several survivors as the infamous Auschwitz doctor, Josef Mengele. He would ask one or two cursory questions and then direct deportees left or right with his stick. Those who seemed physically fit were sent to the left, the elderly and infirm to the right. Some of his decisions seemed whimsical. At first he wanted to separate twenty-year-old Eva Benda from her fifty-two-year-old mother. After Eva's mother addressed him in perfect German—"Please leave us together, we are mother and daughter"—he waved them both to the left.

Anybody with glasses was considered an intellectual or a weakling and therefore sent to the right. Irena Kirkland and her twin sister Alena were both beautiful and nearsighted. "The normal thing when we got off the train would have been to put our glasses on, so as not to lose them. But we were both too vain, so we didn't wear them," recalled Irena. "Had we been wearing them, we would certainly have gone to the gas chambers." A kindhearted *kapo* later told Irena and Alena to say they were different ages so that Mengele would not select them for his sadistic medical experiments.

For each person who was directed to the left, six or seven were sent to the right. Most of the people sent to the left were young women in their twenties and thirties. The oldest person sent to the left was fifty-three years old; the youngest fourteen. Olga, aged sixty-six, and Milena, aged eleven, were automatically sent to the right. Others directed to the right included hundreds of children, most of the remaining physicians in Terezín, the artist Karel Fleischmann, and the youth leader Gonda Redlich.

A dermatologist by profession, Fleischmann was one of a handful of artists who dedicated themselves to chronicling the grim reality of Terezín as a way of countering Nazi propaganda. His drawings capture for posterity the humiliations heaped on the residents of the ghetto, life in the attics and cellars of Terezín, the arrivals and departures of transports, the endless lines. As a doctor, he joined the daily battle against filth, hunger, and overcrowding. A book about the artists of Terezín describes him as a man "with a talent for laughter . . . who transmitted his own capacity for joy and wonder." He spent much of his time with the children. "One of us will teach these children how to sing again, to write on paper with a pencil, to do sums and multiply," he wrote in 1942. "One of us is sure to survive." Although he was only forty-six when he was taken to Auschwitz, his own chance of survival was virtually nil. As a hunchback, he was automatically considered "unfit" for work.

Redlich was another man of enormous talent and potential. Put in charge of the youth department in Terezín, he was responsible for the welfare of fifteen thousand children who passed through the ghetto, only one hundred and fifty of whom survived the war. His personal diary, which was discovered in a Terezín attic in 1967, has become one of the classic accounts of the Holocaust. Redlich remained optimistic to the very end, buying a baby carriage for his son to take with him on the transport. In a letter to his son before leaving for Auschwitz, he wrote: "We will travel on a transport like thousands before us. As usual we did not register for the transport. They put us in without a reason. Never mind, my son, it is nothing. . . . Hopefully, the time of our redemption is near."

Once in Auschwitz, everything happened very quickly. The 1,700 people who failed the selection were marched off in the direction of a redbrick building with a tall square chimney, tapering toward the sky. The dead and the dying were loaded onto trucks, which also headed for the redbrick building, a hundred yards from the end of the ramp. The remainder were taken to a barracks in another part of the camp, behind the barbed-wire fences. Irena Kirkland asked a *kapo* what had happened to the other prisoners. "You see the smoke over there," he replied, gesturing in the direction of the redbrick buildings. "That is from your people."

"We felt that something unnatural had happened," said Helga Kinsky, at fourteen one of the youngest prisoners from transport "Et" to pass the selection. On the way to the barracks, she saw a pile of crutches, one of the vast piles of clothing and other objects abandoned by victims before entering the gas chambers. "I thought, There are people who need those crutches."

Finally, she understood.

The SS had significantly refined the technology of mass murder since 1942, when Ružena Spiegel and others were dispatched to the death camps of eastern Poland. At that time, the main killing techniques were shooting and exhaust gases. Neither method was efficient enough for the annihilation of millions of people. The SS needed to find a gas that would kill large numbers of people cleanly and effectively. After some experimenting, they came up with Cyclon B, which had been invented for destroying vermin. In the words of Rudolf Höss, the commandant of Auschwitz, "Cyclon B caused death with far greater speed and certainty, especially if the rooms were kept dry and gas-tight and closely packed with people."

In order to implement the Final Solution, the Germans constructed an annex to the Auschwitz concentration camp in southern Poland at a farmstead called Birkenau. Birkenau was a purpose-built death factory. A spur from the main railway line led right into the camp. At the head of the ramp were four buildings with chimneys, each with its own undressing room, gas chamber, and crematorium. The gas chambers were furnished with showers and water pipes to resemble a bathhouse, with signs such as "One louse can kill you," "Cleanliness brings freedom," and "To the disinfection room." A squadron of prison laborers, known as the *sonderkommando*, or "special detachment," was always on hand to coax people into the gas chambers. Keeping the victims ignorant until the last moment was vitally important to the Germans. Any outbreak of panic could disrupt the timetable of the extermination operation, which depended on the rapid unloading of transports and the rhythmic activity of gas chambers and ovens.

When the gas chamber was packed, SS men would pour in five or six canisters of gas from the ceiling through hollow pillars with perforated holes. A Czech member of the *sonderkommando*, Filip Müller, described what happened next. "The gas rose from the ground upward. . . . It was dark so no one could see. The strongest people tried to climb higher. They probably realized that the higher they got, the more air there was, and the more they could breathe. The result was a terrible struggle. Many people tried to push their way through the door. It was a psychological reaction. They knew that where the door was, that was the way out. This is why [when the door was opened], the children, the old people, the weak ones were always at the bottom, while the strongest were on top . . . When the door open, they fell out like blocks of stone, like rocks falling out of a truck. Near the center, where the Cyclon gas fell, there was always a void. The victims realized that the gas worked strongest there." The *sonderkommando* shoveled the bodies directly into the crematoria.

Two weeks before Olga and Milena arrived at Auschwitz, the *sonderkommando* had staged a revolt. Understanding that their own days were numbered, they attacked SS men in Crematorium IV with axes, picks, and crowbars. They managed to set the crematorium ablaze before being machine-gunned by German reinforcements. Revolts in two neighboring crematoria were quashed by the SS.

On October 30, a week after Olga and Milena were sent to the gas chambers, the last transport of Jews from Terezín arrived in Auschwitz-Birkenau. By now, the sound of the heavy artillery of the advancing Red Army could be heard in the distance. Much of Hungary had already been liberated. After the processing of transport "Ev," the SS understood that the game was up and set about destroying the evidence of their crimes. They blew up the remaining crematoria and burned as many individual case files as they could. The 2,038 prisoners on the last transport to Auschwitz included Karel and Grete Körbel, whose son Chaim had emigrated to Israel at the beginning of the war.

For the fortunate few who avoided being sent to the gas chambers, the ramp at Birkenau was just the beginning of an intense struggle for survival. Average life expectancy for inmates of forced labor camps was six months. As the Germans fled the advancing Russian armies, they herded their prisoners alongside them in the most appalling conditions. Tens of thousands of people were sent on these "death marches," among them Gert Körbel, whose younger brother Chaim had escaped to Israel in March 1939.

A Zionist like Chaim, the gangling, bespectacled Gert had stayed behind in Czechoslovakia to train young Czech Jews for emigration to Palestine. By all accounts, he was both brilliant and charismatic. A fellow pioneer remembers him as "tall and thin, a very clever person, an intellectual who knew how to work hard with a pitchfork, loading manure with his long pianist fingers, but with an iron will to succeed." Shortly before leaving for Terezín, he married a fellow Zionist named Eva Tučová. A picture taken in the spring of 1942 shows them seated in front of Gert's books: two smiling, idealistic young people, in love with each other and seemingly without a care in the world. At Terezín, Gert was regarded as one of the leaders of the Zionist youth movement. Aged twenty-six when he was transported to Auschwitz-Birkenau, Gert was one of just 250 men to pass the selection.

Gert was sent to work in a coal mine at Furstengrube, about twelve miles from Auschwitz, under the supervision of German convicts. Many of his fellow deportees died of hunger and maltreatment. When the Germans evacuated the camp in January 1945, they machine-gunned 250 prisoners rather than let them fall into the hands of the advancing Russians. Malnourished and sick with typhoid, Gert was sent on a forced march that brought him and a few companions to the town of Litoměřice, just a few miles from Terezín. By now, his ordeal seemed almost over. The SS guards accompanying the marchers had vanished into thin air. Germany had lost the war.

According to a friend who accompanied him on the march, Gert lay down in a barn because he desperately needed rest. He never got up. He died just days before Russian troops liberated the area.

Madeleine Korbel, aged nine, in the courtyard of the Czechoslovak embassy in Belgrade after the war. *Courtesy of the Janković family.*

The Ambassador

By comparison with London and Dresden, the Czech capital had escaped the war with relatively little damage to its gorgeous baroque and medieval architecture. The cobblestones in the city center had been ripped up to make barricades in the final days of street fighting with the fleeing German army. Before leaving, the Germans had bombarded the Old Town Hall, preventing the plaster Apostles in its famous clock from making their hourly appearance to delighted tourists. Allied bombs had destroyed a factory or two. Otherwise, the city was remarkably well preserved.

"There were lots of Russians everywhere," recalls Madeleine. "People were afraid of them. There were jokes about Russian soldiers wearing watches up their arm." In a dispatch to London, the British ambassador, Philip Nichols, reported that the Russian soldiers "look tough, but are slovenly in appearance. Some of the traffic is being directed by Russian girls in military uniform who seem efficient. There have been many stories of rape, looting, and requisitioning in the provinces [by the Red Army], and there have been cases of rape in Prague. But discipline has now been enforced, particularly in the Prague district. . . . There is an absolute prohibition on the sale of liquor."

As president, Beneš occupied Hradčany castle, and Masaryk was appointed foreign minister. But there was no doubt who was ultimately in charge. "The Russian army was master of the situation. They did whatever they wanted," Josef wrote later. The new coalition government contained both Communists and Benešites, but the Communists held the key security posts, controlling both the police and the army. Out in the provinces, unelected Communist-dominated "national committees" were springing up everywhere. In Josef's words, "Communists were given guns and money by the Russians and spread fear by accusing every opponent of being a reactionary." Josef was struck by the way Russian soldiers helped themselves to whatever they pleased. Accompanying a group of ambassadors on a trip to Slovakia, he saw a trainload of war booty headed for Russia. "Furniture was piled in a disorderly pyramid, and on top of it was an easy chair, in which a Russian officer was sitting smoking his pipe proudly and peacefully." The U.S. ambassador turned to Masaryk. "Look, Jan," he remarked sarcastically, "the liberators." Masaryk could only smile painfully.

Soon after returning to Prague, Josef and Mandula decided to make a final break with their Jewish past. The name Körbel had a Germanic, Jewish ring to it. By merely dropping the umlaut, it would sound much more Czech. Many of their friends had changed their surnames in a much more radical fashion. The change of name was formally registered with the Czechoslovak foreign ministry in July 1945.

There is some confusion about the job that Josef held at the Foreign Ministry after he returned to Prague from London. Eager to stress his democratic credentials, he himself claimed that he was *chef du cabinet* to Masaryk, an assertion frequently repeated by Madeleine. His friend Eduard Goldstücker says that, when he visited Prague in June 1945, Josef was running the office of Masaryk's Communist deputy, Vladimir Clementis. "I was there for about a week, and I saw him there every day," says Goldstücker. Madeleine says she believes her father worked for both Masaryk and Clementis, and adds that the situation at the Foreign Ministry was more than usually chaotic in the immediate aftermath of the war. While this is no doubt the case, it is also clear that Josef preferred to stress his connections with the democrat Masaryk rather than the Communist Clementis.

In Prague, the Korbels lived in an elegant, luxuriously furnished apartment on Hradčanské Square, above a famous restaurant known as "At the Swan," with a gorgeous view over the rooftops of the old city. Half a century later, it would become a stage set for the film *Amadeus*. Just a few minutes' walk from the presidential palace and the Foreign Ministry, the apartment was one of several commandeered by the government for senior officials. It had previously been occupied by a family of Austrian industrialists named Nebrich. As the Red Army advanced on Prague, the Nebrichs moved a particularly valuable collection of paintings to a nearby apartment for safekeeping. But many of their belongings—antique furniture, Oriental rugs, and silver—were still in the apartment when Josef moved in.

What happened next is a matter of dispute between the Korbel and Nebrich families. The Nebrichs claim that Josef "stole" their property and took it with him, first to Yugoslavia and then probably to America. The Korbels acknowledge that at least some of the artworks claimed by the Nebrichs are in their possession, but they insist that Josef was an honorable man who could not possibly have stolen someone else's property. They believe that the Nebrich property was legally expropriated by the Czechoslovak state as part of postwar reparations exacted from former German citizens and Nazi collaborators. The original protagonists in the drama are dead, making it difficult to establish the precise facts.

The Nebrich side of the story is recounted by the siblings and children of the original collectors, who now live in Austria. According to their story, passed down from one generation of the family to another, Josef noticed some pale oblong marks on the silk-covered walls of the apartment. It was evident that paintings had once hung on the walls. He questioned the maid, who had also worked for the Nebrichs, and was told that the paintings had been removed to the nearby apartment of one of the Nebrich daughters. Hilga Nebrich Déteindre was married to a Swiss citizen whose father was a consular official. Hoping that the Swiss connection would protect her, Hilga had hung a sign on the door stating that the apartment and its contents were "under the protection" of the consulate.

Josef paid no attention to the sign, according to the Nebrich account. Instead, he demanded to see the paintings that had been removed from the apartment at 11 Hradčanské náměstí. Frail and fearful, Hilga did not have the will to resist the demands of a senior Czechoslovak government official, even though it was unclear on whose authority he was acting. She showed him the painting collection, which included valuable works by the old Dutch masters Adrian van Utrecht and Gerard David, as well as paintings in the style of del Sarto and Tintoretto. It also included some modern paintings and family portraits by Czech artists such as Alfonse Mucha and Anton Filkuka. Josef demanded that all the paintings with the exception of five family portraits be returned to the Hradčanské apartment. Hilga remonstrated with him, saying that her family had never belonged to the Nazi Party. According to the Nebrichs, Josef said he was entitled to the paintings because his family had "lost everything" to the Germans during the war and his parents had died in the concentration camps.

In September, Josef was appointed Czechoslovak ambassador to Yugoslavia, and the Korbels left Prague for Belgrade. The Nebrichs believe they took the contents of the apartment on Hradčanské Square with them. A worker at the Nebrich factory in Prague helped Josef load the truck with the paintings and furniture. The Nebrichs were expelled from Czechoslovakia as members of the country's German-speaking minority. In 1947, they filed a claim with the Austrian authorities for their expropriated possessions, mentioning that they had been taken over by a "Josef Körbel." They say they never received an official confiscation order for their possessions, even though their compensation claim states the apartment was seized by a Czechoslovak state organ.

The Nebrichs spent years trying to track down the "Dr. Körbel" who, they claimed, had illegally taken their property. There were rumors that he had gone to America with his family, but the Nebrichs were unable to trace him. Finally, in 1996, they heard that the U.S. ambassador to the United Nations, Madeleine Korbel Albright, had shown a group of journalists her childhood home at 11 Hradčanské Square during a visit to Prague. Only then did they make the connection between Josef Körbel and Madeleine. In January 1997, they wrote to the State Department to demand the paintings back.

The State Department put the Nebrich family in contact with a lawyer for Madeleine's brother, John. In a letter to the family in October 1997, the lawyer insisted that "there is no credible basis for a claim by your family against our client." He pointed out that the Nebrich family could not conclusively prove ownership of the paintings. Even assuming that the artworks were once owned by the Nebrichs, the evidence suggested that they had been expropriated legally by the Czechoslovak authorities rather than by Josef.

There is little doubt that some of the artworks that once belonged to the Nebrichs followed the Korbel family first to Belgrade and then to the United States. Madeleine's brother, John Korbel, says he has identified at least two of the paintings from a list provided by the Nebrich family as being in his possession. (The paintings are *Interior of a Cathedral* by Hendrik van Steenwijk, a sixteenth-century Dutch painter, and *Seascape* by Ludolf Backhuyzen, a seventeenth-century pupil of Rembrandt.) He says that he may own two or three paintings on the Nebrich list, and one of the paintings could be in the possession of his sister Kathy. He insists that Madeleine does not own any of the disputed artworks. John and Kathy were given the paintings by their mother following their father's death in 1977.

It is unclear to John how these paintings came to belong to his parents. He thinks it possible that his father could have been given them by the Czech government as a form of compensation for his service to the government-in-exile. Alternatively, Josef might have bought the artworks from the Czech government. The idea that his father showed up at Hilga's door and demanded that she hand over her family's painting collection strikes John as "inconceivable." "My father was a totally non-materialistic person," he says. "Although he could be a stern person and a strong person, I cannot imagine that he would go about acquiring property in this way."

Former friends of Josef Korbel take a similar view. "Josef was a man of character," said Josef Marek, a boyhood friend from Kostelec who worked under Josef at the Czechoslovak embassy in Belgrade. "He would never do such a thing."

According to John Korbel's research in Prague, the Czechoslovak foreign ministry helped organize the shipment of artworks and furniture from the apartment on Hradčanské Square to Belgrade. The Belgrade embassy had been looted by the Germans during the war, and needed to be refurnished and redecorated. When the family left Belgrade in 1948, after the Communist coup in Czechoslovakia, some of the paintings followed them to America. Josef's former secretary in Belgrade, Lidia Nováček, says she arranged for a British diplomat to take several crates of Korbel family possessions out with his own shipment. A Serb journalist friend, Pavle Janković, recalled getting into trouble with the Communist authorities for assisting Lidia in packing up the art objects and shipping them out of the country. "In addition to other things, there were also some paintings by Dutch masters," Janković told a Yugoslav news-magazine in 1995. "[Lidia] and I helped get all these valuables out of the embassy and to America. . . . At that time it was very dangerous."

Josef and Mandula told their children that they had some of their pos-sessions shipped back to Prague "to make it look as if we were going back to Czechoslovakia." One crate of belongings, including a lot of books and papers, never made it to America. But fifteen to twenty paintings did arrive in Denver, and adorned the walls of the Korbels' home on South Madison Street. The fact that there were nice Old World pictures on the walls of the Korbels' otherwise very modest bungalow made their house in Denver "a little bit of an oddity," in John's words.

In addition to any artworks that may have once belonged to the Nebrich family, the Korbels had a number of other Czech, Yugoslav, and Russian paintings that were clearly never part of the Nebrich col-lection. These included a couple of works by the modern Czech painter Josef Čapek, which were given to Madeleine after the death of her father in 1977.

John says he is eager to do the "right thing" over the artworks—and would respect any adjudication made by the Czechoslovak authorites— but was dismayed by what he saw as the offensive, threatening tone of communications from the Nebrich family. He points out that Czechoslo-vakia took action after the war to confiscate the property of Germans and suspected Nazi sympathizers, and believes that the Nebrich property might have fallen into this category. The fact that there is no official record of such a confiscation is not unusual, given the chaos of the postwar period and the destruction of relevant archives, he argues.

"These people probably enjoyed a lot of privileges during a terrible period in Czechoslovakia," says John Korbel. "I would venture to guess that my family's losses in the war were a lot more significant than theirs, so I don't feel particularly sympathetic [to their claim]."

.   .   .

Madeleine's father was just thirty-six years old when he was appointed Czechoslovak ambassador to Belgrade. It was an important assignment. The Yugoslav Communists, led by Marshal Tito, regarded themselves as second in stature only to the Soviet Communists, led by Joseph Stalin. Beneš wanted someone he could trust in the post. "Keep your eyes open," he told Josef before his departure. "I am greatly interested in Yugoslavia; she will again play an important role in European politics." Aware that the Czechoslovak Foreign Ministry was subject to Soviet penetration, Beneš instructed Josef to report to him orally. After arranging for his niece, Dasha, to stay with a relative, Josef set off for Belgrade with his wife and two young daughters. Madeleine was then eight years old.

Returning to Belgrade after six years' absence proved quite a shock. More than 10 percent of Yugoslavia's prewar population of sixteen million had been wiped out in the course of three wars rolled into one: a war of liberation against the Nazis; a civil war between ethnic groups; and a Communist revolution. Thousands of towns and villages had been destroyed. Marshal Tito's victorious Communist partisans were busy imposing Soviet-style discipline on the war-shattered country, ruthlessly eliminating any opposition.

As the Czechoslovak ambassador, Josef was in a curious position. The Yugoslav Communists did not know quite how to deal with Czechoslovakia, which had one foot in the Soviet camp and the other in the West. The new ambassador was half friend, half enemy. He enjoyed an enviable degree of access to Tito and other senior Yugoslav officials. But his democratic, pro-Western sympathies and long London exile made him automatically suspect.

When Josef tried to look up old friends whom he had known as press attaché before the war, he found that many now shunned him. In the new Yugoslavia, keeping the company of a foreign diplomat could be dangerous. Among other people, he tried to contact his old friend Jara Ribnikar, the wife of the publisher of the leading Belgrade newspaper and a Czech citizen by birth. He called at her house and sent her flowers, but she was always unavailable. The once elegant Belgrade society queen had spent much of the last three years trudging through the Bosnian mountains with Tito's partisans, being pursued by the Germans. When they finally met again at a government reception hosted by Tito, she wore a partisan uniform with a pistol stuffed into her belt, and no makeup. "Jara, for me you are still a Czech," he told her. Ribnikar looked at her former compatriot haughtily and delivered a classic put-down line: "Don't count me any more among the Czechs. I am a Yugoslav partisan." They never met again.

Recollecting this incident more than fifty years later, Ribnikar laughs at her insouciant arrogance toward a man she had been half in love with. "I felt a little beat of my heart. I was so, so sorry. There was an emptiness. I knew that something was lost. I really liked him, but who knew for whom he was working? Remember, at that time the world was divided into two camps. We had the idea that any foreigner was an enemy."

In the summer of 1946, Josef was appointed a member of the Czechoslovak delegation to the Paris peace conference. He wanted to take Madeleine with him, but she was so frightened of airplanes by this time that she refused to go. In Paris, he was initially assigned a room in a modest hotel with ordinary members of the delegation. According to a fellow delegate, however, he succeeded in wangling a room for himself in the hotel where Masaryk and Clementis were staying. "I remember [Korbel] as a self-important guy who wanted the best room with the ministers," said Ctibor Rybár, a member of the Czechoslovak secretariat. In addition to being aware of his own importance, Josef was also a good family man. He refused to take part in a visit to Paris brothels organized for some other delegation members.

As chairman of a conference commission dealing with economic reconstruction in the Balkans, Josef had to perform a delicate political balancing act. He could not afford to antagonize the Communist members of his own delegation or their Soviet masters. At the same time, he impressed Western diplomats with his reasonableness and integrity. Years later, members of the U.S. delegation to the Paris conference would remember him with respect. "He tried to maintain a balanced, professional position at a time when the Soviets were filibustering on every issue," said Jacques Reinstein, the U.S. representative on the Balkan commission. Back in Belgrade, Josef kept in close touch with the ambassadors of the United States and Britain, feeding them tidbits of information that came his way.

For Madeleine, being an ambassador's daughter was like living in a gilded cage. She was pampered by servants, tutors, and nannies but also subjected to the stern, old-world European discipline imposed by her father. In terms of sheer luxury, she would not live like this again for many years. The Korbels had an apartment in the Czechoslovak embassy, a huge, luxuriously appointed palace opposite the central post office, complete with chandeliered ballroom and marble walls. At parties and official receptions, Madeleine was often required to turn out in Czechoslovak national costume and smile sweetly at the guests. When she returned to Belgrade as secretary of state in 1997 and revisited the embassy, the one room that really stuck in her memory was the toilet. When she was naughty, her father would lock her in the toilet. There were occasions when she spent several hours on her knees in the tiny cubicle waiting for her father to let her out.

One day, Madeleine went to a party with other diplomatic children. Her parents were frantic because they did not know where she was. When she returned, in the early evening, she saw her father at the top of the circular staircase leading up to their private apartment. He was so furious that he threw books at her, shouting, "How can you do this?" Josef decided to punish his daughter by confining her for three days to the room where she received private tuition. She had to sleep, eat, and study in the room. Mandula, who was much less of a disciplinarian than Josef, went along with the punishment. It was usually "my mother [who] managed to get us punished, my father [who] did the punishing," Madeleine recalled. After the first day, Mandula's will crumbled. She began sneaking raspberries to Madeleine and doing whatever she could to make up for the harsh treatment.

Looking back, Madeleine describes her father as "very strict" but also "unbelievably loving" and "very supportive." There is no doubt that Madeleine was the object of her parents' hopes and dreams from an early age. She was the oldest, the brightest, the most driven. Her younger sister, Kathy, lived in Madeleine's shadow. So did her brother John, who was born while the Korbels were in Belgrade. Josef's Serbian journalist friend, Pavle Janković, said Madeleine stood out from her siblings and contemporaries by her industriousness and ambition. He remembered Kathy saying, "Madlenka is a real lady. I am a nothing." Recalled Josef Marek, the embassy press attaché: "Madeleine was always in the forefront. She was better looking, cleverer than Kathy."

Since the Korbels did not want to expose Madeleine to Communist propaganda at the local schools, they arranged for a succession of tutors and governesses. There was a professor of Czech, hired by the embassy. Marek taught her mathematics and singing. Although nobody really discussed the subject in front of her, Madeleine gradually came to understand that a political struggle was under way in Czechoslovakia between the Communists and the democrats, and her parents were on the side of the democrats. When the Czech foreign minister, Jan Masaryk, paid a visit to the embassy, she noticed that his right arm was in a sling. When she asked her father the reason, he replied, "He doesn't want to shake hands with Communists."

In the fall of 1947, at the age of ten, Madeleine went to a private boarding school in Switzerland, like her mother before her. The Prealpina school was in a little town near Lake Geneva called Chexbres. Although she came to love the school, it was difficult at first. She had no friends and did not speak French. As she later recalled, she had to learn the language "in order to eat." Her parents insisted she remain in Switzerland that Christmas rather than come to Belgrade.

Belgrade proved an excellent place for Josef to see how a Communist party consolidates its power. During the immediate postwar years, before the break with Stalin in 1948, the Yugoslav Communists followed the Soviet model slavishly. Factories were nationalized. The press was subject to strict Communist control. Large farms were confiscated. Opposition politicians were thrown into jail. Wages and prices were established by government decree. Uncooperative priests were silenced. The secret police enjoyed virtually unbridled authority.

By his own account, the new ambassador went to Belgrade with "progressive" political views. He was reluctant to believe the dire warnings of his anticommunist friends who said that Tito was determined to crush his political opponents. Little by little, however, he lost his "faith" and became convinced that "communism cannot succeed, but only brings hardships that people will not accept."

As he shuttled back and forth between Belgrade and Prague, Josef worried that the same process might be repeating itself in Czechoslovakia. On one of these trips, he expressed his fears to President Beneš. By then gravely ill, Beneš brushed the ambassador's concerns aside. "I shall defend our democracy till the last breath," he told Josef. "They [the Communists] know it and therefore there will be no putsch . . . the army is fully behind me."

Events in Prague came to a head in February 1948, soon after this conversation. Fearing that they might lose power in an election, the Communists decided to stage a preemptive coup. Already in control of the police force, they armed a 15,000-strong workers' militia and urged their supporters to attend a series of mammoth demonstrations in Prague. The Social Democrat leader, Zdeněk Fierlinger, revealed himself as a Communist sympathizer. Communist-dominated "action committees" sprang up everywhere, including the Foreign Ministry. The purpose of all this political pressure and maneuvering was to force Beneš to accept the resignations of the democratic ministers in the coalition government, leaving total power in the hands of the Communists.

While the Communist putsch was unfolding on the streets of Prague, a miniature version of the same drama was taking place inside the Czechoslovak embassy in Belgrade. The embassy was divided between supporters of Beneš and supporters of the Communist prime minister, Klement Gottwald, whose daughter Marta had earlier worked in the press office. The number-two man in the embassy, Arnošt Karpišek, was sympathetic to the Communists. The Benešites, led by Josef, were in the minority.

Events came to a head at the embassy on the evening of February 24, on the eve of a monster rally in Prague's Old Town Square in support of Gottwald. Karpišek formed an "action committee" to support the demands of the Prague "workers." He brought a telegram to Josef addressed to the "action committee" in the Ministry of Foreign Affairs in Prague, expressing solidarity with the Communist party and "loyalty to Comrade Stalin." The telegram was drafted in Josef's name as ambassador. Horrified, Josef struck his name out and told his deputy that the only loyalty he and his staff could profess was to "President Beneš and the constitutional government of Czechoslovakia."

The following day, in Prague, as hundreds of thousands of armed

Communist supporters flocked to the Old Town Square, Beneš finally gave in to Gottwald's demands. "You are talking to me the way Hitler talked," he complained. The only non–Communist sympathizer in the new government was Jan Masaryk, the foreign minister. In Belgrade, Josef sought out the British ambassador to appeal for political asylum in Britain. He was panicked by the prospect of being taken away by "a posse of Communist secret police." That evening, the ambassador, Charles Peake, sent a "Most Immediate—Top Secret" cable to London, asking the Foreign Office to issue visas to the Korbel family.

> [Korbel] and his wife are in great distress. He tells me that he is now being closely watched and followed when he leaves the Embassy. He had, however, taken most careful precautions in coming to the rendezvous where he met me today. (I had also done the same.) . . . He tells me that if, as he supposes, President Beneš . . . is forced to throw in his hand, his (Korbel's) only hope would be to get to United Kingdom. . . . Since I took up this post eighteen months ago, I have observed that he has been uncompromisingly pro-British in season and out of season, and he has never failed to provide me with any information which came his way which he thought would be of use to my government. . . . I have found him in every way decent, honest, and respectable, and I have no hesitation in recommending him to you as a particularly deserving case.

With Czechoslovakia dominating the news, Peake's telegram was treated with due urgency in London. "What have we done?" wrote the foreign secretary, Ernest Bevin, across the top of the cable. Two days later, the visas were authorized, including one for Madeleine, then at boarding school in Switzerland.

The final act in the Czechoslovak tragedy took place on March 10 when Jan Masaryk was found dead in the courtyard of the Foreign Ministry in Prague. It was unclear whether he threw himself out of the 200-foot-high window or had been pushed. Josef was always inclined to believe that Masaryk committed suicide. He had visited the foreign minister just a week before the Communist takeover and found him lying in bed, "very pessimistic and depressed." Although Masaryk agreed to join the new Communist-dominated government, he later regretted this decision. His father's dream of a democratic, independent Czechoslovakia had been crushed. For the second time in a decade, Czechoslovakia had lost its freedom.

Josef heard of Masaryk's death while escorting a Czechoslovak delegation on a sight-seeing trip out of Belgrade. He had known Masaryk well in London and kept a portrait of him in his study. "He was devastated," said Josef Marek, who telephoned him with the news. "When he came back, he practically fell to pieces. He did not talk at all. He regarded Masaryk as the last hope for democracy." "He cried openly," said the embassy butler, Ferdinand Langus. Josef told Langus to go to his wardrobe and select one of his suits as a memento "in memory of my best friend." Josef and Mandula flew back to Prague for the funeral.

While in Prague, Josef had discussions about his future with Vladimir Clementis, who had become foreign minister in succession to Masaryk. He was still pondering the British offer of political asylum. Although he was a Communist, Clementis was a pragmatic bureaucrat who had been on friendly terms with Josef since their work together as broadcasters in London during the war. He had incurred the suspicion of more orthodox Communists by opposing the Hitler-Stalin pact in 1939. He and Josef were close enough to each other to go out and buy two identical black cocker spaniels during the Paris peace conference. Madeleine recalls that Clementis stepped in to "save the dog" after the family left Belgrade and were unable to take their cocker spaniel with them.

Clementis understood very well that professionalism was in short supply at the Foreign Ministry. He urged Josef to accept the post of Czechoslovak representative on a United Nations commission to mediate the Kashmir dispute between India and Pakistan. Aware that such an appointment would "get him through the iron curtain," Josef was inclined to accept the offer. He told the British ambassador he felt "he could accept without too gravely compromising his conscience and that when it came to an end he would find other ways of making a living."

Later, once he got to America, Josef would repeatedly claim that he was named to the U.N. Kashmir commission *before* the February coup. The perception that he had been appointed to such a sensitive position by a Communist regime that had seized power in an undemocratic manner evidently made him uneasy. But the archival evidence strongly suggests that, while the possibility of Josef's working for the Kashmir commission was raised before the coup, the appointment itself was made weeks *after* the Communist takeover. It is unclear whether the initial suggestion came from the democrats or the Communists. Josef told the British in late February that he was being considered for one of two posts: Czechoslovak representative on the Kashmir commission or ambassador to France.

The language used by Josef to describe his appointment to the Kashmir commission became increasingly unambiguous over the years. In a February 1949 letter requesting political asylum in the United States, he said he was "selected" to be a member of the commission before the coup, which is technically correct although misleading. In a 1954 book, *Danger in Kashmir*, he said he was "assigned" to the commission on February 5. In an official Denver University biography issued in the late fifties, he said he was "appointed" a member of the commission at the beginning of February, which is inaccurate. According to his official Czechoslovak Foreign Ministry biography, Josef Korbel was "named" to the commission on May 13, nearly twelve weeks after the coup.

At the same time, the archives show that from the beginning of April British officials strongly encouraged Josef to accept the position on the Kashmir commission for fear it would otherwise go to a Communist hack. In the words of one Foreign Office official: "Considering the person we might have got, we were very lucky in having Korbel." Madeleine believes that her father accepted the Kashmir appointment as a way to get his family to freedom but also because he was "intrigued" by the problems involved. "He saw it as an opportunity to do an interesting job, not be in touch with his own government, and get out," she says. "He saw it as a challenge."

Josef's relations with the Communists were complicated. On the one hand, people who knew him well had no doubt about his democratic political convictions and opposition to the coup. On the other, he shied away from open confrontation. He was very friendly with Clementis and even had some good words to say about Gottwald, whom he described, at the time of the coup, as "much more sanguine and civilized than the majority of his brethren."

"He was afraid of the Communists," said his former Foreign Ministry colleague Avigdor Dagan. "He was a very good husband and a very good father, but I would not describe him as being very courageous." Dagan remembers an occasion when he and Josef were both talking with a senior Foreign Ministry official who happened to be a Communist. Dagan made a passing remark about Polish foreign policy being controlled by Moscow. Later, Josef reproached him for his lack of caution. "Please be careful, do not say what is on your mind. You could end up very badly."

By the time Josef discussed his new assignment with Clementis, he had firmly decided not to return to Czechoslovakia. One way or the other, he was determined to take his family to the West. One problem, however, remained: What to do with his niece Dasha? Dasha had returned home from London to find herself an orphan. According to her account, Josef became her guardian. By the time of the coup, Dasha was a student at Prague University, twenty years old and increasingly independent. There had been an unpleasant argument the previous summer, when she visited the Korbels in Belgrade. She wanted to invite her Czech boyfriend, Volodya Šima, to stay at the embassy. The ambassador made it clear he did not want a "stranger" in his house.

"Uncle Josef was very patriotic, very ambitious, and very intelligent. But he did not really seem to know how to handle someone like me," Dasha recalled later. "He already had three children, so an extra teenager must have been quite a burden."

According to Dasha, she met her uncle and aunt in Prague shortly after Masaryk's funeral. They were staying at the Alcron Hotel, around the corner from Wenceslas Square. As she recalled the conversation, the Korbels talked vaguely about a "new appointment," but there was no discussion about whether she should join them abroad. Had they asked her to accompany them, she would have gone, despite her romance with Volodya, whom she later married. Several months later, she received a letter from Mandula suggesting that she go to London to stay with the family of her uncle Jan. "I think it was for the sake of her conscience," Dasha said in 1997. "She told me to go to London, but did not explain how I was meant to get there."

Dasha's version of events is disputed by Madeleine, who cannot believe that her parents would have willingly left their niece behind in Czechoslovakia. Such a step would have been out of character, she insists, particularly since they took a young Yugoslav maid with them to the United States. She says her parents told her explicitly that they had invited Dasha to go with them to the West, but that she declined because she wanted to pursue her studies and had moved around enough in her life. "I'd be really, really surprised, in fact shocked . . . if my parents had not offered to bring her." Madeleine has said she believes Dasha stayed behind in Czechoslovakia because of her involvement with Volodya.

More than half a century later, it is difficult to sort out what really happened. The truth may lie somewhere between the two accounts. The atmosphere in Prague in March 1948 in the wake of the Communist coup was one of total paranoia. Madeleine's London cousin, Alena Korbel, believes that Josef and Mandula may have hesitated to tell Dasha of their plans to escape to the West because they were not sure whether they could trust her boyfriend. "They didn't know if Volodya was a Communist sympathizer. Anyone who knows Czechoslovakia at that time knows that they would have been afraid to mention their plans to a third person. It would have been far too risky." According to this version, it was not until Josef and Mandula had got their own family safely to the West that they urged Dasha to join them. When she failed to come, they assumed that she wanted to stay in Czechoslovakia with Volodya.

Whatever really happened in March 1948, it is clear that Dasha suffered under the Communist regime because of her relationship with Josef. After the Korbels went to the United States, she was summoned before an investigation commission at the university, where she was studying English and French. "There were two questions," she recalled later. "Why did you not go to the meeting in the Old Town Square [convened by Gottwald in February 1948]? And where is your guardian?"

In January 1949, Dasha was thrown out of the university. For the next twelve months, she was rejected for one job after another, before finally being assigned to menial work on the railways. She made a little extra money on the side teaching English to the children of "bad class origins."

Two decades would pass before she met the Korbels again.

The Korbel family in Denver in 1951. From left to right: Josef, Kathy, Mandula, Madeleine, and John. *Courtesy of Dagmar Šima.*

Promised Land

The U.N. Kashmir commission proved the ideal cover for the Korbels' carefully planned escape from the Soviet bloc. In Winston Churchill's memorable phrase, an "iron curtain" had fallen across Europe "from Szczecin on the Baltic to Trieste on the Adriatic." Although Josef had an offer of political asylum in Britain, leaving Yugoslavia for the West without authorization would have been risky. His fear of being trapped behind the Iron Curtain was dramatized in early March—after the Communist coup in Czechoslovakia and shortly before Masaryk's death— when he was summoned back to Prague "for consultations." By accepting the offer of the U.N. post, he could get his family to freedom relatively painlessly.

After a last visit to Prague at the beginning of May, Josef returned to Belgrade to say his good-byes. There was a flurry of excitement before he left when Mandula picked up word of the arrest of a Yugoslav leader named Andrija Hebrang who had particularly close ties to Moscow. At the time, foreign diplomats in Belgrade had no idea how to interpret this development. In retrospect, it was one of the first authoritative signs of a history-making event: the split between Yugoslavia and the Soviet Union, which was itself a harbinger of the great schism within the previously monolithic Communist movement. Like much of the best diplomatic gossip, the tip-off came from a lowly domestic source: Hebrang's cook. As the U.S. ambassador reported in a Top Secret telegram to Washington, Mandula tried to "make a farewell call on the Hebrangs," but "found furniture cleaned out and tearful housekeeper who said whole family [was] in detention." The news of Yugoslavia's expulsion from the Soviet bloc would not become public until late June.

From Belgrade, the Korbels went to Switzerland, where Madeleine was in boarding school. Josef took Madeleine to see the United Nations buildings in Geneva and explained that he was getting a new job. They would not be going back to either Czechoslovakia or Yugoslavia. Leaving Madeleine behind in Switzerland to finish school, the rest of the Korbel family then went to London. They stayed for several days with their old friend, Eduard Goldstücker, now number two at the Czechoslovak embassy, and then moved into an apartment in Mayfair. "They were very, very tired," Goldstücker recalled. "The children slept endlessly." Madeleine flew to London by herself at the end of June for her summer vacation. Soon, the family moved into a basement apartment in Earl's Court, a much less desirable part of town than Mayfair.

Decades later, Madeleine could still vividly remember the gas stove and the bathtub crammed into the damp kitchen of their Earl's Court apartment. It was so different from the palatial ambassadorial residence in Belgrade. She also remembered taking classes at the French Lycée, which she described as "the single hardest school I ever went to." Aged ten, she had to walk back and forth from the school with a suitcase full of books and study eight different subjects, including Latin. She hated it.

Josef immersed himself in the study of the Kashmir problem, an issue he knew nothing about. "He feels rather helpless at being pitchforked in media relations, and is anxious to mug the past history up," a British Foreign Office official reported. Like his daughter, Josef hated situations he could not control. In July, the U.N. commission traveled to the subcontinent with the virtually impossible task of finding a solution to the Kashmir dispute acceptable to both India and Pakistan.

Almost immediately, Josef began expressing fears that he was about to be replaced by a loyal Communist. Messages flew between London and Delhi over how to prevent the commission from going into recess, thereby depriving the Prague government of the opportunity of switching representatives. A Foreign Office friend from Belgrade, George Clutton, wrote a private letter to Josef urging him to hang on as long as possible. "I have seen Mandula once or twice and she and the children are flourishing. A small kitten has just decided to make its home with them, and this is regarded as a good augury."

In the meantime, Josef also lobbied U.S. officials for safe passage to America. Thanks to his U.N. connections, he had been able to get American entry visas for Mandula, the children, and an eighteen-year-old Yugoslav maid, Fanci Mencinger. After the Kashmir commission returned to Europe, Josef decided to send the family to New York aboard SS *America*, leaving Southampton on November 5.

Two days before departure, Madeleine got her first taste of American politics. She sat in the bathtub in the kitchen of the Earl's Court apartment, listening to the U.S. presidential election returns over the radio. Despite predictions, the Democrat Harry Truman succeeded in winning an upset victory over the Republican Thomas E. Dewey. The Korbel family cheered. "I was a Democrat, no question," says Madeleine. "It would never have occurred to us [to be anything else]." Her parents had always considered themselves to be progressive on social issues. Even more important than domestic policy was the foreign policy record of the Democrats. Franklin Roosevelt had led the struggle to bring America into the war and defeat Hitler. Truman was taking a tough line against the Soviet Union.

Madeleine still has vivid memories of crossing the Atlantic. The first leg, between Southampton and Le Havre, was calm. Everybody looked forward to a wonderful trip. As soon as the ship left Le Havre and sailed out into the ocean, the seas turned rough. The rest of the voyage was a nightmare. Mandula and Fanci were seasick the whole time. The family spent the entire trip in their first-class cabin. "I had to take care of everything," Madeleine recalls. "It was November out on the ocean." Finally, after five days of misery, they caught sight of the Statue of Liberty for the first time.

The immigration authorities at Ellis Island reported the arrival of "Marie Korbelova, 11 years old" at 10:10 A.M. on November 11. The future secretary of state was traveling on a Czechoslovak diplomatic passport. The family were chiefly distinguished from the other passengers by the twenty-one pieces of luggage that they carried with them. Clearly, they were planning to stay for some time.

Josef remained in Europe to attend a U.N. General Assembly session in Paris. The issue of his loyalty to the new regime in Prague finally came to a head in late November at a meeting with his old friend Clementis, who was also attending the U.N. session. The foreign minister began by asking a question that Josef had evaded for nine months: "What is your attitude to the changes in Czechoslovakia?"

"I must tell you frankly that communism and the Communist regime are unacceptable to me," Josef replied.

What followed, according to a memorandum prepared later by Josef, was a philosophical discussion on the nature of communism. Josef was deeply pessimistic. Drawing on his experiences in Yugoslavia, he argued that the Marxist system of central planning was creating shortages and social discontent, which would lead inevitably to more political repression. "It begins with a small-scale measure and ends with the most violent action against a whole class. . . . It is the end of freedom." Deepening mistrust between Russia and the West would result in a new war, he predicted. Clementis conceded that the country was experiencing some "temporary" difficulties but insisted that the hardships were a "negligible" sacrifice for the construction of a socialist utopia. When Clementis asked Josef whether he was willing to return home once the Kashmir commission finished its work, Josef replied that he did not see a place for himself in the new Czechoslovakia.

Within two weeks of this conversation, Josef was formally dismissed from the Czechoslovak Foreign Ministry. Three years later, Clementis was himself purged and executed by the Gottwald regime, after a show trial in which he was accused of "high treason, sabotage, and espionage."

With no reason to remain in Europe, Josef left for New York on December 17 aboard HMS *Queen Mary*. Other passengers included Somerset Maugham, Walter Lippmann, and several senior diplomats. Before leaving, Josef had told an American diplomat that his funds would run out in "perhaps three months." The Prague government had stopped paying both his salary and living allowance. He took advantage of the Atlantic voyage to discuss his case with Jan Papánek, a former Czechoslovak ambassador to the United Nations who had resigned immediately after the February coup. Papánek, who later said that he did not know "what to think" about Korbel, told U.S. officials that Josef was thinking of applying for political asylum.

Josef arrived in America three days before Christmas, determined to begin a new life for himself and his family.

America had been the promised land for Jews from Central Europe long before anybody seriously proposed the idea of a separate Jewish homeland in Palestine. "Off to America!" Leopold Kompert urged his fellow Prague Jews in 1848 after a spate of anti-Semitic excesses. "Years ago, when the persecution of the Jews was most violent, a Genoese envisioned the original idea of a new world . . . It is this America that we now yearn for, and that is where you should go!"

The postwar period witnessed the third great wave of Jewish immigration to the United States from Europe, each of them inspired by persecution back home. The first wave, which coincided with the dissolution of the European ghettos in the middle of the nineteenth century, consisted mainly of German Jews in search of economic opportunity. The Guggenheims were typical of this wave of migration. For the most part, the German Jews set their sights on becoming prosperous, full-fledged Americans as rapidly as possible. Social acceptance was more important to them than preserving a distinctive Jewish identity. The most successful Jewish immigrants were absorbed into the American elite. In the words of Dorothy Schiff, whose grandfather Jacob had come to America in 1865, "as to being Jewish . . . once you reach a certain financial level, people don't think of you as anything but rich."

The Jewish community in America tripled between 1880 and 1921 with the arrival of three million Jews from Eastern Europe and Russia. The newcomers were poorer, less well educated, and more obviously Jewish than the original immigrants. Fears were expressed in the *Hebrew Standard* that the influx of "miserable, darkened Hebrews" could jeopardize the hard-won privileges of the "thoroughly acclimated American Jew" by provoking an anti-Semitic backlash among the Christian majority. A rift developed between the supporters of total assimilation and the advocates of a more assertive Jewish American identity. A typical

representative of the first group was Walter Lippmann, Josef's transat-
lantic traveling companion. Born to wealthy German-Jewish parents in
1889, Lippmann rarely addressed Jewish topics in his columns and writings. When he did, the tone was usually negative. "I do not regard the
Jews as innocent victims," he wrote as a young man. He complained
about their "distressing personal and social habits," which he attributed
to "a bitter history . . . intensified by a pharasaical theology." The second,
much smaller group was represented by Supreme Court Justice Louis
Brandeis, who insisted that "to be good Americans we must be better
Jews, and to be better Jews we must become Zionists." The debate
between assimilationists and Zionists in the United States echoed the
debate in prewar Europe over how to react to the rise of Hitler.

While anti-Semitism in America was much less pronounced than in
Europe, it nevertheless existed in the form of clubs, hotels, and residential
neighborhoods from which Jews were barred and professions and universities that were difficult for Jews to enter. Many American Jews were wary
of protesting against such slights for fear of drawing attention to themselves. For much the same reason, the American Jewish community
adopted a largely passive attitude toward the persecution of Jews in Nazi
Germany and did not lobby effectively for increased Jewish immigration
into the United States. Even after World War II, when the extent of the
genocide became known, Holocaust survivors arriving in America found
remarkably little interest in the horrifying stories they had to tell. A film
like *Schindler's List* would have been difficult to imagine in the fifties and
sixties, when Hollywood's Jewish elite were preoccupied with being seen
as super-Americans.

Although Josef Korbel went further than many in denying his
Jewishness, his action was very much in tune with the times. His great
goal in coming to America was to find a country that would allow
him and his family to make the most of their talents. Like many first-
generation immigrants, he remained almost naively grateful to America
for the gift of acceptance, an attitude he passed on to his children. In
an interview with a Denver newspaper in 1954, six years after his arrival
on the *Queen Mary*, he contrasted the welcome he had received in America
with the rebuffs he had experienced in Europe. "When I lived in France,
I couldn't find a job. When I lived in England, the community did not
accept me," Josef complained. "No country has gone as far as the United

States in the spirit and fullness of democracy. No country compares with America." In later life, Madeleine delighted in telling the story of how the English kept on asking her parents "When are you leaving?" while the stock American question was "When are you becoming a citizen?"

The Korbels' quest for assimilation in America was a repeat performance. As a young man, Josef had embarked on a similar journey in Masaryk's Czechoslovakia. For a time, it appeared that he had succeeded: He was one of the few Jews accepted into the Czechoslovak diplomatic service. But the quest for acceptance ended in disaster. He was thrown out of the Foreign Office after Munich; his parents were murdered by the Nazis; he was forced to flee a second time after the Communists seized power. From his point of view, hiding his origins was an entirely logical reaction to such devastating setbacks.

For an insight into Josef's mind-set, one need look no further than the experiences of other Holocaust survivors. Arnošt Lustig, a Czech Jewish writer who survived the concentration camps and is well known for his novels and short stories about the Holocaust, tells the story of a friend who was with him in Auschwitz. "This friend—let us call him George— was a famous soccer player in Czechoslovakia. I admired him as a sportsman. He emigrated to the United States in 1948 and married a beautiful woman. When I came to America in 1970, he invited me to visit him. He lived close to Chicago. I arrived at the airport, and he collected me in a nice Porsche. He told me it had been difficult for him when he first arrived in America. He had spent time digging graves, but he was now doing very well. As we approached his house, which looked like a castle, George said to me, 'Don't say anything about my past. Don't say that I am Jewish. I married a non-Jewish wife, we are now Unitarians, my children don't know about my past.'

"It was a pleasure to meet his children, who were then sixteen and eighteen, and to spend time with such healthy, beautiful people. We had a nice dinner. At the end of the dinner, one of his sons came to me and said, 'Explain something to me. Why does my father buy your books, which are only about Jews?' " George had every one of Lustig's books in his library but had never told his children the reason for his obsession with the Holocaust.

Such stories are commonplace. As I researched the fate of a single transport to Auschwitz—the transport that took Olga and Milena to their deaths in October 1944—I came across several similar tales. One in particular was hauntingly reminiscent of the story of the Korbels. The deportees on transport "Et" included Max and Gertruda Zweigenthal and their six-year-old son, Otto. After the war, an American cousin of the Zweigenthals, Carol Zsolnay, tried to trace her relatives. Max's brother, Paul, had spent the war years in England—like the Korbels—and then emigrated to the United States. He had then disappeared. Through the Red Cross, Carol eventually discovered that Paul was living on the West Coast of the United States under a different name. In May 1996, she wrote to him to ask for information about her relatives. A few days later, Paul wrote back:

> Your letter . . . brought back very sad memories. . . . One never forgets one's loved ones, nor the atrocities that we all lived through during the war. However, it is not good to live in the past and when we came to America many years ago, we decided to start a new life. We were very lucky that we made it over here, thanks to the affidavit we received from my wife's old nanny. At the time when she offered to help us, she also gave us very strong advice. She told us that we would meet the same prejudices here that we were trying to escape from in the old country. She advised us to change our name and to deny our religious background. So it is that we moved here using a different name and practicing a different religion. We have tried to live a good life and to be accepted for who we are. We have not experienced hate or anti-Semitism here in this country and would not like to now by acknowledging any of our past.

In many cases, hiding the truth from children proves very difficult. As Lustig's story about "George" suggests, little hints and clues are often thrown out inadvertently. The refusal to discuss a certain topic—for example, how your parents died—is itself an important clue. Research has shown that children latch on to these taboos and often devise ways of subtly challenging their parents' story. "The children of Holocaust survivors often understand that something happened to their parents, but they get a strong message that their parents don't want to talk about it," said Ken Jacobson, an American writer who has researched the lives of many such children.

In Madeleine's case, the strength of her ties with her parents, and particularly with her father, may have served as an inhibition against asking too many questions. "She senses that her parents saved her life and protected her during turbulent events, so who else is she going to trust?" In later life, Madeleine would say that one of the great motivating forces in her life was the sense "that somehow I had been saved—I thought only from the Russians." From her childhood, she felt an obligation "to repay the fact that I was a free person . . . I had this feeling that there but for the grace of God, we might have been dead."

Madeleine's English cousins found out about their Jewish roots when they were in their teens. Like his brother Josef, Jan Korbel converted to Christianity and brought his children up as Catholics after their escape from Czechoslovakia in 1939. Jan's daughter Alena, who was two years older than Madeleine, first encountered the word "Jew" at school in England during World War II. She remembers joining other children in taunting a little Jewish girl who had cheated on a test. "You're a Jew, you're a Jew," the children chanted over and over again. Alena did not know what "Jew" meant and felt rather ashamed about taunting the poor girl, but she joined in because "I didn't want to be left out." Later on, as a teenager, she took her parents to midnight Mass and was embarrassed because her father seemed to have no idea how to behave. It was not until her parents were divorced, when she was eighteen years old, that she finally discovered the truth about her origins.

Her discovery came about because of the anti-Semitic remarks of her fellow students. One of her girlfriends kept on talking about "the nasty Jewish girls" at school. A boy she knew ventured the opinion that "the trouble with Hitler was that he didn't kill enough Jews." The remark confused Alena, who thought that Britain had gone to war to stop Hitler. She didn't want to ask her friends for an explanation in case they ridiculed her, so she went home and asked her mother.

"Jews are scapegoats," her mother told her. "And in case you are thinking of becoming anti-Semitic yourself, I had better tell you that we are Jewish."

The discovery left Alena "confused" and vaguely "embarrassed," even though she felt attracted to other Jewish people. "It was terribly complex, I didn't know what it meant to be Jewish," she said. It was not until a few years later that she began to consciously explore the question of the family's relationship with the Holocaust. During a visit to Czechoslovakia in 1967, Alena made a trip to Terezín with a relative on her mother's side and saw a room where family members had been imprisoned.

Like Walter Lippmann, Josef studiously avoided Jewish themes in his writings. In six books, written over the course of thirty years, he dealt extensively with the cruelties inflicted on the Czechs by the Nazis and Communists but barely mentioned the Holocaust. One book, *The Communist Subversion of Czechoslovakia,* is dedicated "to the memory of my parents," but offers no clue as to their fate. Another work, *Twentieth Century Czechoslovakia,* contains only one passing reference to the "tortuous trek" of 140,000 Czech and Slovak Jews to the gas chambers. In conversations with friends and colleagues, Josef was relentlessly forward-looking. "He never wanted to talk about the past except occasionally to reflect on the fall of Czechoslovakia," said his Denver University colleague, Arthur Gilbert. "Like so many immigrants, he wanted to fit in."

And yet, despite his determined rejection of his Jewish origins, Josef was molded by his past in ways he could never escape. Another assimilated Jew, Sigmund Freud, once posed the following question to himself: "Since you have abandoned all these characteristics of your countrymen (language, religion, nationalism), what is there left of you that is Jewish?" Freud's answer: "A very great deal, and probably its essence." It is an answer that could equally apply to Josef Korbel.

Josef shared several characteristic traits of assimilationist Jews. His eagerness for acceptance was reflected in an eagerness to please, particularly people who were in a position to help him or his family. Americans were impressed by his pragmatism and rational outlook. Unlike many Soviet-bloc exiles, he did not waste time fighting lost political battles or retreating into an ethnic ghetto. He placed enormous store on the education of his children, which he viewed as a means of assimilation. He set his sights on becoming an American citizen as swiftly as possible. While he never lost his heavy Central European accent, he insisted that everybody call him "Joe." Combined with an almost exaggerated identification with the mores of American society was the ironic detachment of the outsider. Like the German Jewish poet Heinrich Heine, he saw his conversion to Christianity as an "entry ticket" to Western civilization rather than as an end in itself. He was a man of strong political convictions balanced by a strong streak of self-preservation and ambition.

Madeleine would inherit many of these same characteristics. She, too, would feel a constant need to prove her own worth and please other people, beginning with her own father. She, too, would combine a fierce commitment to abstract principle with an equally striking ability to bend with the prevailing wind. She, too, would become a super-patriotic American while maintaining an ability to laugh at herself and marvel at her own situation. Throughout her life, she would be attracted to people with a similar outsider-insider outlook on life, which is perhaps one reason why she has so many Jewish friends.

The first place that the Korbels lived in the United States was once described by F. Scott Fitzgerald as "one of the strangest communities in North America." The Korbels chose to live in Great Neck, on Long Island, because it was close to Lake Success, the temporary home of the United Nations. Situated on a peninsula jutting out from the North Shore, Great Neck in the late forties was also a place of social, economic, and religious distinctions so complex that they made European society seem simple by comparison.

At the top of the Great Neck social structure were the luxurious mansions and fake French châteaux immortalized by Fitzgerald in *The Great Gatsby*; at the bottom were the cottages of struggling migrants from Queens and the Bronx. Great Neck peninsula ("West Egg" in Fitzgerald's novel) was divided into a crazy quilt of nine incorporated villages, each with its own bylaws and lists of prohibitions and exclusions. On some parts of the peninsula, Jews were welcome; a hundred yards away, they were prohibited from buying houses. At school, Jewish children were sometimes taunted for "killing Jesus." If Josef had any doubts about the

correctness of his decision to abandon his Jewish roots, they were probably dispelled by his eight-month stay in Great Neck.

The Korbels lived in a gatehouse on a larger property at 149 Station
Road, straddling the boundary between fashionable King's Point and
down-at-heel Great Neck Village. Madeleine was enrolled in nearby
Arrandale public school. She joined the sixth-grade class of Mrs. Attanas,
remembered by her students for swallowing large quantities of Pepto-
Bismol. "She was very dynamic, but obviously she had a lot of stomach
problems," said Madeleine's classmate Winnie Shore Freund. The first big
celebration was Thanksgiving. In later years, Madeleine would remember
joining the other children in singing the Thanksgiving hymn, and "all of
a sudden hearing somebody who sounded very different." She quickly
realized that the person who sounded different was herself. It did not take
her long to get rid of her "weird" British accent. "I am a mimic, and I
soon developed a standard American accent," Madeleine recalls. Says
Freund, "She consciously tried to become an American, and talk like an
American."

The assimilation process was not limited to learning to speak American English. She also wanted to dress like her friends and absorb American popular culture. Madeleine and her mother spent a lot of time
listening to soap operas on the radio, waiting for the end and always being
disappointed. "I wanted so much to be like everyone else. I had spent a
very weird childhood. I had been through the war, been a diplomat's
child, been to boarding school. I think that a lot about my personality
has to do with the fact that as a child I had to adapt to a lot of different
situations."

While Madeleine struggled with her vowels, her father commuted
to U.N. headquarters at Lake Success. In February, word finally arrived
that Czechoslovakia wanted to replace him as its representative on the
Kashmir commission. Eager to display his anti-Communist credentials,
Josef prepared a fire-breathing press statement accusing the Russians of
engineering his dismissal as part of a plan of "Communist infiltration
in Southeast Asia." An American U.N. delegate, Thomas Power, persuaded him to redraft his statement on the grounds that it was unnecessarily inflammatory. "I assured him that we were well aware of his
anti-Communist feeling and that . . . it was not necessary to drag in the

Russians so forcefully in order to assure asylum for himself." Power reported to the State Department that Josef "was most receptive to [our] suggestions."

A few days later, Josef called in a reporter of *The New York Times* and openly said he would never go back to Czechoslovakia. He also applied formally for political asylum in America. "I cannot, of course, return to the Communist Czechoslovakia as I would be arrested for my faithful adherence to the ideals of democracy," he wrote in his application. It took four months for the asylum application to be approved. Some Czechoslovak exiles expressed doubts about Josef, in part because he had failed to resign immediately after February 1948. "Some of us thought that Korbel and others remained longer than necessary in the service of the Communist government," said Pavel Tigrid, who had worked as a broadcaster in London and later joined Radio Free Europe. Others believed that Josef had been too close to the Communists in London, and particularly to Clementis. The animosity ran so deep that when Josef returned to London in the early 1970s, some of his former colleagues refused to see him.

Such opinions were not shared, however, by Western officials and senior aides to Beneš. Hubert Ripka, a leading supporter of Beneš in the outgoing government, testified to Josef's "political reliability" when he applied for asylum in the United States. Ripka said he and others had urged Korbel "to remain at his post for the time being in order to serve as a source of information for the anticommunists." He added, however, that Korbel's real opposition to the Communist regime was known to the Czechoslovak democratic leaders and to representatives of Western countries. Cavendish Cannon, the former U.S. ambassador to Belgrade, described Josef as someone who "has long been known to us as a friend of the West." Cannon said Korbel was unable to resign his post as Czechoslovak ambassador to Belgrade immediately after the coup "because he felt he would never be able to get out with his family."

Back in Prague, a court formally confiscated all Josef's property because he "left the country illegally." The political situation in Czechoslovakia had gone from bad to worse. A wave of persecutions was under way against anybody deemed to have associated with "enemies of the revolution." Many of Josef's old Foreign Ministry colleagues were put on trial. Some were hanged. "If he had not left, the same thing would undoubtedly have happened to Korbel," says Antonin Sum, Masaryk's private secretary, who spent thirteen years in jail in Czechoslovakia after being found guilty of high treason. Later, Madeleine would tell journalists that the Communist regime in Czechoslovakia also put her father on trial in absentia and sentenced him to death. A search of the archival records, however, turns up no evidence to support this assertion.

Now that he had lost his U.N. position, Josef's most pressing priority was to find a job. The State Department put him in touch with Philip Mosely, a professor of political science at Columbia University and consultant to the Rockefeller Foundation. Long rumored to have ties with the Office of Strategic Services, a forerunner to the CIA, Mosely had an almost legendary reputation as an action-oriented academic. Among other things, Mosely acted as godfather to impecunious émigrés from Russia and Eastern Europe, paying them for their reminiscences of life under communism and helping them find ways of staying in the United States. Intelligent, energetic, and obviously well informed, Josef was exactly the kind of person whom Mosely liked to help. He paid for a series of memoranda from Josef on his diplomatic career and then arranged an appointment at the University of Denver as visiting professor of international relations. Mosely suggested that the university split Josef's $5,000 salary with the Rockefeller Foundation.

Josef hurried home to tell his family the good news. "That's wonderful," said Mandula. "Where's Denver?" Recalls Madeleine, "None of us had a clue where Denver was." In order to find out where they were going to live, they had to look up Denver in the atlas.

The family set out for the Rocky Mountains in a new green Ford coupe. Josef and Mandula sat in the front. "We drove and drove and drove," Madeleine recalled. The children sat in the back, occasionally fighting with each other, "like all children do." America was still a deep mystery to them. Out of habit, Josef kept on giving motel owners his passport, and they kept on asking for his driver's license. Madeleine and the other children spent much of the trip trying to figure out why Denver was called "the mile-high city" when "we never went up." When they crossed the Colorado border, according to his own much-repeated account, Josef "flung open the door of the car, stepped out and, with the Rockies on the skyline and a rainbow arching the heavens, solemnly took off his hat." The trip took five days, with Josef at the wheel the entire time.

Madeleine would return to Long Island's North Shore a decade later, this time not as a penniless immigrant but as a member of the moneyed elite.

Madeleine presided over the international relations club at Kent. *Kent Denver School.*

"I Wanted So Much to Be an American"

By the time Madeleine arrived in Denver at the age of twelve, her family had moved house more than a dozen times since her birth in 1937. Sometimes the family stayed no longer than a few months in an apartment before moving on. The longest Madeleine had ever lived anywhere was two years in Walton-on-Thames during the war and two years in the Czechoslovak ambassador's residence in Belgrade after the war. She had attended half a dozen schools. Even in Denver, the Korbel family moved four times in four years. "The part I think about most in my childhood is that we were constantly going somewhere else," Madeleine told a reporter in 1997.

The uprooted existence had the effect of making Madeleine more than usually dependent upon her parents, particularly her father. From a very early age, she modeled herself on him, did things she knew would please him, and talked about him incessantly. To a large extent, his interests and political views were also hers. "I tried to pattern myself after him," she once said. "When he was with the U.N. commission [on the India-Pakistan dispute], I wrote a paper on Gandhi. When he wrote books on eastern Europe, I wrote school papers on similar topics." "A great deal of what I did, I did because I wanted to be like my father," she told another interviewer. Her siblings agreed. Madeleine is "Daddy reincarnate," says her sister Kathy Silva. Adds her brother John: "Madeleine had a special relationship with our father partly because she followed so closely in his footsteps."

The object of all this devotion was, by all accounts, a remarkably complex and in some ways contradictory personality. In Denver, where he lived half his life, there is an extraordinary range of opinions about Joe Korbel. Many of his university colleagues and former students speak of him with great respect as an inspiring teacher and brilliant administrator who built up a top-class graduate school in international relations from virtually nothing. But others remember him as a "control freak" who displayed little tolerance for dissent among his subordinates while being excessively deferential to his superiors. Friends recall the charming, witty host who loved to tell jokes and regaled his guests with old Czech songs sung in his rich baritone voice. Former neighbors complain that he was aloof and difficult to get to know.

In many ways, Mandula was the opposite of her husband. She made a habit of blurting out whatever was on her mind and was nearly always exuberant and lighthearted. Her idiomatic butchery of the English language would reduce her friends to fits of laughter. If Josef was excessively analytical, looking at a problem from all sides, Mandula would often act out of pure emotion. The neighbors loved her because she always had time for them and would go out of her way to help them. She was "the antithesis of stuffiness," in the words of a family friend. Raised to a life of privilege in a boarding school in Switzerland, the former ambassador's wife adapted quickly to the family's reduced economic fortunes in America.

Somehow the very different characters of Josef and Mandula melded into a happily married couple. It was a very traditional marriage. "I was amazed by the difference between Dr. Korbel and his wife," said Marion Gottesfeld, a University of Denver trustee and family friend. "She was a plain-looking lady. He was always absolutely correctly dressed, quite the European professor. She saw to it that he made a great front for the family." Josef almost always had a starched white handkerchief in the breast pocket of his three-piece suit. Even when skiing in the Rockies, he wore a jacket and tie.

If Josef and Mandula had one trait in common, it was their extreme solicitude for their children. Madeleine would later describe her parents as "protective . . . overly so in terms of worrying about us and all kinds of things." Josef went to extreme lengths to supervise every aspect of his daughter's upbringing and education. He corrected her essays, screened her boyfriends, fretted about whether she would get into the best schools, plotted her future. Kathy and John would occasionally rebel against the firm discipline imposed by their father, but Madeleine almost always went along with his wishes. "Madeleine was the responsible one," Kathy later recalled.

The pressure to fall into line was intense. If a child was late for the dinner table, she would be sent to her room. "He was a strict European parent," said John. "The most severe form of punishment was when our father wouldn't talk to us for a week." A neighbor, Jack Newman-Clark, remembers John coming to him once in a panic because he could not keep up with his studies. "He was scared to death of his father. He said, 'My father's going to kill me for it, what am I going to do?' I sat with him for a good hour trying to encourage him, saying, 'Don't worry, you'll make it.' "

Superficially, Mandula seemed more relaxed than Josef and was certainly less of a disciplinarian, but she too was constantly worrying about the children. At her funeral in 1989, Mandula's friend, Rita Kauders, told the children, "You were all constantly on her mind. She would say to me, 'Rita, quick, turn on Channel Six, Madla [Madeleine] will be on.' 'Katie, she works so late every night.' 'Jenda [John] travels too much.' 'They work too hard, they all work too hard.' "

Overprotectiveness is a common characteristic of Holocaust survivors, and it is likely that at least some of this parental concern was the result of the Korbels' wartime experiences. A 1968 Canadian study of the families of survivors showed that the parents were often "excessively protective, constantly warning their children of impending danger." A related trait is exceptionally high expectations. In the words of another 1967 study, "The parents, in an attempt to justify their survival, demanded qualities of the children which were the accumulation of their expectations of all the dead who were murdered. The love and ambitions of whole families were resurrected in memory and imposed as hopes on the children."

As the oldest child, Madeleine had been through the most with her parents and was therefore the focus of their most intense ambitions. She was the survivor. "Madeleine must have been very special to that family," said Robert DuPont, a childhood friend from Denver who went on to become a prominent Washington, D.C., psychiatrist. "I don't think that her parents' relationship with her was the same as with her brother and sister. Much more was poured into it."

Pushed on by her father, Madeleine channeled her energies into excelling at school and absorbing the values of her adopted country. "I spent a lot of time worrying, trying to make sure that I would fit in. I wanted very much to be an American. That was the big, defining thing of my life," she told an interviewer soon after her appointment as secretary of state. She returned to this theme in an interview for this book in 1998, in which she depicted herself as a firm believer in the "melting pot" approach to ethnicity. While she was proud of being a Czech-American and spoke Czech at home, the emphasis was "more on the American" than on the Czech. In her words, "I wanted very much to belong. Everything about me wanted to be like the other kids."

The Denver that provided the Korbel family with a refuge in the early fifties was a much less sophisticated, more egalitarian place than it is today. Originally settled in the Gold Rush of 1859, Denver had gone through several cycles of boom and bust but remained in essence a cow town on the eastern edge of the Rocky Mountains. The mining bonanza and crisp mountain air had attracted an ethnically diverse population. Around 4 percent of the population were Jews, many of them descendants of sweatshop migrants from the East seeking cures for tuberculosis. Yarmulkes and beards were a common sight in Jewish West Denver. The black population was small, around 5 to 6 percent, and there was relatively little overt discrimination. For a refugee from Europe, or even from Long Island, Denver still seemed imbued with the frontier spirit.

The first place the Korbels lived in Denver was a two-story house at 995 South Williams Street, which they rented from a biologist on leave. Their next-door neighbors, the Spensleys, were ardent Republicans. "We would have arguments about politics. They were quite the opposite of us," recalled Ruth Spensley. "My husband was in advertising. He believed in making money. The Korbels were much more socialistic. Josef didn't seem to approve of making money, even though he liked money." The Spensley daughter went to the local Morey Junior High School with Madeleine. Mandula and Ruth got on very well, but Josef had little interest in making small talk with neighbors. "I once made an innocent remark about something in his past that I thought was humorous, and he really took offense," recalled Ruth Spensley. "He came back at me so hard that I walked out of the room. It was childish."

After a year on South Williams Street, the Korbels moved to a succession of modest apartments and bungalows lent to them by the university. None of the houses compared with their original house on South Williams Street, let alone the ambassador's residence in Belgrade. The house on South Gaylord Street was next to a cemetery that "terrified" Madeleine and the other children. The basement of the house on South Race Street, where Josef had a little office, was perpetually flooded. It was not until 1957 that the family settled down in their own house at 2314 South Madison Street, a bungalow that they bought for $15,500 ($92,000 at 1999 prices). They remained there until 1973, when they moved across the street to a more attractive two-story house with gables.

After sending Madeleine to Morey Junior High for seventh and eighth grade, Josef decided that his daughter needed a better education. He had heard about a private girls' school that was willing to offer her a scholarship. Madeleine wanted to stay with her new set of friends. For the first time in her life, she rebelled. "We had screaming fights over this," she recalled. As usual, her father got his way.

The Kent School for Girls had been founded by a group of spinsters known as the "Three Marys" who specialized in preparing girls for acceptance by the eastern women's colleges. The campus was located right at the edge of Denver, with nothing but scrubland between the school and the mountains. The buildings were fifties-style functional and very spartan, with pastel-colored cinder-block walls. "It was like going to school in a factory," said Madeleine's classmate, Stephanie Allen. There were only sixteen girls in Madeleine's class. For anyone coming from the East, it took time to get used to the wide-open spaces and the lack of people.

"When I took the children to the park, I used to think 'Gosh, I will never find them again.' It was just scrub oak and great plains," said Marie Valance, one of Madeleine's favorite teachers, who arrived in Denver from Washington, D.C. "The air was bright and crisp, and you could really see the mountains. I remember the meadowlarks springing up and soaring off, ever singing, as in Shelley."

The school ethos was unashamedly Republican. In Madeleine's second year at Kent, a mock election was held to coincide with the Eisenhower vs. Stevenson presidential race. "Miss Val" remembers that there were only seven votes for the Democrats in the entire school. One of the votes was certainly Madeleine's. "She was our living, walking Democrat in a school where everyone else's father was a raging Republican," Stephanie Allen recalled. The principal, Mary Bogue, sat up all night watching the election results on television and celebrating the end of two decades of uninterrupted Democratic rule. The next morning, she had the children sing "Happy Days Are Here Again" as they pledged allegiance to the flag. "It was just awful, but that's the way it was," said Melanie Grant, one of the few Democrats in the school besides Madeleine.

The leader of the "Three Marys," Mary Bogue, was "a very serious, non-playful, matriarchal tyrant," in the words of Stephanie Allen. "Miss Bogue was scary," agreed Julika Ambrose, the daughter of a Hungarian doctor and the only other "refugee child" in the class. "I did not see her smile very much. She was the prototypical grande dame with the big chest and the hanky. She could level you with an eyebrow, and you would think 'Oh, God.' " At the same time, Miss Bogue was fiercely proud of her charges. "I remember meeting her later and she said, 'You and Madeleine really accomplished something.' "

By the time she got to Kent, Madeleine had lost most of her British accent and was well on the way to becoming a full-fledged American. Her friends called her Maddie. "I would not have had a clue about Madeleine's East European origins if she had not told us about them," said Stephanie Allen. "She must have worked very hard on her American accent. I don't even remember a funny word here or there."

Madeleine is chiefly remembered at Kent for her debating talents and the intensity with which she did everything. "She would take on the Republicans in the school in formal debates," remembered Allen. "She was always extremely well prepared, knew how to use her wit, and was undaunted in the conviction that what she was about was right." Recalls another classmate, Kyle Reno: "My whole image of Madeleine from the day she arrived was that she had all the answers. She either knew the answers or knew how to get them. She was very serious, very dedicated, very researched." Madeleine played hockey the same way she debated the Republicans. "I still have a visual image of Madeleine coming down the field and thinking, 'I'm glad she's on my team,' " remembers Allen. "She had that look about her. She was formidable." Agrees Reno: "Whether it was field hockey or chemistry, it was the same amount of intensity."

Even at the age of fifteen, the future secretary of state was a fanatical student of foreign affairs. In the eighth grade, she had won the Rocky Mountain Empire United Nations contest on the strength of being able to memorize the fifty-one U.N. member countries in alphabetical order. At Kent, she founded an international relations club. "I made myself president," she told Kent-Denver students in 1997. "I made these poor girls come once a week to have discussions. I tortured them. All I ever wanted to talk about was foreign policy." Club members used to take their lunch to an upstairs classroom and hold intense discussions on international topics. Madeleine sat at the teacher's desk with a pile of newsmagazines and newspaper clippings. "She was more serious than the rest of us giggling teenagers," said Julika Ambrose, a fellow club member.

Although Madeleine was one of several academically ambitious students in the class, she was not the most outstanding. Two other students did better than she on the SAT tests in 1955, the year she graduated. But Madeleine did well enough to win a scholarship to Wellesley and be accepted to four other colleges, including Stanford. In the Kent School yearbook of 1955, her classmates made affectionate fun of the way she "takes a definite stand on matters, staunchly saying, 'You guys, this just proves it!' " The entry went on: "Her constant interest in anything she is doing, and the drive with which she does it, keep all interested in the activities of our 'emaciated' companion." "Emaciated" was an allusion to Madeleine's attempts at dieting: losing weight was always a major preoccupation, even as a teenager. There was another cryptic reference in the yearbook to her interest in "Princeton," one of the few subjects on which she was a bit "incoherent."

To decipher "Princeton," it is necessary to know about Elston Mayhew.

With no boys in sight, and sixteen very different girls with few common interests, Madeleine's class at Kent School offered little in the way of social life. "I was arguably the poorest [girl in the class]. We didn't own our own house. I always felt out of it. We wore uniforms, thank God, otherwise I would have been very uncomfortable. I could not stay out late. The [other girls] would have country club parties. I didn't like it." She showed up for the potluck dinners on Friday nights, usually with the same dish, garlic bread. Apart from that, she spent most of her free time with a group of teenagers from East High School, a Denver public school known for its high academic achievement. Her most serious date was Elston Mayhew, a skinny math and science whiz with closely cropped hair, as intense about his studies as Madeleine was about hers.

"Madeleine and Elston were such a couple," recalls Robert DuPont, Elston's best friend at high school. "They did everything together, they cared about each other, they spent a lot of time together." They were both overachievers. "Elston was not a person of tremendous gifts. He was just a guy who was going to work ten times harder than the next person. That is also the important thing about Madeleine."

Like Madeleine, Elston had been obliged to struggle hard to achieve what he wanted in life. His family background was much more modest than hers. He was an orphan brought up as the only child of doting step-parents, both of whom were largely uneducated. His father worked at a meatpacking plant. His mother devoted herself to his education, super-vising his contacts with the opposite sex as closely as Josef Korbel super-vised Madeleine. According to another high school friend, Charles D. Vail, "His mother was almost a smothering type. . . . I am sure that she was as alarmed about Madeleine as Professor Korbel was about this young American lad who was courting his daughter. She wanted to know about everybody's background, and make sure that they were the right sort of kids to be fooling with Elston."

Madeleine and Elston double-dated a lot with Bob and Charlie and their girlfriends. They studied together. They went to movies together. They danced the jitterbug at Elitch Gardens, a teenage hangout in Denver, and listened to big band Glen Miller music. On weekends, Elston sometimes grabbed a few steaks from the factory where his father worked, and they headed up to the mountains for steak over a campfire. But wherever they went, they were kept on a short leash by their parents, and particularly by Josef. "Dr. Korbel had an absolutely inviolable curfew, based on the time of the movie, the time it took to eat a hamburger, malt, and french fries, and the time it took to get back home," said Vail. "Sometimes, when Elston was the driver, that could be a bit inconvenient. Everybody would have to call it a night because we were out of wheels." Vail recalls that "Dr. Korbel was pleasant enough, but very stern underneath it all and very suspicious of young men coming to see Madeleine."

Madeleine met Elston at a friend's house while in her second year at Kent, when she was in the tenth grade. Given Josef Korbel's suspicious nature, making friends with boys was difficult. The previous year, he and Madeleine had had a big fight when he insisted on chaperoning her to a student prom with her date. Eventually, they reached a compromise. Josef permitted his daughter to go to the prom in the boy's car, but followed them in his own car. That particular prom was embarrassing for another reason as well. Without a suitable dress of her own, Madeleine had had to borrow a dress from a sixty-year-old university professor, Elizabeth Fackt. (With their thick accents, the Korbel parents habitually called their friend "Miss Fucked.") The dress was awfully dowdy, resembling a huge lampshade. Hoping to look a little more up-to-date, Madeleine fixed a red velvet ribbon across the front. "I looked like a lunatic," she laughs. "I never saw that boy again."

Elston quickly figured out that the surest way into Madeleine's heart was via her father. Like Madeleine, he did things that would please Professor Korbel. Josef had written a book with the title *Tito's Communism*, so Elston wrote his high school thesis on the same subject. "Elston got all his ideas [about Yugoslavia] from Madeleine's father," DuPont recalled. "He was smart enough to know that Josef Korbel was a very special asset." Josef was suitably impressed. "Elston and Dr. Korbel got along very well," said Vail. "Elston developed a view of the best way to approach

Professor Korbel. He would not go in and say, 'Hey, how about those New York Yankees?' "

Elston graduated from East High School in 1954 after winning a full scholarship to Princeton. His high school yearbook contains elliptic references to "Kent," just as Madeleine's alludes to "Princeton." "Here's hoping these Kent women don't give you too much trouble," scrawled one friend. Madeleine graduated magna cum laude from Kent a year later, with a scholarship to Wellesley. In the eyes of many of their friends, they seemed made for each other. Says DuPont: "The thing about Madeleine is that she wasn't the smartest, she wasn't the prettiest, but she was the most determined, the hardest working. She would get there by having a focus, by doing the job, whatever it took."

The same was true of Elston Mayhew.

Wellesley College was founded in 1875 in order to prepare women to fill teaching positions vacated by men who had gone off to fight the Civil War. But this was only the pretext. Right from the start, Wellesley's founder, Henry Fowle Durant, had loftier goals in mind in creating a women's college imbued with Christian principles in a pastoral setting by a lake outside Boston. "The higher education of women," he declared, "is one of the great world battle cries for freedom, for right against might." He believed that God was "calling to womanhood to come up higher, to prepare herself for great conflicts, for vast reforms in social life, for noblest usefulness." The ethos of Wellesley had changed little by the time Madeleine Korbel arrived on campus in the fall of 1955.

Madeleine was one of thirty-five freshmen assigned to a small dormitory called Homestead at the entrance to the college. "You will find yourself in a maze of excitement the minute you enter the large autumn campus," enthused the welcoming handbook. "Hats of different colors will be the first thing you'll see. The purple ones will perch atop the sophomores; the green cover juniors; in a couple of days, the red-capped seniors will arrive. Some of the purple hats will be labeled 'ask me' and that's what they want you to do—ask them." As a member of the Class of '59, Madeleine was given a yellow felt cap to wear. Room assignments went strictly according to religion. Episcopalians roomed with

Episcopalians and Jews with Jews. Madeleine found herself in a room with another Roman Catholic, Mary Jane Lewis. The only black student at Homestead was put in a room by herself.

Coming from the American West made Madeleine exotic enough, let alone her coming from Czechoslovakia. On her first day at Wellesley, a fellow student asked her in all seriousness whether there were paved roads in Denver. As at Kent, she worked hard at becoming indistinguishable from everyone around her, at least in the way she looked. "It was a very conformist era. We all dressed alike," recalled her friend, Emily Cohen MacFarquhar. "Everybody had to have the right camel hair coat, the right Bermuda shorts, the right crew neck sweaters. Madeleine had the right camel's hair coat, but it was a little large. There was some teasing about getting her to dress the right way, so that she had the Wellesley look." According to MacFarquhar, Madeleine's focus was on becoming "wholly American," as it had been at Kent. She remembers teasing her new friend about being "an enemy alien." One day, Emily and her roommate found a notice at a local post office instructing "aliens" to "register" with the authorities. They tied the notice to a light cord above Madeleine's bed, so it would dangle in her face when she woke up.

By this time, Madeleine was as American as her friends. Since she had a boyfriend at Princeton, she wore a Princeton scarf over her camel's hair coat, an important status symbol. Soon after her arrival at Wellesley, she was invited to join other "foreign students" on a shopping expedition to Boston organized by the ladies of the alumnae society to equip everybody in the proper American wardrobe. The ladies quickly realized that Madeleine had little need of their help when she appeared downstairs in all the right gear, beginning with the Bermuda shorts.

There were a number of initiation rituals designed to correct any deficiencies in the way newcomers to Wellesley comported themselves. The weirdest of these rituals was the requirement that all freshmen students pose for a "posture picture." Part of a pseudo-scientific experiment originally intended to classify America's best and brightest into different physiological types, the photographs were traditionally shot in the nude with pins sticking out from the upper body. As a concession, by the time Madeleine got to Wellesley, the students were permitted to pose in undershorts rolled up to display the top of their pelvic bone. The breasts were left exposed. Students were invited to pose in their "best position." According to a college handbook, the purpose of the photograph was to find out whether the student had "an understanding of good body alignment and the ability to stand well." Any student who received a "posture grade" of lower than C minus was required to take remedial exercises. In later life, the "posture pictures" were a source of much mirth for Madeleine and her friends. When she became secretary of state, her former classmates sent her a congratulatory telegram saying they knew she would "sit up straight" in her new job.

Some of Madeleine's classmates took the posture photographs in their stride, but others found them humiliating. "For those of us who were modest, it was strange and disorienting. It really bothered me," said Shirlee Taylor Haizlip, who lived on the same floor as Madeleine in Homestead. It is indicative of the conservatism of the era that nobody dared challenge a ritual that now seems absurd. According to Haizlip, "We were all bright girls, but we were taught to be nice and not to question authority." Other initiation rites were less degrading. Madeleine took an obligatory course in the "Fundamentals of Bodily Movement"— popularly known as "fundies"—which set her straight on such matters as how to get out of a taxicab without showing her legs, how to get her suitcase down from a luggage rack, and how to rise from a squatting position with a champagne glass. Her enunciation was good enough to pass the speech test on the first try, in contrast to her friend Emily MacFarquhar, who had to take remedial exercises to get rid of a very slight Bronx accent.

As a scholarship student, Madeleine was noticeably less well-off than most of her Wellesley contemporaries. In order to earn money, she took a job with a laundry company, sorting through bags of dirty sheets and pillowcases. Her parents were shocked. "We may be poor, but you do not have to do other people's laundry," they wrote her. Madeleine was certainly unusual in this respect. Some students went to the lengths of sending their clothes home to be laundered by their parents. The U.S. Postal Service even had a special laundry rate back in the fifties.

Taking girls from different backgrounds and transforming them into proper young ladies was what Wellesley was all about. Sunday-afternoon tea was an important institution, as were formal dinners, with freshmen and sophomores taking turns as waitresses. Chapel was regarded as a central part of the Wellesley experience, even if it was no longer mandatory. Freshmen were expected to be back in their dorms by ten o'clock. If they missed curfew, they were expected to report themselves to their housemother under the "honor system," which was seen as the glue holding the Wellesley social fabric together. Chaperones were provided for visits to Boston. One of the oldest Wellesley traditions was Tree Day, a mixture of pagan rite and Miss America contest, culminating in the crowning of a "Tree Day Mistress" to the strains of Elgar's "Pomp and Circumstance." For a long time, before Madeleine rose to public prominence, the most famous member of the Class of '59 was Judith Martin, better-known as "Miss Manners." The self-appointed arbiter of good breeding is remembered as rather acerbic and antisocial at Wellesley, a somewhat mysterious figure who flitted around campus dressed in black like a beatnik.

For all its quaint rituals, Wellesley was also a place of high academic standards, with an excellent faculty. Durant's injunction about producing "free and intelligent citizens" was taken extremely seriously. Many of Madeleine's classmates went on to distinguish themselves in a wide variety of fields, ranging from federal judges to leading writers and educators. As at Kent, Madeleine stood out not for being the smartest but for being the most dedicated. At political science lectures, she always sat in the front. After the lecture, she recopied her notes into a color-coded binder. If a student skipped a lecture, she could rely on Madeleine for a fill. "I occasionally used to borrow her notes. They were exhaustive, very meticulous," recalled Nada Westerman, a fellow political science student. "Madeleine was definitely one of the people who were more goal-oriented than the rest of us. That she should have accomplished so much is not terribly surprising. Everything was there at Wellesley: her intelligence, her drive, her thoroughness."

For her senior year thesis, Madeleine picked a subject that was dear to her father's heart: the subversion of Czechoslovak democracy by the Communists. She focused on the Social Democrat leader Zdeněk Fierlinger, who sided with the Communists during the crucial days of the February 1948 coup. Meticulously sourced and footnoted, and dedicated to her future husband, Joe Albright, and "To my Parents Who Taught Me To Speak Czechoslovakian," the thesis impressed her academic supervisor, Barbara Green, as an original piece of work. "She was able to challenge the popular notion that if you have a strong social democratic party in a country, it would act as a barrier to a takeover of power by the Communists." Forty years later, Green would remember Madeleine as a diligent, "somewhat shy" student who seemed destined for a worthy career in academia. "If you had asked me then to predict what she would become, I would have said a serious scholar."

In addition to being serious about her studies, Madeleine was also serious about her religion, both at Kent and Wellesley. One of her favorite subjects was Bible study, a compulsory course at Wellesley, but taught from a standpoint of comparative theology rather than religious dogma. She went to Mass every Sunday with her roommate, Mary Jane Lewis. When she went on holiday to the home of a Jewish friend, she made sure she ate fish on Good Friday. At Wellesley, she was a member of the Newman Club, a Catholic discussion group. "I was a very serious Catholic," she said later, after the story broke about her Jewish origins.

There were no real rebels at Wellesley. To the extent that there were people who looked at the world slightly differently from the massed ranks of debutantes and Republicans, they clustered around the college newspaper. The *Wellesley College News* was a liberal stronghold in a bastion of conservatism. At the core of the newspaper was a group of smart, self-aware Jewish women who seemed more mature than the average Wellesley student. According to Susan Dubinsky Terris, who went on to become a poet and writer of children's books, these women had the perspective of "outsiders." It was to such people that Madeleine, the practicing Catholic, was ineluctably drawn.

Neither Terris nor her roommate, Emily MacFarquhar, was particularly religious. Their secular Jewish backgrounds were similar to Madeleine's, even though they did not realize just how similar at the time. At Wellesley, Catholics were almost as much outsiders as Jews, and it seemed to Terris that Madeleine's Catholic upbringing could account for their intellectual affinity. For Terris, who is left-handed, being Jewish was a little like being a lefty. "There was a famous athletics coach who said that left-handers see the world two frames off to the left. In a sense, we also saw the world two frames off to the left. We were more formed than many of the other girls. Emily and I were treated as adults by our parents. We were more or less grown-ups when we arrived on that campus, and Madeleine was too. We did not look at our lives in the same way as our classmates. We did not discuss hairstyles. We were interested in issues, books, what we were going to do with our lives."

"It is interesting to me that many of Madeleine's best friends were Jewish," said Shirlee Taylor Haizlip, the one black woman in Homestead, who lived on the same floor as Madeleine and Susan and Emily. "The people who were closest to her in our class were Jewish, without realizing that there was a common parentage." Shirlee's family story was almost a reverse image of Madeleine's. The product of an Irish-African heritage, she came to Wellesley thinking she might somehow be able to find some long-lost relatives who, in black terminology, were "passing" as whites. "I fantasized that one of my white cousins might be in my class," she wrote later. Shirlee's relatives had rejected their African heritage for much the same reasons that Madeleine's parents had rejected their Jewish ancestry: They feared it would expose them to endless discrimination. After leaving Wellesley, Shirlee spent decades tracking down her "white" relatives.

In a best-selling book about her quest for her roots, titled *The Sweeter the Juice*, Haizlip describes the pressures on Wellesley students to remold themselves in the dominant WASP image. In her case, the immediate problem was how to straighten her naturally crinkly hair. After some disastrous experiments in which her scalp turned bright red, she finally found a revolutionary new chemical that delivered on its promise to straighten Negro hair. "Everybody aspired to be like the upper-middle-class white person. It was a Ralph Lauren kind of environment, but in a very unself-conscious way," she recalled.

Jews, blacks, and Catholics were all the subject of what might be called "genteel discrimination" at Wellesley in the form of informal admission quotas. By the time Madeleine got to Wellesley, the college had been prohibited by the Massachusetts Supreme Court from asking perspective applicants their religion. Nevertheless, the number of Jews was restricted to between 15 and 20 percent of the total student body.

When it came to guessing the religious affiliation of students for room assignments, Wellesley never made a mistake. Nonpracticing Jews like Susan and Emily felt little overt discrimination, other than improved dating prospects at nearby Harvard, which was 40 percent Jewish in the late fifties. Observant Jews had a tougher time of it, because Wellesley refused to make any concessions to their religious practices. "The first time I encountered any anti-Semitism at all was at Wellesley," said Alice Arsham Moskowitz, who worked on the newspaper with Madeleine. "By putting people together by their religious affiliation, they essentially created cliques." Moskowitz cited the case of a friend who was picked upon by other students because of her Jewish mannerisms.

Madeleine joined the staff of the *Wellesley College News* in the fall of 1956, her sophomore year, as a "candidate reporter." Her first article was about a student hangout called "The Well," which had just introduced dietary food. Accompanied by a photograph of students in cashmere sweaters drinking coffee, it was typical of her early journalistic efforts:

HAMBURGERS AND HARVARD, DIETS AND DATES: MISS GRUSZYNSKA OVERSEES ALL AT THE WELL

by Madeleine Korbel '59

Calorie conscious? Hate liver and fish? The Well answers all these needs, according to Miss Aniela Gruszynska, supervisor.

"The girls come to the Well because it is like mother's kitchen," remarked Miss Gruszynska, adding that they are able to order what they want the way they want it.

Over the next three years, Madeleine wrote articles for the *News* every few weeks. One searches in vain for anything remotely controversial in these writings. For the most part, she stuck to campus themes such as the teaching of foreign languages at Wellesley and the opening of a new arts center. Occasionally, she displayed an interest in foreign policy, as when she reviewed *The New Class* by the disgraced Yugoslav leader Milovan Djilas. She also revealed her passion for politics, covering John F. Kennedy's campaign for reelection to the U.S. Senate in 1958. When Kennedy visited Wellesley in October, Madeleine was in the crowd of banner-waving supporters at the train station. Her subsequent report suggested that she had fallen under the spell of the "handsome candidate" who patted the head of any child within reach. She was part reporter, part political groupie.

> Taking advantage of the Senator's late arrival, this reporter asked questions of the rather varied crowd, which was gathering in the oval in front of the railroad station. General comments gathered from interviews: "Kennedy has a great following in Wellesley, but many people will not admit it in this Republican community and so they are not down here." "I don't even know the name of his opponent." "He won't have any trouble, I don't even see why he is bothering to campaign.". . .
>
> In the general spirit of a political rally, the loudspeakers blared music and there were police escorts. The Senator was surrounded by autograph hunters. Smiling, he signed a great many for them—one for me too.

Madeleine's journalistic role model was James Reston of *The New York Times*. "We were all in awe of James Reston," said her friend, Ann Einhorn. "Madeleine would joke that she would like to become the female equivalent of James Reston." Madeleine's stock among her fellow *News* reporters rose sharply when she confided that her father had once been interviewed by the great Reston.

She worked hard to be on good terms with everybody. In her junior year, the *News* was riven by a bitter power struggle. One faction was led by Emily MacFarquhar, one of Madeleine's best friends at Wellesley, a vivacious, outspoken student who had set her heart on becoming editor of the newspaper. Since Emily was already the associate editor, she seemed the natural choice. But the incumbent editor campaigned against her election on the grounds that she was too "radical" for a conservative place like Wellesley. The job went instead to Ann Einhorn, who was regarded as more moderate. Einhorn is now a prominent judge and MacFarquhar a well-known writer and journalist, but the bad feelings provoked by their four-decades-old rivalry have not entirely disappeared. "She used various underhanded, unpleasant tactics against me," says MacFarquhar. "It was the first devastating blow of my life." Somehow, Madeleine managed to remain on friendly terms with both women and was rewarded with the number-two position on the masthead.

In later life, Madeleine and her friends would depict themselves as members of a tiny group of beleaguered Democrats at Wellesley, swamped by the Republican majority. Her longtime friend Winnie Shore Freund remembers that the student body was "ninety percent Republican." It is true that they were in a minority, but the number of Democrats was larger than these recollections suggest. In a straw poll conducted on the eve of the 1956 presidential election, the Republicans collected 745 votes to 310 for the Democrats. In Madeleine's dorm, Severance, the vote was 56–22 in favor of Eisenhower. Seven out of every ten students voted the same way as their parents.

What the Wellesley Democrats lacked in numbers, they made up in fervor. As a Student for Stevenson, Madeleine spent the fall of her sophomore year traveling to Boston to collect money for the Democrats and chanting pro-Stevenson slogans at public rallies. The Republicans were a lackluster lot, reflecting their smug conviction that victory was inevitable. As Madeleine's fellow Democratic activist, Sara Lippincott, later recalled in *The New Yorker*, the Republican students "showed *esprit de corps* only when they were irresistibly goaded by the S. for S., who took advantage of every public event at the college to form a snake dance—the most practical formation for a group too small to muster a full-scale parade. On these occasions, the Eisenhower people would rumble and mutter, then rise to their feet from all corners of the hall or the hockey field or the quad . . . and chant 'We like Ike . . . We like Ike . . . We like Ike,' gradually deafening us, and sometimes nudging one or two of us into Lake Waban in their proselytic fervor."

The 1956 Stevenson campaign was Madeleine's first real taste of grassroots political activity in her adopted country. It was an exhilarating experience. Years later, she would remember being threatened with arrest on Boston Common while she was collecting "dollars for Democrats." An elderly woman accused the Stevenson students of "begging." Other voters berated them for campaigning for a "divorced man." The local Democrats welcomed as much help as they could get, dissolving the traditional barriers between students and the local population. "We learned a great deal about grass-roots political action," Lippincott wrote. "How to pacify strangers whose dinners have been interrupted by a telephone canvass, how to avoid nasty types while collecting funds on the street, how to keep confetti from cohering into a useless ball, how to keep a donkey from getting surly in a parade (you feed it unfiltered cigarettes every ten minutes or so)." The former mayor of Boston, the legendary James Curley, was an education in himself. The Wellesley Democrats noted with awe the way the former mayor managed to upstage everybody, including Governor Stevenson, with his showmanship and the "papal quality of his gestures."

Madeleine was one of fifty Wellesley students selected to accompany Stevenson and other Democratic bigwigs down the aisle at a rally in Boston's Mechanics Hall three weeks before the election. They were each issued a "Students for Stevenson" sash, which they wore crosswise across their chests. They also wore little silver pins made in the form of a shoe with a hole in the sole, an allusion to a widely published photograph of Stevenson during the campaign. During the rally, the bowler-hatted Mayor Curley made one of his grand entrances, appearing in the spot-lighted center aisle at the penultimate moment and taking much of the confetti meant for Governor Stevenson.

Foreign policy was a big issue in the days leading up to the 1956 election. The Soviets had just invaded Hungary to put down an anti-Communist insurrection, and the British and French had occupied the Suez Canal. Stevenson blasted Eisenhower for giving the Hungarian rebels the false hope of "liberation" and then failing to come through with any concrete support when their uprising was crushed. But the expected pro-Stevenson surge never materialized. Far from hurting Eisenhower, the crisis had the effect of encouraging the American people to rally behind the president.

Stevenson showed up in Boston again on the eve of the election, changing his plans at the last minute in order to visit a newborn grandson. Boston's Hotel Statler was filled with his supporters, including a poster-waving Wellesley contingent. The welcome was as ecstatic as before, but there was despondency in the air. Down in the polls, Stevenson decided to gamble on the politically sensitive issue of Eisenhower's health. Alluding to the fact that Ike had recently had a heart attack, Stevenson predicted that "a Republican victory tomorrow" would make Richard M. Nixon "guardian of the hydrogen bomb" sometime in the next four years. Exploiting concern over the president's health was Stevenson's last chance of turning the election around, but it left an unpleasant taste with his own supporters. "It was a desperation move," recalled Lippincott. "When he brought up the heart attack, the audience groaned. We did not want our man to sink to that level."

Eloquent and idealistic, Stevenson was a figure of hope for a generation of young people turned off by the self-satisfaction of the Eisenhower era. "We admired Adlai because he wasn't just a run-of-the-mill politician," said Madeleine's fellow Democrat Lucy Leinbach Robb. "He was sophisticated and savvy, an intellectual with a good sense of humor and a sense of self. Those of us who were politically active felt that Eisenhower was just a figurehead, whereas Adlai had a real persona."

Madeleine's decision to become a Democrat seems virtually predetermined, given her father's political beliefs and her admiration for him. Josef Korbel had always considered himself a man of the left. His personal experience with communism made him a hawk on East-West relations. Even on this subject, however, he was less strident than other exiles, having no illusions about America's willingness to "free" Eastern Europe from Soviet domination. On domestic politics, he was progressive. He was opposed to any form of ethnic or religious discrimination and was an advocate of integrated public schools, while insisting on a private-school education for his own children. Madeleine followed in his footsteps. "My memory is that she was a liberal Democrat. That is what we all called ourselves back then," said Emily MacFarquhar. "At the same time, she was more worldly wise than the rest of us." It seemed quite natural that political émigrés from Eastern Europe would support the party of Roosevelt and Truman.

After the excitement of the Stevenson campaign, campus politics seemed humdrum. Madeleine had the satisfaction of supporting a winning candidate two years later, when Kennedy ran for reelection to the Senate. She went out canvassing for him and covered some of his local appearances for the college newspaper. Even in Republican-dominated Wellesley, Kennedy was a popular candidate. He beat his Republican opponent by a margin of 5,398 to 4,943 in the town of Wellesley. Other Democratic candidates were defeated by margins of up to four to one.

During her junior year at Wellesley, Madeleine fulfilled another dream. Her family's request for U.S. citizenship was granted in March 1957, during her sophomore year. Since Madeleine was away at college, her ceremony was postponed until August. The little refugee girl had finally become an American.

At Wellesley, Madeleine worked for the college newspaper. Here she is seated second from the right, facing the camera. Her close friend Emily MacFarquhar is standing on the left. *Wellesley College.*

The Feminine Mystique

During Madeleine's first semester at Wellesley, the college newspaper ran a big takeout on the latest fad to sweep the campus: marriage mania. The number of married and engaged students was higher than ever before. " 'Why wait?' is the prevailing opinion on the question of when to marry among Wellesley's matrons," reported the lead story. Other stories described the plans of the newlyweds, most of which boiled down to "being a housewife." Among the minority who planned to work, most insisted that their jobs would be temporary. "I will teach for a year or two, then start our family" was a typical reply.

A series of informal polls over the next few years confirmed these findings. As a reporter for the *Wellesley College News*, Emily MacFarquhar remembers standing in the college snack bar and asking students what they wanted to do with their lives. "The first twenty-seven wanted to be married and become mothers and housewives. Perhaps three women wanted to have careers." The social pressures to marry, raise children, and look after the home were relentless, despite the first-class education offered by Wellesley. "It was a bit of a mixed message," says MacFarquhar. "Wellesley definitely conveyed to us the importance of learning, the importance of academic achievement. This was not a finishing school, despite all the stuff about posture pictures, proms, and everything else.

It was a very serious academic environment. At the same time, we were also receiving a message from our peers that the appropriate end to our four-year education was [not only a degree but] also a wedding ring."

Sometimes the two messages got mixed up. Students habitually took their knitting to class, in order to complete the pullover or scarf for their boyfriend at Harvard or Princeton. One of the rare members of the faculty willing to put a stop to the constant clacking of knitting needles was the formidable Margaret Ball, who taught Madeleine international relations. "Ladies, I will not have any knitting in this class," she told her students. "I know if you drop a stitch before you do." The college motto was *Non Ministrari sed Ministrare*: "Not to be Ministered unto, but to Minister." Madeleine and her friends joked that an equally good translation would be "Not to be Ministers, but Ministers' wives." "We had a very good education, but there was a sense that you needed to identify yourself by being married," she recalls.

The marriage mania at Wellesley reflected the ethos of the times. By the late fifties, the average age of marriage in the United States had fallen to twenty. Anyone who had not snagged a husband by the age of twenty-five risked being considered an "old maid." College-educated women tended to marry slightly later than the average. Even so, more than 80 percent of Madeleine's class were married within five years of leaving college.

Perhaps because Wellesley was a single-sex college on an isolated campus, Wellesley women had the reputation of being even more obsessed with finding a boyfriend than their counterparts elsewhere. There was a stigma attached to girls who did not have dates on weekends. Harvard students were constantly teasing Wellesley women for being willing to go out with anyone. "Cliff-dwellers [Radcliffe women] Choose Cautiously, Wellesley Girls Take Any Date" was a typical headline in the *Harvard Crimson* in November 1955.

Madeleine was one of the rare Wellesley women who did not permit the marriage obsession to interfere with her studies. She simply pursued both goals. "Madeleine was more serious about her studies than a lot of people," said Emily MacFarquhar. "She was at Wellesley to learn. She had gotten a message from her father that education was extremely important." But she also managed to ward off social disgrace by having a boyfriend most of the time she was at Wellesley.

The first boyfriend was Elston Mayhew at Princeton, a four-hour train journey away. The distance precluded them from getting together every weekend, but they saw quite a bit of each other in Madeleine's freshman year. "On big weekends, like the football games in the fall and the house parties in the spring, she would be here," said Richard Seabass, Elston's roommate at Princeton. "Elston was shy, and did not talk about girls very much. But it was clear that, among the girls he knew, Maddie was his favorite." Madeleine invited Elston up to Wellesley on several occasions, including the Freshman Prom, for which she bought a new black dress. To Seabass, they seemed very much alike. "Elston was quiet, but he had a wonderful smile, both on his mouth and eyes. That is how I remember Madeleine too." Even when she was not with Elston, Madeleine wore the Princeton scarf around Wellesley, so everyone knew she had a boyfriend.

Madeleine and Elston had an on-off relationship. "We grew apart, split up for a while, and then got together again," says Madeleine. She says he met "a girl from Connecticut." Elston's friends speculate that Madeleine was looking for someone with more prospects than the impoverished chemistry scholar from Denver. Although he went to Princeton on a full scholarship, he got behind in his studies and risked losing it. "Madeleine had her eyes set very much higher than Elston," said Robert DuPont, Elston's best friend from Denver. "By the time [he was at Princeton], he was not the winner he had been some time before. His star was falling by then. He was not going up, he was going down."

According to another friend, Charles Vail, Madeleine told Elston that "she cared a lot about him, but she had a different direction for her life, which involved if not more social status at least more m-o-n-e-y." Whether or not this is the case is unclear. What is certain, however, is that the final disappearance of Elston from Madeleine's life coincided with the appearance of a representative of one of America's wealthiest and most colorful families.

Madeleine had spent the summer of 1957 working in the library of her hometown newspaper, the *Denver Post*. She had been very excited to get the internship, the first rung on what she hoped would be a successful newspaper career. For the most part, the work consisted of sitting around a large table with other librarians and tearing out stories from the first edition with long steel rulers. The stories would then be stuffed into brown envelopes and filed away in cabinets. In addition to working in "the morgue," Madeleine helped out with society reporting, covering parties, weddings, and other events around town, mainly on the phone. "She was witty, bright, and willing to do anything I wanted her to do. She was very enthusiastic," recalled the society editor, Pat Collins Smedley. "She seemed to like the work, and got a kick out of the people we wrote about."

The library at the *Post* was on a mezzanine floor, just above the city desk. One of the reporters on the city desk was a young man named Joseph Albright. He was a month older than Madeleine, slim and short, with a cherubic face. People often could not believe that this shy, unassuming, slightly klutzy young man was the heir to a sizable newspaper fortune. A student at Williams College, Joe was interning at the *Post* for the second year running, reporting floods and break-ins and calling his stories in to the rewrite desk. In his case, the internship had been arranged through a friend of Alicia Patterson, the editor and founder of Long Island's *Newsday*, who also happened to be his aunt. Alicia was married to Harry Guggenheim, inheritor of a mining empire. It was assumed in the family that one day, after he learned the journalistic ropes, Joe would become a newspaper publisher, like his aunt, his grandfather, his great-grandfather, and his great-great-grandfather before him. In addition to *Newsday*, the family newspaper holdings included the *Chicago Tribune*, the *New York Daily News*, and the defunct *Washington Times-Herald*, now part of *The Washington Post*.

Joe came up to the library every evening to work on his honors thesis, which he had devoted to his grandfather, Joseph Patterson, founder of the *New York Daily News*. He struck Madeleine as "very attractive . . . very tweedy-looking." Initially, however, she thought he must be married as he wore a ring on his left hand. (The ring turned out to be his fraternity ring.) One day, she asked him where he went to college. "Williams, Williamstown, Mass.," he replied. "Oh, I go to Wellesley, in Wellesley, Mass.," said Madeleine. They soon discovered they had friends in common, including Joe's best friend at Harvard, Roger Cipriani, an occasional date of Madeleine's when she was not going out with Elston. Soon, Joe was inviting his fellow intern out to lunch almost every day and driving her to and from work.

Elston was also back in Denver that summer, presenting Madeleine with a difficult juggling act. "Joe worked Saturday nights, so I went out with Elston on Saturday nights and Joe on Friday nights," she recalled.

One day, Madeleine took Joe home to meet her parents. When a prospective boyfriend appeared in the house, he was often subjected to backchat in Czech within the Korbel family over his intelligence and general suitability. Typically, the boy would remark on Josef Korbel's fine art collection, saying something like, "Gee, you have a lot of pictures, is your father a painter?" Mandula or Josef would then say in Czech, "This boy is obviously an idiot." When Joe Albright appeared in the house, his line was somewhat different. "Oh, I see you have a lot of pictures; my stepfather is a painter," he told the Korbels. There was the usual backchat in Czech. "This one is really the worst," murmured Mandula. When the Korbels discovered that Joe's stepfather was the celebrated American artist Ivan Albright, they were suitably mortified.

Joe Albright was so unassuming that it took the Korbels some time to grasp the fact that he came from a super-wealthy family. Thinking that Joe was a poor student, Josef insisted that he stop paying for Madeleine's lunch and they go Dutch instead. The secret finally came out into the open when Josef mentioned that he was on a six-month Guggenheim fellowship. "Madeleine, I don't know how to tell you this," said Joe, acutely self-conscious of his family connections, "but my uncle *is* Harry Guggenheim."

After Joe and Madeleine separated in 1983, the Albright-Patterson clan began looking for the culprit who had originally brought them together. One theory favored by some of Joe's relatives was that Josef Korbel pushed Madeleine into marrying Joe because of his wealth and social standing. Another was that it was all the fault of the book editor at the *Denver Post*, Stan Peckham, the family friend who had organized Joe's internship on the newspaper. "I was blamed for Madeleine," Peckham told an interviewer after the divorce. "That was a disaster. . . . Hell, I didn't even know Madeleine until Joey introduced me to her."

Madeleine's friends insist that she was deeply in love with Joe and that his wealth had nothing to do with it. "She definitely married for love," says Danielle Gardner, who was Madeleine's next-door neighbor in Georgetown in the early sixties. "She did not go out and say, 'This is Joseph Medill Patterson Albright, let me get him.' "

Others believe that the motivations were more complicated. Robert DuPont, who used to double-date with Madeleine and Elston Mayhew in Denver, said Madeleine called him one day and announced she had met "the man of her dreams." She made the point that she was joining "a very important family." A psychiatrist, DuPont believes Madeleine wanted to restore the lost grandeur of her family, a common fantasy of someone whose family has fallen on hard times. "There was a time when the [Korbel] family was special. That had been lost. Now they were not special. Madeleine's passion was to recreate that status." There was nothing "random" about the way in which Joe and Madeleine found each other, DuPont insists. "Madeleine was not starry-eyed. She was able to see where her interests lay."

Joe represented an escape from the provincial atmosphere of Denver, which her parents reveled in but Madeleine found "very boring." According to Robert DuPont, she was doing much more than simply marrying money by marrying Joe. "For some people, money means a life of ease and luxury. For Madeleine, I think it meant something else. Right from the beginning, she thought of money in terms of the opportunities it would bring."

Just six weeks after meeting Joe, Madeleine returned to Wellesley for the beginning of her junior year wearing the pin of the Theta Delta Chi fraternity on her bright red Shetland sweater. To be "pinned" was an important ritual at that time, one step short of a formal engagement. "It meant you were engaged to be engaged," said MacFarquhar. "We were all shocked and amazed when we saw this pin [on Madeleine]. It was right after the summer. She just showed up in class with it on."

According to his friends, Elston was upset by his breakup with Madeleine but did not let it bother him for long. "He went on, dated other girls. I don't think he pined away," said DuPont. After graduation from Princeton, Elston could not find work as a chemist, so he joined the U.S. Navy as a navigator. In 1961, he crashed a new car late at night in Florida after returning from a date. The police concluded that he was drunk and put him in a cell to sober up. He died overnight of a head injury from which he would almost certainly have recovered with prompt medical attention.

If Madeleine was virtually ignorant of her family tree, Joe could trace his roots back many generations. He had cousins and relatives galore. His great-great-grandfather, Joseph Medill, was editor of the *Chicago Tribune*, mayor of Chicago, and a patron of Abraham Lincoln. According to family folklore, Lincoln once made himself a little too comfortable in Medill's office, prompting the patriarch to growl: "Take your goddamned feet off my desk, Abe." Control over the *Tribune* was eventually divided between Medill's two sons-in-law, Robert W. Patterson and Robert S. McCormick. The Medill-Patterson-McCormick dynasty developed into one of the great forces of American newspaper publishing.

During the years before America's entry into World War II, the family newspapers struck a xenophobic, isolationist theme. Joe's grandfather, Joseph M. Patterson, was known as one of the "Three Furies of Isolationism," together with his sister, Cissy Patterson, and cousin, Robert R. McCormick. The "Three Furies" used their papers to attack Franklin Roosevelt viciously and campaign against American involvement in any European war. Patterson's own paper, the *New York Daily News*, had a daily circulation of more than 2 million, making it America's most widely read newspaper. Joe's grandfather, who had gone to Groton Prep School with Roosevelt, accused the president of being a "dictator." After Pearl Harbor, FDR had his former classmate stand at attention in front of his desk while he berated him for his editorials. Humiliated, Patterson told his family that his main goal left was to "outlive that bastard Roosevelt," which he managed to do by thirteen months.

Joseph Patterson had three daughters, all of whom worshiped their father and sought to follow in his footsteps, in one way or another. The younger two, Alicia and Josephine, were particularly flamboyant and headstrong. Like their father, they were passionate about outdoor activities, particularly the new sport of flying. Josephine, Joe's mother, got her pilot's license at the age of sixteen and at eighteen became the youngest pilot flying the mail route between Chicago and St. Louis. Rather than hang around for the debutante season, she absconded with Alicia to India,

FAMILY OF JOSEPH ALBRIGHT

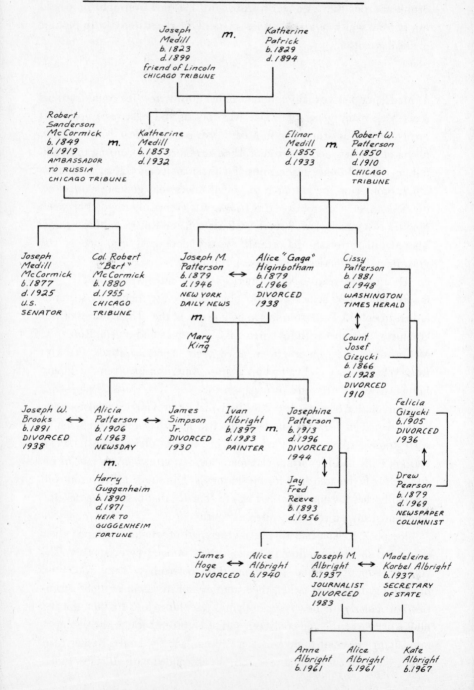

where they went tiger and pigsticking with the Maharajah of Baroodah while simultaneously fending off his advances. "He wanted to make us his concubines," Josephine recalled later. Joe was the oldest child of Josephine and a Chicago lawyer named Jay Fred Reeve. His parents divorced when he was seven, and Josephine married the hyperrealist painter Ivan Albright. At the age of sixteen, Joe formally took the name of his stepfather.

Joe had a curious upbringing, a bizarre mixture of privilege and hardship. As an adolescent he was one of the main characters in a weekly column that his mother wrote for *Newsday*, entitled "Life with Junior." Readers of *Newsday* were treated to detailed descriptions of Joe's various adventures and misadventures growing up, ranging from his disastrous attempts to get a gas-driven model airplane to work, to arguments over whether he was old enough to drive, to the time he went missing and could not be found. A teenager "can make your life a pleasure and a hell in the space of a short hour," Josephine wrote of her son. "[He] is impatient, arrogant, moody, argumentative, self-centered and often as irritating as scratching a nail across a blackboard. He is gay, good company, optimistic, helpful, and often so sweet that he breaks your heart." All this had the effect of making Joe even more self-conscious than he already was. "I found it embarrassing," he said later.

During the summer, Josephine would take her children off to her dude ranch in Wyoming. Joe was known on the ranch as "the little cowboy from Chicago" and subjected to the toughening influence of the West. "He was sent off to work when he was thirteen, fourteen," remembered his sister, Alice. "He worked on the Indian mission, poor guy, haying for the priest. . . . There were some very tough guys out there. It was like being put in the streets from a whole different environment. He had this stoic thing. They used to beat the shit out of him. . . . I remember he had a black eye at the table in the morning, and he was just, like, 'It didn't happen.' " According to Alice, both she and Joe became "guilt-ridden human beings" because of their family's wealth. There was always the feeling that they had things that they "didn't earn or didn't deserve." But while Alice reacted to her upbringing by being expansive and outgoing, Joe was withdrawn and introverted, albeit with a tough inner core.

Joe already had a strong-willed mother and a strong-willed sister. He was about to get a strong-willed wife.

Back in the East, Joe took Madeleine to meet his aunt Alicia and her husband, Harry Guggenheim. This visit would later become the stuff of family legend. Mandula loved to tell friends the story of how Madeleine was picked up by a "rather scruffy young man" who seemed "very nice," but did not appear to have a penny to his name. As told to the Korbels' neighbor in Denver, Jack Newman-Clark, the story has Madeleine and the impecunious young man arriving in front of a set of huge cast-iron gates on the outskirts of a big city. "They drive in and, lo and behold, there are butlers and waiters. He is a multimillionaire. Everybody is floored. And that is how Madeleine became very wealthy."

The story may have been embellished over the years into a Cinderella rags-to-riches fable—the Korbels knew at least the bare essentials about Joe's background before he took Madeleine to meet his relatives—but it captures the wonder of her first visit to Falaise. It is difficult to imagine a setting more fairy tale–like than the Guggenheim estate on Long Island. A Normandy-style manor house built on the edge of a cliff overlooking the Sound, Falaise could be the backdrop for a novel by Daphne du Maurier or F. Scott Fitzgerald.

One of Harry's other nieces-in-law, Dorothea Straus, described Falaise as "the most romantic house" she ever knew. From the terrace, two hundred feet above the sea, "could be seen triangles of sails and the choppy festoons of waves that murmured softly like discreet servants laying a carpet beneath the tall turreted wall of the house . . . The property was separated from the public road by a high grille enclosing woods, lawns, gardens, paddocks, and enough subsidiary lodgings to form a complete village. But these were scattered, partly concealed by old trees and winding paths. In the spring the ground was covered with daffodils, a golden sea leading to the cobbled front courtyard of [Falaise]. Here you were met by more flowers in great earthenware pots: lilies, fuchsia, and azaleas in the spring, geraniums and orange trees in summer, chrysanthemums in the fall . . . One wing of the house was the garage enclosing [Harry's] shining cars, as the stables beyond sheltered his sleek thoroughbred horses. Opposite the garage was a swimming pool enclosed on four sides and set in the midst of blooming oleanders. The atmosphere in this court branching from the main court was hothouse—a Roman bath fit for the Caesars."

Just a thirty-minute train ride from Manhattan, Falaise was one of the fabulous properties on Long Island's North Shore that Fitzgerald described in *The Great Gatsby*. At the turn of the century, industrial magnates like F. W. Woolworth, J. P. Morgan, Harry P. Whitney, and William K. Vanderbilt competed against each other to build ever more magnificent and original residences. The result was a string of English castles, Italian villas, and French châteaux, each of them set in hundreds of acres of land. Falaise is far from the most grandiose of these residences—indeed, it is one of the smallest—but its intimate scale and incomparable setting make it one of the most charming. By the fifties, as death taxes took their toll, many of the mansions had either fallen into disrepair or been sold to institutions like the Russian mission to the United Nations. But Harry Guggenheim remained master of Falaise, living a semifeudal existence with a staff of at least twenty butlers, maids, gardeners, and drivers. He divided his time between Falaise, a Manhattan apartment, and his stud farm at Cain Hoy in South Carolina.

Harry was the grandson of Meyer Guggenheim, a Jewish peddler who immigrated to America in 1848 to escape religious oppression in Switzerland and founded a mighty mining dynasty. Harry's father, Daniel, was the most dynamic and ruthless of Meyer's eight sons and the natural leader of the family after the patriarch's death. At one time, the Guggenheims enjoyed a virtual monopoly in copper mining and could make or break South American governments with a telegram. Daniel played a key role in the early development of rocketry, creating a foundation that sponsored the work of the rocket pioneer Robert H. Goddard. By the time Harry came of age, the emphasis in the family had shifted from making money to spending it. A former fighter pilot and U.S. ambassador to Cuba, Harry considered himself an all-around Renaissance man, with interests ranging from aviation to horse racing to the promotion of world peace. He liked people to address him as "Captain," his rank in the U.S. Navy.

Alicia Patterson, Joe's aunt, married Harry in 1939. It was the third marriage for both of them. In order to keep the restless Alicia occupied, Harry started a small Long Island newspaper called *Newsday* and set her up as publisher. By a fortuitous combination of circumstances—Harry's business acumen, Alicia's journalistic instincts, and the suburban population boom on Long Island—the paper became extraordinarily profitable. Alicia loved her work at *Newsday*, which provided her with a means of escape from a life of stifling privilege. "The people that work down in this office may not be adept in all the social requirements but, by God, they are the first real people I have ever met," she wrote her sister Elinor in 1946. "It has taught me what a rotten parasite I have been all my life and what a lousy bunch of people I have been playing around with."

Although not as wealthy as Harry, Alicia had inherited her own fortune from her father, Joseph Patterson. Known as "the boss lady" at *Newsday*, she lived a life that was quite separate from Harry in many respects, communicating with him by memo and meeting only at Falaise. For many years, she had carried on a secret love affair with Adlai Stevenson, Madeleine's childhood hero. Harry and Alicia had completely different views about politics: He was an ardent Republican, she an independent with a liberal point of view. Working out a common editorial line involved heated family negotiations. They feuded with each other constantly. Sometimes, when they could not reach agreement, they simply ran competing "his" and "her" editorials. The contrasting personalities of Alicia and Harry are reflected in their adjoining bedrooms at Falaise, which has been preserved as a museum. Her bedroom is filled with light and echoes with the sound of waves beating against the rocks below. His is dark, decorated with heavy mahogany furniture, and seems cut off from the outside world.

Joe was more than just a nephew to Alicia. Since she had no children of her own, she regarded him as a surrogate son. She went hunting and fishing with him in Wyoming and encouraged him to think of himself as her successor. Joe was mentioned in the press as the "heir-apparent" at *Newsday* as early as 1951, when he was still only fourteen. Later, Alicia would go back and forth between him and his sister Alice, sometimes favoring one, sometimes the other. In February 1959, a few months before Joe's marriage to Madeleine, Alicia said publicly she hoped that the next generation of her family would take over "when the time comes for me to retire," but added that Joe and Alice would both have to work hard "to prove" they had the necessary "spark." Any appointment would obviously need the approval of Harry, who owned 51 percent of *Newsday*'s stock. (Alicia owned the remaining 49 percent.) Since Harry had no sons of his own, it was generally assumed that Alicia's wishes would prevail. Besides, she was seventeen years younger than Harry and seemed likely to outlive him.

Entering the Gatsby-like world of Harry and Alicia was an eye-opener for Madeleine. She remembers arriving at the house to be greeted by a butler. She and Joe then went for a walk to admire the property and the magnificent views over Long Island Sound. When they got back, Aunt Alicia suggested that she "dress for dinner." Madeleine went up to her room and immediately fell into a panic because she was unable to find any of her formal clothes. "What had happened was that the butler had taken all my clothes away and [the servants] were re-ironing them. That was my first introduction to [Joe's relatives]," Madeleine recalled. "They were quite an overwhelming family."

Madeleine later told friends about the confusion she felt during her first formal dinner party at Falaise: There were so many pieces of silverware on the table that she had no idea which to use for which course. But she soon overcame her embarrassment. In some ways, she was less self-conscious than Joe. Alicia's friend Jackie Gebhard, who worked as a sports reporter on *Newsday*, remembers meeting Madeleine and Joe on the terrace of Falaise at the beginning of the Thanksgiving holiday. They were staying with the Guggenheims. Later, Gebhard took the two of them for drinks with a prominent journalist for *The New York Times*, Tom Hamilton. Joe asked Hamilton what he thought of going into the newspaper publishing business. Hamilton, who had no idea who Joe was, replied: "I think it's a great idea, as long as either your grandfather or your uncle owns a newspaper." Joe got a "stricken look" on his face, Gebhard recalls. He passed on both counts, but that was not how he wanted to get to the top.

Madeleine was also required to pay court to Joe's grandmother. A tiny lady known to the family as "Gaga," Alice Higinbotham Patterson was a supremely elegant matriarch of Chicago society with a terrifying reputation. "She could just freeze anybody out," recalled her granddaughter Alice. The second woman to fly with the Wright brothers, Alice

Patterson once faked having a baby to get her husband out of making a speech. In order to be properly attired for her trip to Chicago, Madeleine needed a formal hat. "It was the kind of hat she would not have had any use for at Wellesley, so she had to scurry around to find it," said her friend Ann Einhorn. "I remember thinking it was amazing that this girl who had literally nothing was able to adapt to her new situation with so much poise."

Madeleine remembers Grandmother Alice as a tiny woman, about four foot nine, who lived in a beautiful apartment on Chicago's Lakeshore drive. Conversation was difficult at first because they were moving in different worlds. Alice's idea of a conversation opener was something like "How does your mother deal with the servant problem?" Madeleine was obliged to confess that her mother did not have any servants. Later, Alice took Madeleine to a very expensive hat shop to be outfitted for an Easter bonnet. The price was $200, a lot of money in those days. Since Madeleine was not sure who was going to pay for the bonnet, she started raising objections. She didn't like the color. The shop assistants promised to make a new one in a different color. She didn't like the raspberry decorations that were attached to it. No problem, they said, they would find some other accessories. In the meantime, they insisted on measuring her head.

"I didn't know what to do," Madeleine recalled. "If [Grandma Alice] had bought me the hat, should I thank her? If she hadn't bought me the hat, that would be insane. Finally, we got to the house and had some tea and she said, 'I hope you like your Easter present.' I still have that hat."

The trips to Falaise and Chicago were all part of a whirlwind romance. By March 1958, nine months after they first met, Joe was already dedicating his college thesis on his grandfather Joseph Patterson "To Madeleine, with whom . . ." The following October, at the start of Madeleine's senior year at Wellesley, the *Wellesley College News* carried an announcement of her engagement to Joseph Medill Patterson Albright.

In June 1959, Madeleine joined 363 other Wellesley seniors in marching across the college lawn in gown, mortarboard, and high-heeled shoes to receive her degree. She was one of twenty-six students to graduate with special honors. The commencement address was given by the secretary of defense, Neil McElroy, and it would be remembered for decades by members of the Class of '59 as the epitome of male chauvinist thinking.

McElroy tried to grapple with a problem that was being discussed increasingly at the end of the fifties: the role of educated women. A few weeks earlier, the *News* had framed the question with the headline "Marriage or Career?" "The modern young woman who has the same education as a boy asks herself: to what use shall I now put my education? Why all this knowledge when all I have to know is how to diaper babies? The difficulty for the twenty-year-old girl is to know what she wants. In her daydreams she desires everything: a brilliant marriage, a successful career, intelligent children. Time brings her to the point where she must choose."

For McElroy, the solution to this conundrum was quite simple. The role of an educated woman was to raise the next generation of scientists, scholars, and politicians. Some of the Wellesley graduates in front of him would become teachers, while others would focus their educational efforts on their own family. "No responsible person in America would suggest that young women curtail that most important of careers— homemaking," McElroy told the graduates. "Your education here at Wellesley in the liberal arts tradition has given you an ideal preparation to serve as the very heart of a home, for the betterment of your family and of your community. . . . You have a duty to foster and multiply the society of educated men and women. This you can do most effectively in your own home, where education really starts." The notion that a member of the audience might aspire to become a federal judge, let alone America's top diplomat, seemed beyond the comprehension of Eisenhower's secretary of defense.

Madeleine and her friends had been used to hearing such platitudes for so long that, for many of them, McElroy's words went in one ear and out the other. The only thing Muriel Fleischmann remembered about the speech was the defense secretary's quip—"I hope that is one of ours"— when some planes flew overhead. Others were more offended. "Even then, some of us felt that educating the next generation was not the reason why we had got our Wellesley education," said Winnie Freund. While McElroy's words sound patronizing today, in the context of the times they were merely realistic. Survey after survey showed that most Wellesley women expected to marry soon after college. For those who thought about careers at all, teaching was an overwhelming first choice. This was not just how the commencement speaker saw the "Class of '59." It was how they saw themselves.

A few years earlier, the standard-bearer of Democratic liberalism, Adlai Stevenson, had made very similar points in an address to students at nearby Smith College. Dismissing the desire of educated women to play a role in "the crises of the age," Stevenson insisted that American women had "never had it so good." A woman's role was "to help her husband find values that will give purpose to his specialized daily chores" and teach their children the "uniqueness of each individual human being." "If you're clever, maybe you can even practice your saving arts on that unsuspecting man while he is watching television," said Stevenson. "I think there is much you can do about our crisis in the humble role of housewife. I could wish you no better vocation than that."

A few days before the commencement ceremony, the *Harvard Crimson* engaged in another round of its favorite sport: Wellesley-bashing. It published an article comparing Wellesley women to the Tunicata, "thin, lithe animals that move about the sea in their youth, investigating their surroundings [until one day] they grow fat, settle down on the ocean floor never to move again, and reproduce." The writer assailed the "cult of gentility" at Wellesley, the elevation of "facileness" over "conviction," and joked that the college offered students a first-class "terminal education": As soon as they graduated, they could forget everything they had ever learned. The Tunicata comparison touched a nerve at Wellesley, sparking fierce denunciations from faculty and students, but there was little argument with the broad conclusions of the article.

Such was the future that seemed to await Madeleine Jana Korbel on the day of her graduation.

In order to clear the way for her marriage to Joseph Albright, Madeleine had to change religions. His family were Episcopalians and were adamantly opposed to his marrying a Catholic. "It would have been easier if you were a Jew than a Catholic," Joe's mother Josephine told

Madeleine. Although there was a strong strain of anti-Semitism in the Patterson family, the anti-Catholic strain was if anything even more virulent. It stemmed in large part from the family's experience with Catholics. Joe's natural father, Jay Reeve, was a Catholic who had divorced his first wife to marry Josephine. In the eyes of the Catholic Church, the divorce was illegal. Reeve was committing adultery when he married Josephine. Josephine was indignant. To add insult to injury, Reeve later remarried his first wife after divorcing Josephine.

Grandmother Alice also had problems with Catholics. Joe's grandfather, Joseph Patterson, had divorced her in order to marry a Catholic woman named Mary King. Alice and her children regarded her as a usurper, referring to her derisively as "Bloody Mary," after the devoutly Catholic Mary I of England who persecuted the Protestants. "Bloody Mary" compounded her sin, in the family's eyes, by persuading Patterson to convert to Catholicism.

Since she was still a practicing Catholic, Madeleine's conversion to Episcopalianism was more than just a formality. After her divorce from Joe, she would be drawn back to Roman Catholicism, at least briefly. As Geraldine Ferraro's foreign policy adviser, she attended Mass regularly with the Democratic vice presidential candidate during the 1984 election campaign. The two women talked about how hard it had been for Madeleine to walk away from the Catholic Church. "She believed in the Blessed Mother," said Ferraro, a practicing Catholic herself. "If you took away my religion and made me say all of a sudden that the Blessed Mother is no longer a virgin, I would say, 'Hey, give me a break.' "

The wedding, which took place in Wellesley three days after Madeleine's graduation from college, brought together two very different families. "It was a little bit of a mismatch," acknowledges Madeleine. Harry and Alicia motored up from New York in their chauffeur-driven Cadillac; Alice flew in from Chicago; the Korbel family had all traveled from Denver. The Albrights paid for a very elaborate rehearsal dinner on the eve of the wedding. The wedding itself, in St. Andrew's Protestant Church, was small but formal. By working in the Wellesley cafeteria, Madeleine had saved up enough money for wedding apparel for the bridesmaids. She herself looked ravishing in what the *Rocky Mountain News* described as "a gown of peau de soie, fashioned with a square neckline and lace appliquéd bodice" and a long veil falling from "a tiara headpiece appliquéd with lace and seed pearls."

The reception was held in an old-fashioned English inn called the 1812 House in Framingham. After it was over, Alice Albright, Joe's rebellious younger sister, took off the bridesmaid's dress that Madeleine had bought for her and ripped it into pieces. The incident gave Madeleine yet another insight into the eccentric family of which she had become a part.

By marrying into one of America's best-known families, Madeleine became the envy of many of her Wellesley classmates. Ironically, her achievement came at a time when the very institution of the "happy housewife" was coming under attack. As Madeleine was graduating from Wellesley, Betty Friedan was researching her groundbreaking work *The Feminine Mystique,* which would soon become a feminist bible. Friedan did much of her research among Madeleine's generation of East Coast college women in 1959. She discovered that the number of women college graduates with career plans had actually dwindled since the 1940s, when she herself graduated from Smith. Her conclusion was that the ideal of the "happy housewife," perpetuated by countless women's magazines, novels, and advertisements, was a sham designed to keep women in permanent subordination to men. Women, Friedan believed, wanted something more out of life than merely being the perfect mother or the perfect wife. But they were trapped in a culture that penalized overeducated women. She quoted a student who dropped out of an honors course at Smith:

> I got so excited about my work I would sometimes go into the library at eight in the morning and not come out till ten at night. I even thought I might want to go on to graduate school or law school and really use my mind. Suddenly, I was afraid of what would happen. I wanted to lead a rich full life. I want to marry, have children, have a nice house. Suddenly I felt, what am I beating my brains out for? So this year I'm trying to lead a well-rounded life. I take courses, but I don't read eight books and still feel like reading the ninth. I stop and

go to the movies. The other way was harder, and more exciting. I don't know why I stopped. Maybe I just lost courage.

The girl who insisted on having both a happy marriage and a fulfilling career was a rarity, at Wellesley as much as at Smith. Although she never read *The Feminine Mystique*, Madeleine Korbel Albright would become the prototype of Friedan's "new woman."

While at Wellesley, Madeleine met Joseph Medill Patterson Albright, heir to a newspaper fortune. They were "pinned" six weeks after they first met in the summer of 1957, engaged the following year, and married in June 1959. *Chicago Sun-Times.*

Young Married

After a honeymoon on Caribbean beaches, Madeleine and Joe embarked on married life together in the great American heartland. Joe had signed up for the Army Reserve and was required to do six-month military training at the Army base at Fort Leonard Wood, Missouri. Madeleine spent the first few weeks at home in Denver, finding temporary work booking reservations at the Greyhound Bus Depot. She then went to Missouri to join Joe, getting a part-time job as a reporter for the *Rolla Daily News* for a salary of $35 a week. Although she says she wrote obituaries and handled the social page, she did not leave much of an impression. A search of the newspaper archives forty years later did not turn up any bylines.

Both Madeleine and Joe were focused on raising a family and making a living. Although Joe came from a very affluent family, much of his own wealth was tied up in trusts. In an article for the *Chicago Sun-Times* soon after his marriage, Joe wrote that it seemed "out of the question for us to buy a house." Describing himself as "young and . . . very much in love," he wrote that he and his new bride had entered into the "venture of marriage" with a stockpile of resources in the form of "clothes, some money, wedding presents, education." Over the next few years, he added, "we must acquire other assets of family life—furniture, rugs, pots and pans."

Back in Chicago by the end of 1959, Joe resumed his job at the *Sun-Times*. The *Sun-Times* was the liberal alternative to the conservative *Tribune*, the newspaper founded by Joseph's great-great-grandfather, now under the control of the McCormick branch of the family. Although Joe's family owned a large chunk of *Tribune* stock, the McCormicks were barely on speaking terms with the Pattersons. The *Trib* remained in the posthumous shadow of Colonel Robert "Bertie" McCormick, its eccentric and unashamedly partisan publisher who had died in 1955. Published under the slogan "the World's Greatest Newspaper," the *Tribune* had no qualms about using its dominant position to promote the Colonel's pet causes and skewer his enemies. *Trib* reporters took delight in clobbering the opposition, by fair means or foul. Joe would later remember covering one of his first murders and being promised a helping hand by a veteran *Trib* reporter. They waited together outside police headquarters for a briefing that never took place. What Joe didn't realize until the papers appeared the next day was that his competitor had already received a private briefing from the lieutenant inside the police station.

The Chicago newspaper wars were not quite as vicious as they were in the twenties, when they were immortalized in Ben Hecht's play *The Front Page*, but they were still pretty frenetic. "It was a very intense news town," recalled Jim Hoge, another reporter on the *Sun-Times*, who married Joe's sister, Alice. "The race was on for scoops, for changing stories between editions to make sure you had caught up with whatever the other guy had."

At the 1960 Republican convention, which took place in Chicago, Joe succeeded in getting a world scoop that more than wiped out his earlier humiliation. Finding himself at a loose end, he had hidden out in the bathroom of a suite used by Republican leaders for political deliberations. After waiting for several hours, he was rewarded when Richard Nixon and other Republican leaders held a discussion in the next room on the vice presidential candidate. Unfortunately, he was seated in the bathtub and could not reach his notebook, so he had to resort to other means of recording what he was overhearing. Occasionally, Nixon or some other Republican luminary would rattle the bathroom door in frustration. Joe later told friends that the physical needs of Republican leaders were not "my problem. My problem was how to write in the dark on toilet paper." The next day, the *Sun-Times* came out with a verbatim record of the proceedings beneath a six-inch-deep banner headline stripped across the front page:

Exclusive Story of Meeting
HOW GOP LEADERS
AGREED ON LODGE

As an aspiring journalist, Madeleine wanted very much to be part of Joe's world. She applied for a job at the *Sun-Times* but was turned down on the grounds of the company's anti-nepotism policy. As she later recollected the conversation, one of the newspaper's editors, Emmett Dedmon, took her out to dinner and told her, "Honey, you may want to be a reporter, but you can't be on a competing paper, and you can't be on the paper that your husband works for, so why don't you find another career?" "It made me mad, but not mad enough to fight," she said later. Instead, she went to work for the publicity department of *Encyclopaedia Britannica*, researching answers to subscribers' questions. Being turned down for a job in journalism proved a blessing in disguise for Madeleine, who now says "I would have been a lousy reporter."

At this time, Madeleine was still not thinking in terms of a "career with a Capital C," in the words of her friend Winnie Freund. "The last thing she ever thought of was that she would have a spectacular career. Our generation of women went to school, were active in the community. . . . Sometime down the road, she probably saw an academic career for herself, like her father. But she was primarily focused on Joe's career." On the other hand, she certainly did not see herself as a full-time housewife. "I thought that I had an obligation to do something more with my life than just be happy," she said in 1998. At this stage in her life, wanting to be anything other than a housewife was ambitious in itself.

Living in Chicago meant dealing with the in-laws, all of whom were pillars of local society. Grandmother Alice lived on swanky Lakeshore Drive. Josephine and Ivan Albright lived in a large town house at 55 East Division Street, on the city's fashionable near-north side. A revered figure in the Chicago art world, Ivan was best known as the painter who drew the grotesque and harrowing *Picture of Dorian Gray* for the 1944 movie adaptation of Oscar Wilde's novel. He could spend weeks working on a tiny detail of his meticulously painted portraits, recording every single blemish on the human body with seemingly macabre delight. The titles of his paintings were works of art in themselves. When Joe and Madeleine got to Chicago, he had been working on his masterpiece, *Poor Room— There Is No Time, No End, No Today, No Yesterday, Only the Forever, and Forever and Forever Without End,* for more than two decades. He had erected a cross section of a brick wall in his studio, pierced by a window hung with dusty curtains and framed by wasps' nests and dead apple-tree branches. A slashed, lace-cuffed hand rested on the windowsill, suggesting that something violent and terrible had occurred inside the room. "I compose in motion," he explained. "I wish to create tension and conflict."

Ivan and Josephine had a curious marriage. Like her mother, Alice, Josephine could be very intimidating. Their former son-in-law, Jim Hoge, describes Ivan as a kindly if eccentric loner who escaped his wife's rages by locking himself in his studio. "He was a kinetic bundle of energy, always moving around. Sometimes you could not understand what he was saying. Whenever we visited, he and Josephine would almost invariably have some big fight. . . . It was easier for me to get on with him than with her." Josephine, adds Hoge, "could be impatient, very upfront with her emotions. You could tell when she didn't like you. She sizzled a lot. . . . There were days when you just couldn't do anything right, as far as Josephine was concerned. She would give you the cold shoulder and mutter 'Stop off somewhere.' You just felt that you should be some place else." Madeleine's relationship with her in-laws was similar to Hoge's. She says she liked Ivan but had a "tough" time with Josephine.

At the beginning of 1961, Madeleine escaped this intense familial atmosphere when Joe was summoned to Long Island by his aunt Alicia to work at *Newsday*. Alicia's friends feared that she was working herself to death. After long consideration, she finally decided to put her prospective heir through his paces. Josephine was opposed to the move. She felt that her son, then only twenty-three, needed more experience before being thrust into the world of newspaper publishing. But Joe insisted he was up to the challenge.

In April, Madeleine and Joe moved to Garden City, Long Island, renting an apartment at 360 Stewart Avenue. Madeleine was pregnant with twins, who arrived six weeks premature on June 17, each weighing no more than three and a half pounds. Since they both had collapsed lungs and were exceptionally vulnerable to infection, they had to be placed in incubators. Madeleine had nothing to do but gaze at them through the glass.

Bored and restless, she enrolled in an eight-week, eight-hour-a-day Russian-language class. When her father came to visit the following month to see his first grandchildren, she greeted him in Russian, her fourth language in addition to English, Czech, and French. He was delighted and suggested she pursue a teaching career.

The christening took place in the oak-paneled drawing room of the Guggenheim estate at Falaise in the presence of both families and Madeleine's Wellesley friends. The twins were named Alice Patterson and Anne Korbel after Joe's grandmother and Madeleine's mother. When they came back home, Madeleine found she had to feed them three times a night. "I kind of sat there during the day, feeding them, watching soap operas, and I thought, 'I didn't go to college to do this.' " Excited by her progress in Russian, she decided to enroll in graduate school. "My life has been an alternately exciting and frustrating mixture of housewifery and studying," she wrote in a Wellesley alumnae classbook. "After one year of a regular job, and one year of coping with premature twins, I decided that the best route to sanity was to dilute housework with some studying and vice versa."

While Madeleine was looking after the twins, Joe was making the rounds of *Newsday*, gaining practical experience in the various departments. Despite his efforts to fit in with the boys, he could not quite shake the image of the privileged heir apparent. One of his first assignments was to deliver bundles of newspapers along the North Shore, in order to get acquainted with the distribution system. Most of his coworkers reported for work in battered station wagons, but Joe showed up in a new, fire-engine red Mercedes-Benz. It was one of an identical pair given to him and his sister by Alice, who had decided that her grandchildren were driving cars that were way beneath them. On another occasion, he was selling advertisements but was too shy to ask for a check. When he got back to the office, around seven P.M., his supervisor, Dave Targe, told him to go back and get the check. "I'm supposed to meet my aunt to have dinner," Joe protested. "Get the check first and meet your aunt later," said Targe.

Alicia was amused by her nephew's tribulations, and later called Targe to say, "I'm so glad you did that to Joe."

Joe and Madeleine were frequent visitors to Falaise. They would go over to the estate practically every weekend for Sunday lunch and a swim in the pool or a game of tennis. Although Harry was away half the year, Alicia was always there. "I spent a great deal of time with her," Madeleine recalled. "She was a really earthy, funny, strong, great woman. . . . She was larger than life. I really liked her. . . . She played a huge role in our lives."

"Alicia went out of her way to include them in her fancy parties," said Jackie Gebhard, Alicia's tennis partner from *Newsday*. The Guggenheim set included the theater director George Abbott, the magazine illustrator Neysa McMein, the socialite Marietta Tree, and the publisher Bennet Cerf. Gebhard describes the atmosphere at Falaise as "formal-hilarious." Harry liked to have black-tie parties, served by liveried butlers. "The general format was knock-off English country life," said Jim Hoge. "On Sundays, we always had Yorkshire pudding and big slabs of beef. Harry was very taken with the English style."

Alicia, by contrast, was a great practical joker who loved to gossip. One of her favorite pastimes was known as "The Game," a dumbed-down version of charades. A label was pinned to the back of a black-tied guest with a name like Mickey Mouse or Rin Tin Tin or Greta Garbo; the partner was required to act out the part. "It was the silliest thing in the whole world," recalls Gebhard. "The most fun was watching stuffy people running around acting silly." Katharine Graham, whose family owns *The Washington Post*, recalls a party given by Alicia in New York in which she made the guests give mock funeral orations over each other's bodies. The publisher of the *Los Angeles Times*, Otis Chandler, left in disgust, saying the evening was not for him. (Harry Guggenheim would later sell *Newsday* to the Chandler family.)

As the two children-in-law, Madeleine and Jim Hoge were the outsiders in these goings-on. "I think it was a bit much for both of us," said Hoge, a coldly handsome man nicknamed "The Hog" by Alicia. "My father did very well as a New York lawyer, but we were definitely not in that league. It was probably less unfamiliar to me than it was to Madeleine. But Madeleine, being the daughter of a diplomat, probably had a little better sense of the wider world than me."

Joe and Madeleine were also occasional guests at the hunting lodge at Kingsland, Georgia, on a sweeping bend in the St. Mary's River, where Alicia went three or four times a year to unwind. Alicia had bought the 1,800-acre estate in 1936 during a previous marriage because of the excellent quail shooting, and it played a very important role in her life. Here, she was totally independent of Harry, holding court with friends like Adlai Stevenson and George Abbott. She loved to sit by the black, brooding river, watching the alligators, and drew an almost religious inspiration from the serenity of the setting. The modest, one-story house was made out of clear cypress wood, with shutters painted a pale bluish-pink to match the fungus on the surrounding trees. At the bottom of the lawn leading down to the river was a magnificent live oak, with great clumps of Spanish moss hanging down from its spreading limbs. When Madeleine's children were older, Kingsland became one of their favorite vacation spots.

In the spring of 1962, Joe was transferred to Washington to cover the State Department. He and Madeleine rented a mews house at 3421 R Street, in the heart of Georgetown, two blocks from Dumbarton Oaks. It was an exciting time to be in a place that had previously been considered a rather slow-moving southern backwater. A new generation of politicians had swept into town with Jack Kennedy, and change was in the air. The journalists who flocked to Washington with the Kennedys felt that they too were part of Camelot, the shining city on the hill. "In the fifties, people our grandfathers' age had been in charge," said Ward Just, a reporter for *Newsweek* and a friend and neighbor of the Albrights. "We tended, in a rather snobbish way, to think of these people as Babbitts. All of a sudden, the Babbitts were swept out of Washington, and in the Oval Office you had Marco Polo and his cohorts."

Because of her high-powered neighbors and Joe's journalistic contacts, Madeleine was a tangential part of this world. Their Georgetown friends included Worth Bingham, heir to several Louisville newspapers, and his wife Joan; Jay Iselin, a journalist on *Newsweek*; and the lawyer John Zentay. According to Just, who later became the preeminent Washington novelist, Georgetown society at this time was organized in a series of socio-archaeological layers. The top layer consisted of the great hostesses like Katharine Graham and Polly Wisner, commentators like Joe Alsop and James "Scotty" Reston, and the "wise men" in the shape of diplomats Chip Bohlen and Tommy Thompson. The crust below that was made up of the odd senator and assistant secretary of state. "Then there was the third crust, which was where we were," said Just. This layer consisted of young people still in their twenties, including junior members of newspaper and newsmagazine bureaus, eager to make their reputation. "Occasionally, the upper crust would dip down into the pot and drag one of us up for a meal to see what the younger people were thinking. As a result, we would find ourselves around the dinner table with people like Joe Alsop or Polly Wisner, listening intently."

The Albrights' immediate next-door neighbors were Danielle and Richard Gardner, a law professor from Columbia University who had responsibility for international organizations at the State Department. An Italian Jew whose family fled to America during the war, Danielle Gardner shared a similar immigrant background with Madeleine, along with a similar drive for total assimilation into American society. "Both of us had tried very much to Americanize ourselves," recalls Gardner. "Neither of us had the slightest accent by that stage." They rapidly became good friends. The Gardner daughter was a year older than the two Albright girls. A pair of Peruvian sisters, Felicia and Margarita, worked as housekeepers for the two families and chattered across the fence in Spanish. It was almost a "communal life," Gardner says. "We were literally in and out of each other's houses the whole time." They or their housekeepers would take the children to nearby Montrose Park, where they would often run into Teddy Kennedy's children.

Madeleine did typical housewifely things like cooking dinner for Joe and looking after the children on weekends, when the housekeepers were off. By the end of the weekend, she was often exhausted: Dressing and feeding one-year-old twins and dragging them up and down steps in their double-stroller was a major production. She gave Danielle practical tips on looking after the house, such as putting plastic sandwich bags on the top of glasses while they are stored in the cupboard to prevent them from gathering dust. "That is something I still do," says Gardner. "It was her idea. She is highly organized, and has a very inventive mind."

At the same time, Danielle detected a certain "restlessness" in her friend. "This was a woman who wanted to do more than just take care of her children," she recalls. "She felt something was missing from her life." One day, Madeleine told Danielle that, since she and Joe had enough money to hire full-time help, she wanted to study for a Ph.D. She enrolled at the School for Advanced International Studies at Johns Hopkins University. One of her first classes was a graduate seminar on Soviet foreign policy taught by the Sovietologist Vernon Aspaturian, whom she impressed as "very serious." Gardner believes that the Albrights' position on the fringes of Georgetown society was a motivating factor in pushing Madeleine to return to her studies. "She was a little bit envious of the fact that we were moving in higher society," said Danielle, who received more "A list" invitations than Madeleine because of her husband's position at the State Department. "If she had enough excitement in her life, she might not have felt the same intellectual push."

To casual acquaintances, Madeleine often seemed a little shy. But she could hold her own in serious conversations, particularly if the subject was foreign policy. "She had no hesitation in saying what she thought," said her brother-in-law, Jim Hoge. "A lot of the characteristics of Madeleine today are just an evolution of things you could have seen during those early years, if you were looking closely. You were struck by her great energy, her focus on going up the ladder, the way she would do what was needed to take the next step."

At the same time, Madeleine tended to be taken for granted by many of the men in Joe's circle. Ward Just remembers an occasion in which the members of the Albrights' Georgetown set were engaged in a favorite game: guessing which of them would end up first on the cover of *Time* magazine. At that time, a *Time* cover story was even more of a status symbol than it is today. At one point, as the argument between the men grew more intense, Joe turned to his wife and said, "You know, you can fetch us another bottle of wine, Madeleine." The idea that sweet little Madeleine might one day be a cover subject for *Time* was obviously too ludicrous to contemplate. "It was not that anyone thought she was dumb, but it was hard to conceive of any woman of our circle ever showing up in the affairs of the world," says Just. "That was the most unlikely of events." As events turned out, Madeleine would be the only member of the group to make the cover of *Time*.

Madeleine was left to discuss her ambitions with her women friends.

Danielle remembers her saying one day that the job she really wanted was chief of protocol at the State Department. "No, Madeleine, that's the job I can do, that's the job I want," said Danielle, whose husband served as U.S. ambassador to Spain during the first Clinton administration. The future secretary of state put a stop to the daydreaming. "Well, maybe we can do it together."

Late at night on July 2, 1963, Joe Albright was telephoned from New York with tragic news. His aunt, Alicia Patterson, was dead at the age of fifty-six. It was entirely unexpected, although everybody told her that she drank, smoked, and worked too much. A few weeks before, she had begun to feel nauseated and vomit blood. Suffering from stomach ulcers, she had been given a choice by her doctors: radically change her lifestyle or have an operation to remove part of her stomach. She chose the second option, not wanting to subsist on "mashed potatoes and skimmed milk" for the rest of her life. The surgery was unsuccessful. After two more operations in swift succession, she died in the recovery room.

Joe was appointed funeral supervisor. He flew to Long Island and stayed at Falaise. By the time Madeleine and the rest of the family began to assemble, Fourth of July fireworks were going off in the bay beneath the Guggenheim mansion. It was one of those magical evenings that Alicia loved so much. At one point, Harry took Joe out onto the porch and read him a letter written by Alicia. "You have been wonderful in giving me a chance in the newspaper," she told Harry, "I want Joey now to have that same chance." Moved by the note, Harry said he was determined to honor Alicia's wishes. (Alicia had always lamented the fact that she was the minority shareholder in *Newsday*, with 49 percent of the stock, compared to the 51 percent controlled by her husband. "That son of a bitch Harry will not let me have the other 2 percent of the stock," she complained.)

The funeral was held the following day in the Episcopal cathedral in Garden City, in accordance with Alicia's wishes. It was a brisk day, and the flags were flying buoyantly in the wind. There were messages of condolence from President Kennedy, Nelson Rockefeller, and Averell Harriman. Adlai Stevenson, Kennedy's ambassador to the United Nations, sent a cable from Paris describing his former lover as "one of my oldest, dearest friends" and praising her "bravery and gallantry." There were no eulogies, but many of the *Newsday* staff were in tears as the organist played Alicia's favorite hymns, including "Abide with Me" and "Rock of Ages." The service ended on an upbeat note, with the organ booming out the "Battle Hymn of the Republic." A few weeks later, Madeleine and Joe flew down to Alicia's beloved hunting lodge in Georgia with an urn containing her ashes. Flanked by other members of the family, they buried the ashes in a box under the spreading oak tree by the river, and then threw the urn into the pitch-black water. Harry had a plaque erected to mark the spot with an inscription that read:

> A beautiful and spirited lady lived on this land until she died on July 2, 1963. Under this oak tree she watched the river that she loved. She dreamed and thought: "If there be a paradise on the face of this earth, it is this! It is this! It is this!" A wish has been fulfilled that her ashes mingle here with the earth. Her name was Alicia Patterson Guggenheim. She was born October 15, 1906.

Alicia's death meant an immediate change in the fortunes of Joe and Madeleine. Harry took over as publisher of *Newsday*, and Joe, at the age of twenty-five, was brought back to Long Island and named "assistant to the publisher." This was a clear signal that he was being trained for the succession. Joe was also one of four principal beneficiaries of Alicia's will, along with two other nieces and a nephew. Joe inherited a 12 percent share of the very profitable *Newsday* operation; a quarter share of Alicia's holdings in the rest of the family newspaper business, including the *Chicago Tribune*; and a quarter share of the hunting lodge in Georgia. Alicia also gave him her fishing rods and guns in memory of their hunting expeditions together. When her father Joseph Patterson died in 1945, Alicia's pre-tax share of the Patterson-McCormick Trust had been valued at around $2.5 million, or around $22.5 million today. While the precise figure is difficult to calculate, Alicia's bequest to Joe, including *Newsday*, must have been worth well over $15 million in 1999 prices. Much of this money, however, was not immediately accessible. Several million dollars of Alicia's fortune would go to Madeleine after her divorce from Joe in 1984.

• • •

Moving back to Long Island from New York with two young twins, Joe and Madeleine lost little time using some their newly acquired wealth to buy their first home. The rambling stone house, at least a century old, was in a beautifully secluded position on a winding country lane near the village of Oyster Bay, about twenty minutes' drive from Falaise. The house was built on two floors with an attic, with a swimming pool and cabana out back. For the house and five-acre lot, the Albrights paid $87,000— worth roughly $460,000 today—and took out a $40,000 thirty-year mortgage with an interest rate of 5.5 percent. Two years later, they bought an adjoining five-acre lot for $23,000 in the name of a dummy corporation, a legal device that had the effect of maintaining separate ownership of the two lots. They chose a humorous-sounding name for their new company, Snob Hollow Real Estate Development Corp., with offices on New York's Lexington Avenue. Madeleine was appointed vice president of the corporation; the post of president went to her mother, Mandula. The company even had its own corporate seal. Today, the combined property is worth well over a million dollars.

The return to Long Island put Madeleine and Joe back in the almost feudal atmosphere of the Guggenheim court, this time without Alicia. Harry treated his relatives and employees in the benign, patrician manner of an English country squire dealing with his underlings. Everyone was assigned a precise station in life, as reflected in their place on Harry's Christmas gift list. The annual gifts ranged from cartloads of manure for tenants on the Falaise estate to Christmas bonuses for the staff and turkeys and cases of whiskey for senior members of the family. In return, they were expected to symbolically touch their caps in the form of fulsome notes of gratitude, which Harry read carefully and filed away meticulously year after year. Decades later, the Harry F. Guggenheim collection at the Library of Congress boasts a large collection of thank-you letters from both Madeleine and Joe. They provide an interesting reflection of contrasting personalities. Madeleine's "Dear Uncle Harry" notes are carefully composed and painstakingly neat, as if written out several times in advance. Joe's letters, by contrast, are stream-of-consciousness missives scrawled in a childish, ungainly hand.

During their first few months in Long Island, Harry piled attention on Joe and Madeleine. He sent them boxes of fruit and homemade jams, invited them to dinners at Falaise, bought a firescreen for their new home, and gave Joe a large Christmas raise and bonus. "That was quite a party you gave on Saturday night," wrote Madeleine after a dinner for the novelist John Steinbeck and the publisher of *The New York Times*, Arthur O. Sulzberger. "Undoubtedly, you give the best toasts of anyone anywhere." A few weeks later, she wrote to thank Harry for "that marvelously generous bonus you gave Joe," which "will pay for our vacation and for so many other items we have been waiting to get for our house." Joe's four-page Christmas thank-you letter went into greater detail about their domestic needs:

> We have finally decided (as of three weeks ago) that we couldn't get along with just one car. Madeleine needs one to go to Columbia or shopping, and I need one to go to work. We have gotten by so far by borrowing (for a fee) the car of Mrs. Lieberthal, the children's nurse. But she is irritated (properly) because we put too much mileage on her car. Assessing all our requirements (lots of space, ability to drive to work after a snowstorm, long-lasting, useful for odd jobs around our house and garden), we have almost decided on a jeep station wagon. In addition to these special requirements, we would of course use it for normal driving just like any car we might buy. All this long technical discussion has been leading up to this: your generosity, past and present, made it possible and we are highly grateful. Grateful for what the dough makes possible. Grateful also, I must tell you, for the sense of accomplishment that goes along with it.

Joe expressed his appreciation to Harry for "the way you have brought me into the inner workings of the paper" in the months following Alicia's death. He ended the letter with a description of a Christmas party given by him and Madeleine. "Our house is big enough to accommodate a hundred people at a cocktail party. But our driveway is not nearly big enough to hold their cars. These two lessons we learned Sunday afternoon. The consequence was a massive traffic jam."

The following Christmas, the party went more smoothly, despite several inches of freshly fallen snow in the driveway. A few days later, both Joe and Madeleine wrote to thank Harry for a $250 Christmas check, which was paying for a winter vacation at the Rockefeller resort in the Virgin Islands. "The water is turquoise and absolutely the right temperature and the sand is white; if you sit on the beach and look out, you can see other islands and you feel a million miles away—and you made it all possible for us," wrote Madeleine. Added Joe: "This was a really wonderful Christmas for us this year, because the kids really figured out what Christmas was all about. 'What's the big idea, Christmas?' asked Anne, somewhat belligerently. We proceeded to tell them all about Jesus and the Wise Men and the Manger. 'What is Jesus Christ's middle name?' asked Alice. We left them the day after Christmas, and we are hoping that by the time we return (after three more days in Georgia on the way home) at least a few of their toys will remain intact."

Despite their upper-crust social connections, Joe and Madeleine led very un-Gatsby-like lives. Their interests centered around their children, Joe's work with *Newsday*, Madeleine's studies at Columbia University, and a group of like-minded friends. For relaxation, Madeleine looked after the garden, went to movies, played bridge and tennis, went swimming in the pool. "When they came here, Madeleine did not know anybody in the area, so I introduced her around. She became part of my tennis gang," said Jackie Gebhard, the *Newsday* sportswriter who had been friendly with Alicia Patterson. "She was shy, quiet, and somewhat withdrawn, not like she is today."

"They were not really part of the Guggenheim set," said Winnie Freund, Madeleine's friend from Wellesley, who lived close to the Albrights on Long Island. "Joe was not someone who wanted to be part of that world. . . . Madeleine had always been poor. She watched her pennies." Joe's wealth enabled them to have a large, comfortable house with a full-time housekeeper and two cars, but they did not live ostentatiously. In some ways, they were rather frugal. Madeleine did not spend a lot of money on clothes. When they went to the theater in Manhattan, they usually bought cheap tickets.

"Joe was so rich, but he was also so unassuming, so unprepossessing," said Marty Schram, a *Newsday* colleague. "He would not dominate any room he was in, even though he could buy the room, the building, and everything in it." Schram likes to tell the story of a pool party that Joe and Madeleine gave for *Newsday* staff in the mid-sixties. At one point, Madeleine came up to Joe to report that they were "out of beer." After a slight hesitation and an anxious glance at his wife, Joe replied, "OK, bring out the Michelob," in the tone of a wine connoisseur parting with a rare vintage. "Bring out the Michelob" became a humorous catch-phrase at *Newsday* to describe the self-effacing stinginess of the presumptive heir. Whatever beer they had been drinking until then was cheaper than Michelob.

Madeleine drove back and forth several times a week to Columbia, where she was enrolled in Zbigniew Brzezinski's graduate seminar on comparative communism. The Polish-born Brzezinski was one of the rising stars at Columbia, having been recruited from Harvard to be director of the Research Institute on International Change, which specialized in the Soviet bloc. "It was like sitting at the feet of the master," said Steven Goldstein, who took the seminar along with Madeleine. "He was terrific. He was not so much virulently anti-Communist as virulently analytic. He loved to put things in boxes. We would talk about different ways of coming to power, different types of transformation."

Brzezinski had little time for students who failed to keep pace with his lightning intellect and rapid-fire delivery. When students complained that he was speaking too fast for anybody to take decent notes, the imperious Brzezinski shot back that they must be "writing too slow." He loved to get the students to role-play, assigning them parts in the Soviet Politburo. "OK, you have just removed Khrushchev," he would tell them. "What do you do now?" Brzezinski remembers Madeleine as a "very pleasant, amiable, easy-to-get-along-with graduate student," but hardly "a special student." If she stood out, it was because of her East European background. Brzezinski knew Madeleine's father, Josef Korbel, from the academic circuit. His wife, Muska, was the grand-niece of Czechoslovak leader Eduard Beneš. "All of that created more contact than would otherwise have been the case," said Brzezinski.

Studying for a master's degree at Columbia meant that Madeleine was able to spend quite a bit of time in Manhattan. She would go to movies and theaters with Steven Goldstein and his then wife, Marcia Burick. Her friend from Georgetown, Danielle Gardner, has a vivid memory of a luncheon appointment with Madeleine at the University Club on Fifth Avenue on the day President Kennedy was assassinated. She greeted Madeleine with the news as she stepped out of a taxi. "It was a scene. We were crying and embracing each other. The waiters there were Irish, they were also crying. We kept hugging each other, saying, 'Oh my God, my God.' "

Politically, Madeleine felt close to both JFK and his brother Robert. During the 1964 Senate election in New York, she did volunteer work for Bobby Kennedy, who was running for the Senate for the first time, against Kenneth Keating. "Madeleine and I were the only ones [among our friends] who openly supported Kennedy," said Marcia Burick. "At that point everybody thought that Bobby Kennedy was a carpetbagger, but he appealed to us." By her own account, Madeleine's work for Bobby consisted mainly of "licking stamps." Madeleine and Joe were invited to Falaise to watch the election results on a huge board, a biannual ritual followed religiously by Harry Guggenheim.

Holidays with the children were often spent at Alicia's estate in Kingsland, Georgia, or in Woodstock, Vermont, where Josephine and Ivan Albright had moved from Chicago. (Ivan's Chicago studio had been bulldozed in 1963 to make way for a development project.) Joe and Madeleine liked to go up to Woodstock for Christmas because they could take the children skiing on the nearby slopes. Uncle Harry could always be relied upon to send up a huge turkey. "We had a marvelous time in Vermont and managed to get some skiing in," Madeleine wrote Harry in December 1967, describing the progress made by the six-year-old twins. "The children have mastered the tow themselves and spend hours riding up and skiing down. They left the man operating the tow quite confused because for quite some time he didn't realize there were two of them."

The Albright family was by now complete. Madeleine had her third daughter, Katie, in March 1967. A little over eighteen months previously, she had lost a child while in labor. It was a tragedy, but in some ways a relief. Doctors had warned that there was a high risk of the baby's being born abnormal. For a time, she considered flying to Sweden for an abortion, but her doctor told her that she was too far along in the pregnancy and her own life might be in danger from the operation. There was nothing for it but to wait for the baby to be born. She now says, "It was horrible, absolutely the worst time in my life." She whiled away the time knitting an "unbelievably complicated" Irish sweater. Later, she went home to her parents.

Her own experience giving birth to a stillborn child helped make Madeleine a firm advocate of a woman's right to choose when the abortion debate raged later in Congress.

Prague, Madeleine's birthplace. She returned to the city in 1967 for the first time since the 1948 Communist takeover.

Roots

One of the luxuries that Madeleine and Joe permitted themselves was foreign travel, which they saw as a reward for "slaving away at the job, the house, the garden." In the summer, they would leave the children in the care of the housekeeper and get away to some exotic destination. One year it was Greece. Another it was Egypt, where they toured the Valley of the Kings, spending three nights at Claridges Hotel in Paris on the way back to New York. In 1967, the year that Katie was born, their friends Steve Goldstein and Marcia Burick persuaded them to take a three-week car and train trip around Eastern Europe, revisiting Madeleine's old childhood haunts and some new places as well.

They started off in Vienna, a capitalist outpost surrounded on three sides by the menacing drabness of communism, where they rented a car to drive to Budapest. Penetrating the Iron Curtain was quite an experience in those days, somewhat akin to entering a gigantic concentration camp. Even ordinary tourists were subjected to lengthy searches and interrogations by steely-eyed Communist border guards, making them feel that they must be guilty of something even if they had nothing to hide. The Cold War acquired real meaning for Madeleine and her friends as they drove across a 2,000-foot-wide strip of carefully plowed land, protected on either side by high watchtowers, trenches, and barbed-wire fences.

Once they got into Hungary, a psychological weight of oppression descended upon them that would not entirely disappear until the end of the trip, as if they were being constantly watched and supervised. At the same time, they also experienced the thrill of meeting interesting people in exotic settings. Madeleine's own nervousness and excitement increased the closer they got to her native Czechoslovakia, the last leg of the trip.

Budapest, the once-glittering twin capital of the Austro-Hungarian empire, was now part of the Soviet empire. But it still boasted grandiose Hapsburg architecture and a majestic position on the Danube. Marcia and Steve had visited the city three years earlier as part of their own "back to the roots" tour, which had included trips to synagogues in Hungary and Czechoslovakia and a visit to the Auschwitz death camp. As practicing Jews, they wanted to show their friends some of the Jewish sights of Eastern Europe, while also visiting places that had a special meaning for Madeleine. "We took them to all the synagogues and we went to the cathedrals with them," said Marcia.

In Budapest, the Goldsteins took the Albrights to visit a home established for elderly victims of the Holocaust. Many of the residents had Auschwitz numbers tattooed onto their arms. Madeleine persuaded Joe to leave behind a $100 donation. They then moved on to Romania, where they toured the medieval churches and castles of Transylvania. Along the way, they amused themselves by making up newspaper headlines about their trip. "Young Couple Stops in Castle, Never Seen Again" was Madeleine's contribution as they were passing through Dracula country. The following day, Madeleine wrote a postcard to Harry Guggenheim: "This trip is even better than we expected. We are seeing a great deal of the country and meeting people in restaurants and on the streets who are very friendly. We have just hit Bucharest, which is an amazingly active city."

The only person in the group who had no connection at all to Eastern Europe was Joe. "We felt sorry for him for being such a WASP. He could not relate to it," said Marcia. In the Bulgarian capital, Sofia, a tour guide provoked gales of laughter from Madeleine, Steve, and Marcia by describing the Czechs as "the Jews of Eastern Europe" over tea in a restaurant. "With one fell swoop, he had insulted three of the people at the table," laughed Marcia. "Poor Joe was left out of it."

In Belgrade, Madeleine took the others to see the Czechoslovak embassy, where she had spent two years of her childhood. As they stood outside the embassy, Madeleine wondered out loud if she should go inside and ask to see her childhood scrapbooks, which had been left in the basement. Over dinner, in a local restaurant, they listened politely to someone extolling the greatness of Tito and the wonders of Yugoslav communism, cracking up with laughter as soon as they were by themselves.

After returning the rental car in Vienna, they set out by train for Czechoslovakia. This was the emotional highlight of the trip for Madeleine, and she was very nervous about returning to a country that regarded her father as a traitor. The Czechoslovak embassy in Washington had not raised any difficulties about giving her a visa, even though they were well aware of the Korbel connection. Even so, she was a little paranoid. "We were afraid that she would be followed," said Marcia Burick. "They knew that she was Maria Jana Korbel." Making the atmosphere even more tense was the fact that an anti-Zionist campaign was under way in Czechoslovakia in the wake of Israel's victory in the Six-Day War. The authorities were rounding up anyone who took part in pro-Israel demonstrations. In August, the body of an American-Jewish activist was found washed up on the bank of the river Vltava.

Beautiful yet melancholy, Prague seemed more than usually conspiratorial. Undercurrents of dissent were beginning to disturb the monolithic surface of Czechoslovak political life. The Writers' Union was becoming a focus of opposition to the hard-liners in the Czechoslovak Party led by the Stalinist Antonin Novotny. The following year, 1968, these liberal stirrings would emerge with full force in the reform movement known as the "Prague Spring."

It was impossible to travel outside Prague without special permission from Čedok, the Czechoslovak tourist agency. The Albright party managed to get themselves transferred from a dreary, out-of-the-way hotel to the Alcron, around the corner from Wenceslas Square, an establishment favored by diplomats, spies, and journalists. The Alcron was where Josef Korbel had stayed when he came to Prague in 1948 after the Communist coup. Concerned about drawing too much attention to herself, Madeleine was reluctant to use her Czech. But she took her friends to see the apartment on Hradčanské Square where the Korbel family had lived for a few months after World War II between returning from England and going to Yugoslavia. "She kept on saying how beautiful the crystal used to be,"

Marcia Burick recalled. They knocked on the door of the apartment and were amazed to discover that it was now occupied by no fewer than three families. "It was a shock to see it all destroyed," says Madeleine.

Marcia and Steve took the Albrights to visit the Jewish museum and an old Jewish cemetery. The Nazis had planned to preserve the museum as a monument after exterminating all the Jews. In the event, of course, they succeeded in killing only roughly half the Jews in Czechoslovakia. However, most of the survivors had fled the country after the war, reducing a once-thriving community to little more than a rump. In 1967, the Jewish museum in Prague was still set up on the Nazi model as "a museum to a dead race," according to Steven Goldstein. "There would be a table set for a Passover dinner, and they would explain everything on the table. I felt I was some sort of Egyptian visiting the British Museum and seeing my history and culture there. I found that very creepy."

After visiting the museum, they went around the corner and visited an exhibit of children's pictures from Terezín entitled "I have not seen a butterfly around here." In a remarkable twist of fate, the exhibit included a drawing by Madeleine's cousin, Milena, who was killed in Auschwitz (page 92). It depicted the bunk beds in the children's dormitory at Terezín, with a menorah and a vase of flowers. It seems unlikely that Madeleine would have paid any attention to Milena's name scrawled in the upper left-hand corner of the drawing. After all, it was just one of forty or so drawings in the exhibit. If she did notice the signature, she showed no sign of it.

Madeleine had some important family errands to run in Prague. Before she left America, her parents had given her the names of their remaining relatives and close friends left behind in Czechoslovakia in February 1948 after the Communist coup. Madeleine saw as many of them as she could. The conversations were depressing. "They talked mostly about what they had been doing and how terrible things had been" in the two decades since the Communist takeover. The experience made Madeleine realize how lucky she was "to have been raised in a free country."

Among other people, Madeleine saw her cousin Dasha, who had been partly brought up by the Korbels after escaping to England at the beginning of the war. Dasha remembers calling on the Albrights in the Alcron

Hotel. Since contacts with foreigners were still frowned upon by the authorities, she stayed only for about half an hour. "I popped in and out," she recalled.

While in Prague, Madeleine also went to see a first cousin of her mother, Petr Novák, who had survived the concentration camps during the war. (Petr's mother and Mandula's mother were sisters.) She says she did not know at the time that Petr was related to her, even though he had lived with the Korbel family in the apartment on Hradčanské Square for several months in the summer of 1945.

By 1967, Petr Novák was forty years old and gravely ill with stomach cancer. A child prodigy, he had been an accomplished cellist before the war, playing in concerts all over Czechoslovakia. In 1942, at the age of fifteen, he was sent to Terezín, along with his parents and older brother. The rest of Petr's family were killed in the Holocaust, but Petr himself was selected for hard labor at Auschwitz. At the end of the war, he and other Jewish prisoners were sent on a forced march to another concentration camp. As the Russians were approaching the camp, SS guards began massacring the prisoners. According to Dasha, who knew him well, Petr was in a group of men lined up in a row and machine-gunned. He fell to the ground, pretended to be dead, and then spent hours lying beneath a pile of dead bodies, until the Germans went away. He survived the massacre but was wounded in his left wrist. The wound prevented him from ever playing the cello again.

Madeleine was more than usually nervous when she went to see Petr. Concerned that the secret police might be following her, she asked Joe and Marcia to accompany her part of the way. Joe then went off in one direction to confuse any pursuers, while Madeleine and Marcia took a taxi to the part of town where Petr lived. Marcia remembers waiting near the apartment while Madeleine went in alone. An hour or so later, she reappeared, very distraught.

Back at the hotel, Madeleine told her friends that Petr was "a friend" of her parents who had been sent to the camps with his family along with other Czech "patriots." She says that she was brought up to believe that Czechs were also "fodder" for the Nazi concentration camp system "after Jews." According to Madeleine's version of the story, as told to her friends, camp guards had deliberately slashed Petr's wrist to prevent him from ever playing the cello again. As Marcia recalls the incident,

Madeleine gave her a graphic description of Petr, sallow and gray, wasting away from cancer. "There but for the grace of God, there but for the grace of God," she sobbed, distraught that Petr had lost his entire family.

While Madeleine was telling her story, Joe clinked his car keys on a table in order to thwart the hidden microphones. Madeleine explained that Petr was a disillusioned Communist who had become a Zionist. A few weeks earlier, he had attended a banned public celebration of Israel's victory in the Six-Day War and had been briefly arrested. Knowing that he had not long to live, Petr was defiant. "I can die in the putrid air of your prison or in the putrid air of Prague," Madeleine quoted him as telling his jailers.

In addition to meeting Petr, Madeleine met two elderly women who were looking after him, both of whom had been friends of her parents. She says they told her that her father had been sentenced to death in absentia by the Nazis. She had never heard of this particular incident before, and it upset her greatly. Madeleine adds that she might have been upset for a variety of reasons, including the news about her father, the meeting with Petr, and "the kind of stories that they were telling about their suffering while we were living abroad."

Madeleine's own memories of her meeting with Petr Novák are much less vivid than Marcia Burick's secondhand recollections. Her version of why the Novák family was sent to Terezín, and how Petr lost the use of his wrist, is not supported by independent evidence. While it is true that some Czechs were also sent to the concentration camps with Jews, the deportations were not on as massive a scale, and it was exceedingly rare for children to be rounded up with their parents. Given the fact that Petr later became " a Zionist" and was only fourteen years old at the time of is deportation to Terezín, it would seem reasonable to conclude that he was rounded up as a Jew rather than as a Czech patriot. Madeleine, however, says she did not "put the pieces together" at this time.

Interviewed by *Time* reporter Ann Blackman in February 1998, she said she did not have a strong memory of the afternoon and could not remember if she saw Petr. Interviewed for this book in November 1998, she said she did meet Petr in Prague in 1967 but had no recollection of his living with her family in the summer of 1945.

The incident with Petr Novák, and Madeleine's various recountings of it, raise questions about precisely when she found out about her family's connection to the Holocaust. I shall address these questions in a later chapter.

Petr Novák died of cancer in June 1968, the year after his meeting with Madeleine.

In addition to being a physical barrier, the Iron Curtain served as an information barrier between East and West, making it possible for the Korbels to build a new identity for themselves in America. As the years went by, however, the barrier became increasingly porous. Despite the fact that Madeleine's parents kept quiet about their Jewish origins, many of their friends either knew or guessed their secret. While Josef rarely talked about the past except in general, political terms, Mandula talked openly to close friends about the tragedy that had befallen the family during the war. She also kept in touch with relatives like Petr Novak.

After the war, several members of the extended Körbel family had tried to contact Josef. The first was Joža Gruber, Josef's first cousin, who had escaped to Israel during the war, leaving the rest of her immediate family behind in Czechoslovakia. She says she wrote to Josef at the Czechoslovak embassy in Belgrade seeking his help in tracing her parents, who had been murdered by the Nazis. "I never heard back from him." She later learned from other relatives that Josef had emigrated to America with his family.

Sometime around 1958, Josef received a visit in Denver from another first cousin, Karel Mahler, whose family had fled to Brazil during the war. Since he worked in an export-import business, Karel had contacts all over the world and was able to track down many of his relatives. A year after his meeting with Josef, Karel visited Chaim Körbel in Israel and passed on Josef's news and address. "I wrote Josef a letter, but never got a reply," Chaim recalled. "I concluded that he wanted to stay distant from me, or perhaps he thought I was looking for a favor. When I didn't get a response, I dropped the matter."

Although Josef was estranged from his older brother Jan, he spent time with Jan's family when he went to England for a sabbatical at Oxford University in 1963. Jan's daughter, Alena, considered herself very "close" to her uncle and at one point wanted to go and live with Josef in America, because of strains in her own family. Alena believes that she reminded Josef of his murdered mother, Olga, to whom she bore a close physical resemblance. At the end of the sixties, Alena went to the United States to make the rounds of her American relatives and visited Madeleine and Joe on Long Island. She had made a visit to Terezín two or three years previously—in 1967—but says that the question of the family's Jewish origins did not arise while she was with Madeleine.

The two brothers, Jan and Josef, eventually became friendly again in the late sixties. By this time, Jan was married to a second wife and living in Malta. Josef and Mandula went to visit them. Madeleine later recalled that it was "a big deal" in the family when they all made up.

Several neighbors of the Korbels in Denver concluded that the family must be of Jewish origin from chance remarks by Mandula. "Once she brought out an album that she had and began showing me pictures. She pointed to her father and told me his name [Spiegel], which sounded very Jewish," said Ruth Spensley, the Korbels' first neighbor on South Williams Street. Hilda Newman-Clark, who lived next door to the family on South Madison Street, had a similar impression. "I always thought that Mandula and Joe were Jewish, although they never actually mentioned it. I just assumed it was because many of her friends from Czechoslovakia seemed to be Jewish."

While Josef's Jewish background was not widely known at the University of Denver, several close colleagues were in on the secret. One such person was George Barany, a Hungarian Jew who fled to America after the failed 1956 uprising in Budapest and became a professor of history at Denver. Barany's wife and mother-in-law had both been at Auschwitz, and both became friendly with Mandula. On one occasion, Mandula asked Barany's mother-in-law about the Auschwitz tattoo on her arm. "At a certain point, I think Mandula told my mother-in-law that most of her relatives had been killed in the concentration camps," said Barany. Even before this revelation, however, Barany said he had "a gut feeling" that Josef and Mandula were of Jewish origin.

While Barany made no secret of his own Jewish identity, he sympathized with Josef's decision to hide his background. "Many Jews protected their offspring in the way they thought best. They thought it was better to err on the side of defending their children from the disastrous

The gravestone of Josef and Auguste Körbel (great-grandparents of Madeleine Korbel Albright) in the Jewish cemetery at Nový Bydžov. *Michael Dobbs.*

The match factory in Letohrad, where Arnošt Körbel (Madeleine Albright's grandfather) got his start. *Letohrad Museum.*

The house in Letohrad where Madeleine's father, Josef, was born and grew up. Josef's childhood friend Jan Koloc is standing outside. *Michael Dobbs.*

The warehouse in Kostelec where Madeleine's maternal grandparents, Alfred and Ružena Spiegel, ran a wholesale business. *Michael Dobbs.*

Picture of Arnošt Körbel and his dog, Drollo, and Madeleine's cousin Alena. Photo taken around 1938. *Courtesy of Alena Korbel.*

Wedding picture of Josef and Mandula Körbel in Prague, April 1935. To the left is Olga Körbel, wife of Josef's brother, Jan, with her daughter, Alena. *Courtesy of Alena Korbel.*

Portrait of Arnošt Körbel.
Courtesy of Alena Korbel.

Portrait of Olga Körbel.
Courtesy of Dagmar Šima.

Arriving at Terezín. Drawing by Ferdinand Bloch, who was deported to Terezín on the same transport as Arnošt and Olga Körbel in July 1942. *Jewish Museum, Prague.*

Jews arriving at the new ramp at Auschwitz-Birkenau in May 1944. The scene when Olga Körbel and Milena Deiml arrived at Auschwitz in October would have been very similar. *Yad Vashem, Courtesy of the U.S. Holocaust Museum.*

Josef and Jan Korbel, in Malta, in the 1970s, after the two families had made up. *Courtesy of Dagmar Šima.*

The children of Jan and Josef, Berkhamstead, England, 1943. From left, Madeleine, Alena, Kathy (small child), and George. *Courtesy of Alena Korbel.*

The apartment at Hradčanské náměstí 11 in Prague, where the Korbel family lived between July and November 1945. *Michael Dobbs.*

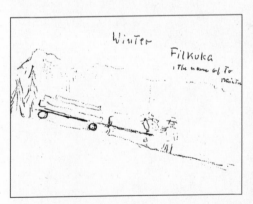

A drawing from memory by Doris Nebrich Renner of family pictures that she says were illegally expropriated by Josef Korbel and taken to Belgrade. *Doris Nebrich Renner.*

Picture of Madeleine, aged eleven, in Switzerland in 1948, soon after the Communist coup in Prague. *Courtesy of the Albright family.*

Mandula, Madeleine, and Josef Korbel swimming in the Sava River, near Belgrade, around 1947. *Courtesy of the Janković family.*

Josef Korbel, Czechoslovak ambassador to Belgrade, looks over the shoulder of deputy Czechoslovak foreign minister Vladimir Clementis as he signs a treaty in Belgrade. *Courtesy of Josef Marek.*

Portrait of Madeleine's mother, Mandula. *Courtesy of the Janković family.*

Picture of Madeleine (squatting) and sister, Kathy, in the courtyard of the Czechoslovak embassy in Belgrade with Nikola Janković, son of their Serbian friends. *Courtesy of the Janković family.*

Madeleine, Kathy, and unidentified friend in Belgrade. *Courtesy of the Janković family.*

Madeleine attended the Kent School for Girls in Denver, from 1952 to 1955. *Kent Denver School.*

Like other children at Kent, Madeleine was required to take part in school plays. Here she is costumed as a man, complete with fake moustache. *Kent Denver School.*

At Denver and later at Wellesley, Madeleine dated East High School student Elston Mayhew, a straight-A student from a poor background. They broke up finally after Madeleine met Joseph Albright. *East High School yearbook, 1954.*

MADELEINE KORBEL

International relations, Princeton, or any other topic brings forth a flood of comment from Madeleine, expert if on the first subject, and a bit incoherent if on the second. You will often find her taking a definite stand on matters, staunchly saying, "You guys, this just proves it!" Her constant interest in anything she is doing, and the drive with which she does it, keep all interested in the activities of our "emaciated" companion.

Madeleine's entry in the Kent 1955 yearbook. *Kent Denver School.*

The Albright family in Wyoming, 1945. Back row: Alicia Patterson, Blandina, Ivan, Josephine, and Adam Albright. Front row: Alice and Joseph Albright. *The Art Institute of Chicago.*

Madeleine with the twins, Alice and Anne. *Courtesy of the Albright family.*

Representative to the United Nations, Madeleine Albright, greets an old friend, Edmund Muskie, a former secretary of state, in 1993. *The Washington Post.*

As secretary of state, Madeleine moved to repair relations with Jesse Helms, the conservative chairman of the Senate Foreign Relations Committee. He was instrumental in approving her Senate confirmation. *The Washington Post.*

Madeleine and Czech president Václav Havel and Hillary Clinton in Prague in July 1996. Madeleine's relationship with Hillary was a factor in her nomination as secretary of state five months later. *White House.*

Madeleine Korbel Albright, Warren Christopher, and Boutros Boutros-Ghali at the United Nations. *United Nations.*

Secretary Albright at her swearing-in, with her family and friends. Left to right: John Korbel, brother; Kathy Silva, sister; Pamela Korbel, sister-in-law; Josef Korbel, nephew; Geoffrey Watson, son-in-law [Anne's husband]; Peter Korbel, nephew; Jesse Helms; Bill Clinton; Albright; Al Gore; Barbara Mikulski; daughters, Kate, Anne, and Alice. *White House.*

Madeleine relished the showman side of the secretary of state job. Here she is, dressed in a Baltimore Orioles uniform, throwing out the ceremonial first pitch on the opening day of the baseball season. *The Washington Post.*

legacy of hundreds of years of anti-Semitism. Once you had that feeling in your blood and bones, it was difficult to get rid of it. There were still unspoken quotas in America when he arrived here [in 1948]. The question he would have asked himself is: 'Why instill this fear and anxiety in my children?' "

There were career considerations as well. Denver University was a Methodist institution, and the Church had influence over senior appointments. While the university employed many Jewish professors, it is an open question whether Josef would have been promoted to senior administrative positions, including the deanship of a new Graduate School of International Studies, had his Jewish origins been known. Marion Gottesfeld, who was for a long time the only Jewish member on the DU Board of Trustees, believes that Josef was "better off not being Jewish. He might not have gone so far had he been an acknowledged Jew. Today, it would not make any difference, but this was a couple of decades ago."

Over time, Josef seemed to become less preoccupied with hiding his Jewish background. During a sabbatical at Stanford University in 1956, having left his own family in Denver, he was regularly invited to the family of a Stanford professor for spaghetti dinners. Susan Aspaturian came from a family of Jewish refugees from Vienna, and one evening they started talking about their similar wartime experiences. "He didn't seem to be hiding anything," said Vernon Aspaturian. "He didn't talk a lot about it, but he mentioned that he was Jewish."

The Korbels' Jewish background was known to several of Josef's subordinates at the graduate school. Bernard Abrahammson, a Swedish Jew hired by Josef to teach economics, said his suspicions were confirmed when he ran into a former Czechoslovak diplomat during a sabbatical at Haifa University in 1971. "You must know Joe Korbel," Abrahammson exclaimed. "I don't know any Korbel, but I know somebody by the name of Körbel," the former diplomat replied. He then told Abrahammson the story of Josef's conversion to Catholicism during the war in London and his subsequent change of name. Abrahammson never raised the matter directly with Josef. "I felt it was none of my business, it was irrelevant in the context of the graduate school." After Josef's death in 1977, Mandula told the Abrahammsons about the deaths of her family members in the Holocaust.

Many of the Korbels' old friends from Czechoslovakia, who came to visit them in Denver, were Jewish. In the early seventies, the Korbels arranged for some particularly close friends, Rita and Otto Kauders, to move to Denver from Buenos Aires. Otto had first met Josef in Paris in the thirties and was one of his oldest friends. Naturally, Otto knew all about Josef's background and was used to referring to him as Körbel rather than Korbel. Both he and Rita were proud of their Jewishness, so they were somewhat taken aback when Josef took Otto aside early on and told him about his conversion to Catholicism. Rita says she felt "a little indignant. I said to my rabbi at one point, 'It's outrageous.' He said, 'Rita, if they don't want to be Jewish, it is nothing to be alarmed about.' The rabbi was more understanding than I was." Rita found it difficult to understand why her husband—who was "very passionate" about his beliefs—did not fall out with Josef over the question of his conversion. "I was always amazed that he did not say 'To hell with Korbel.' I could never understand it, and I didn't want to bring it up, because they were our very good friends."

On occasion, Rita recalls, she was asked by other friends of the Korbels if they were Jewish. "People would ask me, 'Are they really not Jewish? Just look at their noses.' I can't remember whether I was loyal to his lie or not."

In some respects, Rita's spiritual journey was the almost the reverse of her friends'. She came from a long line of Czech Jews but was baptized at birth. Despite the progressive views of leaders like Masaryk, there was still an undercurrent of anti-Semitism in Czechoslovakia, and her parents felt that the children would have more opportunities if they were raised as Christians. They taught Rita and her siblings not to respect Jews and made derogatory remarks about the local rabbi. "At first, I didn't even know I was Jewish. Then, when I found out, I was ashamed of admitting it," says Rita. She eventually discovered her Jewish origins when she asked for a day off from work to mark a Lutheran holiday. Her request sent her supervisor into fits of laughter. "Look at her," the supervisor kept on saying in amazement, referring to Rita. "She looks like a real Jewess, and she won't work on Martin Luther Day." Shortly before the war, Rita escaped to England with her father, and it was there that she finally lost her "embarrassment" about being Jewish. Her Chinese boyfriend, accustomed to the British perception of Asians as somehow inferior, could not believe that a Jewish girl could have a similar hang-up. "From that moment on, I never bothered to hide the fact that I was Jewish."

After the deaths of their husbands, Rita and Mandula became extremely close. Mandula talked openly about the murder of her relatives in the concentration camps, and Rita talked about the loss of her mother and brother. She is convinced that the initiative for switching religions came from Josef rather than the more easygoing Mandula. "I think she just followed in his footsteps."

Deciding what to tell their children about the Holocaust, and when, must have posed an agonizing dilemma for Josef and Mandula. If they spoke about the tragedy that had befallen so many of their own relatives, their children would carry a psychological burden for the rest of their lives. If they said nothing at all, they would spare the children the trauma experienced by many second-generation Holocaust survivors. But they would also deprive the children of their own history and run a risk of their finding out later, perhaps by accident, and being shocked by the mendacity of their parents.

Years later, Madeleine's cousin Dasha would try to imagine herself in the situation of Mandula and Josef, who had looked after her in England. She tried to think what she would have done if entrusted with the responsibility for raising three young children in a strange new land.

"I know from my experience what assimilation involves, and I am certain that they took it as their parental duty to let bygones be bygones and protect [their children] from the trauma that has been with me all my life," Dasha later wrote. "When all is quiet and I close my eyes I still hear my grandmother whispering those loving words of which the Korbel children were deprived. In this I pity them. They were spared the trauma, and in this I envy them."

Joe Albright, with his uncle Harry Guggenheim, as he was being groomed to take over *Newsday. Reprinted with permission. Copyright ©️ Newsday, Inc., 1963.*

13

A Child of Munich

As Madeleine entered her fourth decade, her world was shaken by a series of revolutions. The late sixties saw the birth of women's liberation, the flowering and subsequent crushing of the Communist reform movement known as the "Prague Spring," and the student rebellion in both America and Europe.

Closest to home was the revolt on American campuses. As Madeleine was cramming for her Ph.D. orals at Columbia in the spring of 1968, the university was taken over by left-wing students. Buildings were barricaded with furniture and filing cabinets, classes were suspended, and the Red Flag flew over several university buildings. The campus was plastered with portraits of Che Guevara and graffiti such as "Lenin won, Fidel won, we will win." The climax to these events came with a police bust in the early-morning hours of April 30, in which nearly seven hundred people were arrested and dozens of students were injured. While some of her friends spent nights on the barricades, Madeleine kept away from the protests. She drove in from Long Island in the morning, did whatever she needed to do around the campus, and then drove home in the evening to be with her family.

From Madeleine's point of view, the protests were an unwanted distraction from her studies and parental responsibilities. It was infuriating to make the one-hour drive to Manhattan from Oyster Bay, search for a place to park, and then find the libraries blocked by student protesters. "I was very motivated to work," she recalls now. "I was not part of the sixty-eight stuff." The day before she was due to take her orals, another graduate student had been forced to enter the examination room through a window. Madeleine was luckier, but she still had little sympathy for the protesters.

"Madeleine was distant from it all," said her friend Steven Goldstein, who had become a junior member of the Columbia faculty by 1968 and was involved in mediation efforts between the students and the university. "I don't remember us ever having a political conversation on either the Vietnam War or the moral issues of communism." Madeleine's passivity can be explained partly by her age—she was ten years older than the average student and had three young children—but also by her political convictions. She did not share the rebels' cynicism about American society. Quite the opposite, in fact. She remained touchingly grateful to the United States for granting her family asylum.

The disillusionment felt by many students was reflected in a letter from student leader Mark Rudd to the president of Columbia as the protests got under way. Among other things wrong with America, Rudd cited the "war of aggression in Vietnam . . . our meaningless studies, our identity crises, and our revulsion with being cogs in your corporate machines. If we win," he warned Grayson Kirk, "we will take control of your world, your corporations, your university, and attempt to mold a world in which we and other people can live like human beings." He concluded his letter with the slogan that became the rallying cry of Columbia radicals, "Up against the wall, motherfucker, this is a stick-up."

Like many of the most articulate student leaders, Rudd came from an impeccable middle-class Jewish background. His father, whose name was originally Rudnitsky, had emigrated from Poland and created a successful real estate business in New Jersey. Before coming to Columbia, the younger Rudd had been a troop leader in the Boy Scouts and goalie on his high school soccer team. By calling for a "war of liberation" against an oppressive "power structure," he was rebelling against the very country that had provided his parents with a sanctuary from the murderous anti-Semitism of Eastern Europe.

Madeleine later joked about her somewhat smug patriotism at a time when many of her fellow students were busy questioning everything. "Sometimes we are depressed with being over thirty and not alienated, but most of the time we love it," she told her Wellesley classmates in 1969. While she was beginning to have some reservations about the Vietnam War by 1968, her doubts were overwhelmed by her vision of America as a land of freedom and opportunity. It was a position largely shared by other first-generation immigrants at Columbia. "Those of us from Eastern Europe felt that the students were rebelling against the only country to serve as a barrier against Communism," said Istvan Deak, a history professor from Hungary who later served on Madeleine's Ph.D. committee.

One of Madeleine's principal academic advisers at Columbia was Zbigniew Brzezinski, one of the few members of the faculty to strongly oppose the students. Brzezinski, who had fled Poland with his family at the start of World War II, would later write a celebrated article denouncing the "revolution" as a "counter-revolution." In his view, the "revolutionaries" were simply modern-day Luddites unable or unwilling to adapt to the changes occurring in post-industrial America. The students, in turn, denounced Brzezinski as a tool of the military-industrial complex. Leading a pig by the snout, they marched down 118th Street toward his institute chanting "a pig, a pig, for Professor Zbig." Brzezinski, who had visions of the pig defecating in his office or being thrust into his face while cameras flashed, urged the university authorities to call the police. "The deans were all scared shitless," he recalled. A few minutes later, Brzezinski revised his opinion of the deans when two police cars screeched to a halt in front of the demonstrators and ordered the students to back off. But it turned out that the police had been summoned not by the university but by an animal-protection society. The students returned without the pig a few days later to confront "the war criminal" Brzezinski. By his own account, he came downstairs to confront them, casually munching an apple. "You have ten minutes in which to ask me any question you want, and then I have to go back to my office and plan some more genocide," he told them.

Brzezinski's administrative assistant, Christine Dodson, remembers Madeleine as "fanatically pro-American." A Fulbright scholar from Greece who had experienced the turmoil of the Greek civil war, Dodson shared with Madeleine and Brzezinski a sense that "the '68 generation did not realize how lucky they were." While she had some sympathy for the antiwar views of the students, Dodson was appalled by what she saw as their spoiled-brat behavior. She remembers seeing an elderly woman— who turned out to be Mark Rudd's mother—arriving at the barricades with a plastic bag full of chicken soup and telling everyone in earshot, "Mark is used to having his chicken soup." "I don't believe this," Dodson thought to herself, "they are going to make a revolution with chicken soup."

The "power structure" knew how to reward loyalty. Ten years later, Brzezinski would invite Madeleine and Christine to join an inner core of Columbia-trained academics working for the White House.

Madeleine's views on Vietnam, like her views on so much else, were shaped by her father. Until 1968, Josef Korbel was a strong supporter of American involvement in Vietnam. A firm believer in the "domino theory" of one Asian country after another succumbing to communism, he drew an analogy between the expansionist policies of Russia and China and those of Nazi Germany. If the West failed to stand up to Communist aggression, Korbel believed, it would be repeating the mistakes of the thirties.

"The American action appears to be absolutely sound," Josef told a Denver newspaper in August 1964, after President Johnson ordered U.S. air strikes against North Vietnam in retaliation for an alleged North Vietnamese attack on the cruiser *Maddox*. If the United States did not respond, he went on, it would be reduced to the status of "paper tiger." Three years later, Josef conceded that the initial decision to intervene in Vietnam might have been "unwise" in view of the ideological disintegration of the Communist camp. This was not a monolithic enemy the West was fighting. Having gotten involved, however, there was no way back. "We are now in the position in which we would endanger all of East Asia if we withdrew. We cannot withdraw."

"Joe was a big supporter of the war," recalls his Denver University colleague Ron Krieger, who opposed the war. "He kept on invoking the Munich analogy: If we don't stop them in Vietnam, they will be marching down 16th Street." Josef's pro-war views put him at odds with some of the younger members of the DU faculty. The argument came to a head in November 1966 when Secretary of State Dean Rusk—who frequently spoke of the need to avert "an Asian Munich" in Vietnam—came to Denver to dedicate the building of the new Graduate School for International Studies. Josef had spent a huge amount of time and effort raising more than $3 million for the new school. In some ways, Rusk's visit was the crowning achievement of his academic career. He was mortified when some of his own handpicked assistants joined students in protesting the secretary of state's visit and holding a teach-in to critique administration policy. Compared with what was happening on campuses elsewhere in America, the anti-Rusk demonstration at DU was very tame, but Josef was shocked by the lack of respect shown to his guest. "Imagine how embarrassing this was for me," he told his colleagues afterward.

"Joe was a control freak, and wanted to make sure that everything went exactly according to script. He did not care for any deviations," said Vince Davis, one of his subordinates at Denver. "As long as you were well behaved and didn't challenge him, he was the most lovable man you can imagine. But if he thought you were doing anything against his sense of fitness or appropriateness, he was distressed." When Krieger wrote a letter to the university newspaper arguing that the United States did not have the moral right to intervene in Vietnam, Josef was offended and accused him of being "hysterical." Josef was motivated in part by a superpatriotism that people who had been born and raised in America had difficulty understanding. "What he had been through made him a great and fierce lover of America," said his colleague Arthur Gilbert. "He kept on saying 'This is a wonderful country, I love this country.' "

Josef's distaste for the antiwar movement was cultural as much as political. "He was a traditional diplomat of the old school," said DU history professor George Barany. "He didn't think it was right to embarrass people like Dean Rusk by confronting them in public." When he visited Columbia on sabbatical, Josef was disgusted by the antics of the student rebels. "It was a matter of style for him," said Catherine Kelleher, who sympathized with the students. "It was a very scruffy revolution. He took the view that the state had every right to impose its power. His attitude was, 'You are not as old as I am and you haven't been through what I have. If you had, you would appreciate the need for order.' "

After the devastating setback of the Tet offensive in early 1968, Josef began reluctantly to rethink his views on Vietnam. While he had no moral qualms about intervention, he could see no light at the end of the tunnel. Perhaps, after all, it would be better for the United States to cut its losses. A negotiated settlement was the only way out. "I am a victim of the Tet offensive," he said that summer. "It came as a shock to me that we could be taken by surprise at a time when our officials told us we were well on the way to a military solution." Says his colleague Bernard Abrahammson: "His views changed from hard-line to less hard-line, but never moved to really vigorous opposition to the war. He was a pragmatist." Adds Arthur Gilbert: "It was devastating for Joe to speak out against U.S. policy. He finally did, but it wasn't easy for him."

Madeleine's views on Vietnam underwent an almost identical evolution. Flying to Hanoi in June 1997 for the first time as secretary of state, she explained to reporters that she had initially seen the war as part of a necessary worldwide struggle against the "Communist monolith." "Having come from where I had come, I was more likely to view it that way." Over time, however, she was troubled by the dissension that the war was causing in the United States. She eventually concluded that the image of a war to contain a steadily expanding Communist monolith was oversimplified. "I came to see what everybody came to see—that it was not that kind of a war." The North Vietnamese were motivated by nationalism as much as communism. For Madeleine, as for her father, Tet was a key turning point.

In short, both father and daughter came to view the war as a mistake, but a noble mistake on the part of a country that remained the champion of freedom.

Josef's relationship with his subordinates at the Graduate School for International Studies was a little like his relationship with his children. He was the family patriarch, the charismatic leader who took great interest in what everyone was doing but was intolerant of dissent and easily offended by real or imagined gestures of disrespect. As the sixties wore on, this paternalistic style began to grate with the junior faculty. It became more and more difficult for Josef to enforce his discipline, and in the end he gave up in frustration.

The graduate school was Josef's monument. The idea of building a world-class institute in international relations at the foot of the Rocky Mountains, far from the traditional centers of foreign policy debate on the East and West Coasts, reflected his ambition for both his adopted city and for himself. He hoped that Denver would compete with places like Columbia and Johns Hopkins to turn out the next generation of Kennans, Nitzes, and Bundys. The method he used to create the school was ingenious. In 1923, an investment banker named James H. Causey had set up a philanthropic body in Denver called the Social Science Foundation to "advance liberal causes" and help students gain a better understanding of "the great social, industrial, and international problems of the present and future." Disturbed by the strikes that had racked Colorado during the early part of the century, Causey donated the income from an office building to fund an academic exchange program and a series of public lectures on contemporary issues. Josef himself had come to Denver under the auspices of the Social Science Foundation and was appointed its director in 1959. In alliance with DU Chancellor Chester Alter, he wound down the lecture program and used the money to launch a foreign policy research institute. Matching funds were provided by the Ford Foundation.

"Joe Korbel wanted to build something out here, and he set about it by using his contacts and his charm. Very cleverly, he brought in young people who would not challenge him for many years," said Arthur Gilbert, one of the first recruits. "Once you taught here you were part of a family, and you were never allowed to forget that." Josef invited his subordinates to his home for intimate soirées, serenading them with Bohemian folk songs while Mandula read their palms. In return, he demanded 100 percent loyalty. When Ron Krieger went on vacation and failed to send him a postcard, he became very upset. The penalty for such infractions was similar to the discipline he meted out to his real children. An expression of cold anger would come over his face, and he would not talk to the offender for several days, except in the most clipped, brusque manner. "There was no shouting, just a stony silence," recalled Vince Davis. "You didn't know you were out of the doghouse until you met him a day or two later at the coffeepot or the water fountain and it was all very friendly. . . . He was an old east European autocrat. He wanted to be the boss, run his show, and not have anyone tell him otherwise."

Josef had a horror of being embarrassed in front of people he was trying to impress, a trait he passed on to his oldest daughter. He put a lot of effort into making sure that everything went according to plan. At meetings of the board of the Social Science Foundation, Krieger and other faculty members joked that they were the "dancing bears," summoned to impress the trustees by performing a carefully rehearsed script.

Despite his liberal views and his hopes for Madeleine, Josef was initially reluctant to accept female graduate students or hire women professors. His reasoning was largely pragmatic: In the early sixties, it was difficult for women to find good positions in government and academia, particularly in international relations. "He thought we were throwing our money away because the women would not get jobs," said Gilbert. As late as 1972—after stepping down as dean—Josef opposed hiring the first woman faculty member. He later conceded that he had been mistaken. "He had a role reversal about how women could fit in, and told me I was more professional than some of my male colleagues," Karen Feste recalled.

Eventually, Josef became a great champion of talented women students, just as he had been a champion of blacks and other minorities. One of his star students was Condoleeza Rice, a black woman who went on to become President Bush's principal adviser on the Soviet Union and provost of Stanford University. Rice credits Korbel with inspiring her to pursue an academic career. When she applied for an internship at the State Department, he badgered officials on her behalf. "He was nothing but supportive and insistent, even pushy, about me going into this field and being aggressive about getting the best jobs." It was the same with Madeleine. "He was as proud of her, and as aggressive about her prospects, as he was about me," Rice recalls.

By the end of the sixties, several faculty members were rebelling against Josef's brand of authoritarian paternalism. He began to lose support from his own protégés. There were grumblings about personnel policy. The dissent came out into the open at a faculty meeting in early 1969, when one of his deputies suggested that he had shaded the truth in applying for a foundation grant on behalf of the school. Josef seemed taken aback by the accusation and the failure of other professors to rush to his defense. At the next faculty meeting the following week, he announced he was quitting at the end of the academic year. "He made it very clear this was the end of the meeting. We kind of gasped, got up, and walked out," said Vince Davis, one of the dissidents. "It was clear his mind was made up. There was very little point arguing with Joe." While resigning the deanship, he remained a senior member of the faculty. He later told friends that he had "had enough" of pacifying his squabbling colleagues.

In hindsight, some of the professors who opposed Korbel in 1969 now look back on his deanship as almost a golden age. "The school went downhill after him, and hasn't come back," said Davis, who left DU for the University of Kentucky. Arthur Gilbert, who remained at Denver, has come to see Josef's resignation as a case study in futile academic in-fighting. After siding with Korbel's critics in the late sixties and serving under a half dozen other deans, he now sees his former boss as "the best of the lot."

While one generation gap was emerging in Denver between Josef Korbel and his younger colleagues, another was becoming apparent in Long Island between Harry Guggenheim and Joe Albright. Initially, Harry seemed enthusiastic about introducing his nephew to the inner workings of *Newsday*, in accordance with Alicia's wishes. But as the years went by, he began to find fault with his presumptive heir. Joe was given a succession of ever less important assignments. He and Madeleine were invited to Falaise less frequently.

In part, Joe's decline from favor was the result of his own professional inadequacies. His talents were those of a reporter rather than an editor, and he had practically no management experience. He did not do well at his first big job, that of night city editor with responsibility for running the city desk when the daytime editors went home. "My cockiness led me to jump into a job which I hadn't been sufficiently prepared for," he said later. He had difficulty making decisions on deadline and was often late getting the paper to the composing room. His next job was day editor for Suffolk County, and that was not a success either. He seriously underesti-mated the importance of a major fire and the number of reporters needed to cover it. "He was a nice man, but sort of wimpy," said one of his reporters, Pat Byrne. "Joe had a rough time at *Newsday* because he was considered a young fellow not up to the big job ahead," said *Newsday* magazine editor Lou Schwartz. "In terms of office politics, he was not a strong figure."

There were other problems. Harry had great ambitions for *Newsday* and was thoroughly enjoying his new career as newspaper publisher. Pompous and self-important, he was very much impressed by political connections. He wanted a successor in his own self-image: a Renaissance man who could throw a party for senior government officials or leading New York publishers. The quiet and unassuming Joe Albright lacked the glitz and gravitas that Harry regarded as essential qualities for running a newspaper. His political views were uncertain. The idea that Joe should be deciding what stories played on the front page of *Newsday* at the height of the Vietnam War made Harry very uncomfortable. In a way, Madeleine was more Harry's type than Joe. She was certainly equipped with more of the social graces than her somewhat klutzy husband. He liked the way she flattered him. He flattered her in return, passing on a letter from a friend that described her as "a gem." "From now on, you can't cease to glitter," Harry told Madeleine in August 1964.

In early 1967, Harry surprised everybody by announcing that LBJ's press secretary, Bill Moyers, was taking over as publisher of *Newsday*. Harry himself would continue as president and editor-in-chief. He saw Moyers as a big-name politico who would put *Newsday* on the map. Moyers was sophisticated, well connected, and clearly at ease in the world of high officialdom, qualities that Joe seemed to lack. Harry was so happy with the appointment that he was even willing to overlook the fact that Moyers was a Democrat.

Joe and his family were deeply disappointed, even though it had been apparent for some time that he was out of the running. Joe told Harry that he thought of applying for a Nieman fellowship or moving to the *New York Daily News*, another family-owned newspaper. In reply, Harry said that he had "opened every door" for his nephew at *Newsday*, but that it would be unfair to other shareholders "if I attempted to do more." In a letter to Joe's mother, Josephine, he was more blunt. "I fear that your expectations and Alicia's hopes and encouragement . . . have created a belief that Joe would become editor or publisher of *Newsday* on Alicia's death or certainly on mine. . . . He is today inexperienced and incapable of such responsibilities. His appointment would have been a disaster for him and a serious setback, perhaps irreparable, for *Newsday*." Joe continued to hold out hopes for his own promotion. On his thirty-first birthday, in April 1968, he wrote to Harry asking to be given "another chance" at a top management job. "It would be desirable for all of us to find out within the next couple of years whether I have been dreaming the impossible dream." A few weeks later, he was sent to Washington as associate bureau chief.

Madeleine put in a good word for Joe whenever she could. At this point, his career was more important to her than her own. With student strikes raging at Columbia, she took a day off from cramming for her orals to go to the races with Harry. The opening of the new racetrack at Belmont Park was a glittering social occasion, and Harry was in his element. Afterward, she wrote to thank Harry for his hospitality and attached a private memo to Joe from a *Newsday* editor praising his work. "Joe is in Washington and I found it on his desk and thought you might be interested in seeing it," Madeleine wrote. "Could you have it sent back to me, since Joe does not know that I am sending it to you." The incident provides a revealing insight into Madeleine's frustrated ambition for Joe: She was willing to go behind her husband's back in order to trumpet his virtues to Harry. Former *Newsday* reporter Marty Schram says he had the sense that Madeleine was "a little frustrated that Joe was not more assertive. . . . Joe was not the kind of guy who was comfortable banging his fist on the table. I always thought that Madeleine was one of Joe's balls, if not two of them."

It did not take long for Harry to become disillusioned with Moyers. They had arguments over Vietnam. Moyers favored a moratorium on the bombing, while Harry wanted to bomb the Vietnamese to the negotiating table. Harry began to suspect that his new heir apparent was a dangerous radical. In November 1968, Harry threw his usual election-night party for *Newsday* staffers at Falaise. As he later wrote to Moyers, the "looks of dismay" on the faces of senior *Newsday* editors suggested to him that they were "pathetically praying for the defeat of Richard Nixon." He instructed Moyers to "free" the newspaper from "the clutches of propagandists and polemicists who are so deeply prejudiced that they cannot see what is right for the country. . . . Nixon is going to be the next president. He is going to have to crack down on the permissive society. We must support the president. . . . Anyone who cannot support the new president should leave *Newsday* and find a place that will tolerate their prejudices." Over the next two years, he would return ever more persistently to this theme.

As Harry grew older and more frail—he had a mild stroke in 1969—he became more cantankerous. He began seeing enemies everywhere. Although he remained on civil terms with his in-laws, he regarded the Albrights as members of the opposing ideological camp. "Your children are all New Left, and I don't approve of that," he told Josephine in 1970. He was damned if he would ever put Joe in charge of *Newsday*.

Madeleine and the children joined Joe in Washington in September 1968. Since there was nothing decent on the market to rent, they bought a second home in Georgetown, at 1318 34th Street. They paid $103,000 for the house, the equivalent of $490,000 today, and took out a $50,000 mortgage. Distinguished from neighboring buildings by circular stairs leading up to the front door, the new house boasted a living room with two fireplaces, a library, and plenty of space for entertaining. "Our new house is a brick, three-story rowhouse of the federal period," Joe wrote Harry that summer. There is "a small garden out back with four magnificent southern magnolias and a couple of crepe myrtles. It is nowhere as big as our present house, but it is a very nice house." Madeleine would keep the 34th Street house after she and Joe were divorced in 1983, and live in it as a professor at Georgetown University and as secretary of state.

After five years in Long Island, Madeleine was happy to be back at the center of things in Washington. "We hope for a longer stay this time," she wrote her Wellesley classmates soon after making the move. She went on to report that the children and Joe were "thriving under my sporadic and not very orthodox care. . . . Even after the horror of Orals, [Joe] says he enjoys having a perpetual student wife."

With her master's degree from Columbia under her belt, Madeleine now had to choose a subject for her Ph.D. dissertation. As she was making the move from Long Island to Washington, Soviet tanks were rolling into Czechoslovakia to suppress Alexander Dubček's experiment in "communism with a human face." The Soviet invasion of her native Czechoslovakia was a terrible blow, dashing hopes of an early end to the Cold War.

Like her father, Madeleine had wanted to believe in the reformability of communism. As Czechoslovak leaders set about reimposing totalitarian rule under intense pressure from Moscow, Madeleine decided to make a systematic study of the Czechoslovak press during the eight months of relative freedom between January and August 1968. Her background and her fluency in Czech made her well qualified for the task of analyzing the role of journalists in the "Prague Spring." She started making daily trips to the Library of Congress to study back copies of Prague newspapers. To help her with her project, she also cultivated Czech journalists in Washington who were sympathetic to Dubček. One such journalist was Jiří Dienstbier, the correspondent for Czechoslovak radio.

Madeleine and Dientsbier had long talks about the political situation in Czechoslovakia and the way the gains of the "Prague Spring" were being reversed by politicians desperate to salvage something from the wreckage. There were obvious parallels between the actions of Beneš in 1938 and 1948 and the actions of Czechoslovak leaders in the months after August 1968. "I said to myself that I will never behave like these politicians," recalled Dienstbier. "The whole nation peacefully challenged the Soviet occupation. It was fantastic. The moral unity of the nation was broken not by the occupier, but by the attempts of the politicians to save at least something." According to Dientsbier, Madeleine had similar views. "Perhaps her instinct for strong behavior in a crisis is influenced by this background. She always opposes capitulation in face of evil activities."

At the end of 1969, Dientsbier was recalled to Prague and dismissed from his post. He would spend the next twenty years in a succession of menial jobs, such as stoker and night watchman, but his fortunes would change dramatically after the "Velvet Revolution" of 1989. The next time Madeleine heard from him, he would be foreign minister of Czechoslovakia.

In the meantime, the struggle for control of *Newsday* was coming to a head. Disillusioned with Moyers and dying of prostate cancer, Harry Guggenheim took decisive steps to prevent the newspaper from lurching leftward. Without telling the Albrights, who controlled 49 percent of the stock, he negotiated a deal for the sale of *Newsday* to the Times Mirror Group, owners of the *Los Angeles Times*. He was so impressed by the staunchly Republican credentials of the Times Mirror patriarch, Norman Chandler, that he was prepared to overlook the more liberal outlook of his son, Otis. After the negotiations were complete, Harry called Joe to tell him that the deal was done and that there were powerful tax reasons for the Albrights to go along with it. "It was a surprise, we had no idea he was thinking about this. We thought he would leave us the extra two percent to [give us] control, as Alicia indicated he would," Joe recalled later. The news hit the *Newsday* staff like a bombshell. Fearing that the newspaper would lose its independence if the Chandlers took over, they signed petitions urging the Albrights to oppose the sale. "Pray for Joe" read a sign on the employee bulletin board.

The Albrights' town house in Georgetown quickly became the focal point of the "Stop Harry" movement. While Madeleine was not one of the principal players, she was more than just a bystander. "I would go to their house on 34th Street, and we would sit about discussing how to defeat the sale of *Newsday* to Times Mirror," said Marty Schram, a reporter in the newspaper's Washington bureau. "Madeleine was all for [stopping the sale], but she was never the bold, brassy type. She would go to the kitchen, and come out with coffee and cookies. She was a strong, supportive influence on Joe, and seemed to have some good ideas." Sometimes, Joe's ingrained caution made him push Madeleine out front. When a reporter from *The New York Times*, Jack Rosenthal, came over to the house to talk about the sale, Joe refused to meet him for fear of "screwing up the cause." Rosenthal stayed all evening talking to Madeleine.

Despite a financially attractive offer from the Albright family, Harry remained adamant about selling *Newsday* to the Chandlers. The money did not matter to him as much as the ideological principle. He was furious with Joe for opposing his wishes. "You created a Frankenstein with Joe Albright when you made him Washington bureau chief," he told Moyers. "He is using his position to lead the procession against me." When Moyers suggested that Joe was guided by his own interests as a minority shareholder, Harry exploded, "It doesn't seem to me he's working for *Newsday* now. He's spending all his time plotting against me. . . . Well, I'll be finished with them all before long."

The Albrights were unable to prevent the sale of *Newsday* to Times Mirror. By holding out against the sale, however, Joe and his siblings managed to get a significantly better deal for themselves. Harry sold his

51 percent share of *Newsday* for the equivalent of $31.6 million in Times Mirror stock. For the 49 percent owned by the Albrights, the Chandlers offered the equivalent of $37.5 million. Joe's own share was worth approximately $9 million, or an estimated $7 million after taxes.

The Albrights had lost a newspaper, but they had gained a fortune.

Madeleine as president of the Beauvoir school board with the principal, Frances Borders. *Courtesy of the Albright family.*

Dirty Tricks

Navigating the close-knit world of Georgetown society was easier the second time around. While Joe tried to sort out his relationship with *Newsday* and Uncle Harry, Madeleine threw herself into the duties of motherhood, philanthropy, and political campaign work that were the staple occupation of well-connected Washington women. Doors seemed to open automatically for her. Family connections earned the Albrights an automatic listing in the Blue Book, the indispensable guidebook to American high society. They enrolled the twins at the National Cathedral's Beauvoir school, alongside other children of the Washington elite such as the Kennedys and the Heinzes (of ketchup fame). For the Albright children, Beauvoir was the first rung of a high-powered educational conveyor belt designed to lead directly to elite East Coast colleges like Williams and Wellesley. For Madeleine, the school would become a springboard for her entry into the innermost sanctum of American politics.

Soon after arriving in Washington in the fall of 1968, Madeleine was co-opted onto the Board of Trustees for Beauvoir school, an unpaid but much-sought-after appointment. Her ability to leapfrog dozens of other deserving candidates is testimony to her energy and networking abilities, but also to the social pull of the Patterson family. As Joe's wife, Madeleine helped control the disbursement of funds belonging to the Cissy Patterson Trust, named after the eccentric publisher of the *Washington Times-Herald*, Joe's great-aunt. For many years, the Trust had supported a charity called the Black Student Fund, which gave scholarships to under-privileged children to enable them to attend exclusive private schools like Beauvoir. It is likely that Madeleine owed her appointment to the Beauvoir board so soon after her arrival in Washington to the fact that she was already a member of the board of the Black Student Fund by virtue of her family ties.

In the world in which Madeleine was now operating, one opening led to another. Once on the Beauvoir board, she was roped into fund-raising, a traditional activity for stay-at-home mothers. Even though she had never before raised money, she showed she had a talent for persuading parents to contribute to the new roof or the reconstruction of the play-ground. She was methodical, persistent, and charming into the bargain. One of her fellow fund-raisers at Beauvoir, Jim Goodbody, was also rais-ing money for the presidential election campaign of Democratic Sena-tor Edmund S. Muskie. Impressed by Madeleine's organizational skills, Goodbody asked her to become the co-coordinator of a big fund-raising dinner that he was organizing for Muskie at the Washington Hilton. "That's how the whole thing started," Madeleine recalls.

Madeleine liked Muskie. She regarded him as the "quintessential American politician," someone who had come from a very modest back-ground and worked his way up through a series of elected offices, from mayor to governor to senator. She admired his "honesty and forthright-ness." Furthermore, she already had an indirect connection with Muskie through Joe, who had got temporary work as an investigator for one of Muskie's Senate committees after resigning from *Newsday*. She accepted Goodbody's offer.

Perhaps without realizing it or making any conscious career decisions, Madeleine was doing what her genes and upbringing had prepared her to do best. She was making the most of the opportunities that came her way while at the same time creating a network of friends and contacts who would remain useful to her for the rest of her life. It would be incorrect to say that she did this effortlessly, as she invested a lot of hard work in the cause of self-improvement. But the effort itself came naturally, because it had been bred into her.

Just as her father and grandfather succeeded in escaping the Jewish ghetto by making themselves indispensable to the majority Christian society, so too would Madeleine escape from the female ghetto by making herself indispensable to men. The politics of confrontation and bra-burning advocated by the radicals of women's lib were not for her. She would climb to the top of America's male-dominated society not by rebelling against that society but by insinuating herself into its ranks and adapting herself to its sometimes archaic rules and rituals. As the rules began to change, and pressure grew for women to be admitted to occupations previously reserved for men, the refugee's daughter from Eastern Europe was well placed to take advantage of the new opportunities.

By the time Madeleine joined the Muskie-for-President campaign in early 1972, the primaries were already under way. After being acclaimed the Democratic front-runner, Muskie was reeling from a string of political embarrassments, including the celebrated "crying" incident in New Hampshire, when he appeared to crack under the pressure of personal attacks from his opponents. The dinner at the Hilton had a twofold purpose: to raise desperately needed funds and to demonstrate that the Senator from Maine was still a viable candidate. If the dinner went well, it could restore momentum to a flagging campaign. If it went badly, it would be even more difficult for Muskie to resist the growing political tide in the Democratic Party in favor of the most radical antiwar candidate, George McGovern.

Madeleine began organizing her friends and acquaintances to sell tickets to the dinner. Most of her fellow volunteers were wives of well-heeled Washingtonians like herself, many of them recruited from the Beauvoir parking lot. For them, working for Muskie was a way of demonstrating their social conscience without doing anything too overtly radical. Muskie was very much the candidate of the Democratic establishment, moderate in all things, including his opposition to the Vietnam War. His most important political contribution as a senator had been his work on environmental issues, which led to the passage of the 1970 Clean Air Act. Green was the preferred color of the Muskie campaign. "We all sat at long metal-top tables with green pencils, addressing envelopes and chatting about each other's lives," recalled Pie Friendly, who worked with Madeleine on the dinner. Julie Finley, a disillusioned Republican who also had children at Beauvoir, remembers Madeleine issuing a stream of suggestions along the lines of "We have to get these invitations out," "Who else can we think of?", and "These people should be good for $1,000."

There were three thousand tickets to sell at $125 a ticket, or $1,250 a table. Invitations to a more exclusive pre-dinner cocktail party with Muskie were priced at $1,000 a person. "This is an enormous task requiring the immediate creation of a vast network of solicitors," Madeleine memoed fellow organizers. "Each solicitor must sell an average of ten tickets, plus one couple for the cocktail party, to assure maximum financial success." Solicitors were given a set of specific instructions:

- Emphasize that this dinner is the major fund-raising effort in the Washington metropolitan area on behalf of Senator Muskie.
- Emphasize that this will be a fun and exciting evening. We will have top-flight entertainment. Prominent political and show business personalities will be at as many tables as possible.
- Early money is vital. Collect checks yourself and collect them as soon as possible. We can't wait until the last few weeks.

In pre-computer days, Madeleine's organization consisted of dozens of cardboard boxes stuffed with handwritten index cards. She compiled huge mailing lists of would-be invitees, culled from the rolls of the Great and the Good, as reflected in the boards of Washington charities and companies, the directories of private schools, club membership lists, and the address books of friends of friends. "That was easy enough, but it took a lot of work to ensure that we did not mail the same person six times," said Goodbody, her fellow dinner organizer. Each contributor had to be thanked personally by letter, even though Muskie's signature could be added by machine. Big contributors merited a special letter from the candidate. In addition to raising money from her friends, Madeleine also made her own campaign donations. She and Joe contributed a total of $3,250 to the Muskie campaign during the three months leading up to the dinner.

The 1972 Muskie campaign established a pattern for Madeleine's involvement in subsequent political campaigns. By the standards of big donors, her own contributions to a succession of Democratic presidential and congressional candidates would remain modest. But they were large enough to elicit personal gratitude from the candidate, and their effect was multiplied by her willingness to contribute endless hours of hard work to the campaign. She was contributor, activist, fund-raiser, hostess, and cheerleader all rolled into a single, seemingly tireless, package.

The big event was set for eight P.M. on April 17 at the Washington Hilton. Dress was black tie. Averell and Pamela Harriman were enlisted as Honorary Chairmen. The list of cochairmen read like a congressional roll call, from Frank Church to Thomas P. O'Neill Jr. The press was on hand to witness the political and financial resurrection of Edmund S. Muskie of Maine in defiance of the newspaper pundits who had concluded that the early Democratic front-runner had run a singularly inept campaign. Madeleine was more than usually nervous. In personal terms, she had staked more on the success of the dinner than anyone, including Muskie. This was her debut in the exotic, cutthroat world of Washington politics, and she was determined to make the most of it.

As the guests circulated in the glittering ballroom of the Hilton, champagne glasses in hand, it soon became clear that not all was going according to plan. The first sign that something was wrong came with the appearance of half a dozen African ambassadors in ceremonial tribal attire, accompanied by spouses who were, if possible, even more colorfully dressed. "These people don't go to political fund-raising events," thought Goodbody. "Who the hell brought them here?" The same thought occurred to Berl Bernhard, the charismatic Washington lawyer who was serving as Muskie's campaign manager. He went over to the ambassadors and asked them what they were doing at a campaign fund-raiser. From deep inside their multicolored robes, the ambassadors produced official-looking invitations. "The Honorable Edmund S. Muskie, United States Senator, candidate for the Presidency of the United States, cordially invites you . . ."

"What the hell is going on?" Bernhard asked Madeleine, who was equally perplexed. "Did you invite these people?"

"No, I didn't invite them."

No sooner had they apologized to the African ambassadors, telling them they were welcome to stay for dinner, than huge bouquets of flowers and crates of liquor began to arrive at the hotel along with demands for payment. This was followed by the appearance of deliverymen carrying armfuls of cardboard folders containing two hundred extra-large pizzas, with assorted toppings. The accompanying slip showed that they had been ordered that morning. Once again, Bernhard turned to Madeleine for an explanation.

"We're not having pizzas, are we?"

"No, we've already served the hors d'oeuvres."

"Well, they're here, and they have my name on them and your name on them, so somebody knows we are having this event."

"I had nothing to do with it."

On the surface, Bernhard was doing his best to present a smiling face to the dinner guests and reassure everybody that everything was going just fine when quite evidently it was not. Inside, he was ready to crack up from one final indignity after weeks of accumulated stress. He wanted to find the person responsible and kill him. He was meant to be lining up VIPs to meet with Muskie. Instead he was dealing with African ambassadors and pizza deliverymen. "It's all under control, there's no problem, just a little confusion," he repeated to the press people and big contributors who asked what was going on.

Naturally, the pizza men wanted to be paid. The Muskie campaign was already in terrible financial straits, and it was unclear where the money for the pizzas would come from. When Madeleine and Bernhard told them politely to get lost, they summoned hotel security.

"These people are refusing to pay."

"We are not paying for things we didn't order."

As the dinner got under way, two magicians from the Virgin Islands showed up in the lobby of the hotel, saying that they had been recruited to entertain "the children." Also clamoring for payment were half a dozen limousine drivers who said they had been hired by the campaign to drive the ambassadors to the dinner.

It was beginning to dawn on Bernhard that the mix-up was not the result of Madeleine's or anybody else's incompetence, but was part of a deliberate plot to embarrass Muskie and rob him of a moment of triumph. Strange things had been happening to the Muskie campaign over the last few months. Counterfeit letters had been circulated on Muskie campaign stationery denouncing the senator's Democratic opponents as homosexuals and accusing them of being in the pay of "Fat Cats." At a rally in Florida, stickers had been distributed, proclaiming, "If you liked Hitler, you will love Wallace—Vote Muskie." Confidential campaign information was finding its way into the hands of right-wing columnists. Schedules had been thrown into disarray. During the New Hampshire primary, people purportedly representing the "Harlem for Muskie Committee" had telephoned voters in the middle of the night, urging them to support Muskie because he "will be so good to the black man." (The black vote in New Hampshire is less than 2 percent.)

At first, Bernhard suspected his neighbor and old political sparring partner, Frank Mankiewicz, an aide for the rival McGovern campaign. It did not occur to him to suspect Richard Nixon and the Republicans. After all, Nixon was far ahead in the polls and seemed to be coasting to reelection. It was only much later, after the unraveling of the Watergate scandal, that the truth came out. The attempt to sabotage the Hilton dinner was the work of a clandestine operative for the Committee to Re-Elect the President, Donald H. Segretti. Despite Nixon's seemingly invincible lead, CREEP was determined to make sure of victory by sowing confusion in the ranks of the opposition.

After the pizza men and the magicians had been sent away and the limousine drivers paid off, Muskie got up to make his big speech. He thanked Madeleine and the other organizers of the dinner for their stupendous hard work. Discarding a planned speech on the environment, he roundly attacked the Nixon administration for resuming the bombing of North Vietnam, promising to withdraw every American soldier from Indochina within sixty days of his inauguration as president. "If the President will not change course in 1972," he thundered, "it will be up to a new president to settle the conflict in 1973."

The newspapers scarcely noticed Muskie's speech, even though it marked a significant hardening of his position on the Vietnam War. Instead, the talk of Washington was of pizzas and African ambassadors.

Despite the attempts at sabotage, the Hilton dinner turned out well for Madeleine. For an aspiring Democratic Party activist, to have been the victim of dirty tricks by CREEP was almost as good a credential as inclusion on Nixon's personal enemies list. Years later, Madeleine would proudly cite "being sabotaged by Segretti" as her "claim to fame."

Perhaps most important, Madeleine gained a reputation for fierce personal loyalty and selfless hard work. Whatever ambitions she may have had for her own advancement were kept well hidden at this stage. "Most of the men were already picking out their seat in the White House," said her friend Sheppie Abramowitz. "Women did not do that in those days." Madeleine stuck with Muskie long after his campaign had begun to disintegrate, at a time when many more prominent supporters were deserting him. After the Hilton event, her fellow dinner organizer, Jim Goodbody, raised a toast to "Madeleine's steadfastness" at a time when "some of us had feet of clay." "She was incredibly patient and a bit stubborn," he said later. Goodbody remembers running into Madeleine at the Democratic convention in Miami. By that time, he had bailed out of the campaign and was campaigning for McGovern.

She was still working for Muskie.

As the Muskie campaign drew to an ignominious close, Madeleine gained a distinction of a different sort. In the fall of 1972, she became the first woman to be elected chairman of the board of Beauvoir school. It turned out to be an immensely important step for her. Her fund-raising efforts for Muskie had served as a kind of crash course in presidential elections. Beauvoir was a real political apprenticeship. As she later remarked, with only slight exaggeration, the time she spent on the Beauvoir board was her "introduction to American politics."

Her political education took place in the shadow of Washington's unfinished Episcopal Cathedral, a full-scale replica of the great Gothic cathedrals of Europe, down to the gargoyles and stained glass windows and cherubic choirboys in the stalls. Since the early years of the century, the children of the Washington establishment had been brought to this idyllic spot, high on a hill looking down on the rest of the city, for an English-style upbringing. They would go to Beauvoir between the ages of five and eight to learn how to socialize with one another. The girls then went on to the National Cathedral School, where they played hockey and prepared for entry to the women's colleges of New England. The boys went to St. Albans, a prep school steeped in the traditions of muscular Christianity, where pupils were expected to excel on the playing fields as much as in the classroom.

As Washington transformed itself from a southern backwater to the capital of a world superpower, it became more and more difficult to get into Beauvoir. Not only did the school seem to offer a straight shot to Harvard and Yale, but it provided students and parents with a lifelong network of influential friends. Since many places were reserved for children of Beauvoir alumni, the competition for the remaining places was fierce, despite the high fees. Parents were known to resort to desperate measures to get their children into Beauvoir, and equally desperate measures if they were turned down. Upset by the rejection of her child, the wife of a prominent English diplomat caused a scandal by depositing a box of cow dung on the front doorstep of the school. Competition to get onto the Beauvoir board was equally intense, attracting some of the most influential people in the city, in addition to rising stars like Madeleine and Charles Ruff, a prominent lawyer who went on to become chief legal counsel to President Clinton. Some of these people—such as the lawyer Harry McPherson, a former top aide to LBJ, and the Democratic political operative Doug Bennet—would play important roles in Madeleine's future career.

The principal of Beauvoir was a warm but rather scatterbrained woman named Frances Borders, who looked a little like Miss Frizzle of the Magic Schoolbus, with gray hair piled on top of her head and sticking out uncontrollably in all directions. An excellent teacher but hopeless administrator, she was much influenced by the progressive educational theories then in vogue. Miss Borders introduced Madeleine to the teachings of the Swiss educator Jean Piaget, who had little time for the traditional school activities of reading, writing, and arithmetic. "We were all supposed to read Piaget's works," said Julie Finley, a member of Madeleine's board. Much attention was paid to the inner feelings of the children, to the frustration of some Beauvoir parents, who felt that good old-fashioned discipline would often be more appropriate. Finley still recalls with astonishment the time when her five-year-old son bit a girl student on the leg. Instead of telling the boy that biting was bad, and not to do it again, the teacher sat him down on the floor and attempted to explore his feelings, asking questions like, "What made you do that?"

Arguments over Piaget landed Madeleine in the middle of a fierce turf battle between Beauvoir and the other schools on the Cathedral Close. Miss Borders thought it was wrong to send children off to intensely competitive schools like St. Albans or the National Cathedral School at the age of eight. According to Piaget, young children absorb data about the world in an indiscriminate way, inhaling colors, poetry, music, and stories like the air they breathe. It is only later—between the ninth and eleventh years—that they begin to organize all this information in a systematic, "grown-up" way. One way to implement Piaget's ideas, Miss Borders believed, was to expand Beauvoir by at least one grade. That way, the little dears would be kept in a loving, nurturing environment for as long as possible before being sent out into the harsh adolescent world where seven times seven equals forty-nine and homework is done on time or else. According to Harry McPherson, it was not long before Madeleine became as articulate an exponent of Piaget's philosophy as Frances Borders herself. Together, they launched a campaign to convince the Cathedral chapter that Beauvoir needed to be expanded.

Their lobbying effort met determined resistance led by the headmaster of St. Albans, Canon Charles Martin. In both philosophy and appearance, Canon Martin was almost the exact opposite of Miss Borders. Short and stocky, with a forceful personality, he looked a little like the pet bulldog that used to accompany him on his daily rounds. He believed in building character through tried and proven methods, notably competition on the sports field and tough, no-nonsense learning. Canon Martin had no intention of allowing the theories of some Swiss educator to interfere with the running of his school. Furthermore, he knew that he could count on the solid backing of the boards of St. Albans and National Cathedral School. There was no way they would agree to give up the income represented by an entire classful of children, let alone the annual financial donations of their parents and grandparents.

"Their reaction was, 'This is unbelievable,' 'What are you talking about?' " said McPherson, who supported the attempt to expand Beauvoir. "It was a great political lesson for Madeleine. She gave it her best try, but she came up against a lot of lawyers and bankers who were sitting on the boards of the other schools." Recalled Madeleine's friend Bitsy Folger, "They believed that St. Albans was the best and Beauvoir was wishy-washy, and they needed to get those boys in there and shape them up."

Frustrated in the campaign to add another grade to Beauvoir, Madeleine turned her attention to other issues. She consistently supported efforts to increase the representation of minority children by encouraging the school to offer scholarships to poor families. "She has a strong sense of social justice, like her parents," said Lois Rice, a prominent black Washingtonian who served on the Beauvoir board at the same time as Madeleine. "The fact that she came from modest means herself may have had something to do with it. She would often say that marrying Joe was a bit like living a fairy tale." Despite these good intentions, the Cathedral schools remained an island of white privilege in an overwhelmingly black city. The former deputy principal of Beauvoir, Sherri Migdail, recalls an occasion when Canon Martin invited the city's leading blacks to dinner in the great hall of St. Albans to encourage them to enroll their children in the school. At the end of the dinner, he introduced his teaching staff. With the exception of a sports coach, they were all white. He then introduced his kitchen staff, who were all black. "He did not see anything peculiar about that at all," said Migdail. Needless to say, the drive to recruit more black kids was a flop.

The Beauvoir board met monthly in the Cathedral library. Madeleine seemed to enjoy sparring with the high-powered people on the board and made an effort to recruit more of them. "She really believed that she was truth speaking to power," recalled Frances Borders. Some of the powerful men she persuaded to serve on the board—such as the millionaire publisher Joseph Albritton, the lawyer Joe Califano, and former LBJ aide Jack Valenti—turned out to be ineffective and had to be eased out. Madeleine took delight in sifting the wheat from the chaff and was renowned for her sharp observations about colleagues and would-be colleagues. "My clearest memories are of the nominating committee that chose additional board members. I remember her being quite funny about it," said Doug Bennet, an aide to Senator Muskie. "We used to accuse her of character assassination." Adds Frances Borders, "Madeleine was able to say to people, 'Sorry, you are not pulling your weight, get out.'"

Attending to the affairs of Beauvoir was almost a full-time occupation for Madeleine. She would sometimes drop in at the school two or three times a day to check on what was going on. Toward the end of her four-year term in office, the situation at the school began to deteriorate, through no fault of hers. The National Cathedral did not have an effective fund-raising program and was more than $11 million in debt because of the huge costs of cathedral construction. Church leaders routinely dipped into tuition money to pay the builders. The accounts were a mess. In the view of many Beauvoir parents, Frances Borders seemed to be losing control over the school, and key decisions were being taken by the more forceful Sherri Migdail. "We were in crisis mode all the time," said Julie Finley. "There were a lot of dike holes, and Madeleine was running around putting her fingers in the dikes." The crisis came to a head after Madeleine's departure from the board, when both Borders and Migdail were asked to resign.

The mid-seventies may have been troubled years for Beauvoir, but they were productive ones for Madeleine. She discovered the power of the old boy network, learned how to run a meeting efficiently, and gained confidence in her own judgment. Above all, she made many invaluable contacts. Beauvoir was her launching pad for big-time politics.

It is an open question whether Madeleine's subsequent career would have taken off the way it did had she gained her early political training on a school board in the suburbs. Had she not married a wealthy man, she would not have been able to send her children to one of the most exclusive private schools in the nation, and she would not have had the same easy entrée into the heart of the Washington establishment. But in some ways that is beside the point. Plenty of privileged people make nothing of the advantages that they have been given. Madeleine was attracted to power as a swan is attracted to water. She had an instinctive understanding of what she needed to do to accomplish the next step. In the words of her friend Danielle Gardner, "Beauvoir helped Madeleine learn how to work the phones. . . . She is like a sponge. She has a particular knack for networking with people. She says to herself, 'Here is Ed Muskie. If I am going to get to him, I have to meet so and so, who knows Ed Muskie.' She knows how to reach whatever person she wants to reach. It is a whole jigsaw puzzle: Someone is here, I need him for something, I have to make such and such a contact, I am going to get to him because I have made the contact."

Madeleine's life may have been "a fairy tale," in her phrase, but it was a fairy tale of her own making.

A woman's required talent, Madeleine likes to say, is "juggling." Men have the luxury of concentrating on their careers. If a woman wants to get ahead, she has to become an expert in many different fields. "There are those who think that because we juggle, we don't do anything seriously," she complained to Bronx High School students in 1997. "The truth is that we need to use our ability to do many things at the same time to our best advantage." Or, as she said on another occasion, "women's careers don't go in straight lines. They zigzag all over the place."

Perhaps at no time in her life did Madeleine have so many balls in the air as during the mid-seventies. She was working at Beauvoir, fundraising for politicians, sitting on the board of the National Cathedral, throwing dinner parties for her Georgetown contacts. On top of all this, since 1968 she had been attempting to complete her Ph.D. thesis for Columbia University on the role of the Czech press in the "Prague Spring." Toiling away in solitude in the Library of Congress was an agony for her. It seemed such a fusty place. "There were little old people there, older men, who were doing work in the Slavic section," she recalled. "They kept calling each other 'Your Excellency' and saying, 'As I have said to Beneš . . .'"

In order to find time to write up her findings, she would frequently get up at 4:30 A.M. She later described work on her Ph.D. as "the hardest thing I ever did." Because she craved human contact, she much preferred what she called "people activities" to academic research. "Most of my friends know that it took me an embarrassingly long time to get my Ph.D.," she told her Wellesley classmates in 1979. "The reason it took me so long was that I got over-involved in community activities and politics." "She really struggled to complete her Ph.D.," recalled her friend Winnie Freund. "It was very hard for her to closet herself away and do the research and do the writing. She is a people person. She likes to talk, hold discussions, think about things in a dialogue with other people."

In addition to her volunteer work and academic studies, Madeleine had three young children to raise, a full-time occupation in itself despite the assistance of a live-in housekeeper. The twins, Alice and Anne, were entering their teens and into hockey and softball. The youngest daughter, Katie, was also a bundle of energy. "Madeleine was a very involved mother," says Stephen Hess, a former Nixon speechwriter and family friend. "These weren't three little girls in frilly pink dresses. They were athletes. They were hellions." There were never-ending scrapes and bruises. Madeleine and Joe devised a hectic schedule to keep the girls occupied. There were visits to museums and puppet shows and soccer games. On Sundays, after tennis, they would meet their friends the Rices at Hamburger Hamlet for foot-long hot dogs. While both parents doted on the children, Joe tended to be willing to let them do almost anything while Madeleine, perhaps remembering her own upbringing, was the disciplinarian of the family. "She was always stricter than he was. Her attitude was 'let's live by the rules,' " recalls Danielle Gardner.

Enforcing discipline was always a problem, Madeleine remembered later. She herself had received a strict European upbringing. While she was never as strict with her own children as her father had been with her, she did try to establish well-recognized limits. The challenge was being consistent. At one stage, she even thought about writing "a dictionary of punishments." "At certain moments, I would get mad at my kids for spilling the milk, and would say 'You can't watch TV for two weeks.' At the moment of the spilling of the milk for the fifty-fifth time, I would get furious. At that moment, you say whatever occurs to you." In Madeleine's proposed "dictionary of punishments," everything would be worked out in advance. Spilling milk would be punished by one day of withholding television, and so on. In the end, the dictionary remained a fantasy. "I tried to work out a system of being strict, and found it was useless."

For a wealthy couple, Madeleine and Joe were rather frugal when it came to spending money. They splurged on things like a farm in Virginia, vacations at Aspen, and season tickets for the National Symphony Orchestra, but otherwise they counted their pennies. "They lived a fairly modest life, if you can say that about a family which had a beautiful home in Georgetown and access to several other homes. There was nothing pretentious about them," said Hess. Hess recalls going with the Albrights to the races at Charlestown and standing "with our noses pressed to the fence" in order to save the entry fee. On family outings to restaurants, the children would invariably want the most expensive item on the menu, only to be told that they would have to make do with hamburgers.

They spent summers in Long Island, at the house in Oyster Bay, which they hung on to until 1974. (They sold the house for $172,500, double their initial investment.) They also liked going to Alicia Patterson's hunting lodge on the winding St. Mary's River at Kingsland, Georgia, which had been inherited by Joe and his siblings after Alicia's death.

The Albrights frequently invited another family, such as the Freunds or the Hesses, to join them at Kingsland. From the hunting lodge, they made side trips by boat up the river to the Oakanoake swamp or by car to Savannah to see the old mansions. Another favorite excursion spot was the nature reserve on Cumberland Island, just off the Florida coast. Surrounded by thousands of acres of forest, the Kingsland estate offered total tranquillity and seclusion. It was a marvelous place to take children. Alligators sunned themselves by the side of the river, which was black from the tannic acid of cypress trees that grew on its banks. The manager of the estate, Walter Merck, who used to take the Albright children water-skiing, still remembers the shrieks of terrified delight as they caught sight of the alligators. "There was one particular alligator that would always be in the same spot on the sunny side of the river. We would pass it when we went water-skiing. The girls on the bank would jump up and down, pointing at the alligator, trying to scare the one on the skis. The one on the skis would look the other way, pretending it wasn't there. It was funny."

The Freunds joined the Albrights in Kingsland for spring break most years during the sixties and seventies. Joe and the other men shot for quail, which were plentiful in the forests around the St. Mary's River. Madeleine and Winnie organized treasure hunts and riding expeditions for the children. In the evenings, the adults liked to play a game called "Fictionary," which consisted of finding an obscure word in the dictionary and inventing various fictitious definitions for it. The person who guessed the real definition was the winner. While the adults played "Fictionary," the children organized shows. "To this day, the kids still talk about the shows they put on at Kingsland," said Freund. "The big girls would make the small girls do funny things."

The Georgia estate was also a great place to network. As a fund-raiser and socialite, Madeleine had more relaxed access to influential politicians than members of their professional staff, who were usually kept at a distance. When she invited Ed and Jane Muskie down to Kingsland, they accepted willingly. In a way, she was following in the footsteps of Alicia Patterson, who had entertained Adlai Stevenson at Kingsland. Even though he was an outdoorsman, Muskie was ill prepared for expeditions into the subtropical swamp. One day, while walking in the forest in tennis shoes, he encountered a rattlesnake. Fortunately, Walter Merck set a dog on the snake before it could bite the senator. He then killed the snake with his gun. From then on, Joe insisted that Muskie wear tough leather boots when he went out walking.

Despite Madeleine's proven networking abilities and her fascination with politics, her life until the mid-seventies offered few clues to what she would eventually become. She was thirty-eight years old and, with the exception of a few months at the *Encyclopaedia Britannica* when she was twenty-one, had never held a paid job. Her interests still revolved primarily around her family and various forms of volunteer work. "If I could order her priorities at that time, I would have said that she was first of all a mother, then a hostess and socialite, then a volunteer, and then an academic," said her friend Stephen Hess.

"She had a modest sense of herself," agrees Doug Bennet, one of several people she turned to for advice about her career. "Her objectives for herself were still unformed, and had a lot to do with raising her kids and being Joe Albright's wife, to do what his career required. There was no thought of becoming secretary of state." At the same time, Madeleine's women friends detected a certain restlessness and constant desire to improve herself. "A lot of people do not know what is lacking in themselves, but Madeleine did and she always went right after it," said Danielle Gardner. "Once she had completed a certain step, she didn't just stop there. She moved right on."

After eight years' hard slog, Madeleine finally got her Ph.D. in 1976. Entitled *The Role of the Press in Political Change: Czechoslovakia 1968*, her dissertation has little distinction from the thousands of other worthy tomes filed away and forgotten in the stacks of Columbia University. Replete with dozens of pages of footnotes and a lengthy bibliography, it is a model of academic grunt work, with few flashes of originality or brilliance. Based on an in-depth examination of Czechoslovak newspapers in the period leading up to the "Prague Spring," as well as interviews with dissidents like Jiří Dientsbier, it traces the origins of the movement known as "Communism with a Human Face." The 413-page work contains the obligatory expressions of gratitude to her principal academic advisers, Joseph Rothschild and Seweryn Bialer, and to her father. Madeleine had to make a formal defense of her dissertation in front of a committee of five professors in dark suits. She left nothing to chance, lobbying the committee members she did not already know personally. When she found out that a Columbia professor named Charles Gati was going to be on the thesis committee, "she came in and worked me over," he recalls. "She was very friendly, very interested in me." Neither Gati nor his colleagues have specific recollections of her performance in front of the committee, suggesting that it was neither outstanding nor dismal.

Although a Ph.D. was a prerequisite for a serious academic career, its real value in the short term was the boost it gave to her self-esteem. For perhaps the first time in her life, she was now a professional woman in her own right, and not just an adjunct to her husband. It certainly improved her standing with Ed Muskie, who was already emerging as her principal political patron and mentor. Receiving her Ph.D., she later recalled, made it possible for Muskie to introduce her as "Dr. Albright, instead of Madeleine Albright, little housewife." That meant a lot to her.

Madeleine's first real mentor, aside from her father, was Senator Edmund Muskie of Maine. Her work for Muskie led to a job in the Carter White House. *Carter Library.*

"Perfect Staffer"

A member of the Senate Class of '58, Ed Muskie was up for reelection in 1976. His aides were expecting a tough fight, much tougher than in 1970, when he was just emerging as a truly national figure. Maine can be a perverse state, politically speaking. With fewer than 1.2 million inhabitants, its voters feel they are entitled to a personal relationship with their politicians. While it is quite acceptable for a senator from Maine to enjoy a national reputation, woe betide him if he ever shows signs of forgetting who sent him to Washington in the first place. This was Muskie's problem as the elections of 1976 approached. He was a big figure on the national stage, but his "presidential stature" was working against him in his own state.

Muskie's likely Republican opponent was a handsome young congressman by the name of William S. Cohen, who had earned a name for himself on the House of Representatives Judiciary Committee investigating the Watergate scandal. Public opinion polls showed that Muskie was in serious danger of being beaten by Cohen in the upcoming Senate race. Two conclusions flowed from these polls. First, the senator would have to retool his Washington operation and public image to put much more emphasis on the needs of his Maine constituents. Second, he would have to launch a major fund-raising effort for his reelection campaign to deter challenges from popular, high-profile opponents like Cohen. He would need to raise money not just in Maine, but out of state as well. "Momentum" and "invincibility" were the watchwords of the campaign.

Looking around for someone to head the national fund-raising campaign, Muskie aides soon settled on the name of Madeleine Albright. The initial suggestion came from Doug Bennet, Muskie's representative on the budget committee and a member of the Beauvoir school board, but everybody agreed that she had all the right qualifications. She was on friendly terms with both the senator and his wife. She had an appetite for hard work and excellent connections in Washington. She had a proven track record for raising money, for Muskie and for other Democrats. The previous year, when Walter Mondale toyed with the idea of running for president, Mondale aides had offered her the post of campaign finance director. She had accepted, only to have the offer withdrawn a week later when Mondale decided to pull out of the race.

When Muskie's chief of staff, Charlie Micoleau, called Madeleine with the offer of the fund-raising job, she at first seemed hesitant. She was overburdened with other responsibilities, including finishing her Ph.D., and was reluctant to take on yet more volunteer work. "You don't understand," he told her. "This is a hired position. We are going to pay you." The salary the Muskie campaign was offering—$600 a month—was pitiful for such a wealthy woman. The job was only part time. But the mere fact that she was at last being paid for her work seemed to appeal to her. "That was very important to her," recalled Micoleau. "She wanted the accountability and the respect that went along with not being a volunteer." The national headquarters of the "Maine for Muskie Committee" soon opened for business in Madeleine's Georgetown home at 1314 34th Street, with its own stationery and dedicated telephone line. The goal of the fund-raising drive was $300,000, half to be raised in Maine, the other half nationally. Compared to the huge sums spent on Senate campaigns these days, $300,000 seems trivial, but it was a lot of money in 1975.

Madeleine set about raising the money in the usual way. There were cocktail parties and breakfasts and direct mailings. As in 1972, the job consisted of making endless telephone calls, compiling long lists of potential Muskie supporters, sending out begging letters, tracking contributors, and following up with thank-you notes. She was writing up to sixty letters a day and making an equivalent number of phone calls. Labor unions were another lucrative source. The success of the fund-raising campaign contributed to the impression that Muskie was overcoming his problems. By the end of 1975, the threat from Cohen had receded. Rather than challenge Muskie in 1976, he decided to wait a couple of years and run against Maine's other senator, Bill Hathaway. Muskie ended up facing a much less formidable Republican opponent, Robert Monks, and coasted to reelection.

Among Madeleine's strengths was an ability to get along with Muskie activists in Maine, who could easily have been put off by a wealthy socialite from Georgetown. "A lot of the people from Washington had real trouble dealing with the people in Maine, but Madeleine was able to fit in anywhere," said Phil Merrill, the manager of Muskie's Maine campaign. "The irony is that she was probably the only one of them with a farm in Virginia and a house in Georgetown." Recalled Charlie Jacobs, a worker in the Bangor office, "A week or so before the election, we got word that a well-to-do woman from Washington was coming up to help us. We didn't really expect the folks from Washington to do the grunt-work. We were a little surprised when Madeleine walked in the door, picked up a bunch of leaflets, and said, 'Where do you want me to go leafletting?' "

The Washington-Maine tensions were more than usually sensitive during this particular campaign because it was important for Muskie to rid himself of his presidential aura. His handlers in Maine spent much of their time trying to create a homespun image for the candidate, forcing him to do the round of state basketball games and garage sales and bean suppers. "I went to Ed's bean supper" was chosen as an official campaign bumper sticker precisely because it looked so unpresidential.

The presidential rumors refused to die, despite the best efforts of Muskie activists in Maine, who feared they would harm the candidate locally. Indeed, the rumors were encouraged by his staffers in Washington, who were reluctant to give up the dream of an office in the White House even though Muskie had firmly ruled out any participation in the presidential primary races. Madeleine was one of the daydreamers. She joined a small group of Muskie supporters led by Charlie Micoleau and Berl Bernhard to discuss the possible resurrection of a Muskie candidacy in the event of a deadlocked Democratic convention. In February 1976, four months before the convention, Micoleau wrote to the senator describing how they might "fan the winds of fate" and suggesting a meeting with "this loyal band of merry men (and women) in a secluded Georgetown living room." Muskie did not take up the suggestion.

The talk of a new "Muskie for President" drive was squelched definitively a few weeks later. Muskie had been selected to give the Democratic response to President Ford's State of the Union address. Despite the fact that reforms introduced after the 1968 election made it virtually impossible to win the nomination without winning the primaries, Muskie aides were still hoping for a miracle. If the senator gave a knockout speech similar to the one he had made in 1970 in reply to Richard Nixon, they reasoned, they might be able to relaunch him. In the event, his performance was a disaster. The chief speechwriter, Richard Goodwin, developed a fatal case of writer's block, and the speech had to be cobbled together at the last moment from several competing drafts. Fed into the TelePrompTer while Muskie was getting dressed, it began with a soaring declaration about "remaking American democracy" but then dropped off into a morass of incomprehensible bureaucratese. Madeleine had invited everybody over to her Georgetown home for what she had planned as a celebratory party. It turned into a wake for Muskie's presidential ambitions. "It was not a happy occasion," said Muskie aide Al From. "All I can remember is the long hog-tie sandwich." The hostess was as devastated as everyone else.

Madeleine's personal fortunes took a dramatic turn after the Democratic convention when Jimmy Carter chose Mondale as his vice presidential running mate. Several Muskie staffers joined the Mondale campaign. This left Muskie, who was himself running for reelection, with the task of filling several key positions in his Senate office over the course of a weekend. When Charlie Micoleau suggested Madeleine for the post of chief legislative assistant, the senator readily agreed. The job description made clear that Madeleine would be second-in-charge of the office after

Micoleau and would serve as a coordinator with various committee staffs, the real powerhouse of the Senate. That meant dealing with men like Doug Bennet and John McEvoy on the budget committee, Al From on intergovernmental relations, and Leon Billings on environmental pollution, all of whom had years of experience in the Senate and jealously guarded their fiefdoms.

It was a big step up for a woman who had spent most of her time as an unpaid volunteer and had never had a full-time job in her life. Madeleine accepted immediately, but not without some trepidation. Colleagues remember her expressing "great surprise" that Muskie would entrust her with such responsibilities and wondering out loud whether she was up to the job. For a woman who seemed so confident on the surface, Madeleine could sometimes be strangely insecure about her own abilities. At this and other turning points in her life, she would exhaustively analyze her own strengths and weaknesses and turn to more experienced people for reassurance. "She was always asking me if she could do things like this," said Bennet, who later served as president of National Public Radio and president of Wesleyan University. "My answer was yes, she could."

Her women friends were delighted by the appointment. Virtue and loyalty had been rewarded. They knew how difficult it was to make the transition from fund-raising to substantive political work. "We were the changeover generation, and Madeleine represented the change," said her friend Bitsy Folger. "We were surprised and excited when she started working for Muskie on the Hill. We didn't even know she was interested in that kind of work." While Madeleine's marriage and standing in Georgetown society had certainly opened doors for her, in some respects they put her at a disadvantage. "If you were married to someone as rich as Joe Albright, you did not have to work," said Anita Jensen, who worked under Madeleine as a legislative aide to Muskie. "It was not so common for women who did not need the money to be out in the workforce."

The appointment of a woman to a top staff position was a shrewd political move by Muskie. In 1972, the Senate had agreed to a constitutional amendment guaranteeing equal rights for women, but it still remained very much an old boys' club. As a leading supporter of the

Equal Rights Amendment, Muskie was under political pressure to hire and promote qualified women. When he named Madeleine to be his chief legislative aide in August 1976, there were only a handful of women in senior staff positions in the Senate. There were no women senators. At a staff meeting the day after she came on board, Muskie celebrated her appointment with the immortal line: "At last we'll have some sex in this office."

There was stifled laughter. "Jesus, Ed," Berl Bernhard thought to himself, "another felicitous introduction."

Working for Muskie was both a privilege and a nightmare. The son of a poor Polish tailor named Stephen Marciszewski who had come to the United States in 1900 to avoid conscription in the Russian army, Muskie was a man of great intelligence and integrity. As a boy, he had struggled to overcome an almost debilitating shyness. His exceptionally high standards—for both himself and others—made him exceptionally difficult to work for. It was hard to please him, but easy to provoke his wrath. He tested his staffers by yelling at them and ripping their arguments to shreds. Those who could stand up to such harsh treatment flourished under his tutelage and remained incredibly loyal to him. The weak and the mediocre departed in tears. According to Leon Billings, the most faithful Muskie-ite of them all, "He was my mentor, my best friend for many years but, when it came down to it, he was a real sonofabitch."

Stories about Muskie were legion. At his funeral in 1996, Billings told the story of how, after three decades of loyal service to Muskie, he decided to address his former boss by his first name. They were having lunch together, Muskie had long since retired from active political life, and Billings thought a little informality might be appropriate. "So it's Ed now, is it?" Muskie glared. Billings quickly went back to calling him "Senator." In Muskie's world, staff people existed to be abused. He liked to call them "the FBs," the "faceless bastards" who were forever trying to overschedule him and put ridiculous words in his mouth. "Shitagodamn," he would rage, in his great booming voice, upon being handed his schedule. "What do you think I am? A tube of toothpaste that you can just squeeze?" Being able to put up with Muskie's temper was the key to working for him. Another longtime aide, John McEvoy, recalls the senator's asking him at his initial job interview, "Do you cry easily?" When McEvoy asked the reason for the slightly odd question, Muskie replied: "You have to understand that I am a man of enormous frustrations. I can take it out on my [Senate] colleagues, my family, or my staff. The first two options are not available."

Muskie's insistence on excellence and originality made it very difficult to write speeches or manage a political campaign for him. Berl Bernhard, who directed his 1972 presidential campaign, once had a big argument with Muskie over the content of his speeches. In Bernhard's view, and the view of the campaign professionals, the candidate needed to keep hammering away at certain carefully selected themes. Muskie would have none of it. "I am not going to impose on the public by just giving them reiterated garbage," he fumed. "The American people are entitled to my thoughts as they develop." "The problem was that he was probably smarter than the rest of us intellectually," said Bernhard. "Nothing was of acceptable quality." At the same time, Muskie had a vision and sense of legislative strategy that many other senators lacked. His ability to master exceptionally complicated subjects won him the respect of friend and foe alike.

Madeleine appears to have had a knack for dealing with Muskie. "She handled the senator as well as anyone I knew," said Billings. "She had clearly made a decision that she was not going to be intimidated by him." Madeleine was tough enough to put up with his fits of anger, while being feminine enough to appeal to his old-fashioned, gentlemanly side. She says Muskie's rages were usually directed at things that bothered him, rather than at individual aides. "He yelled a lot, but he never yelled at me."

Some of the male staffers suspected that Muskie treated his women employees better than the men. "He was of the old school," said McEvoy. "He could be as curt with her as everybody else, but I doubt that she was subjected to the same intellectual pounding as the men." Not so, says Madeleine's former assistant, Anita Jensen, who describes Muskie as "an equal opportunity disaster." Nevertheless, it was clear to all that

Madeleine enjoyed a special relationship with the senator. This was partly because they knew each other socially, putting Madeleine under the column of "family" as well as "staff," and partly because of her conciliatory, even ingratiating personality. To outsiders, Madeleine may seem confrontational, thanks to a "tell-it-like-it-is" image that has been carefully cultivated in recent years by her PR people. To insiders, she has a quite different image. "There is the inner circle and the outside world," says Jensen. "Within the family, she does not work by confrontation. She works by talking things through, by blabbering on."

Part of Madeleine's role as chief legislative assistant was to save Muskie from himself by deflecting his anger. During his Senate reelection campaign, she consistently advised him "to keep it cool," particularly during the run-up to a televised debate with his Republican opponent. She included "some cheap shots" in the debate preparation book, so that "you can get mad at us and retain your statesmanlike composure before the television audience." A few days later, she and other aides urged the senator to avoid flashes of "anger, hostility, or irritation" that can be magnified on television, and to project instead "a soothing, confident aura of calm leadership."

Muskie had a suite of offices on the ground floor of the Senate Russell Building. Madeleine and three other legislative aides were crammed into one half of the end room in the corridor. The other half of the room was taken over by the press operation. The working conditions were so cramped that Anita Jensen was unable to get out of her chair at the same time as her neighbor, Charlie Jacobs. As the senior person in the room, Madeleine had a desk in the corner, next to the window, with a foot more working space. Although Madeleine had a grand-sounding title, her actual responsibilities were rather mundane. The real power was held by male staffers who had key positions on Muskie's Senate committees. They formed a kind of Praetorian guard around Muskie, dealing with the subjects that really fascinated him such as the environment and the budget process and jealously guarding their access to the senator. Madeleine was left to look after all the loose ends not already taken care of by the committee staffs. The legislative staff was also responsible for dealing with the tens of thousands of letters addressed to Muskie every year. Although Madeleine made valiant attempts to organize an efficient system to deal with this vast tide of incoming mail, it ended up defeating her, as it defeated all her predecessors.

The political odds and ends assigned to Madeleine included foreign policy. She quickly became an expert on matters like the Panama Canal treaties, urging Muskie to resist political pressure from the right to keep the canal under total American control. Her bailiwick included what was irreverently known around the office as "shoes and Jews." Although Muskie was a believer in free trade, he was under constant political pressure to protect the shoe industry, once a major supplier of jobs in Maine, which was losing business to countries like Israel and China. It was easier for him to take a stand on matters like human rights and freedom of immigration for Soviet Jews that did not directly involve his own constituency. Another perennial headache for the staff was abortion. As a practicing Catholic, Muskie had a generally pro-life voting record and was the target of endless lobbying by the Bishop of Portland. Madeleine, who had gone through the trauma of giving birth to a stillborn child, tried to nudge him gently to vote in favor of Medicare funding for abortions when there was a risk to the health of the mother. It was a difficult pitch. Anita Jensen recalls an occasion when Madeleine went in to try to convince the senator that the so-called health exception would not undermine his pro-life position. A few minutes later, she heard a buzz on the intercom. Madeleine was summoning up reinforcements.

"Anita, explain to the senator why a health exception is important."

Jensen cited the case of a woman with high blood pressure, whose health could be in danger if she had a baby. It was an unfortunate example. Muskie exploded.

"High blood pressure, what do you mean, high blood pressure? I have high blood pressure. What else? What else? Hangnails?"

Unsure of her own opinions, Madeleine sometimes wrote deliberately vacuous memos or prefaced her arguments with remarks like "Charlie thinks that . . ." or "Anita had the idea that . . ." She rarely took strong positions that could expose her to criticism. Part of Madeleine's caution, according to Anita Jensen, stemmed from the fact that she was surrounded by a shoal of male sharks willing to do anything to advance their careers. For a woman to avoid drawing attention to herself was a natural defense mechanism. "Back then, Congress was a boys' club. If a woman screwed up, it was much worse than if a guy screwed up. There was no place to hide. . . . If you feel at risk from being humiliated by some guy who puts you down or calls you an idiot, you end up tiptoeing around a lot of the time. You end up shutting up and keeping your head well down. The boys were chummy enough on the surface, but every one of them carried a knife. They were very, very serious careerists. The way to survive in such a situation is to be pleasant and smarter than the others, but not to show it. Madeleine was wary of being knocked down if she got too uppity."

As a Senate veteran with twenty years' experience behind her, Jensen was more willing than Madeleine, a relative newcomer, to be outspoken and stand up to the men. She believes that Madeleine made a tactical decision not to try to beat the guys at their own game but "to join them and then sneak up on them afterward. . . . Madeleine wanted to work, she wanted to create a persona for herself that was more than just Joe's wife and a mother." Madeleine has described herself to others as "the world's perfect staffer." It was a proud self-portrait, but also a self-deprecating one, as though her mission in life consisted of making powerful men look good.

The men seemed unaware that their behavior might be perceived as patronizing or threatening by their women colleagues. At the same time, they concede it was hard for women to break into the old boy network of the Senate. Key to this network was a group of administrative assistants and staff directors of the most important committees who referred to themselves as "the secret government" and exercised their power by inviting cabinet officers for breakfast and grilling them mercilessly. As a chief legislative assistant, Madeleine was one rung below this inner group. "I am sure that Madeleine was frustrated about not being able to penetrate the secret government [which] was pretty maledominated," recalls Charlie Micoleau. "She was out of the charmed circle," agrees Al From. Even though her job description stated that Madeleine was meant to "coordinate" the work of the powerful committee staffers, From says he cannot remember her doing much in the way of "coordination."

Working for Ed Muskie was a little like "working for Mount Rush-more," in Anita Jensen's phrase. At his funeral, Madeleine spoke of him as her political "role model," saying that she would never have accomplished what she had in public life without his support. Later, when she became secretary of state, she placed his portrait on the wall immediately outside her office. These were more than acts of ritual obeisance. Madeleine learned a great deal from Ed Muskie. As she said in her funeral ora-tion, for her and other members of the expanded Muskie clan, Muskie represented "our link" to America's "proud democratic heritage." For all his personal quirks, there were few politicians more eloquent than Muskie on the meaning of public service and the validity of the demo-cratic process.

While Madeleine's personality is obviously very different from Muskie's, they had certain things in common, beginning with an immi-grant's faith in America as a shining beacon for the rest of the world. Like Muskie, Madeleine may seem outwardly rigid and confrontational. Like him, however, she is a compromiser at heart, willing to make a deal with her worst enemy in the interest of getting something accomplished. Like Muskie, she has an acute sense of the art of winning over political oppo-nents. Observing Madeleine's very public love fest with Jesse Helms, the archconservative chairman of the Senate Foreign Relations Committee, former Muskie staffer John McEvoy says he is reminded of the way Muskie used to operate. "Muskie might have fulminated about Helms in public, but he would also have found ways to work with him in pri-vate. . . . He understood that you have to recognize the legitimacy of the other guy. You can't be fixed in your position. Politics is baseball, not lob-bing hand grenades."

After the Carter election victory in November 1976, Muskie staffers put together a list of deserving candidates for posts in the administration. The list was headed by the senator's longtime aide, Leon Billings, who was recommended for the post of head of the Environmental Protection Agency. There were eighteen other names on the list, all but one of them men. Madeleine's name was not among them.

As it turned out, Madeleine was the only Muskie staffer to get a job in the Carter White House. In early 1978, Zbigniew Brzezinski, Madeleine's old mentor at Columbia University, decided that he needed to improve his ties with leading senators and congressmen, which were rather strained. Until that time, congressional relations for the National Security Council were handled by the regular White House staff. Brzezinski wanted someone in the job who would report directly to him. Since Madeleine already had some experience on Capitol Hill working for Muskie, he decided that she would be ideal.

The choice surprised some of the more experienced people around Muskie, particularly the men. In pursuing their own careers, they had paid little attention to the quiet little woman in the back office who seemed to make a career out of being pleasant and helpful to other people. It was not the last time that Madeleine would be underestimated by her male colleagues. In particular, they failed to take into account her diligence at forming a network of people who would be helpful to her when the time came.

Whatever the personal jealousies her appointment may have provoked, the Muskie staffers gave her a great send-off. There was a ceremony in the office and everybody hugged her. Leon Billings had some amusing advice on how to conduct herself in her new NSC job under Brzezinski, popularly known as "Zbig."

"Just remember," he told her, "he is zbig, and you are zmall."

Not to be outshone in the department of outrageous puns, Muskie joked, "You are going from Pole to Pole."

Shortly before moving to the White House, Madeleine had to deal with the pain of her father's losing fight with pancreatic cancer. The last year of Josef's life was an agony for him and his family. He seemed drained of his usual vitality and energy. "You know, I'm tired," he would say to his university colleagues. "Really tired." He was researching a new book on the Czechoslovak legionnaires who joined the Russian army at the end of World War I, but he had to cut back his travel plans sharply in order to undergo treatment in a hospital. He was trying to get his strength back when his health took a sudden turn for the worse. In July 1977, he was rushed to hospital in Denver with pneumonia. It was the end.

The memorial service took place in the Phipps House in Denver, an ornate, Georgian-style mansion. Tributes flowed in from students and fellow academics. Brzezinski sent a telegram praising him as "a valued friend and respected colleague." A graduate student described Josef "as the most stimulating and most exacting teacher I've encountered." The eulogy was given by his colleague Russ Porter, who had worked with him on his books, turning the rather stilted language of an immigrant into colloquial English. Porter, who was closer to Josef than anyone else at the university, talked about the complex character of a man who had overcome adversity "beyond the understanding of us who have lived so easily and so safely for so long." At one point in the eulogy, he mentioned the "contradiction" in Josef's spiritual life: "Though a baptized Christian, he was not a churchgoer." It was an odd enough formulation to stick in the memory of Rita Kauders, a Czech Jew living in Denver who knew about Josef's Jewish background. She wondered if Porter was also in on the Korbel family secret.

Understanding Josef is the key to understanding Madeleine. While there were other influential men in Madeleine's life, including Muskie and Brzezinski, none of them compared with her father. It is difficult to overstate the impact that he had on her, both consciously and unconsciously, or the extent to which she modeled herself after him. Pleasing her father was one of the great motivating forces of her life. In the words of her friend Christine Dodson, Madeleine "did not need other father figures because she had her father. The others were important to her, but they were not father figures."

Madeleine inherited superficial things—such as her looks and naturally effervescent personality—from her mother, Mandula. Her inner character is surely that of her father. She inherited his easygoing social skills mixed with an iron determination. The combination of gentleness and steeliness was the product of a lifelong struggle for acceptance, both in Europe and America. At times, he had to fight for his family's very survival. In order to overcome shattering setbacks in his personal and professional life, Josef needed a tremendous inner resolve. To win social approval, he had to conceal his inner drive behind a mask of affability and pleasantness.

In contrast to Mandula, who was naturally gregarious and somewhat undiscriminating in her choice of friends, Josef had a highly developed sense of who could be useful to him and who would not. He passed this trait on to his daughter. Anita Jensen was struck by Madeleine's "superior social intelligence" when they worked together in Muskie's office. "You can be intelligent in a logical and abstract way, and you can also have social intelligence, knowing what people want from you and factoring that into how you deal with them. Madeleine has that to a very high degree. She has a hyper-ability to understand what other people are about, where they are coming from, what they are likely to need, and where their limits are."

Most people who knew Josef Korbel agree that he was an exceptionally complicated and contradictory figure, difficult to figure out. His exuberant American optimism was forever doing battle with an ingrained European pessimism and hardheaded realism. "He was very social, very amiable, and yet he was also a very private person. You knew him, but you didn't know him," said Karen Feste, a Graduate School colleague in Denver. The contradictions in Josef's character made it difficult for his friends to sum him up in a single phrase. "He was ambitious, humorous, very intelligent," said Rita Kauders. "I would not call him ruthless. On the contrary, he was always civil, very polite. I was going to say 'soft,' but that is not right." "Uncle Josef played out the charade very thoroughly," said his niece Alena Korbel. "He played his cards very close to his chest, and some people did not like him because of that. But I knew him to be very gentle and kind."

Josef's books and lectures are full of moral judgments on the great characters of the twentieth century. His own direct experience of evil made him a man of high moral principle, yet he did not always live up to his own moral code when it came to ensuring the livelihood of his family. A trivial example was his ardent championship of integrated public schools for everyone except his own children. When a university colleague bought a house in the suburbs in order to give his children a better public school education than they would have received in racially mixed Denver, Josef's reaction was indignant. "Joe felt this was totally wrong and that I had abdicated my social responsibilities," recalls Bernard Abrahammson. The fact that Josef had sent his daughter to the most exclusive private school in the city did not seem to be relevant to him.

A more important example of the hard-nosed side of Josef's personality was the way he rewrote his own past to suit the needs of the present. He gave several versions of his dismissal from the Czechoslovak foreign service after the Munich crisis and hid the real reason for his escape from the Nazis in 1939. A man of strong democratic convictions, he doctored his biography to skate over the inconvenient fact that he accepted an important diplomatic assignment in 1948 from a Communist government that had just seized power in a coup d'état. If one is to believe the Nebrich family, he engaged in a kind of victors' justice after World War II and seized paintings and other valuable items belonging to them to avenge the sufferings of his own family at the hands of the Germans.

How does one explain this apparent contradiction between word and deed? The answer seems to be that truthfulness and morality are fine in the abstract, but in extreme situations other laws take over. When confronted with evil, good men sometimes feel they have a right to resort to questionable acts. In his writings about totalitarianism, Josef frequently talked about the need for the democracies to protect themselves by all available means. Writing about the Cold War between the United States and the Soviet Union, he remarked that "this is no longer an argument between gentlemen." It was the same with individuals. A deeply moral person, Josef strove to live up to his ideals. But if he sensed that his family was somehow in danger, he would take whatever action he deemed necessary to protect the interests of his loved ones, including telling a few white lies. Putting his own family first seemed the natural thing to do in the wake of World War II and the Holocaust at a time when Europe was torn in half by a new ideological conflict. In the words of a Terezín survivor, "The Jews had always been the ones to suffer. In such an evil world, what was the value of clinging to laws and virtue that no one else seemed to observe?"

Having come of age in less tumultuous times, Madeleine has been spared the agonizing moral choices that confronted her father. At times, however, one senses a similar tension between abstract principles and messy reality. When pushed to the wall, as she was in 1997 following the furor over her Jewish ancestry, she can be fierce in defending what she perceives as her own interests and the interests of those close to her. Family loyalties come first with Madeleine, as they did with her father.

For more than a century now, the drama of the Korbel family has been the struggle for assimilation. Each generation has had to find ways of adapting to new languages, new cultures, new religions, new identities. Each has in some way improved on the performance of its predecessors. The ability to adapt to new circumstances has been the required talent of Madeleine's family. Her great-grandfather, the older Josef Körbel, brought the family out of the ghetto. As a functionary of the Austrian state railway system, he was required to learn German and forget Yiddish. Her grandfather, Arnošt, became a citizen of the new Czechoslovak state created in the aftermath of World War I and turned his back on Judaism altogether, only to be forced back into the ghetto by the Nazis and murdered along with millions of others. Her father, Josef, was born a citizen of Austro-Hungary, was a citizen of Czechoslovakia for thirty years, and spent the last twenty years of his life as a citizen of the United States.

Josef was a hybrid. He never entirely lost his thick East European accent. "When he dressed up in his three-piece suit," recalls his DU associate Karen Feste, "he looked like a character out of the old Austro-Hungarian empire." Even so, according to his niece Alena, he was more successful in shedding his past than his older brother Jan. "My father [Jan] was a bit of a mystery to me," said Alena. "He tended to put on a show." Josef was better educated, less gauche, and more self-confident than his brother.

As much as he loved America, Josef sometimes had difficulty adjusting to the strange ways of his adopted country. For Madeleine, by contrast, the adjustment was so complete that it seemed effortless. She became indistinguishable from millions of other Americans. She lost the accent and, thanks to her marriage to Joseph Medill Patterson Albright, she even lost the ethnic-sounding name with which she had been born. "What made Madeleine tick," according to Alfred Friendly Jr., a former Muskie staffer and journalist who would join her in the Carter White House, "was a desire to be part of the Establishment." In this, too, she succeeded brilliantly. So successful was this great-granddaughter of a Jewish stationmaster in penetrating America's WASP

Establishment that she even has a pew named after her in Washington's National Cathedral, in recognition of her services to the Episcopalian church.

The tragedy is that her father, who had done so much to set her on the right path, did not live to see her triumph.

Zbigniew Brzezinski and the staff of the National Security Council. Seated on the right of the table, Madeleine is one of the only two women in the room. *The Washington Post*

From Pole to Pole

Inside the White House, the initial reaction to Madeleine's appointment was one of deep suspicion. Even before she reported for work, she was caught up in a turf fight between National Security Adviser Zbigniew Brzezinski and the network of "good ol' boy" Georgians who had come to Washington with President Carter. The Georgians in the congressional relations office were put off by what they saw as Brzezinski's intellectual arrogance and his ill-disguised contempt for the political arts of wheeling and dealing. He treated them as country bumpkins who knew nothing about foreign policy and should be kept away from sensitive national security matters at all costs. When Brzezinski announced that he wanted to appoint his own congressional affairs person, the Georgians feared he was undermining their authority. Eventually, the president ordered everyone to stop squabbling and work together.

Madeleine moved to the National Security Council in March 1978. Since her job had not existed before, a place had to be found for her to work. She was given a windowless cubbyhole in the bowels of the White House, next to the Situation Room, where the President and his aides manage major crises. There was barely enough space for a chair and a desk. "It was a ridiculous office," said her friend Christine Dodson, Brzezinski's staff director and former aide from Columbia University.

"Her desk used to belong to a secretary. We simply raised the partition to the ceiling so that she had some privacy."

The premises may have been claustrophobic, but—in a system where location is everything—Madeleine enjoyed the most important perquisite of all. Most of the National Security Council staff were across the street in the Old Executive Building, away from the hub of political power. The only NSC staffers with offices in the West Wing were Brzezinski, his deputy, and the four or five aides he consulted most frequently. It was an early lesson in what Madeleine later called "the importance of proximity."

With the West Wing office came a pass to the White House Mess, the best place for exchanging gossip with other presidential aides. "It was the ultimate voyeur's job," she said later. Her immediate neighbors were the press officer, first Jerry Schecter and later Al Friendly Jr., and the military affairs officer, the brilliant but eccentric Colonel William Odom. A former military attaché in Moscow, Odom seemed forever occupied with mysterious top-secret projects, such as devising a new targeting strategy for U.S. nuclear warheads. Visitors to his office were greeted by a huge map of the world covered with an assortment of blue, yellow, and white pins. When asked what the pins signified, Odom would reply disarmingly, "Nothing at all, but it drives people crazy." Madeleine's duties seemed banal by comparison.

Brzezinski ran the National Security Council along the lines of his institute at Columbia, with himself at the center and authority radiating outward like spokes on a wheel. Like other staffers, Madeleine was obliged to submit daily reports to Brzezinski, summarizing her activities and noting any contacts with legislators or journalists. Although Brzezinski was cordially disliked by many people in Congress and on the political side of the White House, and had plenty of enemies in the State Department, he got generally high marks from his own staff for his accessibility and efficient way of conducting business. "Working for Zbig was great," recalled Bob Pastor, the NSC's Latin American expert. "He read everything and gave us feedback. He was very clear in what he wanted and was open to arguments." On occasion, the national security adviser would play one group of aides off against another, alternating between them for advice. Brzezinski viewed this system as one of "creative tension," although it sometimes seemed more like "creative destruction" to the victims.

Although Madeleine occupied prime White House real estate, she ranked relatively low in the hierarchy of brilliant minds around Brzezinski, which included Cold War warriors like Odom, Harvard academics like Sam Huntington, and top-flight regional experts like the China scholar Michael Oksenberg or the Middle East specialist Bill Quandt. Madeleine was regarded as a "process person" rather than a "substance person." While Brzezinski welcomed her advice on how to deal with Congress, her foreign policy views were of little interest to him or anyone else. According to former Brzezinski assistant Les Denend, anyone trying to pick future secretaries of state from the NSC staff would have likely put Madeleine "at the bottom of the list, or at least in the bottom ten percent." Her job did not lend itself to writing dazzling memos on the future of East-West relations, and she had no particular area of expertise.

What Madeleine did have, everybody agrees, was political savvy and a gift for handling personal relationships. The circumstances of her appointment, over the objections of the congressional relations staff, required her to negotiate some treacherous bureaucratic shoals. Yet she quickly succeeded in gaining the confidence of the Georgians without forfeiting the trust of her sometimes imperious boss. "Madeleine is good at people-handling," said Brzezinski. "She knows how to make people feel good about themselves."

Under ground rules worked out with the congressional office, she was not permitted to do her own lobbying on Capitol Hill without prior approval. So instead she carved out a niche for herself as an intermediary between the two warring camps inside the White House, translating the geopolitical gobbledygook of the national security people into a language that the political people could understand and vice versa. Her principal contact in the congressional office was a gregarious lobbyist named Bob Beckel, who had responsibility for pushing the administration's foreign affairs agenda through Congress. A former football player, Beckel detested the intensely cerebral Brzezinski. The feeling was mutual. "I thought his understanding of the Hill was about as complete as a chicken's, and he thought that my understanding of foreign policy was less than that," Beckel recalled. After initially resisting Madeleine's appointment as an intrusion on his turf, Beckel discovered that she could be helpful to him.

Soon, Beckel was telling his fellow jocks in the congressional office, "She is fine, man. We have to put up with this asshole [Brzezinski]. She knows Congress, unlike the rest of that staff of his. Let's take advantage of it." By August, five months after arriving at the White House, Madeleine was claiming "a breakthrough" in her relations with the congressional office in her evening report to Brzezinski. "They actually asked me to help in making calls to get a vote count," she reported proudly. Once she made her breakthrough, Madeleine rapidly became "quite a favorite" of the political people, according to Beckel. She was one of the very few people on the NSC staff who could go up to Capitol Hill and talk to senators and congressmen in a language they could understand without being obnoxious.

Madeleine arrived at the White House at a particularly interesting time. During her first week on the job, the Senate voted 68–32 to approve the Panama Canal treaties, transferring sovereignty over the Canal Zone back to Panama. The long-delayed vote was a major foreign policy victory for the Carter administration, but it came at a heavy political price. Right-wing Republicans led by Ronald Reagan were exploiting the Panama "sellout" to stir public resentment over the decline of American power. Moderate Republicans felt bruised from the beating they had taken for supporting the administration over Panama. Because of defections by Democrats, their votes were vital to the administration's hopes of pushing its foreign policy agenda through Congress. But they were reluctant to put themselves through a similar ordeal again.

Madeleine drew several lessons from the administration's Pyrrhic victory over the Panama Canal treaties, which are relevant to the way she has handled congressional relations as secretary of state. She understood, first of all, that there is a limited reservoir of congressional goodwill, which has to be husbanded carefully. As the person in the White House responsible for pushing foreign policy legislation, Madeleine felt she was "always bad news." The President's political managers made a habit of blaming the foreign policy people for his problems with Congress. Selling foreign aid to Capitol Hill, she later joked, was a little like "selling leprosy." Rather than presenting Congress with a long "laundry list" of policies and budgets to approve, the administration had to be very selective in asking for congressional support, particularly for unpopular foreign affairs projects.

A related lesson was the need for administration officials to build personal relationships with key people in Congress. Having just come from Capitol Hill, Madeleine understood the art of trading favors. In one of her first memos to the national security adviser, Madeleine laid out a "congressional outreach" plan. She told Brzezinski that members of Congress liked to think of themselves as "important policy-makers" with a better grasp of public opinion than appointed officials. The most important senators have probably "run for President or thought about it [and] are not easily awed. . . . From my Muskie experience, I can tell you that he does not just want to be stroked, he wants his advice to carry some weight." She urged Brzezinski not to expect immediate results after just one meeting. "It is a slow process of building mutual confidence." Over time, the investment would pay off.

In addition to the usual meetings with key congressmen, Madeleine suggested a series of social contacts, including tennis games, invitations to the Kennedy Center, and dinners at her house in Georgetown. "If I can guarantee your presence, I think we can produce most anyone." Brzezinski nixed the tennis games—"I didn't want to be wiped out," he recalled later—but approved the dinner parties. Her plan drew heavily on the social connections she had accumulated through her fund-raising work. Many of the prominent Washingtonians that Madeleine invited to dinner were known to her from her time on the Beauvoir school board or from her volunteer work with the National Symphony Orchestra. She liked to mix politicians, journalists, and leading cultural figures, such as the exiled Russian cellist Mstislav Rostropovich, who had just taken over as the principal conductor of the NSO. Organizing dinner parties for Brzezinski turned out to be more difficult than Madeleine had anticipated, given the late hours that everybody worked and senators' reluctance to sit through foreign policy lectures. "The idea was a good one, but I don't think she gave many," said Brzezinski.

Improving Brzezinski's relations with key senators and congressmen was a formidable challenge. In the words of his longtime aide, Christine Dodson, "He did not give a damn about Congress." He made no effort to stroke the overinflated egos of politicians by pretending to be impressed with their knowledge. "Instead of saying something like 'good point, but I have a slightly different view,' he would simply say, 'That's wrong,' " recalled Beckel. "Madeleine, of course, would always cover for him and patch it up." When Brzezinski went to testify before the Senate Foreign Relations Committee investigating allegations that the president's wayward brother Billy had accepted gifts from Libya, he seemed to relish the confrontational atmosphere. He recalls that Madeleine was sitting directly behind him, urging him to be less combative. "Her general demeanor was, 'stroke them, don't punch them.' She was right." Despite Madeleine's advice, Brzezinski could not resist taking a few slugs at the president's opponents, telling Republican senator Richard Lugar that he "resented" his insinuations of dishonesty.

After work, Madeleine would get together with her colleagues and complain about Brzezinski's idiosyncrasies. "It was like a joint therapy session," said Beckel. "We would have a drink in my office at the end of the day and bitch about how we had to teach these amateur politicians how to stroke Congress." Another recurring complaint was being left out of key meetings. "The way she behaved was that of a person who has to be given the right to speak or to be invited into meetings," said Dodson, who frequently intervened on her behalf with Brzezinski. Beckel recalls comments from Madeleine like "I can't get the son of a bitch [Brzezinski] to tell me what is going on."

Despite these petty humiliations, she remained fiercely loyal to her boss, reacting sharply when Brzezinski was criticized in the press. A particular target of Madeleine's ire was the gossip writer Sally Quinn, who claimed in an article for *The Washington Post* that Brzezinski had opened his fly buttons to a female journalist. (*The Post* later retracted the allegation.) "You would mention Sally Quinn and Madeleine would go up the wall," said Al Friendly, the NSC press spokesman. "She could get vociferously unhappy, not necessarily over serious things."

Some of Madeleine's frustrations surfaced in a memo she wrote to Brzezinski after her first year in the job. While insisting that the "accomplishments outweigh the disappointments," she told Brzezinski that she would be more useful to him "if I were kept better informed. I am not a secret information junkie, but I think it would be helpful if I could see additional cable traffic. Most of what I get is about room reservations for Codels [congressional delegations]. I often find out substantive material with congressional impact . . . from the people I deal with at State or Defense. Other than just feeling stupid and put-down, which I can deal with, I cannot be useful if I have to scrounge information." She added that she had been "unsuccessful in persuading you and others to consider the legislative/political angle during the decision-making process rather than after it."

Like many of her colleagues, Madeleine frequently felt overwhelmed by the pressures of the job. She would often be at her desk by 7:30 A.M., having had breakfast at the White House Mess. She would then put in a thirteen- or fourteen-hour day. She would later say that it was impossible for anybody who has not worked at the White House to understand the pace. "You think you're working on the world's most important thing and all of a sudden the world's really most important thing comes to your desk and you set that first one aside, and the coordination . . . all of a sudden disappears." In previous jobs, where she could prepare herself thoroughly for every eventuality, she had a reputation for efficiency. In the White House, by contrast, she had to struggle to keep her head above water. "Her work habits were not the most orderly," recalled Friendly, who sat in the next office. "Sometimes you felt that she was making life harder for herself by not being the most organized person." There were "random moments of heightened tension" with the secretary when Madeleine could not find the piece of paper she was looking for.

She coped with these pressures by keeping her head down and being as nice as possible to the people who mattered. Her modus operandi in the White House was similar to the way she had conducted herself on Capitol Hill. She survived by not being confrontational and by maintaining a "charming and helpful" facade even when she felt "furious" inside. As with Muskie, she rarely ventured her personal opinions, instead playing the role of loyal team player, or "facilitator," as she later described it. "I had to learn to speak out for myself," she said later. "I would be in a White House meeting and I would think of something and not say anything because I wasn't sure it would add to the discussion. Then some man would say what I had been thinking and it would be hailed as a great idea."

Madeleine's present reputation for "telling it like it is" bemuses many of her Carter administration colleagues, who remember her as being generally unwilling to stick her neck out. Some interpreted this reticence primarily as a defensive mechanism. "The lion in her was always there," said Beckel. "The genius of it was that she kept it in check knowing full well that if she stepped out into that male domain she would have been crushed. There are ways they can crush you, particularly when you are just starting out on that ladder. She completely understood that. Her tongue must have bled a thousand times at night from having to bite it while these guys were stealing her ideas."

Apart from Madeleine, the only other professional woman on the forty-person NSC staff was Jessica Mathews, who was responsible for "global issues" such as arms control and human rights. (Christine Dodson was purely an administrator.) It is instructive to compare the two of them, because they represent two different generations of women. Nine years Albright's junior, Mathews seemed less inhibited about arguing with the men. The only child of the historian Barbara Tuchman, Mathews had been working all her adult life and took equality for granted. If anything, she says, she found it "an advantage" being a woman at the NSC. She certainly did not feel at all uncomfortable about speaking out at meetings, as Madeleine sometimes did. Mathews, who went on to head the Carnegie Endowment for International Peace, a leading Washington think tank, sees the difference in approach as partly generational. "The fifties were a rotten time" for a woman to come of age, she says. The other problem was that Madeleine had an "ill-defined" job. "She had little to do with the rest of us, and she had a boss who didn't understand the importance of what she was doing."

While Albright respected Mathews, who came to the NSC a year before her, she may have seen her as a negative role model. Mathews got caught up in the political maneuvering in the White House and came into conflict with Brzezinski, who was pushing for a more confrontational line vis-à-vis the Soviet Union. As a result, Mathews resigned in July 1979. Her departure was an object lesson in the dangers of staking out an exposed position.

If Madeleine had a real area of expertise, it was the domestic dimension of foreign policy. Working with Congress made her understand better than anyone else on the NSC the meaning of House Speaker Tip O'Neill's dictum that "all politics is local." There were trade-offs everywhere. When the administration agreed to a major arms sale program to Saudi Arabia and other U.S. allies in the Middle East, the Jewish community started howling. A promise to lift the embargo on arms sales to Turkey had Greek-Americans descending on the White House by the coachload. "We had two hundred Greeks in the East Room, all boiling mad," Beckel recalls with a shudder. Madeleine had an intuitive sense of when to negotiate and when to stand firm. Knowing that the Greek-American vote was largely confined to states like New Jersey, she had argued against providing the Greeks with a forum to vent their grievances in front of the president. "You don't know Greeks, I know Greeks," she told Beckel. She was overruled, but the angry scenes in the State Dining Room proved her right.

The issue that consumed most of Madeleine's time was the effort to persuade the Senate to ratify a follow-up to the 1972 SALT nuclear arms limitation treaty with the Soviet Union. During a period when the Kremlin was flexing its muscles in the Third World, and U.S.-Soviet relations were even more strained than usual, curbing the arms race was one of the few remaining areas of superpower cooperation. Without arms control, there would be little left of the Nixon-era policy of détente. The SALT II treaty was a high priority for Carter, who saw reducing the risk of nuclear war as part of his historical legacy, but it was exceedingly unpopular with conservatives. Mustering the necessary two-thirds Senate majority for ratification was sure to prove very difficult, particularly with an election approaching.

Much of Madeleine's work on SALT consisted of drawing up long lists of senators and congressmen and dividing them into categories: "For," "Against," and "Undecided." Her remarks about the newly elected Republican senator from Maine, William S. Cohen, make interesting reading in light of the fact that they would become cabinet colleagues during the second Clinton administration. In one memo, she included the future secretary of defense in the "conservative, but some chance of working with them" column. "He is most unpredictable and when he was in the House he had a bad record of supporting the Administration on foreign policy issues," she added. In another memo, she noted that Cohen "is on Armed Services and has already begun arguing about SALT. He has an overestimation of his intellectual capabilities but is a clever self-promoter and will, therefore, be talking more than most. It would be useful to try to influence him."

Together with her colleagues from the congressional relations office, Madeleine kept track of the ratification debate and drafted memos for Carter and Brzezinski on how to sway members of the Senate. "Spent a large part of the day making calls to Members on SALT and working on briefings," she noted in a typical evening report to Brzezinski. "Despite the fact that we were not telling them much more than was in the papers, they were pleased to be called." The lobbying efforts reached a peak in May 1979 with a series of meetings in the Blue Room of the White House, with a dozen senators at a time seated in a large semicircle around the President. Madeleine sat at the back of the room, together with other White House staffers, noting the senators' objections to the treaty. Beckel recalls that "the most uncomfortable chairs" in the White House were used for these briefings in order to discourage the senators from staying too long and asking too many questions. Any momentum that there may have been in favor of SALT was soon lost, however, as a result of intelligence reports (later proved exaggerated) of a Soviet combat presence in Cuba.

In order to brief members of Congress on SALT, Madeleine had to bone up on the arcane vocabulary of arms control and targeting strategy. Along with other NSC staffers, she attended what was known as "SALT school." As a general rule, the more expert a senator felt himself to be on the subject, the more frustrating the conversation was likely to be. White House staffers used to dread briefings with Senator John Glenn because he was forever drawing comparisons with his own experiences as an astronaut. "He thought he knew all about trajectory and telemetry," said Beckel. "Madeleine's patience with him was unbelievable. I just wanted to say, 'Senator, this ain't Friendship Seven. This is a MIRVed, ten-warhead missile we're talking about.' Madeleine would just listen to him, and find a nice way of letting him know that he was wrong." (MIRV stands for "Multiple Independently Targetable Reentry Vehicle." A MIRVed missile is one with several nuclear warheads, each of which can be programmed to hit a different target.)

Despite growing evidence that SALT II was unwinnable, Madeleine maintained a facade of determined optimism. Her reports to Brzezinski were either neutral or upbeat. "To summarize, the opposition tried but did not lay a glove on us," she reported after Senate committee hearings in July 1979. A few weeks later, she reported that "the general mood of SALT proponents is optimistic but not over-confident." It was only *after* the administration was forced to withdraw the treaty from Senate consideration in January 1980, in the wake of the Soviet invasion of Afghanistan, that she gave voice to her doubts, telling Brzezinski "we did not have 67 votes *ever*—even at our best" and that "none of the Republican front-runners is for SALT." There is a whiff of opportunism about this belatedly blunt assessment. By this time, of course, the treaty was dead, and Brzezinski was opposed to any attempt to revive it.

The SALT debate was one occasion when Madeleine allowed her hopes to get the better of her usually acute political instincts. Her ally, Bob Beckel, believes she underestimated the political pressure on moderate Republicans like Howard Baker to vote against the treaty. "If I was going to fault Madeleine on anything during this period, it was that she was blindly optimistic about SALT," says Beckel. "Despite being a good politician, she could not understand how anybody could oppose [a treaty] that would limit strategic weapons. . . . She was not willing to be the bearer of bad news to Brzezinski. . . . This was one of the few times when she felt that the Hill was wrong, and she knew the issue better than they did. She really believed that we got a lot out of the Russians, which we did. She got real discouraged with the Hill. She felt that some people who had shown courage in the past were getting gutless."

While remaining loyal to Brzezinski, Madeleine maintained strong ties to her former mentor, Muskie. It was a difficult balancing act, as little love was lost between the two Poles. Despite a common ethnic heritage,

Brzezinski and Muskie were very different personalities with different views of how foreign policy should be conducted. A first-generation immigrant who fled Poland in 1939, Brzezinski took a much tougher line toward the Soviet Union than Muskie, who was born and brought up in the United States and did not have firsthand experience of Communist repression. "It never occurred to Muskie that he was an Eastern European," said his aide, Leon Billings. "He was a Maine Yankee who happened to be a Polish Catholic. Brzezinski was a Polish Catholic who happened to be in the United States." Although both men had superb intellects, Brzezinski was coldly analytic while Muskie was much more temperamental.

When Muskie was selected to lead a U.S. congressional delegation to China in November 1978, he invited Madeleine to go along. Although she had been working for Brzezinski for only several months, she jumped at the opportunity. In those days, China was still a mysterious, exotic country in the throes of a continuing revolution. The Maoist Gang of Four had been overthrown two years earlier, but great uncertainty still persisted over China's future direction. Despite Nixon's groundbreaking trip to Beijing in 1972, very few American politicians had set foot in the Middle Kingdom. Traveling to China was a bonding experience for the members of Muskie's delegation, which included ten members of Congress and their wives and five staff aides.

The trip left them brimming with impressions—mostly very superficial—about the lifestyle and political orientation of one-quarter of mankind. Muskie was staggered by the number of bicycles in China and the way "the bicycles overflow into the vehicle lanes, and the vehicles fend for themselves, high pitched horns constantly tooting, in the most reckless fashion I have ever seen." And then there were the people. "Simply unbelievable masses of people, all dressed in various shades of blue or gray Mao jackets. They were neat, hardworking, busy all the time, and obviously committed. We saw them building houses, building roads, building walls, irrigating fields, working the fields—in short, a nation of workers." "There doesn't seem to be any overt military fear or oppressive fear driving them onward," another member of the delegation, Senator Robert Packwood, confided to his diary. "There they all are in their blue tunic jackets, riding their black and blue bicycles, looking like great hordes of small ants, scurrying about the landscape." The Americans were struck by how primitive everything was. "Even the toilet is an essence of simplicity," marveled Packwood. "The plunger which releases the water is controlled by a straight rod in the center of the lid. You simply lift it about two inches, let the water run out and drop it, putting the stopper back over the hole."

The tour included meetings with Chinese officials, who kept warning of the common threat posed by Russia, and obligatory visits to tourist attractions like the Forbidden City and the Great Wall. Packwood was one of the few members of the delegation not to be impressed by these tourist sights, preferring to devote his attention to matters like plumbing. "C'mon, folks," he complained to his diary after a visit to an ancient Chinese mummy preserved in a sealed glass case. "We've got better things to do in China than see a two-thousand-year-old woman."

Having been given only a week's leave of absence by Brzezinski, Madeleine had to break away from the trip halfway through. She left Canton on a Saturday and was back at her desk in the White House the following Monday. The crisis of the day was the mass suicide of American cultists in Guyana and the murder of an American congressman who went to investigate. "No time for jetlag today," Madeleine memoed Brzezinski. "Am getting to know new Congressmen in an unfortunate way, as some call to find out if constituents' relatives are among dead. . . ."

Madeleine may not have seen all that much of China, but she saw a lot of some key members of Congress. She would form firm friendships with several of her traveling companions in China, including Senator Patrick Leahy of Vermont and Senator Richard B. Stone of Florida. They would accept her dinner invitations when others turned them down. The Great Wall turned out to be a great place to network. As Madeleine told Brzezinski, the relationships she forged on the trip proved "invaluable. . . . I got letters from those who went saying how glad they were I had gone along and how useful I was—you cannot beat that if you are in my business." The boss seemed less convinced of the value of foreign jaunts. When Muskie invited Madeleine to accompany him on a trip to Europe the following April, Brzezinski instructed her to decline.

• • •

Even though she worked at the White House, Madeleine was constantly looking for ways to be helpful to her former boss, Ed Muskie. She helped organize a series of meetings between Carter and Muskie, including a presidential drop-by on a "surprise" 65th birthday dinner for the senator in March 1979. A White House photograph captured her standing between the two of them in a green-blue dress, locked in an affectionate embrace with Muskie as the president grinned cheesily into the camera (page 246).

In May 1980, Muskie was appointed secretary of state following the resignation of Cyrus Vance over the failed U.S. mission to rescue the hostages in Iran. Suddenly Madeleine found herself playing the role of intermediary between the national security adviser and the secretary of state. It was a rocky relationship from the very beginning. Muskie believed that Vance had been the victim of bureaucratic sabotage by Brzezinski, and he was determined to shift power back from the National Security Council to the Department of State. At his swearing-in ceremony, Muskie depicted himself almost as the coequal of the president in matters of foreign policy. He even kidded Carter about his error-prone diplomacy, saying, "I'm not sure I'm comfortable that you and I will be making mistakes together, Mr. President." The president laughed, but reddened noticeably. "I will never forget the look on Carter's face," Madeleine said later.

Madeleine did her best to smooth things over between Muskie and the White House. NSC staffers credit her with orchestrating the first Muskie-Brzezinski meeting and their much-quoted one-liner to the press, "We will not be Poles apart." She repeatedly urged Brzezinski to defer to Muskie and "make him feel that he is number one." "She would make me understand that batting his arguments down in an NSC session and showing him to be wrong or ignorant was not the best way of getting him to change his mind," recalled Brzezinski.

The tensions between the two men came out into the open during the summer, when Muskie suspected that Brzezinski was cutting him out of the loop on a key national security decision. Odom and other NSC officials had been toiling away for years on a new targeting strategy for nuclear missiles that would get away from the traditional doctrine of

"Mutually Assured Destruction," appropriately abbreviated as "MAD." They were grappling with the possibility of a limited nuclear exchange short of apocalypse. The outcome of this policy review was the top-secret Presidential Directive 59, which emphasized the selection of specific military targets over the old notion of obliterating entire population centers like Moscow or Leningrad. The change in doctrine was a logical response to the growing size and sophistication of the nuclear arsenal of both superpowers. At the same time, the idea that nuclear war might be thinkable for the first time was shocking to many people. Muskie, however, was less concerned with the implications of the new strategy than the fact that he knew nothing about it.

The story that Carter had signed a new nuclear targeting strategy broke in the press on the last day of the Democratic Convention in New York, on the basis of NSC and Pentagon briefings. When Muskie picked up the paper the next day, he was furious. His aides immediately interpreted the affair as a power-grabbing move by Brzezinski. The national security adviser was trying to do to Muskie what he had already done to Vance. Muskie aides decided to strike back in the time-honored Washington fashion, by leaking to the press. A few days later, both *The New York Times* and the *The Washington Post* carried stories orchestrated by Muskie aide Leon Billings saying that the secretary of state had been kept in the dark. "We decided that Brzezinski had to be taken on publicly," said Billings. "We could not allow Muskie's integrity to be lost."

As relations between her two mentors deteriorated, Madeleine found herself caught in the middle. Once again, the key to survival was keeping her head down. Both sides appealed to her to act as a go-between, but she was most reluctant. When Billings asked her to help him sort out the mess, she told him she did not want to "get involved." "She managed to maintain her relationship with the Senator through all of that without injuring her relationship with Brzezinski," said Billings. "That was pretty skillful." Madeleine told other White House staffers that she felt "cornered." "I don't think she felt that either person was in the right," said Brzezinski aide Les Denend.

Looking back on the episode, Brzezinski concedes that Muskie had some reason to be upset but insists that the snub was not deliberate. He attributes the failure to inform Muskie of the signing of the Presidential

Directive to a "breakdown of communication" following Vance's resignation. "His complaint that he did not get the directive was absolutely true because it was top, top, top, top secret and the State Department was not the place to discuss who we are going to bomb and how." As for Madeleine, Brzezinski believes she sincerely tried to "smooth ruffled feathers." He recalls her saying that Billings was trying to push Muskie into a fight. Her advice, as it had been before, was to avoid confronting Muskie head-on. "He was very incendiary and temperamental. She said you can get your way just by schmoozing and massaging him a little bit."

Inevitably, the relentless pressures of life in the White House meant that Madeleine had less time for her family. Working for Muskie had been demanding enough, but she had made a point of getting home in time for dinner with the children. She would rarely stay to gossip with other staffers or drink with them in the Carroll Arms. She would arrive at the office between eight-thirty and nine A.M. and leave between six and seven P.M. "She had a very strong sense that she had to be home for the girls," said her colleague Anita Jensen. At the White House, her working day stretched out at both ends. She frequently ate breakfast in the White House Mess at seven A.M. and was not at home until eleven P.M. or even midnight.

The intense lifestyle took a toll on her marriage, even though everything was fine on the surface. Outwardly, Joe Albright was very supportive of his wife and seemed to take pride in her achievements. They both adored their children and worried about them constantly. In other ways, however, they were drifting away from each other. A friend who visited them at their farm in Virginia for one of their Sunday barbecues and tennis parties was left with a mental image of two people living in different worlds. While Madeleine was holding court at the swimming pool, surrounded by high-powered people like Brzezinski and Georgia senator Sam Nunn, Joe was by himself in the kitchen, fixing drinks. "Madeleine was making sure that everybody was having a good time," the friend recalls. "She was the center of attention, running the show by the pool, and Joe was in the kitchen, running that. It was a little poignant, a little sad. It was not a moral issue, just two people drifting apart."

While Madeleine's career finally seemed to be getting off the ground, Joe's career was sputtering. The scion of one of America's most successful newspaper families, he desperately wanted to prove his own worth rather than be known simply as the inheritor of someone else's fortune. His life-long dream of running his own newspaper had been shattered by his own professional shortcomings and the obduracy of his uncle, Harry Guggenheim. As both a reporter and an investigator for Senate committees, he had earned a reputation for a certain dogged persistence, but somehow he had never got the recognition he was striving for. "I was always a little nervous about his judgment," said Al From, his boss on Capitol Hill. "He could find things out, but I was not always sure that he knew what he had found."

Returning to journalism, Joe got a job in the Washington bureau of Cox newspapers, a regional chain that included the *Atlanta Constitution*. This put him in the middle of the journalistic pecking order, above the wire service reporters but below the reporters for the big newspapers and newsmagazines who consider themselves part of the opinion-making elite. He broke some memorable stories, including an exposé about lax security at U.S. nuclear installations, for which he won a Sigma Delta Chi award in 1978. But the top journalistic prizes, notably the Pulitzer, continued to elude him.

Not only was Madeleine's career beginning to eclipse his own, but Joe was having to make certain sacrifices to permit her to get ahead. When she joined the White House in 1978, Carter administration officials were determined to avoid anything that smacked of conflict of interest. They insisted that Joe promise not to cover the White House as a journalist and to make a full disclosure of his financial holdings. "I recognize that the insulating steps which each of you has agreed to take are significant and have been taken at considerable personal sacrifice," wrote White House Counsel Robert Lipshutz.

Joe Albright has refused to discuss his marriage with Madeleine, so it is difficult to know what was running through his mind during this period. His background and behavior, however, are consistent with someone experiencing a classic male mid-life crisis. He had recently turned forty; he was frustrated in his journalistic ambitions; his wife of twenty years was no longer there to support him in everything he did. For the first time in their life together, Madeleine now seemed to put her career ahead of his. "I think that Joe thought he was being outshone, that she was on the fast track and he was not," said Pie Friendly, whose husband Al worked next door to Madeleine. Whereas he had dreams of becoming a foreign correspondent and living in exotic places in Europe and Asia, her life revolved around Washington and Georgetown. Although they had the children in common—the twins were about to go to university, Katie was in high school—they spent a lot less time together.

On top of all this, a woman appeared in his life who was younger, prettier, and slimmer than Madeleine, had similar interests, and was ready to share in his journalistic adventures. Marcia Kunstel was a thirty-two-year-old reporter for the *Atlanta Journal*. In the summer of 1980, she was assigned to cover the political conventions in Detroit and New York (Joe covered the conventions for the rival *Atlanta Constitution*). Marcia was dark-haired and soft-spoken, with a shy, engaging smile and a less forceful personality than the new, successful Madeleine. In some ways, she was like the Madeleine Joe had first married. The campaign trail—a self-insulated little world where everybody lives on expense accounts hundreds of miles away from home—was an ideal place for romance to blossom.

Madeleine would later insist that she was totally unaware that Joe was conducting an affair with another woman. As far as she was concerned, everything was fine with her marriage. Writing in her Wellesley class record book in 1979, she painted a picture of happiness and fulfillment that many classmates might envy:

> I have been unbelievably lucky in the last twenty years—without sounding too much like Pollyanna—I am married to the same man I met while at Wellesley, I have three daughters—all of them relatively well put together . . . Joe is an investigative reporter—working for a chain of newspapers which owns the *Atlanta Constitution*—now well read in Washington. We have lived in Washington for the last ten years and believe that for us it is the best of all possible worlds.
>
> In terms of my career—all I can say is that my interests have finally come together. [At the NSC] I am able to combine my "foreign policy" background with my fascination for executive-legislative relations. On the negative side, my new job leaves little time for anything

else but family—so have not seen my friends as much as I would like. Also am not getting as much exercise as I should—therefore the perennial weight problem. My excuse is that I use up all my discipline working twelve hours a day. In re-reading this, I am afraid I sound a little too self-satisfied. Believe me—I don't think every thing I do every day is perfect—but I really am having a wonderful time . . . knock on wood!

Madeleine, Mandula, Anne, and Alice at the high school graduation of Katie Albright in 1985. *Courtesy of the Albright family.*

Defeat

In November 1980, Madeleine and Joe hosted their traditional election-night party, inviting their friends to watch the returns coming in from across the country and hopefully celebrate another Democratic victory. The party turned into a wake before it even had a chance to get started. By the time the guests began showing up at the Albrights' home in Georgetown, it was already clear that Jimmy Carter was headed for a humiliating defeat at the hands of the archconservative Ronald Reagan.

Rick Inderfurth, who had worked with Madeleine on the NSC, remembers showing up at the house soon after seven P.M., just as the first results were coming in. He went up to the second floor, where Zbigniew Brzezinski and other Democratic luminaries were gathered around the television set. "How are things going?" he asked cheerfully. "It's over," replied Brzezinski, as he rushed out the door to the White House.

Senior Carter administration officials had been aware of the certainty of a Reagan victory for several days, on the basis of confidential polling, but that did not make defeat any easier to swallow. For Madeleine and her friends, the 1980 election meant more than the simple loss of political power. The scale of the Republican landslide—victory in forty-four states plus control of the Senate for the first time since 1954—was a shattering repudiation of everything the Democrats stood for. "It seemed like the end of the world," recalled Jessica Mathews, Madeleine's old NSC colleague. "The Reagan election was a helluva wake-up call to the Democrats," said Al Friendly, Brzezinski's press spokesman. "The first Reagan term was more of an upset to Washington mores than the first Eisenhower term. For anyone who grew up with the consequences of the New Deal, the Reagan administration brought a profound challenge. They were an appalling crowd, all those hard ladies in fur coats. Fighting them was cultural as much as ideological."

A Democratic loyalist to the core, Madeleine took the defeat even more personally than many of her colleagues. "We all expected the Reagan victory, but we were all sick by it," said Brzezinski aide Christine Dodson. "Madeleine probably felt it much more than I did. She was always partisan." Robert DuPont, a psychiatrist friend from Denver, says there was never any question with Madeleine "who were the good guys and who were the bad guys."

On the last day of the Carter presidency—January 20, 1981— Madeleine and Christine hung around the White House tidying up their offices and waiting for their successors to take over. The Reaganites never showed up. "They decided there was nothing they could learn from us," said Dodson, who was responsible for the orderly transfer of top-secret documents. Madeleine finally persuaded her friend "to forget these people" and take part in a farewell ceremony for Carter. They locked the documents in a filing cabinet, jumped into Madeleine's battered red station wagon, and drove out to Andrews Air Force Base. They got there just in time to see Carter receiving an emotional embrace from the wife of one of the American hostages in Iran. She had just heard that the plane carrying her husband and fifty-one other American hostages had been permitted to leave Teheran. The Iranians had waited until Carter was out of office before ending the crisis that had blighted his presidency.

As Carter flew back to Georgia on Air Force One, the two women drove to a fish restaurant in Silver Spring, Maryland, for a late lunch. Freed from the burdens of office, they spent hours talking about their lives and future plans. At one point, Madeleine said to her friend, "The only thing I am sorry about in our relationship is that you don't have the same Cinderella marriage I do."

. . .

Carter's defeat left Madeleine without a job. This problem was solved in the short term when Brzezinski invited her to work with him on his memoirs. He gave her the task of combing through his 2,500-page private White House diary and marking passages that were too sensitive to use, for either privacy or national security reasons. Halfway through this project, she won a fellowship from the Woodrow Wilson Center for Scholars in Washington to study the role of the press in the Solidarity movement in Poland. She taught herself Polish—her third Slavic language after Czech and Russian—and began combing through stacks of Polish newspapers, from the turgid Communist party daily *Tribuna Ludu* to underground Solidarity journals calling for the dismantling of the Communist state.

The most exciting part of the research came in November 1981, during a two-week trip to Poland, then in the throes of a climactic showdown between Solidarity and the Communist authorities. Madeleine interviewed scores of Polish editors and journalists and traveled to the steel-mining town of Nova Huta, in southern Poland, to see Solidarity leader Lech Wałęsa attempting to defuse a strike. As she later described the scene, the auditorium was "packed shoulder to shoulder with several thousand workers, many wearing red-and-white Solidarity baseball caps." She was struck by the former electrician's "rapid-burst, single-pitch delivery" and his charismatic hold over the workers. Wałęsa had a unique knack for firing his supporters up and making them believe that they had won something, even as he pulled them back from the brink. It was a lesson in the power of popular oratory that Madeleine never forgot. After fifty minutes of question and answer, the strike fever began to cool, and Wałęsa received a standing ovation from the workers.

Back in Washington, Joe was being more than usually solicitous of his wife. He bought her a low-slung Datsun sports car and lost no opportunity to praise her to her friends. Christine Dodson remembers an incident in late November 1981, soon after she returned home from Poland, when she and Madeleine went to meet Joe at the airport. As they were driving back into town, Joe kept kissing and hugging Madeleine, who was driving, and saying how wonderful it was to have her back home. "He couldn't keep his hands off her," says Dodson, who was concerned that they would have an accident.

A similar incident occurred a few weeks later with Marcia Burick, who had accompanied the Albrights on their East European trip in 1967. She and a friend were having brunch at the Four Seasons in Georgetown with Joe and Madeleine, who was full of impressions from Poland about the conflict between Solidarity and the Communist regime. It was the morning of Sunday, December 13, a few hours after General Wojciech Jaruzelski declared martial law, putting an end to Eastern Europe's most hopeful experiment in democracy since the "Prague Spring." As Burick recalls the occasion, Joe kept making comments like, "Madeleine met so many people in Poland, isn't she wonderful?" His attention was so flattering that Burick, who had just gone through a painful divorce of her own, exclaimed out loud, "Imagine having a man who is so proud of his wife."

In retrospect, it seems likely that Joe was making an exaggerated attempt to make up for his infidelity to Madeleine, even as he felt his marriage was falling apart. His request for a divorce came as a huge shock to Madeleine and her friends. Even so, there were warning signals for those who chose to look for them. Sheppie Abramowitz, Madeleine's friend from the 1972 Muskie campaign, remembers a "very, very strained dinner" with the Albrights in the fall of 1981. Her husband Mort wondered if Joe was having a drinking problem. When Sheppie asked Madeleine what was the matter, she did not want to talk about it.

The bottom fell out of Madeleine's fairy-tale world on January 13, 1982, at eight o'clock in the morning. As she later recalled the scene, Joe sat down with her in the living room of their Georgetown home and blurted out, "This marriage is dead and I'm in love with someone else." A storm was raging outside. It was an apocalyptic day in Washington, one that would remain in her memory forever. That afternoon, an ice-coated Air Florida jet that had just taken off from Washington National Airport crashed into the nearby Potomac River after striking the 14th Street Bridge. Minutes later, a Metro train went off the rails, killing three people.

Joe's announcement stunned and bewildered Madeleine. She had been brought up in a particularly close-knit family by parents for whom divorce was unthinkable. Most of her friends were still happily married. In Joe's family, of course, divorce was commonplace. His parents, grandparents, sister, and numerous uncles and aunts had all gone through at least one marriage, sometimes two or three. But Joe seemed different from his eccentric relatives. He was quieter, less flamboyant, more principled, more family-oriented.

Of the two of them, Madeleine had the stronger, more impulsive personality and was used to getting her way. "She was always a winner," said Danielle Gardner. "Everything else had gone right for her. Her career was going fine, her Ph.D. had come in, she had got a dream job. She graduated from one of the top women's colleges. She caught an intelligent man from a very good family with money. They had wonderful children, a fabulous house . . . Whatever happened, some way, she won. Everything. This was the first defeat of her life, a man leaving her and she didn't know why." Whatever her problems with Joe, Madeleine had no intention of leaving him. Accustomed as she was to taking the lead in her marriage, it does not seem to have occurred to her that *he* might walk out on *her*. "She probably didn't think that he would ever make such a move," says her friend Bitsy Folger. "I can imagine she thought he was faithfully part of her world."

Like many people, Madeleine may have underestimated the stubborn streak in her husband's character and the degree to which he was determined to pursue his own dreams. His outer reserve hid a complex jumble of idealism, insecurity, and ambition. Once Joe made up his mind about something, it was difficult to talk him out of it.

Her friends began to worry about her. That summer, Christine Dodson invited Madeleine to visit her at her vacation home on the Greek island of Lésvos in the Aegean Sea, opposite the Turkish coast. She asked a friend to pick Madeleine up at Athens Airport, but the friend had difficulty recognizing her from Dodson's description. "She was in one of her thin phases, gaunt actually," Dodson said later. "She was wearing a white dress, with this white face and blond hair." When she finally arrived on the island, Madeleine was so exhausted that she spent most of her time sleeping on a mattress on the balcony overlooking the sea. During her waking hours, she and Dodson would tan themselves, go swimming, and hold endless discussions about their lives.

After she got over her initial shock, and there was no longer any reason for secrecy, Madeleine became hopping mad. "She was absolutely wiped out, just totally bamboozled," said Pie Friendly, who attempted to comfort her during this period. "It knocked her for a total and complete loop. She was devastated. . . . She walked around looking like the wrath of God." Even peripheral friends and acquaintances were dragged into the drama. "She was a woman scorned," said Estelle Lavoie, who had worked under Madeleine in Muskie's Senate office. "It was not just another woman, it was a much younger woman, and that added salt to the wound. She was furious. She kept on saying, 'Just go ahead, just go.' "

Having made the break, Joe bent over backward to soften the blow by agreeing to give Madeleine a generous financial settlement out of his own family inheritance. He also set up generous trust funds for the children. Madeleine's lifestyle would in no way be cramped by the divorce. Under the terms of the divorce settlement, she got the house in Georgetown, the 370-acre farm near Dulles Airport in Virginia, and a large stock portfolio. She even kept several canvases painted by Joe's celebrated stepfather, Ivan Albright.

By 1993, the year that Madeleine was appointed ambassador to the United Nations, her portfolio would have a market value of $3.5 million. It included stocks in many of America's leading companies, such as Chevron and Walt Disney, but the crown jewel was 11,000 shares of the Chicago Tribune Company, which had been in Joe's family for five generations. (Madeleine sold the Tribune Co. stocks for more than $600,000 when she joined the Clinton administration and converted the portfolio into a blind trust.) The Georgetown house had an assessed market value in 1996 of $809,000, and the farm was valued at more than $1.4 million. By the time Madeleine became secretary of state in 1997, it is likely that her net worth approached $10 million, in view of the run-up in stocks and property values.

By December, everything was finalized. Shortly before Christmas Joe wrote to Senator Muskie to tell him "the sad news that Madeleine and I are being divorced." He told Muskie that he would soon be leaving for Italy to take up a new post as chief foreign correspondent of Cox newspapers. "There isn't much I can say except that it has happened, it is regrettable, and the decision is final," his letter continued. "One factor I haven't mentioned is that I have been seeing another woman, Marcia Kunstel, who is a reporter on the *Atlanta Constitution* down in Atlanta. She has resigned from the paper and will be coming with me to Rome to work as a freelancer. We expect to be married next summer. You should also know that Madeleine has placed considerable emphasis on her desire for me to get out of Washington if I was to be living with Marcia. As things worked out, the Rome job has accomplished that." The divorce came through on the last day of January 1983.

Making Joe part with a large chunk of his money and insisting that he leave town were two ways Madeleine could get back at him for the pain he had put her through. Another was her own career. For the first time in her life, she was free to focus on herself.

Madeleine was forty-five years old when she was divorced. She had been married for twenty-three years. Until she went to college, she had lived with her parents. Now, for the first time in her life, she suddenly found herself almost totally independent. "It was a shock," she says now. "I had never lived by myself. [After college], I stayed in the dormitory with my roommate for the two days between graduation and getting married."

In hindsight, the divorce gave Madeleine both the motive and opportunity to focus her considerable energy on reaching the top. Without a husband to look after or slow her down, and with her children either at college or about to go to college, she finally had the time and freedom to fulfill her ambitions. Had it not been for the divorce, "I would not be sitting here," she says bluntly, warming herself by a roaring fire in the office of the secretary of state. "It was a huge turning point."

Her friends agree. "It's a normal psychological reaction," says Madeleine's friend from Beauvoir, Sheppie Abramowitz. "If your husband goes off with a younger woman, you want to show that you can succeed on your own." Danielle Gardner makes a similar point. "How does a woman scorned react? She says, 'OK, I'm going to show you.' That was part of what propelled her."

"I have no doubt that her divorce was the turning point in her life," says Jessica Mathews, who worked with Madeleine at the NSC. For the previous twenty years, Madeleine's career had taken second place to her marriage. All of a sudden that trade-off seemed senseless. Furthermore, argues Mathews, Madeleine could now "rise as high as she wanted without it being a source of friction with her husband."

Christine Dodson, who was as close to Madeleine as anyone during this period, agrees that her friend "changed dramatically" in the years after her divorce. Her style was no longer cramped by Joe's more reserved and introspective personality. "She became much more forward, much more articulate, much noisier than when she was married." And then there was the simple question of time and energy. "The divorce gave her time to pursue her career. If Joe had not asked her for a divorce, I am sure she would not have become secretary of state. Instead, she would have been a happy wife, a happy mother."

In the fall of 1982, just as she hit rock bottom emotionally, Madeleine received the offer of a job at Georgetown University. A Jesuit university steeped in tradition, Georgetown was under pressure to recruit more women and provide successful role models for women students. By 1982, roughly half the students at the Georgetown University School for Foreign Service were women, but there were hardly any women professors. The Donner Foundation offered funds for a new program designed to help women make careers in diplomacy. It was a temporary position, without full academic tenure, but it offered Madeleine a professional haven.

"From my point of view, Madeleine was perfect," said Putnam Ebinger, a former associate dean of the foreign service school. "We were getting more and more women students at both graduate and undergraduate level. We wanted someone who could not only teach, but who could also help women make choices about their professional lives." Madeleine's practical experience both on Capitol Hill and in the White House made her very attractive to the selection committee. Zbigniew Brzezinski, who had hired Madeleine to sort through his papers, offered a glowing testimonial.

Madeleine told Brzezinski that the time had come for her "to move on and stand on my own feet" rather than remain an extension of him. "I have to develop my own profile, my own personality." Looking back at this episode, Brzezinski believes that his former protégé had already set

her sights on a top foreign policy position in a future Democratic administration. "She was gunning for secretary of state since 1982, or at least
1984," he says.

Precisely how early Madeleine began seriously nurturing an ambition
to become secretary of state is a matter of dispute. Christine Dodson
insists that, in the early eighties at least, such ambitions were no more
than an idle daydream. "She may have wanted to be whatever, but she
didn't think there was much chance of achieving anything. The question
is what her expectations were. She didn't think in grandiose terms at all."
Another friend, Doug Bennet, who had known her since the Muskie days,
agrees. "It is important to remember how vulnerable she was," he says.
"Her career up until then was hardly illustrious. At its best, it was the
'perfect staffer.' At its worst, it was the beneficiary of available part-time
employment. I would be very surprised if she was seriously talking about
becoming secretary of state at this point."

To a large extent, these differing assessments reflect the different sides
of Madeleine's personality. One Madeleine is loyal to a fault, extremely
eager to please, and constantly looking for reassurance from those around
her. The other Madeleine is determined and assertive, brushing aside anybody who disagrees with her, and focusing relentlessly on the goals she
has set for herself. The overall result is a seemingly contradictory mix of
insecurity and assertiveness, vulnerability and determination, pleasantness and steeliness, disorganization and single-mindedness. In reality, the
two sides of her personality are inextricably linked. Because she felt insecure and vulnerable, she redoubled her quest to succeed.

At different times, different people have been struck by different
aspects of Madeleine's character. During the early years of her marriage
and career, she took care to hide her steely side behind a pleasant facade.
But "the lion in her," in the phrase of her Carter administration colleague
Bob Beckel, was always there, and she would occasionally emit a distinctive roar. In recent years, the more assertive side of her personality has
gradually come to the fore. At the same time, the vulnerable side has
never completely disappeared.

Particularly around the time of her divorce, when she reexamined herself and her life obsessively, Madeleine went through many moods and
phases. She veered between ambition and self-doubt. One day she would

dream big dreams, the next she would wonder if she was capable of achieving anything significant at all.

In the summer of 1984, Madeleine and her fellow members of the Class of '59 returned to Wellesley for their twenty-fifth reunion. The weather was blazingly hot, and most of the sessions were held on the lawn sloping down to Lake Waban. The microphones were not working properly, so even more time than usual was spent in intense private conversations.

It was difficult to believe that a quarter century had gone by since a member of Eisenhower's cabinet sent them out into the world with an injunction to focus their ambitions on raising the next generation. The changes that had taken place since Graduation Day were captured in a list of "appearances" and "disappearances" drawn up by class members. "Appearances" included microwave oven, husband helping, the Pill, non-smokers' rights, telephone answering machines, panty hose, blow-dryers, Pampers, bug zappers, seat belts, felt-tip pens, shrink-wrapped food, AIDS, single parenting, and women referring to themselves as Ms. Among the "disappearances": hats for women in church, fins on cars, Peck & Peck suits with matching hats for wearing on the train to Wellesley, dorm rooms without locks on doors, getting pinned, six-foot college scarves, manners, posture pictures, and premarital virginity.

At one level, the mood among the returning Class of '59 was self-congratulatory. "It was at the twenty-fifth reunion that I first looked around my classmates and said, 'What a powerful lot,' " recalls the feminist writer Pam Daniels. Not much had been expected of the class when they graduated, beyond becoming homemakers and teachers. Few of them had embarked on careers after leaving college, preferring instead to get married and raise a family. A quarter of a century later, more than 80 percent were working for a living, mostly full time. They had distinguished themselves in many fields, from politics to scholarship to law to journalism. (Relatively few had gone into business.) Many had waited until their thirties or forties to begin work. "I was surprised by the number of our classmates who had reinvented themselves in mid-life and how many had gone back to school to get new careers," said MacFarquhar, who organized a poll of the Class of '59.

On another level, some members of the class complained that there was a downside to their newfound success and independence. "It was an unhappy time for a lot of us," said Alice Moskowitz, who had worked on the *Wellesley College News* with Madeleine. "Life had not turned out the way we had been told. Many people were feeling that the rules we had been brought up to live by had not worked out for us." The implicit trade-off that Wellesley graduates had accepted back in 1959—I will subordinate my career to that of my husband in return for lifelong happiness and security—no longer seemed to apply. Although the divorce rate remained below the national average, it was significantly higher than it had been for previous generations of Wellesley women. You could play by the rules and make all the traditional sacrifices for your family and still end up divorced. A failed marriage was often one of the most powerful motivating forces for a successful career.

In some ways, Madeleine's zigzag career pattern was typical of many of her classmates. "It is great to be a middle-aged woman in the United States today," she wrote in the 1984 class yearbook. "Although we predated the women's movement, I am a major beneficiary of it. . . . I am now doing just what I prepared myself to do at Wellesley."

But there were disappointments, too. Five years after exulting in her good fortune at working for Jimmy Carter and being "married to the same man I met while at Wellesley," Madeleine listed the "lows" in her life: "Divorce and Ronald Reagan."

Madeleine and Geraldine Ferraro. Madeleine remained on good terms with Ferraro after the 1984 campaign and later appointed her to the UN Human Rights Commission. *State Department.*

Resurrection

A new man appeared in Madeleine's life soon after Joe moved out in the summer of 1982. An amiable Californian, Barry Carter taught law at Georgetown University. He shared her passion for politics and foreign policy and had been buzzing around the fringes of the national security establishment ever since graduating from Yale Law School in 1969. He married the daughter of the former secretary of defense, Robert S. McNamara, and got a job in the Pentagon as an analyst. Although he was a Democrat, he had worked for Henry Kissinger on arms control issues at the National Security Council while doing his military service. "It was either Kissinger or Vietnam," he said later.

Carter believes that he was first introduced to Madeleine by a mutual friend, Toby Gati, whose husband Charles had been a member of her Ph.D. thesis committee at Columbia. The Gatis were living in New York at the time, where Toby worked at the United Nations Association. When she came down to Washington for the annual UNA ball, she would stay at Carter's house on Dupont Circle and would occasionally invite her own friends over for drinks. By this time Carter was divorced, with no children of his own, and was looking for eligible women to date. Gati was struck by his "fatherly" instincts. Her young son loved Carter because he bought him presents and allowed him to play with his dumbwaiter. Later,

Carter would have a similar paternal relationship with Madeleine's children. He was four years younger than Madeleine.

"It was a good match, personality-wise. She would clearly have been
the dominant one," says Toby Gati. "Barry is a real homebody . . . the
kind of guy you would like to bring home to your mother." They were
compatible in another way as well. As a prominent fund-raiser who had
served in the Carter administration and was plugged into the Democratic
elite, Madeleine could smooth his entry into big-time Democratic politics. "I think he really cared for her, but politics was the glue," says Gati.
"They must have only talked about politics. It would have been 'Take out
the garbage and who is going to run the campaign?' "

Carter refuses to discuss the details of his romance with Madeleine
but says he was attracted by her "effervescence" and "rapier wit." "She can
cut to the core of something with a comment. Discussing almost any issue
with Madeleine is fun, intellectually interesting. I like smart, fast, fun
people, and Madeleine was clearly that." An accomplished linguist herself, she would sometimes kid him for his lack of language ability and
poor pronunciation. "I speak your native tongue better than you do," she
joked. "Jesus, you really know how to put someone in his place," he
would respond feebly.

A few weeks after their initial meeting, Carter invited Madeleine to
dinner at Nora's, a fashionable restaurant near his house known for its
upscale organic food. She then invited him to a $1,000-a-plate dinner
that she was hosting for Walter Mondale, Carter's former vice president,
who was the leading Democratic candidate for the 1984 presidential election. The dinner took place at her Georgetown home and brought
together many of her wealthy Democrat friends from her Muskie days and
the Mondale crowd from Cleveland Park, home of many Washington liberals. Once again, Madeleine had the political intuition to support a campaign while it was still in its formative stages, at a time when her
contribution would be most appreciated. Federal Election Commission
records list her as the second contributor to the "Mondale for President
Committee" in November 1982, two years before the election. The only
earlier contributor was the campaign treasurer.

Mondale gave a witty, self-deprecating speech. Carter remembers a
cameo appearance by Joe right at the end of the dinner. He had taken his
three daughters out for the evening and was bringing them home. The

divorce came through a few weeks later. By the spring of 1983, Barry and Madeleine were spending much of their time together, and Barry had become a regular visitor to the 34th Street house. By this time, Joe was in Italy with his fiancée, Marcia Kunstel.

Although Madeleine had an offer to work for Mondale, she already had commitments to Georgetown University and was unable to devote herself full time to the campaign. Furthermore, she was worried about her youngest daughter, Katie, who was only fifteen and a sophomore at the National Cathedral School in Washington. "I used to wander around the house paralyzed with fear that she was out too late," she later recalled. "I worried if [Katie] would come home, if she was doing her homework, if she would get into college." The twins, Anne and Alice, were in their senior year at Dartmouth and Williams, respectively. "I bet she knew every night where her daughters were," said Carter. Madeleine's concern for her daughters is reminiscent of the way in which her own parents constantly fretted over her and her siblings.

Carter became very fond of the Albright girls and tried his best to make himself one of the family. That summer, he took Madeleine and her daughters on a white-water canoe trip in northern Maine. A private seaplane deposited the party and their canoes on the glassy surface of Umsaskis Lake, in a natural wilderness of fir and cedar. They spent the next three days canoeing the rapids of the Allagash River and camping on its banks. Spurred on by Carter's interest in her and the trauma of Joe's walkout, Madeleine was making one of her recurrent efforts to lose weight. Back home in Washington, she began swimming laps at Georgetown University.

Instead of working full time for Mondale, Madeleine gave a series of dinners at her home, inviting Democratic luminaries to discuss topical foreign policy issues. Up to sixteen people could fit comfortably around her dining room table. The hostess would sit at the head of the table, moderating the discussion but rarely taking firm positions herself. The guests, who included strong personalities like Richard Holbrooke and Robert Hunter, competed with one another to display their brilliance. "There was a little bit of jockeying. . . . These are smart people with elbows," says Carter, who was a regular invitee. The food, which was prepared by the housekeeper, was generally something forgettable like beef stew and rice washed down with what Carter describes as "an okay wine."

Each dinner was devoted to a different theme, perhaps Asia one night, arms control the next. Madeleine knew all the different foreign policy crowds. Another venue for foreign policy discussions was Mondale's law firm on M Street, where many of the same people would meet over coffee and croissants.

Since Barry Carter had more time on his hands than Madeleine— classes at Georgetown law school end early—it was he who joined the Mondale campaign first. He rushed around the country with the candidate on the primary trail, while she provided backup in Washington. One of the key tasks of a foreign policy adviser during a presidential campaign is to gain the support of one's fellow pundits by flattering them and holding out the carrot of political patronage. Madeleine proved very good at this. "The goal is to keep the pundit class busy so they won't write nasty op-ed pieces," says Janne Nolan, an arms control expert who worked for the rival Gary Hart campaign. "One of Madeleine's charms is that she could take thirty pages on the Chemical Weapons Treaty and say to the academic writing it, 'Please make sure that your home number is on this in case the candidate needs to reach you over the weekend.'"

Madeleine was also good at overcoming the huge disconnect between the foreign policy wonks who gathered around her Georgetown dinner table and the grassroots activists who actually run political campaigns. The need for plain speaking was driven home to her at a platform committee meeting that took place in a Washington hotel shortly before the 1984 Democratic convention. Gary Hart was trying to find wedge issues to divide the Mondale delegates, who were being whipped into shape by a rough-and-tumble street pol named Paul Tully. His proposal for a nuclear freeze was one such wedge issue. Madeleine and Barry tried to educate the delegates on the arguments for and against various types of nuclear freeze. Finally, Tully lost his patience. "My people aren't academics," he told them. "You have to tell them how to vote, for or against." He instructed the two foreign policy experts to signal which way the delegates were meant to vote with a simple thumbs-up or thumbs-down. Once they had delivered their verdict, the burly Tully would see to it that the delegates voted the proper way.

It was understood that Madeleine would join the Mondale campaign after the Democratic convention in July, but she did not know what position she would get.

. . .

Madeleine watched the nomination of Geraldine Ferraro as the Democratic candidate for vice president of the United States from the floor of the convention center in San Francisco. Barry Carter was by her side, as the delegates erupted into rhythmic chants of "Gerr-eee" "Gerr-eee" and the band played "The Lady Is a Champ" and "New York, New York." It was one of those defining moments in American politics when nothing is quite the same afterward. Ferraro was the first woman ever to be nominated to a presidential election ticket by a major political party, and her breakthrough was widely seen as a huge symbolic advance for all American women. "The mood was so electric that just being female felt terrific," wrote Maureen Dowd, who was covering the convention for The New York Times.

A three-time congresswoman from the New York borough of Queens, the forty-nine-year-old Ferraro was an inspired choice in many ways. She was tough, sassy, and had a special way of connecting with crowds. Her candidacy gave the Democratic ticket overnight excitement. But she had one glaring weakness: She knew very little about foreign policy. For a woman aspiring to a job that was just a heartbeat away from the presidency, this was a major shortcoming. Mondale aides recognized immediately that Ferraro would need someone to guide her through the national security minefield. They proposed she get a series of in-depth briefings from their own experts.

A week after the convention, Madeleine and Barry flew to New York to begin inducting Ferraro in the mysteries of throw weight and the MX missile. The sessions took place over the course of a weekend in Ferraro's Queens home in Forest Hills. They stayed in a local motel, braving the scrum of reporters and secret servicemen who were camped perpetually around the house. They sat down together in a little study off the living room. "It was very informal," recalled Carter. "Gerry's kids would come in and out, and she would make them lunch. We would eat lunch there too, peanut butter and jelly sandwiches or turkey sandwiches." Madeleine concentrated on broad foreign policy issues, while Barry focused on military matters. Ferraro had a cassette recorder and diligently recorded the seminars. "Madeleine was very good. She was able to take stuff and put it in simple language, which I was able to absorb and articulate," recalls

Ferraro. At night, she replayed the conversations while soaking luxuriously in the bathtub.

"Who's in there with you?" her husband John would call through the
bathroom door.

"Oh, just Barry Carter."

Albright and Ferraro quickly established a personal rapport. They
found they had a lot in common, beyond their love of politics. They were
both wealthy women, from immigrant families, of roughly the same age.
(Ferraro is two years older than Madeleine.) They had both embarked on
careers in middle age. They each had three children, either in college or
soon to go to college. They even had a Roman Catholic background in
common. According to Barry Carter, it became "obvious" by the end of
that first weekend that Madeleine would be traveling with the candidate.

Since Madeleine still had teaching commitments at Georgetown University, she and Barry agreed on a tag-team approach. She would join Ferraro on the road for most of the week but would be back in Washington
on Thursdays for her weekly undergraduate seminar in the "U.S. foreign
policy process." He would look after things in Washington but would
take Madeleine's place on the campaign plane on her days off. The logis-
tics were nightmarish, but somehow they made it work. One of Ferraro's
abiding images from the period is of Madeleine commuting back and
forth between Washington and the traveling campaign. She recalls looking out of the plane window in "some very flat place," seeing Madeleine
standing all alone on the tarmac with her suitcase and her raincoat,
and asking, "How in God's name is she ever going to get back home
from here?"

The atmosphere on the plane was a mixture of summer camp and
traveling circus. Vice presidential campaigns are generally more relaxed
than presidential campaigns because the stakes are not quite as high. This
one was particularly exuberant. Ferraro liked joking around with her aides
and took over the role of den mother and tour leader, referring to her staff
as "happy campers." Ferraro staffers prided themselves on their esprit de
corps. They joined reporters in an impromptu conga line down the aisle of
the plane, joked around with Groucho Marx masks, and spent one flight
dancing to the sounds of Motown music. Willie Nelson's "On the Road
Again" became a campaign theme song. When an anonymous Mondale

aide was quoted in the newspapers as saying that defeat was inevitable, the Ferraro camp had T-shirts printed up with the slogan "We will take to the hills and mount a guerrilla campaign."

For the reporters seated at the back of the plane, the big issue was whether or not Ferraro had what it takes to push the nuclear button. The Cold War was still raging, and the United States and the Soviet Union had tens of thousands of nuclear weapons aimed at each other, so this was not an idle question. But the fact that Ferraro was a woman and was running against George Bush, a World War II veteran and former director of the CIA, made it even more difficult for her to establish her credibility. "The reporters decided that foreign policy was the issue on which she would rise or fall," says Francis O'Brien, Ferraro's press secretary. The Ferraro staff began to think of the reporters as jackals, waiting to pounce on the smallest mistake. They needed a foreign policy expert on the plane at all times to make sure that the candidate was up-to-date on all the issues and clean up after her, if necessary.

For the most part, Ferraro avoided the obvious traps. Her biggest gaffe came early in the campaign when she confused a promise of "No First Use" of nuclear weapons with the doctrine of "No First Strike." Although they sound much the same to a layman, the two terms mean different things. "No First Strike" referred to a massive preemptive strike against the rival superpower, a pledge that most American politicians were happy to give. The same was not true of "No First Use," which would commit the United States to rule out the use of tactical nuclear weapons to counter, say, a Soviet conventional attack on Western Europe.

When Ferraro made mistakes, her aides generally preferred dealing with Madeleine than Barry. She was more politically astute and had a knack for sensing and deflecting trouble. "She was always very smart politically," said O'Brien, who frequently sat next to Madeleine on the campaign plane, a couple of rows behind the candidate. "She understood the substance, but she also understood the politics."

In fact, Madeleine was more than just a foreign policy adviser to Ferraro. She was also a soul mate who could be relied upon to bolster Ferraro's spirits when things were going badly, notably when she was under attack over her husband's tangled finances. They became "very close friends" during the campaign, according to Ferraro. "She was probably the person

I confided in most on that plane." They spent hours talking about their lives and their families. Ferraro believes that the intense campaign atmosphere helped Madeleine overcome the pain of her divorce the previous year. "Madeleine was no longer this woman whose husband had taken off on her. Nobody looked at her as the wife or divorced wife of somebody but as Madeleine Albright the expert, a person who was fun to be with. In a way, it liberated her."

In return, Madeleine was fiercely loyal to Ferraro, just as she had been loyal to Muskie and Brzezinski. The way the press kept hammering away at the nuclear button question irritated her. It smacked of double standards. In her view, they were beating up on Ferraro *because* she was a woman. She was particularly furious with Ted Koppel of ABC, when he spent an entire *Nightline* program grilling Ferraro about her views on nuclear disarmament and questioned her command of the facts. "She was a very unhappy woman," recalls Ferraro. The incident continued to rankle with Madeleine. A few months later, after the election, Koppel was addressing a seminar at Georgetown University on the role of the media in foreign policy. Madeleine, who was sitting in the front row, accused Koppel of "doing a number" on Ferraro during the *Nightline* interview.

For a long time, Madeleine clung to the hope that hordes of angry female voters would make the decisive difference by casting their votes for the Ferraro-Mondale ticket. She called it "the X Factor." She imagined a woman whose husband came down to breakfast every day complaining that his collar was dirty, his shoes needed fixing, and that he needed dinner at six o'clock because he wanted to go out bowling with the boys. He would then go off to work while she would sit at home thinking, "Goddamn that X!" The campaign had already been getting letters from such people, and Madeleine hoped that the effect would be magnified a millionfold on election day when women realized the power that was in their hands. It was a kind of "soccer mom" theory of American politics ten years before it became fashionable. "Madeleine talked the gender gap way before people had heard of it," said Bob Beckel, Mondale's deputy campaign manager. "She was one of the big proponents of the idea that there was a big woman's vote out there and that, if we broke the glass ceiling, we could get the vote."

The "X factor" turned out to be wishful thinking, at least in the 1984 campaign. The gender gap had no effect on the outcome. Even though women were cooler than men toward Reagan, they still voted for him by a margin of 54–46. A poll for *The New York Times* suggested that the net benefit to Mondale of adding a woman to the ticket was a statistically negligible 0.8 percent.

The Ferraro campaign put up a brave front to the end, despite total exhaustion and the looming prospect of near-certain defeat. On Election Day, everybody gathered at the New York Hilton. Madeleine had been traveling with Ferraro. The other members of the foreign policy team, including Barry Carter, all flew up from Washington. They had been given a choice of attending the election-night party with Mondale in Minnesota or Ferraro in New York. "It was no choice," joked Richard Betts, an arms-control expert. "We knew that if we went to Minnesota, the party would be over before it started because of the time difference. I wanted a few drinks under my belt before the result was confirmed." On the way up, the staff rehearsed a ditty with the refrain "No First Strike, No First Use," which they performed in front of Madeleine and Barry at the hotel. "It was a parody of all the nightmares we had been through, and the good times too," recalled Nancy Soderberg, a former student of Madeleine's at Georgetown who had joined the campaign as an intern.

Despite the magnitude of the defeat, Ferraro managed to claim a victory of sorts. The very fact that she had run for vice president, she told her supporters in a midnight concession speech at the Hilton, meant that "women will never again be second-class citizens." Campaign manager John Sasso told reporters, "Women will shoot higher because of her." At the very least, Ferraro had demonstrated that a woman can withstand the intense pressure of a presidential campaign. During 118 days of barnstorming around the country, she had transformed herself from a virtually unknown three-term congresswoman from Queens to a charismatic national figure capable of attracting and enthusing huge crowds.

The lessons of Ferraro's self-transformation were not lost on Madeleine, who watched it happen up close. If Ferraro could do it, why not she?

The romance between Madeleine and Barry Carter ended soon after the campaign when he told her that he wanted children. Since he was childless and four years younger than Madeleine, this was reasonable enough from his point of view. But it did not appeal to Madeleine, who was nearly forty-nine and already had three children. Some of Madeleine's friends felt that Carter had ridden upward on her coattails and then presented her with an impossible proposition. "She was not going to tie herself down with more children," said a former confidante, Pie Friendly. "To be shafted by these two men really devastated her." Madeleine says that her friendship with Carter was a "nice relationship" and she had no hard feelings about the way it ended. "He is a nice person. He wanted to have children. I had already had them." Carter, who has since remarried, says he has remained on good terms with Madeleine, although they rarely see each other these days.

By contrast, Madeleine's friendship with Ferraro deepened after the campaign. Over the years, they went to health spas together, took holidays together, visited each other's homes, and attended the weddings of each other's children. In the summer of 1985, Ferraro invited Madeleine to stay at her beach house on Fire Island. While she was there, Gerry got a telephone call at two in the morning saying that her mother had been taken to a hospital unable to breathe. Madeleine insisted on accompanying her to the hospital in the middle of the night, leaving her husband, John, to look after the children.

The following October, Madeleine accompanied Ferraro on a trip to Moscow, the first visit by either of them to the rival superpower. Mikhail Gorbachev had just become the Soviet leader following a succession of geriatrics, but the Communist system was still well in place. With another Ferraro aide, Adi Guttag, they stayed in the National Hotel facing the redbrick walls of the Kremlin, where Vladimir Lenin had resided immediately after the 1917 Bolshevik Revolution. "It was the nicest hotel in Moscow, and it was terrible," recalls Ferraro. The two aides, Madeleine and Adi, shared a room, while Ferraro had a grander room on another floor. The three women were on edge throughout their stay, convinced that their rooms were bugged by the KGB and paranoid about being followed.

A New York rabbi had asked Ferraro to take some prayer books and pills to the family of a prominent Jewish refusenik, Josef Begun, who was in prison. Not wanting to phone the family from their hotel room, they went out into the street, where all three of them crammed into a tiny telephone booth. "It was surreal," laughs Guttag. "We were three foolish

American women who thought we were sneaking away to make a phone call." The next evening, they took a cab through the dreary, ill-lit streets of Moscow to an apartment bloc on the outskirts of the city, where they met Begun's family. They went ahead with the visit despite being told that other Americans had been roughed up by the police for visiting the Beguns. "It was kind of hairy, but Madeleine was game," recalls Ferraro.

Madeleine was diffident about using her Russian, as she had been about using her Czech while in Czechoslovakia twenty years earlier. "I think she felt a little rusty," says Guttag. But when an interpreter made a mistake, she was quick to point it out.

During the trip, they took a train to Leningrad to visit the fabulous tsarist palaces and museums in the city founded by Peter the Great as his "window on the West." Like many travelers from the West, they were struck by how dilapidated everything was. "It was like going back into a time warp," says Guttag. "We would go into department stores and see racks and racks of shoes, but they were all the same shoes. It was amazing to us that Russia was considered a military rival to the United States." When they got back to Moscow, all the restaurants were closed and they were starving, so Gerry sent Madeleine and Adi to scavenge whatever they could. They returned triumphantly from the bar of the hotel with caviar, pretzels, and vodka. It was a memorable party, enlivened by jokes directed at the hidden microphones in the walls. "We acted like teenagers," says Ferraro. "And God, was I sick. It was a long time before we ate caviar again."

Working for Ferraro was a psychological boost for Madeleine that helped her overcome the trauma of divorce and rejection. But it also gave her something else that was equally important in her later career: a network of influential women friends on whom she could rely for advice and support.

At the core of this network were three female politicians who had managed to break through the male-dominated political system through grit and hard work. Geraldine Ferraro, Barbara Kennelly, and Barbara Mikulski had come to power by different routes, but their lives and professional careers intersected with Madeleine's in interesting ways. They were all brought up in Catholic immigrant households—Italian, Irish, and Polish, respectively—where going to Mass and voting Democratic went hand in hand. Like Madeleine, they had all graduated from women's colleges and followed the typical female zigzag career pattern.

Ferraro was a Queens housewife married to a millionaire real estate magnate. Although she graduated from law school, she spent the first fourteen years of her married life looking after her children. It was only in 1974 that she began working full time in the local district attorney's office. By 1977, she had responsibility for prosecuting all sex crimes in the county, and she soon became known as an advocate of abused children and battered wives. One evening, after a political event, New York governor Mario Cuomo suggested that she run for Congress as a Democrat. The following year, she was elected to the House of Representatives, defeating three more experienced politicians.

Unlike the others, Kennelly was brought up in a political household. Her father, John Bailey, ran the Democratic Party machine in Connecticut for almost three decades. She married a politically ambitious lawyer, Jim Kennelly, who served two terms as speaker of the Connecticut House. Although she attended numerous Democratic political conventions, she went as a guest rather than as a delegate. Again, it was not until 1975 that she made the jump from full-time mother to career woman, winning a position on the Hartford City Council. She was elected to Congress in 1982, at the age of forty-six, with the support of the political machine assembled by her father.

The only one of the trio who has never been married, Mikulski grew up in a deprived Polish neighborhood of ethnically mixed East Baltimore. After graduating from college, she came home to work as a child welfare officer. Her big break came in 1970 when she led a multiracial campaign to prevent her neighborhood from being obliterated by a six-lane highway. The publicity generated by that grassroots effort propelled her onto the Baltimore City Council and into Congress in 1976, the year that Madeleine began working full time for Muskie. She was elected to the Senate ten years later.

Ferraro, Kennelly, and Mikulski all knew each other well from Congress, where they were leading members of the Women's Caucus. Both Kennelly and Mikulski lobbied hard for Mondale to pick a woman running mate. When Ferraro was nominated, they became part of her inner circle and traveled with her on the plane. Since she was close to them in age and background, Madeleine quickly became an honorary member of the club. They considered themselves the true loyalists. "There were a lot of people around Gerry who were sunshine soldiers, gliterati pals," said Mikulski. "As long as there was glitz, they wanted to be in on the glory. But when she had problems over taxes, and the campaign had its problems, [the sunshine soldiers] were not so vigorous in their support. This gang never left her."

When the campaign was over, the "gang" decided to meet at least once a month for dinner. Because of the punishing voting schedule in Congress, the dinners were usually held on Capitol Hill, in restaurants like La Colline or the Monocle. Sometimes they were joined by Mikulski's chief of staff, Wendy Sherman, who represented the next generation of women political activists. "We would talk about everything from kids to diets to movies we had seen lately to the struggles that people were having in doing what they were trying to do," Sherman recalls. "It was a place where you could let your hair down. For this generation of women, finding women like you is not so easy."

It was also a mutual support network. Madeleine supported the political ambitions of her friends with her money and contacts, and they pulled for her at key moments in her career. "The guys have been doing that in this town for ages," says Sherman. "Many jobs never appear anywhere. They just get decided in a series of phone calls that the guys make to each other." (When Madeleine became secretary of state in 1997, she appointed Sherman as one of her senior advisers.) Because they were in a minority and trying to break through male barriers, women seemed more self-conscious about their networking than men. "Men network all the time, even if it is not something they are consciously trying to do," says Nancy Soderberg, who went from being a graduate student of Madeleine's at Georgetown University to an intern on the Mondale-Ferraro campaign to a senior National Security Council position in the first Clinton administration. "They play tennis together. They know each other from school. It is difficult for women to compete with that."

Breaking through the glass ceiling in politics was particularly difficult because of the huge amount of money needed to fight a statewide campaign. Fund-raising requirements favored incumbent politicians, who were overwhelmingly male. Existing money attracts more money. In order to overcome this obstacle and help women candidates struggling to establish financial credibility, in 1984 women's groups launched a fund-raising mechanism called EMILY, based on the slogan "Early Money Is Like Yeast." Madeleine became an enthusiastic supporter of Emily's List, with contributions ranging from $250 to $2,500.

Although Albright was part of the Ferraro-Mikulski-Kennelly circle, Wendy Sherman believes that she was never as "competitively ambitious" as her politician friends. "She loves politics, but in a different way from these other women. Mikulski, Ferraro, Kennelly love the rough-and-toughness of politics, the competitiveness of politics. It may make them crazy from time to time, but it is clearly in their blood." Madeleine's love of politics, says Sherman, stems from the way she was raised, from the values and interests inculcated by her parents. "Foreign policy is so much a part of what she is. It is her life."

Madeleine may not have been as competitive as her politician friends, but she certainly had grand ambitions. Her vague thoughts of one day occupying a top position in the U.S. government began to crystallize during this period, perhaps stimulated by watching the rise of women friends like Ferraro. Chatting over lunch around this time with a Georgetown University colleague, Putnam Ebinger, she said flat out that her goal was to become America's first woman secretary of state. "It was then that I realized how big the ambition was, and I started watching her," said Ebinger, associate dean of the School for Foreign Service. "From my vantage point, it was very exciting to watch a woman working toward that large a goal." The single-mindedness with which Madeleine pursued her long-term goal reminded Ebinger of "the way men operate."

Lacking the tough skin that is a necessary part of any elected politician's armor, Madeleine would choose a different route from that followed by Ferraro, Mikulski, and Kennelly. Most politicians understand that they must absorb a certain amount of personal abuse as the price of getting elected. Madeleine, by contrast, has little tolerance for people questioning her motives and can be hypersensitive to criticism. An illustration of this came many years later in February 1998 when she appeared at a televised "town meeting" designed to drum up public support for possible military action against Iraq by the Clinton administration. The occasion was disrupted by hecklers, provoking testy responses from Albright, who seemed taken aback by the ferocity of the attacks. The defense secretary, William

Cohen, did not appreciate the heckling either but, having been through the maw of Senate election campaigns, he took it much more in stride.

The hustings were fun, particularly as an observer. As a principal, Madeleine preferred a forum where she was clearly in charge and people didn't answer back. She had enormous reserves of energy. The question was where to channel it.

Georgetown University was Madeleine's professional home, in between her work for the Carter and Clinton administrations. *Courtesy of Georgetown University.*

Georgetown

Madeleine's appointment at Georgetown University was a temporary one. Georgetown, like other American universities, has an elaborate academic pecking order. Professors are not all created equal. At the top of the academic pyramid is full professor with tenure rights, meaning that employment is virtually guaranteed for life. Lower down is assistant professor on a "tenure track," meaning that tenure is likely to be granted within six or seven years provided the candidate fulfills certain academic requirements, including the publication of original works. At the bottom of the pyramid is the adjunct professor, on a short-term contract. When she got her first job at Georgetown in 1982, running the "women in foreign service" program, Madeleine was a "research professor," a fancy version of "adjunct."

In early 1984, as the Mondale campaign was getting under way, Georgetown announced a nationwide competition for a "tenure track" position. The university was looking for a specialist in Eastern Europe to succeed the legendary Jan Karski, the former member of the Polish resistance in World War II who had alerted Western governments to the Nazis' mass annihilation of Polish Jews. Karski was a very popular professor whose courses were routinely oversubscribed. His lecture style was highly personal and emotional, drawing on his wartime adventures and the shock of watching his native country succumb to Soviet domination. To replace him, Georgetown was looking for someone with deep knowledge of Eastern Europe and the Soviet Union and proven academic credentials. The appointment would be a joint position in both the School for Foreign Service and the government department.

By November, a joint appointments committee had whittled the applicants down to a four-person shortlist. Two candidates stood out. One was Madeleine. The other was Charles Gati, whose wife Toby had introduced Madeleine to Barry Carter. (Ironically, Gati had served on Madeleine's Ph.D. committee in 1976.) A professor at Union College in upstate New York, Gati was a leading scholar in the field of Eastern Europe with a string of publications to his credit. His academic references included Zbigniew Brzezinski, Madeleine's old boss. Madeleine had less teaching experience than Gati and a less impressive corpus of scholarly works. On the other hand, she was already at Georgetown, was well liked by her students, and was much more familiar with the inner workings of government than Gati. To choose between them was very difficult.

Both candidates were required to give research seminars. Madeleine's chosen subject was "Potential Succession Crises in Eastern Europe." She talked about the possibility of a major upheaval, triggered by the deaths of one or other of the aging patriarchs running countries like Czechoslovakia and Hungary. The candidates were grilled by the appointments committee meeting in the glass-enclosed McGhee Library on the ground floor of the Intercultural Center, an ultramodern addition to the traditional brick-and-ivy campus. The committee then met to discuss the merits of the rival candidates. Students walking past outside the library could see committee members arguing among themselves, without knowing what was going on inside.

Usually, such appointments are made by consensus. On this occasion, however, the committee was split down the middle. All but one of the representatives of the School for Foreign Service favored Madeleine. They liked the fact that she had worked in the White House and on Capitol Hill and could help students understand how government works. Associate dean Alan Goodman was impressed by both her "in-depth knowledge of Soviet and East European affairs" and her "outstanding teaching" abilities. The dissenting voice came from Andre Marton, a former diplomatic reporter for the Associated Press, who felt she was an inferior teacher to

Gati. The government department representatives preferred Gati, largely on grounds of "academic excellence." Department dean Karl Cerny had doubts about Madeleine's ability to fill Karski's shoes. He felt she was more interested in American politics than East European politics. His concerns were echoed by Soviet specialist Angela Stent, who argued that Gati was more "scholarly" than Albright and had more impressive publications. The third government department representative, Robert Lieber, gave the edge to Madeleine, citing her policy-making experience and strong academic references. By choosing her, he argued, Georgetown would not be sacrificing its "excellence image."

In the end, the appointments committee voted four to three in favor of Madeleine. Hoping to break the impasse, they appealed to Brzezinski, who had written the standard academic textbook on Eastern Europe and was friendly with both candidates. Brzezinski was in a tough spot. When Madeleine heard that he had written a letter of recommendation for her rival, she phoned him in some distress. He had not realized that his former aide was also a candidate. He phoned Gati to tell him he was writing "an equally strong letter" in support of Madeleine.

Brzezinski's judgment was worthy of Solomon. He felt that both Gati and Albright were "very strong" candidates who knew the region well. In his view, Gati was more of a "political historian" while Madeleine was "more policy-oriented and involved in current issues." The decision on whom to appoint depended on what kind of person Georgetown was looking for.

That, of course, was the problem. The School for Foreign Service and the government department had totally different visions of what a university should be. Like many political science departments, the government department at Georgetown was becoming ever more theoretical and removed from the real world. The School for Foreign Service, by contrast, loved to recruit Washington insiders. The dean of the school, Peter Krogh, had succeeded in raising millions of dollars by emphasizing his connections to the Washington elite. With a budding television career, year-round suntan, and seemingly unending supply of glamorous young girlfriends, Krogh did not fit into Georgetown's traditional Jesuit mold. From his point of view, Madeleine was precisely the kind of "scholar-practitioner" he wanted on his staff. "One of the complaints when I got here as dean in 1970 was that the school was not taking enough advantage of its [Washington] location," he said later. "Madeleine was out of central casting for this school."

The government department refused to give its consent to a joint appointment. "She did not fill the position in a way we wanted it filled," recalled Cerny. "We were not getting a person to replace Jan Karski." The dispute ended with the school's hiring Madeleine as an "assistant professor" and the government department hiring a part-time "adjunct" professor to run its Eastern Europe program. Although she was delighted to be at Georgetown full time, the controversy over her academic qualifications came as a shock to Madeleine. According to Putnam Ebinger, a school administrator, Madeleine got the feeling that she had somehow been placed "in a subordinate category." "I remember telling her that everyone was thrilled with what she was doing at Georgetown and there were no problems, but I do think the stuff at the start made her feel more vulnerable than she need have."

In the spring of 1986, Madeleine took over Karski's undergraduate class at Georgetown in "modern foreign governments," or "MoFoGo" as it was known in student slang. The prospect of teaching a class of more than one hundred students intimidated her initially. "I had to talk her into it," said Cerny, who was responsible for finding someone to teach the course. "She would have preferred smaller, seminar-type classes, at least to begin with." Such large introductory classes are generally considered a thankless chore by many professors. Despite her initial misgivings, Madeleine did an excellent job. She became comfortable in front of big audiences and began to attract a mass following among School for Foreign Service students, who voted her "best professor" in 1988, 1990, and 1991.

She also continued to teach seminars on subjects such as Soviet politics and the role of Congress in foreign policy decision-making. She loved to get her students involved in role-play exercises, the way Brzezinski had done with her at Columbia. She paid particular attention to her female students, encouraging them to join in discussions without raising their hands and inviting them to play the part of national security adviser or secretary of state in class exercises. "Women have to learn to interrupt," she insisted over and over again. Learning to speak out, she told her students, was a little like learning to play tennis. "You just do it. There are lots of shy people in the world and they don't get anywhere."

"She wanted people to argue," said Mike Sheehan, a U.S. Army captain who came out of the jungles of El Salvador to take a master's degree in foreign service. "She would say things to provoke people." Sometimes, Madeleine would provoke a discussion by arguing an extreme position, as when she gave a lecture proposing that the two superpowers get together and divide up the world. "People were going up the wall," recalls Sheehan. Although Sheehan had hawkish Reaganite views on Central America, and Albright was "mainstream Democrat," the two of them somehow hit it off. When she became U.S. ambassador to the United Nations during the Clinton administration, she brought him onto her staff as her military adviser.

Georgetown was a very convenient base for Madeleine. Living just a few blocks from the campus, she was able to walk to work. Following the example set by her father, she invited students home for dinner, or out to her Virginia farm for a barbecue. This increased her popularity among the students. "Everybody liked her because she was not only knowledgeable and a good teacher, but also personable," said Alex Gershanik, who took a graduate seminar in U.S.-Soviet relations.

Being a university professor did wonders for her own self-esteem. She no longer worried about being excluded from important meetings, as she had at the White House, or that she was a victim of male condescension. "I got over that when I started teaching," she said later. "I was out on my own, and I realized that I had to please myself, which is the hardest thing."

Georgetown was also a great place to network. Every summer, the School for Foreign Service offered a program called the Georgetown leadership seminar, modeled on a Harvard program created by Henry Kissinger. The school invited several dozen rising international stars in politics, military affairs, and foreign policy to Washington for a weeklong conference in the fall to meet the counterparts from the White House, the Pentagon, and the State Department. Madeleine was a regular participant, lecturing on such subjects as "Campaigning American style" and "East-West relations at the turn of the century." Leadership seminar graduates included the future prime ministers of France and Taiwan,

Alain Juppé and Vincent Siew, and the future president of Colombia, César Gaviria.

It was at Georgetown that Madeleine learned how to be comfortable in front of a television camera. Dean Krogh hosted a weekly current affairs show on PBS called "Great Decisions," and Madeleine was a member of the panel. She was the in-house liberal. Her conservative opponent was Ronald Reagan's first national security adviser, Richard Allen. Although the viewing audience was small, the show offered her a chance to polish her one-liners and make effective debating points. With her eyeglasses thrust up into her hair, she projected a brisk, no-nonsense image as she sparred with Allen and denounced Reagan for his excessive reliance on military force. "Of course Grenada worked," she bristled on one program, referring to the Reagan administration's invasion of the tiny Caribbean island in 1983 to topple a Marxist regime on America's doorstep. "It was the Redskins versus the Little Sisters of the Poor, and the score was 101 to nothing." When a U.S. warship shot down an Iranian airliner over the Gulf by mistake in July 1988, she blasted the administration for "murdering innocent people." "We have been brought up to believe that we are special, but we have not been behaving as if we are special."

Her early performances were not particularly polished, but she improved with practice. "She gained confidence as she went along," said Krogh. "She learned to speak in sound bites."

Madeleine made a conscious effort to master television. She consulted media experts and journalist friends, including an old *Newsday* acquaintance, Marty Schram. "She had a cassette of a televised debate in which she participated and wanted to know what I thought of it," recalls Schram, a frequent commentator for CNN. "She was not particularly forceful in getting her points across. She tried to answer the other man's points, allowing the whole game to be played on his turf." Schram critiqued her performance. "When you go into a debate like that, think of the five major points that you want to make, and make them over and over again," he told her. She seemed grateful for the advice. Later, after she joined the Clinton administration, Schram was amazed at the transformation in her personality. "One moment I am giving advice to a woman who is very nice, sweet, almost vulnerable. The next I see the emergence of a real public figure."

Madeleine herself credits her mastery of television to her willingness to give endless interviews to foreign television stations. The collapse of communism also helped by creating demand for her expertise. "Georgetown put out a book of experts," she recalled. "Because my name began with A, I would get called a lot, primarily to do foreign television. I would get Finnish TV or something. They would come to my office. I figured nobody will see this, so I got comfortable with the camera."

Madeleine never did get tenure at Georgetown. In the end, it came down to a question of what she wanted to do with her life. To qualify for tenure, a professor has to publish original work, and Madeleine had done little scholarly research since her monograph on the Polish press in 1982. Outstanding classroom performance was not sufficient. With so many other commitments, she had neither the time nor the inclination to closet herself away for a year and write a serious book. "She is not an academic, she is an action-oriented person," says her friend Christine Dodson. According to Putnam Ebinger, the School for Foreign Service administrator, Madeleine decided that she preferred "doing policy" to "writing scholarly books."

The tenure decision came up soon after she took time off to serve as foreign policy adviser to Democratic candidate Michael Dukakis in the 1988 presidential election. Rather than apply for tenure and be turned down, she withdrew from the running. "That is where she was smart," says Ebinger. "She knew that she would not get it." She worked out a new arrangement with Georgetown, reverting to her old title of "research professor," on renewable short-term assignments. The failure to seal her academic career with tenure rankled a bit, but she knew herself well enough to understand that her real talents lay elsewhere. "I think she was bothered by it," said Nancy Tucker, a fellow Georgetown professor, "but she recognized that she was unlikely to write that definitive book."

Around this time, Madeleine organized a series of gripe sessions for women faculty at Georgetown. She was not alone in suspecting that women had a tougher time of it than men at Georgetown. Women professors complained that they were asked to take on a disproportionate burden of committee work, were paid less than their male counterparts, and were not accorded the same respect. It seemed to be more difficult for women to get tenure than men.

The sessions took place at Madeleine's house over potluck dinners. There would usually be eight to ten women academics in attendance. "She would talk about her own experiences which shocked me to some extent," said Tucker, a leading China expert and regular attendee. "This was a senior person with a good bit of gravitas. She would talk about the fact that she would be called 'honey' by some of her [male] colleagues and asked to get coffee at meetings." Other women had similar complaints. Ebinger, who was responsible for running a 1,200-person undergraduate program, had also been overlooked for tenure. As an administrator, she had observed salaries for men "moving ahead" of salaries for women and men getting preferential treatment when they applied for leaves of absence. "It was not so much overt discrimination as men sometimes not realizing that they are discriminating against women. If a woman was demanding, it would make people irritated, whereas if a man walked in and demanded things, he would get his way."

The women professors never presented their concerns formally to Georgetown. Dean Krogh seemed surprised that Madeleine was involved in the gripe sessions and says he was not aware that she had any complaints. "She never brought anything closely resembling that to my attention," he says.

Like other people who have observed Madeleine closely over the years, Ebinger was struck by the two distinct sides of her personality. On one side is the "great Mom" adored by her children, the generous colleague quick to offer financial help to someone in need, the successful woman looking for ways to support other women. On the other side is a person who can be quite "steely in her determination." "Madeleine could always decide whether someone was going to be important to her advancement or not," says Ebinger. "If they were, she would give them the time in a way that was purposeful. She did not waste a lot of time trying to make everyone happy."

If there was a moment when Madeleine began to get even with Joe for the pain of divorce, it was the wedding of their daughter Alice in October 1987. One of the twins, the delicately featured Alice was the first of the Albright girls to marry. Her future husband was a banker like herself. Joe planned to fly back from Rome to attend the ceremony, together with his new wife, Marcia Kunstel. Madeleine was determined that she would not be outshone by her rival, whom she had never met.

No expense was spared for the wedding, which took place in Washington's Episcopalian cathedral, high on a hill overlooking Georgetown. From there the bride and groom would proceed by horse and carriage to a glittering reception at Decatur House, a restored mansion just across Lafayette Park from the White House. The fact that Joe was picking up the bill pleased Madeleine immensely. According to her friends, she spent months preparing for the wedding, going on a rigorous diet to slim down. "She put her heart into it," recalled Pie Friendly. "Her attitude was, 'I'm going to show the SOB.' " Because she had worked so hard for the cathedral and for Beauvoir school, she had the privilege of marrying her daughter in the Gothic splendor of the cathedral choir.

The choir was divided between rival groups of friends and relatives, many of whom were no longer on speaking terms. All eyes were on Madeleine and how she would perform in public. Everybody knew the circumstances of her divorce from Joe and the fury of her reaction when he announced he was leaving. "It was not easy for her," said Friendly, but "she walked into that cathedral with her head high, like a queen." Equally memorable was the "shimmering silver dress" that Madeleine wore for the occasion. "She looked fab, fab, like a size six," enthused Geraldine Ferraro. "We totally enjoyed watching her." Ferraro, whose pro-Madeleine sympathies hardly made her an objective observer, noted that Joe's second wife looked dowdy by comparison. Other guests say that Marcia seemed quiet and a little out of place.

Joe's formidable mother, Josephine Albright, was also in attendance. Never great to begin with, her relations with her former daughter-in-law had deteriorated sharply since the divorce. The Albrights began to view Madeleine as an interloper who had snagged their son for his money. The feelings were mutual. "She was a fat, dumpy lady," says Friendly. "I remember Madeleine knocking her with disparaging remarks."

Not only did Madeleine teach at Georgetown University, she also continued to cultivate her role as a Georgetown hostess. Her "foreign policy salon," which had begun in previous incarnations with Muskie, Brzezinski, and Ferraro, really got going in earnest during the run-up to the 1988 presidential campaign when she became senior foreign policy adviser to Democratic candidate Michael Dukakis. It was then that her house on 34th Street became a gathering place for influential Democrats dreaming of a return to power.

An imprimatur of sorts was given to these gatherings by a tongue-in-cheek article in the Outlook section of *The Washington Post* headlined "Waiting in the Wings; In Georgetown's Salons, Democrats-in-Exile Prepare for Restoration." Noting that Madeleine's salons had become "more popular than ever since almost all foreign policy advice that reaches Dukakis flows through her," social commentator Aaron Latham was reminded of the atmosphere in England after the restoration of the monarchy in 1660. Like restored seventeenth-century English nobles, the exiled Democrats flaunted themselves excessively, according to Latham. "They verbally preen in her living and dining rooms. They overdo their intellectual finery. They try to dominate the conversation and they never shut up."

In recent times, three Georgetown women have captured the popular imagination: Pamela Harriman, Katharine Graham, and Madeleine Albright. They all lived within a few blocks of each other on the cobblestone streets of Washington's elite intellectual enclave. Although they reached the top in different ways, they had one characteristic in common. They all began by pleasing men, albeit in different fashions.

The daughter of English aristocrats who had fallen on hard times, Harriman has often been compared to an old-fashioned courtesan, in the tradition of Madame de Pompadour or Madame du Barry. She not only slept with men, she amused and flattered them, serving as the perfect foil to their intelligence and manhood. She was solicitous of their every need. In the words of her biographer, "she used many talents, only one of which was her sexuality, to charm and hold a man of wealth for years on end." Through being wife or mistress to a succession of powerful men, from Randolph Churchill to Gianni Agnelli to Stavros Niarchos to Averell Harriman, she shared in their reflected glory. By the time she died in 1997, she had become a woman of influence in her own right as U.S. ambassador to France and a major fund-raiser for the Democratic Party.

Graham, by contrast, owed her start in life to inherited wealth. Her father, Eugene Meyer, was a wealthy banker who branched out into the communications business, buying *The Washington Post* in 1933. Although she worked at the newspaper as a young reporter, neither she nor anyone else imagined that she would one day be in charge of it. That was a man's job. Her role was to be the perfect helpmate for her brilliant but emotionally unstable husband, Philip Graham, who succeeded her father as publisher. It was only after Phil had a nervous breakdown and committed suicide that Katharine was confronted with the task of running the family business. In her memoirs, she describes how she spent much of her time trying to please various men in her life, even while she was transforming the *Post* from a struggling small-town newspaper into a highly profitable Fortune 500 company. Frequently described as "the most powerful woman in America," she never entirely rid herself of the housewife complex that had been bred into her from a young age. "I seemed to be carrying inadequacy as baggage," she wrote. "Every time I was the only woman in a room full of men, I suffered lest I appear stupid or ignorant."

Like Pamela Harriman and Katharine Graham, Madeleine Albright devoted a lot of time and energy to making men look good. She insists that her goal was not simply to please men but to please people in general. As a practical matter, however, the people she was trying to please were overwhelmingly male. "The system is very male-oriented," she says. "If you want to become part of the foreign policy establishment, you have to get along with that establishment." She says it was difficult for her to distinguish between the male part and the establishment part, as they clearly "went together." "I do care whether I please people. That I do, for sure."

Madeleine's father was the first in a succession of male mentors and role models that included Edmund Muskie and Zbigniew Brzezinski. Like Harriman, she married into wealth and used her social position to gain great influence. Unlike Harriman, however, she was never the femme fatale. Her success was based on incredibly hard work. "There is a difference between the way in which they got power," said Toby Gati, who knew both women. "Pamela screwed her way to the top while Madeleine lectured her way to the top. Madeleine's power is more legitimate than Pamela's." Sally Quinn, a Georgetown resident and chronicler of Georgetown ways, says Madeleine was "by far the most modern" of the three neighborhood celebrities "in the sense that she is totally self-made."

In the quirky Georgetown world, the fact that Madeleine held academic seminars around the dinner table made her somehow different. The very idea of the "working dinner," a social event perfected by Madeleine, went against the mores of traditional Georgetown society. It sounded slightly arriviste. Real Georgetowners thought of themselves as more relaxed, more fun. They too worked at parties, but they pretended not to. Graham and Harriman both had bigger houses than Madeleine, and their parties were more glamorous. Their guests included a much higher proportion of "A list" people—Washington's movers and shakers—starting with the president and proceeding downward. Madeleine was not part of the mainstream "Georgetown set," which Quinn defines as "people who emerge out of the world of politics, the White House, journalism, the diplomatic corps, who are friendly and fun and enjoy going to parties." She did not attend the Sunday-night suppers organized by Polly Kraft, the widow of newspaper columnist Joe Kraft. Nor was she "seen" at the soirées organized by Katharine Graham.

Graham's parties were the most "mainstream Georgetown" in the sense that there was no overt agenda beyond socializing and having a good time. While a lot of networking went on, work was not the ostensible purpose of the exercise. By contrast, Harriman liked to organize "issues dinners" at which she would raise funds for the Democratic Party. She would get acolytes like Richard Holbrooke or Sandy Berger—who later became President Clinton's national security adviser—to lead the discussion. There was an important distinction, however, between her "issues dinners" and those organized by Madeleine. Pamela's dinners were mainly "glitz," says arms-control expert Janne Nolan, while Madeleine's were "roll-up-your-sleeve affairs." According to Quinn, "The real agenda was to make Pam look serious." Pamela's guests might feign interest in the ABM treaty if that was the subject ostensibly under discussion, but their attention was likely to wander to the Degas pictures on the walls. At Madeleine's, the guests really were interested in the ABM treaty and discussed it with a passion that was un-Georgetown in its intensity.

"Pamela was much more of the grande dame than Madeleine," said Catherine Kelleher, a former Pentagon official and academic. "Her parties were great theater, but usually the magic didn't last beyond the evening. Madeleine's parties were much more of a working affair. You were expected to pitch in. Time was spent organizing everybody, who would do this, who would do that."

Never being fully accepted into the "Georgetown set" irritated Madeleine, even though she rarely let her feelings show at the time. Much later, after she was named secretary of state, she was amused by her sudden elevation to "A list status." The Georgetown crowd that had previously snubbed her were now falling over themselves to invite her to their parties. When Washington media stars Sally Quinn and Ben Bradlee invited her to their annual New Year's Eve party in 1996, she waited until the last moment to accept. Although Ben and Sally had been living within a few blocks of Madeleine for years, they had never before regarded her as part of their crowd. Madeleine let her friends know that she had no illusions about the ways of Washington.

Just as Madeleine had to struggle to be accepted by the Georgetown social crowd, she also had to work hard to be accepted by the foreign policy crowd. She was seen as a "process person" rather than as a "substance person." It was the same problem she had faced at the White House under Carter. Intellectually, she was the equal of most of the men she invited to her home. But the heavy hitters on the Democratic foreign policy circuit were all male, people like Holbrooke, Berger, Jim Woolsey, Walt Slocombe, Robert Hunter, and Richard Gardner. The men tended to hog the conversation.

"There was a definite pattern of condescension to women," said Janne Nolan. "Every year Madeleine had to prove herself all over again. No matter how many campaigns she had been involved with, there were some who continued to patronize her until she became Dukakis's adviser."

When the primary season got under way, most of the Democratic foreign policy crowd supported Albert Gore Jr., a senator from Tennessee who was considered much sounder on national security questions than Dukakis. As the governor of Massachusetts, Dukakis had devoted little time to foreign policy issues. A three-month stint as an exchange student in Peru in the summer of 1954 had exposed him to the dark side of American power, the habit of intervening to prop up corrupt right-wing regimes. He saw no reason why billions of dollars should be poured into the development of new types of nuclear weapons at a time when the Cold War seemed to be winding down. His opposition to the Reagan military buildup earned him the mistrust of the "defense Democrats" who wanted to show that the Democratic Party was at least as responsible as the Republican Party on national security issues.

Madeleine understood that Dukakis would need the backing of the "defense Democrats" in order to be a credible candidate. During one of his trips to Washington in the fall of 1987, she persuaded him to pay court to them. The meeting was a disaster.

It began on a warm enough note. The host was Graham Claytor, the president of Amtrak and a manic toy-train buff. Claytor had converted the den of his large Georgetown home on N Street into a magnificent model railway, complete with antique trains dating to the nineteenth century. Dukakis was impressed. One of his great passions as a politician was the construction of a high-speed rail network along the northeastern corridor, linking Boston with New York and Washington. He believed so strongly in mass transit as the wave of the future that he refused to drive a car to work. Even as governor, he routinely took the T train from his home in Brookline to the State House in central Boston.

The other guests at Claytor's house, who included former Pentagon officials like Woolsey and Slocombe, wanted to talk about nukes. A debate was raging in Washington at the time over how to protect America's nuclear arsenal from a massive first strike by Soviet missiles. One much-discussed idea was to mount nuclear-tipped MX missiles on trains and move them about the country, making it more difficult for the other side to target them. The cost, of course, would be prohibitive. Dukakis joked that perhaps they should load the MX missiles on Amtrak trains, thereby ensuring virtually unlimited public funding for his beloved passenger train service. His hosts were not amused. "An awful lot of American strategic thought had gone into assuring the viability of these systems," huffed Woolsey. "He seemed to make fun of that."

At one point, Slocombe urged Dukakis to endorse an increase in the federal income tax to pay for an increase in the defense budget. "Are you serious, Walter?" said Dukakis incredulously. "Apart from the policy side, which I don't buy, you want me to campaign for an increase in the federal income tax. That's crazy." The meeting went downhill from there.

Dukakis felt that the defense experts were wrapped up in their own world, while they came away with the impression that he was "not serious." "That was not a good night," Dukakis recalled. "Poor Madeleine. I did not win any friends there." Later, several people at the meeting declared their support for his Republican rival, George Bush.

Madeleine's work for Michael Dukakis in the 1988 presidential campaign consolidated her reputation as a leading Democratic foreign policy expert. *The Washington Post.*

Liberation

Working for Dukakis helped Madeleine establish herself as a serious Washington player. The governor's chief of staff, John Sasso, had served as campaign manager to Gerry Ferraro and had been impressed by the way Madeleine had guided an obscure congresswoman from Queens through the national security minefield. Hoping that she could do the same for Dukakis, he set up a meeting between Albright and Dukakis in March 1987 in a Washington hotel. They "hit it off immediately."

Madeleine was one of the first people to sign up for the Dukakis campaign, even before he officially announced his candidacy. At that time, his rating in presidential opinion polls was less than one percent. Although he had earned a reputation as an effective governor of Massachusetts, there was little to set him apart from the other "seven dwarfs," as newspaper columnists were derisively referring to the Democratic primary field. His chances of winning the Democratic nomination, let alone becoming president, seemed remote. Nevertheless, Madeleine found him an "interesting and appealing" politician and liked the people around him, many of whom had worked on the Ferraro campaign. It was a comfortable fit.

The next twelve months were a long, hard slog. Madeleine turned her Georgetown home into the Washington branch of the "Dukakis for President" campaign. Her dining room became the conference room. The little office next door, where Madeleine used to work, was filled with fax machines and Xeroxes. New telephone lines were installed. People were constantly coming and going. Madeleine organized her fellow academics to produce a huge library of foreign policy position papers on everything from missile defenses in space to the Nicaraguan contras. Other members of the Dukakis foreign policy team included Jim Steinberg, a former Ted Kennedy staffer who became deputy national security adviser in the second Clinton administration, and Nancy Soderberg, Madeleine's former graduate student at Georgetown.

As chief foreign policy adviser, Madeleine spent a lot of time commuting between Washington and Boston and accompanied Dukakis on some of his trips to Iowa, crisscrossing the state in a converted utility van. The Iowa trips helped separate Dukakis from the other Democratic candidates. Although he ended up with a somewhat disappointing third-place finish in the Iowa caucuses, he went on to become the Democratic frontrunner by winning the New Hampshire primary.

As Dukakis began winning primaries, and the rival campaigns imploded one after another, Madeleine's own star rose in Washington. Her gamble in the spring of 1987, of going with a lesser-known candidate, was paying off. Her fellow foreign policy experts, who were accustomed to cutting her off at her own dinner parties, started to treat her with more respect. By the time of the convention in Atlanta, Dukakis was the only game in town, and people were flocking to give him advice. "I called it her Brooke Shields period," said her friend Janne Nolan. "It was very interesting to watch. Suddenly people were hanging on every word she said. As she grew closer to the candidate, they would become ever more obsequious." Noted Aaron Latham in *The Washington Post*: "No important Democrat will say anything bad about [Albright]. That could be because she may be very powerful, or because she really is good at her job."

Some of the men tried to make an end run around her, sending their position papers directly to Dukakis. Since Madeleine controlled the foreign policy paper flow to the candidate, such attempts usually did not succeed. One such approach came from Richard Gardner, a Columbia law professor who had been working on the rival Gore campaign. Madeleine loved to tell the story of how Dukakis's staff had intercepted a letter from Gardner to Dukakis offering to give him foreign policy advice and shipped it off to her. She then called Gardner—her Georgetown neighbor back in the early sixties—and read him the riot act. Foreign policy advice to the candidate goes "through me and me only," she told him. Her friends were struck by the "killer relish" with which she told this story and the evident enjoyment she derived from putting a potential male rival in his place.

Madeleine's strength was that she considered herself "one of the grunts." While men like Gardner, Holbrooke, and Hunter liked to dazzle everybody with grand strategy, she did the dreary organizational work. This was one of the reasons Dukakis liked her. "She was my kinda person," he said later. "She was good folks, down-to-earth, roll-up-your-sleeves. She wasn't from the Upper West Side."

She was also a great loyalist. She tended to see the rest of the world in black and white, dividing people into "supporters" and "opponents." Even when she disagreed with Dukakis's foreign policy positions, she went out of her way to demonstrate her loyalty to him. David Broder, a political columnist for *The Washington Post*, recalls an argument with Madeleine over dinner in New Hampshire. Dukakis had just got himself in some trouble by suggesting that the United States resolve any differences with Panama over the canal through the Organization of American States, a multilateral body modeled on the United Nations. His suggestion played into the hands of his right-wing opponents, who argued that Dukakis could not be trusted to stick up for American interests. Even though it was a private conversation and her comments were off the record, Madeleine refused to concede that Dukakis might have made a mistake and forcefully defended his positions. Broder concluded that she was allowing her political loyalty to take precedence over her policy judgments.

Dukakis's failings as a candidate for the presidency became much more apparent after he won the Democratic nomination. His lack of foreign policy experience was underlined by his Republican opponent, George Bush, the outgoing vice president and a former World War II fighter pilot and director of the CIA. As Madeleine later conceded, Dukakis had a serious credibility problem. Quick-witted and supremely self-confident, he resisted reducing his foreign policy positions to a series of neat sound bites. He made the mistake of looking at problems from all sides, and as a result he sounded wishy-washy on core issues of national sovereignty. As Madeleine saw it, "his logic, his intellectual honesty, his nuanced approach . . . would have been very interesting in a seminar" but were a liability when it came to running for president. He was never able to cross "the threshold of machoism" to be taken seriously.

Another glaring weakness was a reluctance to take advice. "He doesn't know much more about [foreign policy] than Gerry [Ferraro] did, but he's a helluva lot more arrogant," Dukakis's deputy campaign manager, Susan Estrich, told Madeleine soon after her appointment. It was difficult to get a word in when you were talking to Michael because he already knew it all, or thought he did. Although he was unusual among presidential candidates in speaking Greek, Spanish, and French, his foreign policy knowledge was limited to certain parts of the world. He later boasted that he had heard about "Greek-Turkish problems before I was weaned." He was such an admirer of the social welfare system in Sweden that aides liked to joke that his favorite bedtime reading was a Swedish planning document. He had strong views about the immorality of U.S. actions in Latin America. On the other hand, he had never visited Moscow or any of America's key NATO allies, such as Britain, France, or West Germany.

Madeleine had the job of making Dukakis look credible on national security policy. His skepticism about new types of nuclear weapons made this an uphill task. There were some high-profile defections from the Democratic camp, notably by Zbigniew Brzezinski, her former boss at the National Security Council. When Brzezinski announced that he was supporting Bush because Dukakis was not tough enough with the Soviets, Madeleine felt personally betrayed. "She was hurt and angry," Brzezinski recalled. Adding injury to insult was the fact that Brzezinski failed to inform Madeleine in advance about his decision, on the grounds that she might feel an obligation "to run off and tell Dukakis." For a time, they stopped speaking to each other. Eventually, she sent word to her former professor through the Eastern Europe expert Charles Gati that she wanted to "make up." After checking with Brzezinski, Gati let Madeleine know that "he is waiting for your call."

Although Brzezinski insists that his opposition to Dukakis was purely principled, some of his friends believe he might have been persuaded to work with the candidate had Madeleine reached out to him. Instead, they say, she jealously guarded her own privileged access to the candidate. "She did not make any effort to get me on board," says Brzezinski. "However, she did tell me that one of the reasons she was so angry was that she was quietly trying to get us on board and I short-circuited that, in addition to being disloyal to her." Brzezinski was not the only former Carter administration official to be left out of the Dukakis campaign for one reason or another. Carter's former Middle East expert at the NSC, Bill Quandt, discovered that he had been declared persona non grata, apparently because of his criticisms of Israeli settlement policy. Dukakis was already under fire from the right because of his refusal to rule out an independent Palestinian state. Madeleine evidently felt that association with Quandt would tarnish the candidate's political credibility still further. "Don't ever talk to him again," she instructed an aide.

Dukakis reacted to Brzezinski's "betrayal" with more equanimity than Madeleine. "I was never a fan of his," he said later. "I thought he was a lousy national security adviser, with an ego as big as a house."

Great thought was given in the Dukakis campaign to how to boost the candidate's "macho image." Understanding that "speeches are not what anybody cares about, what they care about is the picture," Madeleine reacted with enthusiasm when somebody in the Boston office suggested a visit to a tank factory. Visits to military bases were not permitted under campaign rules, so a tank factory was the next best thing. Being photographed with tanks would demonstrate that Dukakis was "strong" on defense—or so the theory went. The mood was upbeat when the campaign arrived at Sterling Heights, Michigan, for a visit to an M-1 tank plant. Madeleine and other Dukakis advisers were gathered with the press corps on the bleachers as the candidate roared past in an M-1 tank, its gun barrel waving around in front. "It was a very funny event," Madeleine remembered. "There was a lot of kidding about the fact that Dukakis was really trying to take out the press corps. It was fun. Everybody was having a great time."

The mood changed that evening. The television pictures of the buttoned-down Dukakis poking his grinning head out of a huge tank made the candidate look ridiculous. The fact that he was wearing an outsize communications helmet diminished him even more. He looked like an accountant going to war. The Bush campaign immediately seized on the ludicrous image and threw it back at Dukakis, re-airing the tank footage over and over again in their own television advertisements. Dukakis has opposed "virtually every defense system we developed," an announcer intoned gravely. "And now, he wants to be our commander-in-chief. America can't afford that risk."

The search for scapegoats began. Dukakis aide Francis O'Brien remembers teasing Madeleine about the incident, even though he knew she was no more to blame than anyone else. "We are now going to demonstrate strength in foreign policy," he would say mockingly. She herself later attributed the fiasco to the candidate's insistence on wearing a helmet. Without the helmet, he would have looked fine. Not to be photographed wearing silly hats is one of the oldest rules of political campaigning. For his part, Dukakis still refuses to accept that it was a mistake to put on the helmet. He was just obeying standard safety procedures. "You gotta wear the helmet," he insists. "They won't let you in the tank otherwise."

Madeleine's attempts to make Dukakis look tough on foreign policy continued throughout the fall, with only mixed success. They became particularly intense during the run-up to the first televised debate with Bush on September 25. Together with Susan Estrich, Madeleine tried to persuade Dukakis to promise "to spend whatever it takes" to ensure that America had the finest military in the world. He objected sharply, saying that the country was already spending enough on defense and he had other, more important, domestic priorities. When Madeleine continued to insist on this point, he brushed her aside with the comment "Madeleine, you are much more of a big-gun type than I am." "I guess I have a problem with being intellectually dishonest," Dukakis said later. "I thought the notion that we had to spend more on defense in 1988 was ludicrous."

In hindsight, it is difficult to argue that America needed to spend billions more dollars on nuclear weapons at a time when the new Soviet leader, Mikhail Gorbachev, was already signaling his desire for deep cuts in nuclear arsenals. The Soviet Union was suffering from terminal economic exhaustion and the Cold War was winding down, yet Bush and his advisers were still bogged down in theological debates about Gorbachev's "sincerity." Dukakis was more right about Gorbachev's intentions than

Bush, and history has vindicated his judgment. But being historically right is not the same thing as being politically right. The 1988 presidential election campaign was the last to be fought in the shadow of the Cold War. The Democrats were vulnerable to Republican charges that they were "weak" on national security issues, and it was important to demonstrate that this was not the case. Dukakis's inability to convince the voters that he had what it took to stand up to the Soviet Union contributed to his overwhelming defeat by Bush, 426–111, in the electoral college vote.

There was no doubt that Madeleine would have ended up in a senior administration position had Dukakis won the 1988 election. During the campaign, her daughters teased her by addressing her as "Madam Secretary." According to Dukakis, however, the position of secretary of state was reserved for former vice president Walter Mondale. The job he envisaged for Madeleine was U.S. ambassador to the United Nations.

Although she did not end up with a big job, Madeleine learned some important lessons from her Dukakis experience, including how *not* to run a successful presidential campaign. She watched his candidacy unravel under relentless attacks from Bush, who accused the Democrats of being "soft" on crime and "soft" on communism. In the end, Dukakis did not seem to want the presidency badly enough to do what it takes to be elected. His highest ambition up until 1987 was to be governor of Massachusetts. Running for president was almost an afterthought. In the words of one of his top aides, "Either you grow into it or you shrink, and Mike Dukakis shrank right in front of us."

In Madeleine's view, Dukakis was never taken seriously, not because he was wrong on substance but because he lacked a sufficiently macho image. He did not make any glaring foreign policy howlers, along the lines of Gerald Ford's statement in 1974 that Poland and other East European countries were not under Soviet domination. His failure, according to her, lay in his inability "to project himself as a strong national security figure." In her own career, she would do everything she could to avoid this mistake. She consciously cultivated the image of someone who can be relied upon to face down dictators and stick up for American interests. Her background as a refugee from communism helped her considerably. According to Wendy Sherman, a congressional aide who also worked on the Dukakis campaign, Madeleine's personal biography gave her immediate credibility when she became secretary of state.

Madeleine's tough, "tell it like it is" image is to some extent an artificial creation, even though it has its roots in her personality and life story. In 1988 at least, her foreign policy views were much closer to those of Dukakis than Brzezinski. "There are misconceptions about her being a hard-liner," says Gati, who later served with Albright in the State Department. "She is not a Brzezinski, this is all wrong. It would never have occurred to Madeleine to support Bush. She is a loyal Democrat, and demonstrated that by working with people whom Brzezinski would never have worked for."

It was during the 1988 campaign that Madeleine first met Bill Clinton, a much savvier and more flexible politician than Dukakis. Dukakis refused to pander to the voters and hated ever to admit that he had made a mistake; Clinton would say almost anything to gain popularity. Dukakis took an inordinately long time responding to Bush's demagogic attacks; Clinton would become the master of "instant response." The Dukakis campaign invited the forty-two-year-old Arkansas governor to come to Boston to help the candidate prepare for his first televised debate with Bush. He was so engaging and witty that Susan Estrich began wondering if she was working for the right man. After working with Dukakis on his briefing books, Clinton took Albright, Estrich, and Dukakis media adviser Robert Squier out to dinner. They ended up back at his hotel room, where they partied until 3:30 A.M., laughing at the inanities of political campaigning.

Madeleine agreed with Estrich that Clinton had a much better sense than Dukakis of the country's shifting political moods. The Arkansas governor impressed her as someone "who was extremely smart, very astute in the advice he gave, with a very broad knowledge base and an ability to integrate material to pass on to somebody else."

The following year, Clinton asked Madeleine to provide a recommendation for him to the Council of Foreign Relations in New York, the premier talking shop for America's foreign policy experts. She was happy to oblige. "Bill and I hit it off right away," she wrote, recalling their work together on the Dukakis campaign and their common connection with Georgetown University. (Clinton had attended the School for Foreign

Service from 1964 to 1968.) She praised his "active mind" and "excellent background" as a Rhodes scholar and the youngest governor in the United States since World War II.

Membership on the Council helped cement Clinton's standing with the East Coast establishment. He owed Madeleine a favor.

While serving as chief foreign policy adviser to Dukakis, Madeleine also had to look after her dying mother. Mandula Korbel suffered from scleroderma, which causes a general hardening of the tissues, not only in the skin but in other organs. As the disease spread to her lungs, she began to have trouble breathing. She frequently had to use an oxygen inhaler. The high mountain air of Denver was clearly not suitable for her. In 1987, Madeleine persuaded her mother to move to Washington and found a place for her to live and a private nurse to care for her.

The move to Washington followed a long period of decline for Mandula. After her husband's death ten years earlier, she began to feel increasingly alone and melancholy. Her letters to friends were filled with yearning for lost happiness, particularly the years when her children were small. "I feel a terrible nostalgia," she wrote to her Yugoslav friends the Jankovićs in the mid-eighties. "I cannot wait for this life's comedy to end. I have been terribly sad ever since Jožka [Joe] died." Although she had many friends in Denver, she missed her family terribly. She complained that her children never paid enough attention to her. Madeleine was always too busy, Kathy was in California, John was traveling too much. She relied on her neighbors on South Madison Street for many of her day-to-day needs, like making her bed and tidying up the house.

Jack Newman-Clark, an Englishman who lived opposite Mandula, recalls a "knock-down, drag-out fight" with Madeleine over caring for her mother. Mandula had been complaining that she could not sleep because her bed was so uncomfortable. After listening to these complaints for weeks, Newman-Clark decided to call Madeleine in Washington. As he remembers the conversation, Madeleine told him, "I can't help it, I send her money all the time." Newman-Clark, who was very fond of Mandula, says he found the daughter's attitude "disgusting." He told her sharply to fly out to Denver "tomorrow . . . or I am going to raise Cain. . . . She doesn't want your damn money, she wants somebody to take care of her."

"I loved Mandula so much and nobody would come and help her," Newman-Clark said later. "I was very rude to Madeleine, and lost my temper with her on the phone." The next day, Madeleine flew out to Denver, returning to Washington the same evening. "She left some more money and ordered a bed for her, and that was all she did. In the meantime, Mandula was still stuck there, with nobody to take care of her."

A more nuanced assessment comes from Rita Kauders, a Czech Jew who was one of Mandula's closest friends in Denver. She confirms that Mandula frequently grumbled that her children did not do enough for her. On the other hand, says Kauders, the Korbel children were either struggling with their own problems or, as in Madeleine's case, were "terribly busy." "I know they were on the phone all the time. It is difficult to find the truth. Was she complaining too much or were they doing too little?" The answer, says Kauders, is probably a bit of "both." Once Mandula moved to Washington in 1987, she adds, Madeleine looked after her mother "in every way."

Madeleine discussed the problem of how to care for her mother with her friends, including Geraldine Ferraro, whose own mother was gravely ill at the time. Ferraro believes that "she did everything she could for her mother. She was running back and forth. She spent a lot of time with her when she was dying. She was not as close to her mother as she was to her father, but she did all the things a daughter does."

Although Mandula lived in the shadow of her husband, she was a remarkable personality in many ways, and some of her character rubbed off on her oldest daughter. She was as straightforward as Josef Korbel was complex. Like Madeleine, she could make pointed remarks about other people, but she could also make fun of herself. Her thick Czech accent and imperfect knowledge of English often got her into unexpected trouble. Friends and neighbors loved to tell Mandula stories. One favorite was the time she and Josef were trying to sell their house. The price was $33,000, but Mandula—like many Czechs—had difficulty pronouncing the English sound *th*. When prospective buyers rang up, she would tell them that the price was "sirtee-sree souzand dollars." Eventually, she got fed up trying to make herself understood and said in exasperation, "OK, twenty-nine souzand dollars." Josef went into fits of laughter whenever he told that story.

"When I think of Mandula, I think of vivacious and lighthearted," said Karen Feste, a Denver University friend. She recalls an occasion when Mandula returned to Denver to dedicate a room at the university to her late husband in the summer of 1989, on the twenty-fifth anniversary of the founding of the Graduate School of International Studies. Although gravely ill, she emitted a certain glow. Feste told her, quite sincerely, that she looked "beautiful." "Ahhh," Mandula replied dismissively. "You tell me that because I'm going to die now. People always say that you look beautiful before you die." She died a few months later, on October 4, 1989.

At a memorial service in Denver, Rita Kauders recalled with a laugh how Mandula would chide her when she was late with her daily phone call, saying, "You couldn't care less whether I'm dead or alive." She then turned to address Madeleine and the other children. "She wanted you to be perfect, just perfect. Hence her demands and occasional reproaches. But then she would pull herself together and say, 'Rita, if you ever again hear me complain, you can slap my face.' "

Just two weeks before her mother died, Madeleine was named president of the Center for National Policy, a liberal think tank that sought to do for the Democratic Party what the Heritage Foundation had done for the Republicans. Although the center's annual budget was just a million dollars—less than a tenth that of the Heritage Foundation—the appointment was a very significant boost for Madeleine. For the first time in her life, she was no longer someone else's aide. She was a principal in her own right. In the words of her friend Barbara Mikulski, from now on "she was not on TV as Michael Dukakis's foreign policy adviser, she was on TV as Madeleine Albright, president of CNP."

The center was in such dire financial straits that it asked board members to make an annual $10,000 contribution for the privilege of serving. The financial sacrifice was easier for Madeleine than for many others on the board, which read like a Rolodex of affluent, well-connected Democrats from Vernon Jordan to Warren Beatty to Cyrus Vance. "Madeline {sic} enthusiastically accepts the $10,000 per annum quota which we set for Board members," memoed center president Ted Van Dyk when she first joined the board in 1985. Van Dyk's successor as president, Kirk O'Donnell, a former aide to House Speaker Tip O'Neill, had tried to get the center more involved in the cut and thrust of political debate. But it remained in the shadow of larger, better-financed think tanks such as the Heritage Foundation and the Democratic Leadership Council, which was Clinton's vehicle for transforming the Democratic Party into a modern political force.

When O'Donnell resigned in 1989 to go back to practicing law, a search was conducted for his successor. Madeleine was on the search committee. The chairman of the committee was a veteran Democratic Party activist named Richard Moe, who had gone to college with Joe Albright and remained friendly with Madeleine, even after the divorce. Nobody was very enthusiastic about any of the existing candidates. At one point in the meeting, Moe turned to Madeleine and said, "How about you? Would you be available?" "It was one of those instantaneous things," he recalled later.

According to her friends, Madeleine was not immediately certain that she was the right person for the position. "She went through an agonizing process," says Wendy Sherman, who was a consultant to the center. "It was one of those moments when she had to take a risk and a chance because it was time for her to emerge as more of a leader." Another obstacle that had to be overcome were the reservations of the chairman of the board, Ed Muskie, her former boss and political mentor. He was more used to thinking of Madeleine as a staffer than as a principal. Even though he had a good record in the Senate for promoting women, Muskie had qualms about accepting a former aide as an effective equal. "It was a complicated relationship," said Maureen Steinbruner, who became president of the center in 1993 after Madeleine left to join the Clinton administration. "He admired Madeleine and wanted her to succeed. At the same time, he came out of an era in which women did not do things in the world he was in."

After wrestling with this dilemma, Muskie came down on the side of giving Madeleine the job. In Madeleine's phrase, the senator was "not exactly a feminist." Back in 1978, when Brzezinski offered her a job at the White House, Muskie had argued that a woman could not do congressional relations. "That made me mad, and I went and did the job." Madeleine recalls that when Muskie finally offered her the job of president of the center, she had just been out on the roof, clearing out the gutters. She came into Muskie's office soaking wet. Muskie told her, "I really believe you should have this job, but I often wonder whether a woman can be president of CNP." "We laughed about that [afterward]," she said. "I was clearly doing a man's job cleaning the gutters."

What swayed Muskie was probably Madeleine's extraordinary energy and continuous striving to improve herself. As he told his longtime aide, Leon Billings, he decided that she would do "a better job than the others because she has more to prove." In the end, says Billings, Madeleine seemed the natural choice. "Number one, she was available. Number two, she was competent. Number three, she was loyal. [Muskie] could depend on her to do the job at the time when the job needed to be done." Because the center was in such financial difficulty, Madeleine accepted a voluntary $40,000 pay cut, bringing her salary down from $125,000 to around $85,000. She renegotiated her status at Georgetown University, agreeing to a part-time job for which she received $22,000 a year.

According to Billings, most of her friends felt she had reached the "pinnacle" of her career.

The fall of 1989 was a great time to become head of a Washington think tank. The familiar Cold War world was changing with dizzying speed, making it necessary to rethink decades-old assumptions of American foreign policy. The Soviet Union had just staged the first semi-free elections in its history. Poland had elected a non-Communist government. The Berlin Wall, the most visible Cold War symbol of all, was torn down in November after months of street protests by ordinary East Germans. Within weeks, Madeleine's native Czechoslovakia was in the throes of a "velvet revolution" that ousted the hard-line Communist regime and installed a dissident playwright named Václav Havel as president.

Soon afterward, Madeleine heard on a news bulletin that her old friend Jiří Dienstbier had been named foreign minister of the new Czechoslovak government. Dienstbier was the former reporter for Czechoslovak radio in Washington who had helped her on her Ph.D. thesis on the role of the press in the "Prague Spring." After the Soviet invasion, he was dismissed from his job and thrown out of the Communist party. He spent the dreary years of "normalization" as a furnace stoker and night watchman. They talked on the phone, and he invited her to come to Prague to observe the transition to democracy. In early January, she packed her bags and went to Prague. Dienstbier sent her to meet Havel, who had moved out of his cramped apartment and was now residing in Hradčany castle.

Havel, who had never run anything in his life, needed advice on how to set up his office. Even the simplest organizational matters, such as how to move paper around, were new to him. Since Madeleine had worked in the White House, she was able to explain what a president's office was meant to look like and how it should be staffed. After meeting with Havel, she walked down the steep hill from Hradčany castle to the Charles Bridge, a route that she had often taken as a child, while living in Prague after the war. A full moon was shining, and the snow lay thick and fresh on the ground. Prague had never looked so magical to her. It was "the closest thing I've ever had to an out-of-body experience," she said later. "There was this instant when I thought, 'I've spent my whole life preparing for this, I've learned all these things so I could help, so I could advise the Czech president.' It was really weird."

The following month, Havel came to Washington on his first trip as president of the new democratic Czechoslovakia. Madeleine served as his advance man. She turned her Georgetown house into an annex of the Czech embassy. "It was a repeat of the Dukakis campaign," wrote Molly Sinclair in *The Washington Post*, "only this time the computer, copier and fax were humming for Havel. And when the phone rang, a student answered: 'Havel advance.' " Soon, Havel was using her as an interpreter for a very intense literary discussion with Arthur Miller, William Styron, Edward Albee, and Norman Mailer. But the part Madeleine enjoyed most was being introduced to Henry Kissinger as an adviser to the Czechoslovak president. "Kissinger looked completely shocked," she recalled later. When she returned to Prague in May with a delegation from the National Democratic Institute, Havel invited her to stay at the castle.

Madeleine made repeated trips to Czechoslovakia, both as an election monitor and as a consultant for the Times Mirror Center for the People and the Press. In 1990, Times Mirror launched a huge project assessing the state of public opinion in former Soviet bloc countries at the end of the Cold War. They hired Madeleine part time for a fee of $45,000 a year to help set up focus groups in Eastern Europe and interpret the poll data. Crisscrossing the region by plane and car, the Times Mirror team came to rely on Madeleine for everything from historical perspective to restaurant recommendations. Her Eastern Europe network appeared to be as extensive as her Washington network. "It got to be a running joke among us," said Don Kellerman, director of the project. "You could stand on any street in a European metropolis and soon someone would come running across the street, shouting 'Madeleine, Madeleine.' "

A born political animal, Madeleine loved the inside gossip on who was up and who was down. Watching the onetime furnace stokers and street sweepers move into luxurious government offices previously occupied by Communist apparatchiks, and seeing how they behaved, was an eye-opening experience for her. A colleague on the Times Mirror project, Stan Meisler, recalls her amazement at the way many of the new "democratic" leaders were getting themselves mistresses, just like their Communist predecessors.

As a consultant for Times Mirror, Madeleine was also in a perfect position to witness the ugly side of Eastern Europe's liberation from communism, the explosion of primitive nationalism. It was as if the region had suddenly woken from a long political hibernation. Flags, national symbols, political parties, even street names were revived from the pre-Communist past. In the West, there was boastful talk about the triumph of the Western democratic model and "the end of history." From the perspective of places like Warsaw, Bratislava, or Kiev, the opposite phenomenon seemed to be occurring. Far from coming to an end, history was just getting started again after a forced hiatus of many decades. The polling undertaken by Times Mirror confirmed that ethnic hatreds were much more deep-seated in the former Soviet bloc than in Western Europe, or between blacks and whites in the United States.

Conducting focus groups in Czechoslovakia, Madeleine came up with an interesting way of measuring the Slovak desire to pull out of the country founded by Tomáš Masaryk in the wake of World War I. She asked Slovaks to think of their national hockey team, which had won numerous Olympic medals in the past. "Imagine you have a choice," she told them. "You can win the Olympics with a mixed Slovak/Czech team or have a purely Slovak team and not win. Which would you prefer?" The overwhelming response was "a Slovak team." The answer disturbed and saddened Madeleine. "I was raised very deliberately as a Czecho-Slovak American," she wrote later. "The Velvet Revolution has turned to sandpaper, and as a result, both parts of the country have been diminished."

The Czech Republic and Slovakia went their separate ways at the end of 1992 after a peaceful divorce. In the Balkans, the breakup would be more violent.

The polling project took Madeleine on several trips through the Soviet empire, from the Moravian highlands of her native Czechoslovakia to the industrial wasteland of eastern Ukraine. "She was a great traveling companion," said Robert Toth, a *Los Angeles Times* reporter who often accompanied her. "We would arrive somewhere that was the pits and laugh about it." The hotels had a dreary, soul-destroying sameness about them. The walls were made out of giant concrete slabs carelessly slapped together, and there was usually a deafening band in the restaurant. Usually, Madeleine did not complain. Once, however, after a long day, she blew her stack at the manager of a hotel in the Ukrainian city of Lugansk, because her bathtub had no plug. "Madame," he said. "Don't you know that hotels in this part of the world never have plugs."

Madeleine told that story against herself, as a way of illustrating the bizarre nature of the "service industry" in the former Soviet bloc. Countless travelers before and since have shown similar flashes of exasperation. What made the story unusual was the sequel. The bathtub anecdote seemed harmless enough to Toth, who used it in a generally positive profile he wrote about her for the *Los Angeles Times* in 1992 after she was named U.S. ambassador to the United Nations. Madeleine sent word that she was furious with him for revealing the incident. They have not spoken since. A loyalist herself, she expected unconditional loyalty from her friends, even if they happened to be reporters.

One person that Madeleine did not seem to be in a hurry to look up on these trips was her Czech cousin Dasha, who was eager to see more of her American relatives after the fall of the Berlin Wall. Dasha recalls only a couple of hurried meetings with Madeleine in 1991 and 1992. She concluded that Madeleine was "not interested" in seeing her. For her part, Madeleine says that their contrasting lifestyles made it difficult to talk to Dasha. She felt inhibited describing her wonderful life in America to somebody much less fortunate. As a result, "when we are together, there is not a lot to talk about," she said in 1998.

Their lives had certainly taken dramatically different directions since the Communist coup of 1948. Like millions of other ordinary Czechs, Dasha had survived the years of Stalinist repression by withdrawing into herself and her family and having as little contact as possible with the Communist regime. After being thrown out of the university because of her association with Josef Korbel, she was given a succession of menial jobs on the railroads, eventually becoming a bookkeeper. She eked out a living by knitting and giving English lessons to children of "bad class origins." She married her teenage boyfriend, Volodya Šima, an engineer by profession. Although their life was hard, after waiting in line for sixteen years, they were eventually given a small apartment. They had two children, one born in 1953, the other in 1958. Dasha says she turned down several invitations to become a Communist Party member.

In Czechoslovakia, as in many Communist countries, there was a double system of values. When they were at school, Dasha's children were taught all about Marx and Lenin and the idyllic life led by workers in the Soviet Union. They were required to become members of the Communist youth organization, the Pioneers, and wear red scarves around their necks. When they came home in the evening, Dasha told them what life was like in Britain and how the citizens of Western democracies were able to vote for their leaders. Then she would worry that her children might be indiscreet. "That's our little secret," she would tell them. "It's between you and me." Although she did not give her children a Jewish upbringing, she did make sure that they knew about the Holocaust. She waited until they were ten or eleven and then told them the story of what had happened to their grandparents and other relatives, taking them down to the Pinkas Synagogue in central Prague to see the names of the dead painted on the walls.

In 1968, the year of the "Prague Spring," someone suggested that Dasha get a job as a translator for the Czechoslovak news agency, which would allow her to use her English. For the first time, it became possible to acquire foreign books and travel outside the country. In June, she was able to travel to Vienna, where she met her uncle Josef for the first time since 1948. Two months later, the gates slammed shut again after Soviet tanks put an end to Alexander Dubček's experiment in "communism with a human face." Travel abroad did not become possible again until 1988, when Dasha was permitted to accept an invitation from her English cousins to visit them in London. Madeleine's mother Mandula, by now old and frail, happened to be visiting London at the same time. One evening, she insisted that everyone watch the U.S. presidential debate on television, explaining proudly that Madeleine was "on the Dukakis team." It was the first inkling that Dasha had of her cousin's political ambitions.

Later, after she went to the United Nations, Madeleine would gain a reputation as a hawk, eager to use American military power to resolve the world's problems. She was one of the first members of the Clinton administration to advocate the bombing of Serb positions in Bosnia to stop the killing of Muslims. During the first major post–Cold War crisis, however, she was very much a dove.

When Saddam Hussein sent his army into Kuwait in August 1990, Albright was a vociferous opponent of using force to kick the Iraqis out. Invited to speak to House Democrats in October, she called on the Bush administration to "think through the fight scenario" because there was little to keep the Iraqi leader from "setting off chemicals before we finish him." Her preferred course of action was a combination of economic sanctions and negotiations with Baghdad. She predicted that any war would have the effect of turning Saddam into the hero of the Arab world. Her opposition to U.S. military intervention was shared by many mainstream Democrats. "She played to their worst instincts," said Barry Rubin, a Middle East expert at Hebrew University who addressed the Democratic caucus at the same time as Madeleine. "I saw her as a chameleon, someone who will take on any particular position that benefits them at the moment."

In fact, Madeleine stuck to the position longer than most. A fellow Democratic activist recalls that she continued to argue that sanctions should have been given more time to work even after the successful liberation of Kuwait by half a million American and allied troops. She later insisted that she was not opposed to using force "ultimately" after other options had been exhausted. "There are a lot of us who know we were wrong," she told Jacob Heilbrunn of the *New Republic* in 1994.

Madeleine's loyalty to the Democratic Party was rewarded. Even though she did not participate actively in the 1992 campaign, she clearly belonged to the inner circle of Democratic foreign policy experts. Bill

Clinton, the winner of the 1992 election, was a fan of hers. In 1991, during the early stages of his campaign, he came back to her Georgetown house after a fund-raising dinner to pick her brains on foreign policy. Sandy Berger, who later became his national security adviser, was also present. Although Madeleine loves to talk late into the night, particularly with important politicians, on this occasion her two guests outstayed their welcome. She had to get up at five the next morning to fly to Taiwan. "They sat and talked for a long time. It was the only time in my life when I wished that somebody would go home."

Clinton had promised to pick a cabinet that "looked like America," with women and other minorities fully represented. When aides presented him with a list of people who were being considered for top positions, he underlined Madeleine's name with a pen and jotted down "good" beside it. Albright was named head of the transition team at the National Security Council. She was given an office in the West Wing basement, where she had worked under Brzezinski during the Carter administration. After twelve years in exile, it felt great to be back at the center of things, even if she did not know precisely what job she would get.

As is often the case, she was almost the last to find out. One day, while she was working on the transition, she received a telephone call from Anne Wexler, a Democratic lobbyist and friend from the Carter days. Wexler had heard on television that Madeleine had been picked as U.S. ambassador to the United Nations and wanted to check on the rumor. Madeleine knew nothing about it. At that moment, her other phone rang. Warren Christopher, Clinton's nominee for secretary of state, was on the other line with an invitation for her to come to Arkansas to meet the president-elect. It was not until she got to Little Rock that she learned officially what Clinton had in store for her.

At the United Nations, Madeleine led a campaign to prevent Egyptian Boutros Boutros-Ghali from getting a second term as secretary-general. In private, their relationship was correct. *United Nations.*

United Nations

Almost the first thing Madeleine did on arriving at her office at the U.S. mission to the United Nations opposite the U.N. skyscraper on the Hudson River was to unpack a framed photograph of her father. It showed Josef Korbel and other members of the U.N. commission on Kashmir setting off for the Indian subcontinent in the summer of 1948. Her father stood in the middle of a group of U.N. officials, an elegant figure in his dark three-piece suit.

For a woman who wanted desperately to follow in the footsteps of her father, Madeleine had achieved a lifelong dream. She had been an internationalist for as long as she could remember. In eighth grade, in Denver, she had gone to the trouble of memorizing all fifty-one U.N. member states in alphabetical order. Even though the world body had grown to an unwieldy 185 countries by 1993 as a result of the breakup of colonial empires, she still saw it as a tremendous force for good in the world. As a professor at Georgetown, she had coined the phrase "assertive multilateralism" to encapsulate her foreign policy philosophy. Now that the Cold War was over, some new strategy had to be found to replace the outdated idea of "containment." The wave of the future, Madeleine believed, lay in international cooperation and "integration."

She outlined her thinking in a major speech at Georgetown University entitled "Strategic Vision for the 1990s," as America was preparing to go to war with Iraq. "Broad-based coalitions, multinational sanctions, internationally approved use of force," she told her students, "will prove to be key tools for dealing with those who threaten their neighbors with weapons of mass destruction. . . . We do not win when we bomb our enemies into the ground, because we only create new generations of malcontents. We can only win if we work to develop a new international community that works together to discipline those who break its rules. Containment has succeeded—integration is next."

One of Madeleine's childhood heroes was Adlai Stevenson, who had helped create the United Nations and later became President Kennedy's ambassador to the organization. Soon after moving into her eleventh-floor suite on New York's First Avenue, she instructed aides to scour the basement for Stevenson memorabilia. They produced a bust of Stevenson, which she placed in a prominent position in her office, sometimes playfully draped with a U.N. peacekeeper's helmet.

The United Nations job came with a $27,000-a-month suite at the top of the Waldorf Towers. Madeleine had the pink and green rooms repainted cream and hung borrowed Jackson Pollock paintings on the walls. She added personal touches, such as photographs of her daughters and a new friend, Barbra Streisand, but the place still looked like a museum. She much preferred her home in Georgetown. When she showed friends around the Waldorf suite, she told funny, self-deprecating stories about the difficulty of adapting to her high-powered life. She had trouble getting organized, she told a group of Wellesley college classmates. "What I really need is a wife."

At first, she seemed a little nervous about her job. U.N. Secretary-General Boutros Boutros-Ghali remembers Albright sitting nervously on the edge of a chair at meetings with him and reading doggedly from a prepared text. "She was a beginner in diplomacy, an academic," he recalls. "She would never give you an answer. . . . From the smallest problem to the greatest, she would always say, 'I have to consult Washington.' "

Over time, she became more relaxed. Although she made a habit of clearing anything at all important with Washington, she became more spontaneous and exuberant at Security Council sessions. She took such a delight in being the only woman in the room surrounded by poker-faced men that she joked she was thinking of writing a book with the title "Fourteen Suits and a Skirt." She flirted gently with her male colleagues, distributing little bags of Hershey's Kisses on Valentine's Day with a note of affection for fourteen "handsome young men." She also developed a knack for memorable one-liners. "You can depart voluntarily and soon," she told Haitian dictators in July 1994, "or you can depart involuntarily and soon." She described a speech by Iraqi foreign minister Tariq Aziz as "one of the most ridiculous delivered at the U.N." Her pithy turns of phrase earned her the reputation as the Clinton administration's most effective foreign policy spokesman. Admittedly, she didn't have much competition. Secretary of State Warren Christopher was painfully shy and wooden. National Security Adviser Anthony Lake shunned the cameras so much that *The New York Times* once referred to him in a picture caption as "an unidentified man" standing next to President Clinton.

Madeleine's colleagues at the U.N. had mixed feelings about her. Compared to her immediate predecessor, Edward Perkins, she was a real personality. She seemed to have the ear of people in Washington. She could be devastating about her political opponents, but she had a good sense of humor. She made fun of herself, not always intentionally. A fellow ambassador recalled a heated Security Council discussion at which she reserved the position of the United States with the corny old line "It ain't over 'til the fat lady sings." "There was dead silence in the Security Council. Everybody else couldn't believe she had said that. They really did think of her as 'the fat lady.' In a way, it was quite attractive. She didn't mind what she said. She was not totally manipulative. She was natural."

On the other hand, there was also resentment at the fact that she spent so much time in Washington at the expense of schmoozing with her fellow diplomats in New York. Albright herself insisted that combining the U.N. ambassadorship with membership on the cabinet and the National Security Council—where foreign policy is actually made—contributed to her authority. "I'm plugged into Washington, I'm in the inner circle, I'm involved in everything," she boasted to a reporter.

She frequently traveled to Washington once or even twice a day. Her chief of staff, Elaine Shocas, liked to tell the story of the time a summons arrived for a meeting at the White House while Madeleine was in the air to New York. "We literally had someone turning her around at the airport," she remembers. Albright jumped back on the next Washington-bound shuttle, telling the pilot, "The President needs to see me, fly fast!"

The results of all this frenetic activity were not immediately apparent to Madeleine's fellow ambassadors in New York. Although she attended numerous White House meetings, her impact on the shaping of policy appeared to be marginal. She often came back from the capital disillusioned by how little had been achieved. "We just churned about" was a favorite phrase. In order to be effective at the United Nations, an ambassador must spend an inordinate amount of preparatory time negotiating with colleagues over the wording of resolutions. Unflattering comparisons were drawn between Madeleine and her predecessor but one, Thomas Pickering, who had helped put together the international coalition that defeated Iraq during the Gulf War. A professional diplomat, Pickering was known as "the magician" at the United Nations. If one resolution failed to gain sufficient support, he would usually have another up his sleeve to deal with any objections. During his ambassadorship, the United States was able to shape U.N. decision-making in a way that it has rarely done before or since.

The Pickering comparisons irritated Albright. She was particularly upset by a magazine article in the *Los Angeles Times* suggesting that the United States was losing its leadership role on the Security Council. The article had been written by Stanley Meisler, whom she had gotten to know from the Times Mirror project on Eastern Europe. She phoned him to complain, starting the conversation with the words, "Et tu, Brute?"

Madeleine's principal interlocutor and sparring partner at the United Nations was the Egyptian-born secretary-general, Boutros Boutros-Ghali. Their relationship—initially friendly and supportive, then strained, and eventually contemptuous and hostile—was in many ways a reflection of the larger relationship between the United States and the United

Nations. Madeleine began by praising Boutros-Ghali as "a man of extraordinary vision" whom she could "really admire." She ended up masterminding the campaign to deny him a second term as secretary-general.

Although their personalities were very different, Boutros and Madeleine had some things in common. They had both been academics. They both wanted to promote the United Nations as an instrument for settling international disputes. Most notably, they were both outsiders who had succeeded in becoming insiders through an appetite for hard work and the sheer force of their personalities. But that is also where the similarities end and the differences begin. Madeleine came from a family of Czech Jews that had set itself the goal of total assimilation with majority society, first in Czechoslovakia and then in America. Boutros-Ghali was the scion of wealthy Christian Copts who had occupied a traditionally privileged place in Egyptian society and held themselves aloof from the Muslim majority.

Boutros-Ghali was brought up in a crumbling, 100-room mansion that had once belonged to his grandfather, a former Egyptian prime minister assassinated by Muslim radicals. During the period of fervent Arab nationalism under Gamal Abdel Nasser, his family fell out of favor. His Copt background effectively barred him from becoming foreign minister, even though he served for fourteen years in the number-two position. He never attempted to shed his Copt identity, an impossible goal in any case given his family's prominence. Instead, he sought to get his way through stubbornness, intellectual consistency, and relying very much on his own resources.

Whereas Madeleine was acutely aware of public opinion and popular culture, Boutros-Ghali was almost indifferent to it. She excelled in public debate; his strength was backstage maneuvering. She was very effective on television; he was hopeless at sound bites. She was friendly and sociable; he was distant and autocratic. She took criticism extremely personally; he regarded it as part of the rough-and-tumble of politics. She resented his "arrogance"; he thought of her as inexperienced and out of her depth.

From the start, they made a great effort to get on with each other, meeting regularly and holding monthly tête-à-tête dinners at each other's homes. Boutros-Ghali went out of his way to emphasize the importance of the United States; Madeleine made it clear she wanted to see a more active United Nations. Underneath the diplomatic courtesies, however, their personalities began to grate. The Albright camp felt that Boutros-Ghali could be patronizing and ingratiating. Sometimes he called her "sweetie." At other times, he would kiss her hand. "She wondered what all that was about," said Albright aide Rick Inderfurth. "He did not recognize the formidable nature of the person directly across the street from him. I think she was more bemused than resentful." Adds another aide, Mike Sheehan, "He tried to charm her, which was obnoxious."

Boutros-Ghali kept his feelings about Madeleine largely to himself, but his aides were quick to sense the underlying friction. He occasionally made comments like "Poor girl, she is out of her league." "He did not rank her particularly high in the world of effective diplomats," said Charlie Hill, an American who served as his chief speechwriter. "He regarded her as a *parvenu*, not as someone who had come up the ladder." In contrast to Boutros-Ghali, who had run a major foreign ministry and had years of experience in the cutthroat world of Arab politics, Albright was a comparative newcomer to international diplomacy. In an interview after he left the U.N., he made clear that he found it much easier to deal with professional diplomats like Pickering. "She was a beginner in diplomacy," he said. "People have the idea that anyone can be a diplomat. That is not true. Being a diplomat is as difficult as being a doctor. It can take twenty years."

There were arguments over the duties and role of the United Nations secretary-general. Albright complained that Boutros-Ghali wanted to grab too much power for himself. Her aides accused the secretary-general of hankering after the role of world statesman pronouncing on global policy at the expense of the more traditional role of uncontroversial implementer of U.N. decisions. They were alarmed by the tendency of the U.N. protocol people to insist that Boutros-Ghali be given precedence over mere heads of state. "He had an incredible entourage that treated him like the king of the world," said Albright spokesman James P. Rubin. "She [Albright] saw the U.N. as a system of countries. They [Boutros-Ghali aides] tended to focus almost exclusively on the role of the secretary-general and the secretariat."

Boutros-Ghali concedes that he sought to build up the authority of the secretary-general as part of a more general effort to strengthen the United Nations. "As secretary-general, I felt that from time to time I should be a secretary, but from time to time I should also be a general." The United States, he says, wanted "a secretary" in the job and not "a general." He also acknowledges that he tried to project an image of "independence" from Washington, even though he understood very well that the United States was the preeminent voice in the Security Council. "You are trying to kill a fly with a gun," he liked to tell Madeleine and other American officials. "The U.N. has a budget of 1.2 billion dollars, roughly what the CIA spends every day. The U.N. is nothing compared with the power of the U.S. It is zero." (He exaggerated the CIA budget by a factor of ten.)

Boutros-Ghali's hopes of working with the Americans were dealt a fatal blow on October 3, 1993, when eighteen U.S. Army Rangers were killed in Somalia in an abortive attempt to capture a warlord named Mohammed Aideed. Clinton administration officials, from the president down, tried to deflect blame for the fiasco onto the United Nations. Even though they had been operating under U.S. command, the Rangers were technically part of a U.N. peacekeeping force in Somalia charged with enforcing U.N. resolutions. Clinton even claimed that he was not aware that U.S. forces were trying to capture the Somali warlord in retaliation for the murders of twenty-four Pakistani peacekeepers. While it is true that Boutros-Ghali had been a leading advocate of hunting down Aideed, he had the backing of the United States and the U.S. ambassador to the United Nations. Less than two months earlier, Albright had written an op-ed piece in *The New York Times* explicitly endorsing the hunt for Aideed.

> Failure to take action [against Aideed] would have signaled to other clan leaders that the U.N. is not serious. . . . The decision we must make is whether to pull up stakes and allow Somalia to fall back into the abyss or to stay the course and help lift the country and its people from the category of a failed state into that of an emerging democracy. For Somalia's sake, and our own, we must persevere.

Even though Madeleine knew it was unfair to blame the United Nations for the deaths of the Rangers, she was quick to accommodate herself to the new political reality. The Republicans were in full cry about infringements on American sovereignty. Inside the administration, Boutros-Ghali had become "a whipping boy," according to Doug Bennet, the State Department official in charge of international organizations and a friend of Madeleine's from Beauvoir days. At White House meetings, top officials talked mockingly about "Booboo-Ghali." "I can imagine that Madeleine got worn down by this," says Bennet. "That is what I hope is true. A less generous interpretation is that there was an opportunistic element as well. She would have concluded, 'If that is the way things are, why fight it?' " Bennet, who left the State Department in 1995 to become president of Wesleyan University in Connecticut, felt that the end of the Cold War offered tremendous opportunities for the United States to mold the U.N. to its liking. "It turned out that there was no enthusiasm for that in Washington."

Sensing that "assertive multilateralism" had become a political liability, Madeleine dropped the phrase from her vocabulary. Translated into ordinary language, it was not such a stupid idea. Her point was that America lacked the resources and the political will to play world policeman all by itself and therefore needed to take the lead in putting together international coalitions, such as the one that had defeated Iraq in the Gulf War. In the wake of the Somalia disaster, however, the very word "multilateralism" became politically suspect. The slogan "didn't catch on," Albright said later. "People thought it didn't work. I got tired of having to explain it. So I just let it go." Instead of "assertive multilateralism," she began emphasizing the need for America to take its own decisions about when to use force in support of diplomacy.

Somalia led to a general reappraisal by the administration on when to use military force to preserve the peace. The political pendulum now swung in the opposite direction. A new policy directive issued in May 1994—Presidential Decision Directive 25—set out a series of restrictive conditions that had to be carefully considered in order for the United States to agree to commit troops to U.N. peacekeeping missions. The conditions included full consent of all parties concerned, no American troops under U.N. command, the ready availability of troops, congressional support for the operation, "acceptable" risks to U.S. military personnel, and a clear exit strategy.

As luck would have it, release of PDD 25 coincided with an appalling spate of massacres in the central African republic of Rwanda. Members of the majority Hutu tribe were slaughtering rival Tutsis by the hundreds of thousands. Soon, the whole country was turned into a killing field. Bodies floated down the river to Lake Kivu, and huge numbers of refugees fled to neighboring countries. In an attempt to curb the bloodshed, Boutros-Ghali proposed sending 5,500 troops into the Rwandan capital Kigali to secure the airport, reinforce the existing U.N. garrison, and then fan out across the country. The plan was vetoed by Albright, acting on instructions from Washington, in favor of a much more modest relief effort. Madeleine doubted that Boutros-Ghali's plan would work. She pointed out that few countries were willing to contribute troops to such an operation, despite the rhetorical support for intervention in the Security Council.

Boutros-Ghali believes that the United States was opposed to his plan because it would have to pay 30 percent of the cost. "The genocide in Rwanda is 100 percent American responsibility," he said later. Had Washington given a clear lead, other countries would have gone along, he insisted. U.S. officials counter that it would have required as many as 20,000 troops to end the slaughter, and that the United States would have borne a disproportionate share of the burden. "It was untenable politically," says Albright military adviser Mike Sheehan. "It was politically impossible to go into central Africa. The American people were not ready for it."

Even though she loyally executed White House policy on Rwanda, Madeleine was upset about appearing too obstructionist. It was one of the few occasions when she sharply confronted Washington, demanding new, slightly more flexible, instructions. "She has been unfairly tarred in this," says former NSC official Susan Rice. "She had to stand up and be the stinker at the party at the Security Council. The public perception is that Madeleine Albright was opposed to the United States being [in Rwanda], but that is absolutely wrong."

"Goddammit, we have to do something." Madeleine screamed at Rice and her boss, Richard Clarke, in one telephone call from New York.

After it was all over, both Albright and Clinton would express regret that the international community had not done more to stop the massacres. Madeleine, in particular, was horrified by the scale of the killing.

In 1996, she flew by helicopter "over some of the most beautiful country in the world" to visit a stone church on Lake Kivu where five thousand people had been massacred and buried in a pit. American volunteers were helping to dig up the bodies in order to reconstruct the massacre for the international War Crimes Tribunal. There were hundreds of skeletons lying on the ground, but Madeleine was struck by one in particular "that was only two feet long, about the size of my little grandson." The detail stuck in her memory, and she mentioned it the following year, during her Senate confirmation hearing to be secretary of state.

Somalia and Rwanda were devilishly difficult problems. But the foreign policy crisis that came to torment the Clinton administration in its first term was Bosnia. In some ways, it was the archetypical post–Cold War crisis, unfolding not in distant Africa but in the middle of Europe. The collapse of communism had left a political vacuum that was being filled by murderous nationalism. Tens of thousands of Bosnians had been killed and a quarter of a million more driven from their homes. Numerous attempts by Western European leaders to negotiate a peace settlement had all ended in failure. U.N. peacekeepers were reduced to doing little more than providing humanitarian relief as the killing continued. Pledges by the United States and other Western governments to create "safe havens" for Muslim refugees turned out to be worthless. The North Atlantic Treaty Organization suddenly seemed powerless.

Madeleine felt strongly about what was happening in Bosnia. This was not just an abstract foreign policy crisis for her. It was something very personal and visceral, directly related to her own family's experiences before and after World War II. There seemed to be clear parallels between the West's inability to prevent "ethnic cleansing" in Bosnia and the Munich crisis of 1938. The drive by Serb nationalists to create a Greater Serbia conjured up memories of Hitler's insistence on gathering all Germans into a single state. While the killings in Bosnia could scarcely be compared to the Holocaust, they did seem to make a mockery of the solemn and much-repeated promise "Never Again." Madeleine told associates that she now understood what it was like to be in Czechoslovakia in

1938, when the West stood aside and did nothing to prevent the Nazi takeover. When Bosnian Serb troops captured the Muslim-held town of Srebrenica in July 1995 and massacred eight thousand people, Madeleine was distraught.

"This happened before," she told her deputy, Edward (Skip) Gnehn. "I just can't believe it. We said in 1945 that we would never, ever let this happen again. It has. Look at us. It did, it did."

"She could not stand the doing nothing on Bosnia," said Toby Gati, an old friend who had become chief of intelligence at the State Department. "It bothered her tremendously. She was like a horse chomping at the bit all the time. She kept on saying, 'We have to do more, why aren't we doing more?' "

Madeleine's insistence on "doing something" to stop the killing in Bosnia bought her into conflict with the Pentagon, and in particular with General Colin Powell. The victor of the Gulf War was still armed forces chief of staff when the Clinton administration took office. A Vietnam veteran burned by the Somalia experience, Powell was determined never again to allow U.S. troops to be dragged into a military quagmire. The conditions he set for the use of U.S. military force were so restrictive that they effectively ruled out any kind of intervention in Bosnia. In Powell's view, the Gulf War was the model of a successful military campaign: Have a clear objective, use overwhelming force, and get out quickly. None of these conditions seemed to apply in Bosnia.

At first, Albright was reluctant to confront Powell. "It wasn't easy being a civilian woman having a disagreement with the hero of the Western world," she said later. According to Doug Bennet, she would come back from meetings at the White House saying "she felt intimidated by the generals." Gradually, however, she gained more confidence in her own judgment. In August 1993, she wrote a memorandum to the president entitled "Why America Must Take the Lead." She argued in the paper that the Bosnia crisis had come to overshadow everything else that the Clinton administration was seeking to achieve in foreign policy. The only language that the Bosnian Serbs understood was force. In order to achieve a peace settlement, America therefore had to apply military pressure against the Bosnian Serbs through a bombing campaign that would force them to the negotiating table.

The debate on what to do in Bosnia came to a head at a meeting of the

Principals' Committee, made up of the president's senior foreign policy advisers, chaired by National Security Adviser Tony Lake. After lengthy back-and-forth discussion, as the meeting was about to break up, Madeleine gave vent to her frustrations. She asked Powell, "What's the point of having this superb military you're always talking about if we can't use it?" It was a reasonable point, but the way she said it sounded heretical to Powell, who felt that Madeleine was advocating bombing for bombing's sake. "I thought I would have an aneurysm," he wrote later in his memoirs. "American GIs were not toy soldiers to be moved around on some sort of global game board."

The general thought that Madeleine's plan was muddled and ill thought out. The European allies, who actually had troops on the ground in Bosnia, were vehemently opposed to bombing. "You don't just say that you bomb because you can bomb. My view is that you bomb because you have a particular political objective you are trying to achieve, and this is the way to achieve it."

Lake shared Madeleine's frustrations over the failure of Western policy in Bosnia and her desire for vigorous action. On this occasion, however, he sided with Powell. As a young diplomat, he too had been seared by the experience of Vietnam. He said that Powell was right to ask skeptical questions about the political consequences of military action, the kind of questions that "the military never asked during Vietnam." Lake's intervention settled the argument, at least for the time being. Madeleine came away from the encounter with a sense that the playing field had been tilted in favor of Powell and the Pentagon. The whole debate revolved around a set of impossible preconditions for military action. As she later sarcastically remarked, "You can use power when the earth is flat and you have six months to prepare and you're facing a crazy dictator with nuclear weapons and someone else is paying for it. But that is not always the situation."

Looking back at this episode, Madeleine says that she ran into two mind-sets: the "Vietnam syndrome" and the "Gulf War syndrome." She defines the Vietnam syndrome as "Don't get involved in anything" and the Gulf War syndrome as "Don't do it unless you can deploy 500,000 marines."

Within the Principals' Committee, Albright was the earliest and most consistent advocate of using American military force in Bosnia to end the war. Secretary of State Warren Christopher was naturally cautious and deliberate. Secretary of Defense Les Aspin was wishy-washy. Lake also veered back and forth, reflecting the indecision of the president. As time went on, Lake tried to curb the free-flowing discussion that was characteristic of the early Clinton days and keep everybody "on script." He would occasionally drum his fingers on the table to express his impatience. Although Madeleine was not the only target of his irritation, she felt that she was being picked on. "Somebody told me that Madeleine thought I was dissing her," Lake recalled. "I had been unaware of it." He says he then went out of his way to allow her to speak up, keeping a constant eye on the electronic monitor if she was participating by video conference from New York.

The upshot of the early debates on Bosnia was a muddle-through policy that satisfied no one. The Clinton administration refused to get behind a U.N. peace plan supported by the Europeans that would have given the Muslims significantly more territory than they were granted two years later at Dayton, but failed to come up with a viable plan of its own. Instead it settled on a policy of bluster and "pinprick airstrikes" against the Bosnian Serbs that only increased their contempt for the outside world and for NATO. As with Somalia, failures were blamed on the United Nations.

Unable to have much influence on the internal policy debate, Madeleine resorted to public diplomacy. She visited the besieged Bosnian capital of Sarajevo in March 1994, proudly proclaiming *"Ja sam Sarajevka"* (I am a Sarajevan), a post–Cold War version of Kennedy's famous *"Ich bin ein Berliner"* speech. (The locals noted that she mangled the word for "Sarajevan." The correct word is *Sarajka*.) In March 1996, she toured the devastated Croatian town of Vukovar, which had been captured by the Serbs after being shelled to smithereens by the Yugoslav army. As she toured the ruins, young Serb thugs began shouting anti-American slogans and throwing tomatoes and rotten apples. *"Kurvo, kurvo,"* they screamed. "Whore, whore." Madeleine, who understood rudimentary Serbian from her childhood, figured that it was time to leave. The demonstrators began throwing stones. As her bodyguards hustled her into the limousine, a rock hurtled through the window of a U.N. van, raining glass on Albright aides. The ebullient American diplomat Jacques Klein later had T-shirts made up with the slogan "I got stoned with Madeleine Albright in Vukovar."

Within Serbia, Madeleine came to be seen as an enemy. Articles appeared in the Belgrade press describing how the daughter of a former Czechoslovak ambassador to Yugoslavia had become the leader of "the anti-Serb faction" in the Clinton cabinet. Her parents' old Serb journalist friend, Pavle Janković, gave interviews recalling how his children used to play with Madeleine in the courtyard of the Czechoslovak embassy. A few months before his death, he wrote Madeleine a letter complaining about the effect of U.N. economic sanctions against Yugoslavia. "Dear Madlenka," he wrote, according to a draft of the letter in his family papers. "The conditions of our life are difficult. Civil war rages, there are large numbers of refugees on all sides. The sanctions that have been imposed on us by the great powers, headed by America, only hurt the small people who often have nothing to eat. You are the subject of harsh criticism."

In her attempts to publicize Serb atrocities and draw attention to misdeeds by dictators such as Saddam Hussein of Iraq, Madeleine frequently tangled with the intelligence community. By its very nature, the CIA is secretive and resistant to disclosing its methods and sources. When U.S. spy satellites revealed evidence of massacres following the capture of Srebrenica, the agency was initially reluctant to make the pictures publicly available. Madeleine, however, badgered the agency for permission to distribute the pictures at a closed session of the Security Council.

"The intelligence community was not very happy with her," said Toby Gati, chief of intelligence at the State Department. "Their view was, 'Why are you giving our stuff away?' But she knew how to use it. She understood the value of getting information out even if it was classified, getting it sanitized. She pushed that very far." Her performance in the Security Council was reminiscent of that of her hero Adlai Stevenson when he revealed pictures of Soviet missiles in Cuba in 1962.

Madeleine continued to argue at every opportunity that Bosnia was "destroying" American credibility both at home and abroad. "Muddle-through makes the president look weak," she wrote in a memorandum in July 1995. The fall of Srebrenica, a so-called safe haven that the United States had promised to protect, was a tragic illustration of her point. After Srebrenica, opinion at the White House swung in favor of intervention. National Security Adviser Lake put together a package of "endgame papers" for Clinton, with Albright's memorandum on top. American "reluctance to lead an effort to resolve a military crisis in the heart of Europe has placed at risk our leadership of the post–Cold War world," she warned.

Madeleine's views on Bosnia eventually prevailed, but more as the result of changing circumstances than through the force of her arguments. By the spring of 1995, Clinton found himself in an impossible situation. Even though he had done everything possible to keep U.S. troops out of Bosnia, he had promised to assist in a withdrawal of European peace-keepers without really understanding the significance of the pledge. Pentagon planners estimated that twenty thousand American troops would be needed on the ground in Bosnia just to get the Europeans out. Failure to keep this promise would have shattered the NATO alliance. The choice was no longer between staying out and going in. It was between going in to get the allies out or going in to impose a peace. As the crisis deepened, a Pax Americana came to be seen as the least unpalatable option.

The paradox is that although Madeleine turned out to be right on Bosnia, her influence was peripheral. The real decisions were taken by a restricted group of people around Clinton headed by Tony Lake. The job of bullying the rival factions into drawing up an actual peace agreement fell to Richard Holbrooke at the State Department. Madeleine's interventions were "highly ritualistic," recalls Ivo Daalder, an NSC aide on Bosnia. "Everybody listened to her interventions, some more politely than others, but no one really was swayed one way or the other by her arguments."

According to other administration officials, Lake found Madeleine excessively ideological. He puts it more diplomatically. "Madeleine had a view and was able to articulate it very well," he says. "Her weakness was

working it through and translating it into real policy terms in ways that
would help convince others."

The Bosnia imbroglio had the side effect of further poisoning relations
between Albright and Boutros-Ghali. The U.N. secretary-general had
never been enthusiastic about intervening in Bosnia, which he regarded
as a "rich man's war." He antagonized the Clinton administration by
his reluctance to authorize air strikes against the Bosnian Serbs under
the cumbersome "dual key" arrangement that required approval from
both the U.N. and NATO. In the fall of 1995, he infuriated Albright
by opposing the dispatch of a small U.N. force to eastern Slavonia, a
Serb-held enclave in Croatia, as part of the post-Dayton peacekeeping
arrangements.

It was around this time that Madeleine first concluded that Boutros-
Ghali had to go. Not only was he obstructing Clinton administration
policies, he was seen by Congress as the personification of everything that
was wrong with the United Nations. As long as he remained secretary-
general, the chances that Congress would ever agree to pay more than
$1 billion in withheld U.N. dues were virtually nil. "Boutros-Ghali
became a symbol of U.N. arrogance and U.N. incompetence," says
Albright adviser Rubin. "Maintaining Boutros-Ghali was not worth losing the chance of paying back the money we owed. . . . Our calculation was that the U.N. was more important than Boutros-Ghali."
Madeleine reminded White House officials that the secretary-general's
mandate was due to expire at the end of 1996. Planning began to deny
him a second term.

An important role in the anti-Boutros campaign was played by
Rubin, Madeleine's press spokesman. A tall, lean man with rugged
good looks, sometimes mistaken for John F. Kennedy Jr., Rubin was
unusually close to his boss. As a staffer for the Senate Foreign Relations Committee, Rubin had helped Albright prepare some testimony
on U.S. assistance to Eastern Europe after the collapse of communism.
Like her, he was passionate about Bosnia and enormously frustrated by
the lack of action on the part of the West. They were ideological soul
mates, but also good friends, despite an age difference of more than

twenty years. When Madeleine was at a loss for something to do on a Sunday afternoon, she would frequently ring Rubin up and say, "Jamie, you want to go to the movies?" In some ways, he was like the son she never had.

Rubin was a controversial personality at the United Nations. U.N. officials and some ambassadors viewed him as an unscrupulous, Rasputin-like figure, whispering advice into Madeleine's ear or sending her visual signals across a crowded room. "The activities of Rubin were completely poisonous," said a NATO ambassador. "There were many times when Madeleine would see Boutros and the next day a piece would appear in *The New York Times* saying that she had knocked him around and put him in his place. Masses of stuff seeped into the *Times* and *The Washington Post* that was critical of Boutros. It was quite easy to see where the fingerprints were." Recalled Sylvana Foa, Boutros-Ghali's press spokesman, "We called him J.R., the idea being that Jamie would walk on his mother's face in order to get something." At the same time, Foa concedes that Rubin was "very, very good" at his job. "Everything he did was to try to make her look better than everyone else, to make sure that the press loved her. And they did. She was a terrific sound bite. He always made sure that she emerged at the right moment, said the right things, and left the microphone at the right time."

Press contacts with the U.S. mission to the United Nations were tightly controlled. With the exception of Madeleine herself, Rubin was the only official permitted to speak to reporters without prior authorization. He was well informed and frequently went out of his way to be helpful, particularly if a reporter represented an influential publication. But he was also quick to react when a reporter wrote something negative. Stan Meisler of the *Los Angeles Times* says that Rubin called him up "more times to complain about a story than the sum total of all the complaints I had received in thirty years of journalism." On or off the record, there was never any doubt that Rubin was speaking for Albright and fulfilling her wishes. Just as he was loyal to her, she was loyal to him, and quick to defend him from his detractors.

The job of working out a plan to prevent Boutros-Ghali from getting a second term as secretary-general was given to Rubin, James

Steinberg, director of policy planning at the State Department, and Richard Clarke, the NSC official in charge of U.N. affairs. Their strategy paper was approved by Clinton in March 1996, along with a recommendation to endorse Kofi Annan, a Ghanaian U.N. official in charge of peacekeeping, as the next secretary-general. In June, Secretary of State Christopher personally leaked the U.S. decision to oppose Boutros-Ghali in a background briefing for *The New York Times*. The decision was depicted as "unalterable."

At the U.N., it was widely assumed that the dump-Boutros campaign was part of Albright's own drive to get Christopher's job as secretary of state. Getting rid of Boutros-Ghali was popular with the Republican-controlled Congress and particularly with Jesse Helms, the conservative chairman of the Senate Foreign Relations Committee. According to Sylvana Foa, Madeleine had developed a reputation as an eloquent defender of the U.N. in speeches around the country. "She realized that she had to give Helms something. He really hated the U.N. Boutros's head on a silver platter was the most easily palatable thing she had to give him."

The Albright camp pours scorn on this theory. Rubin points out that Helms already thought highly of Madeleine and did not need to be persuaded that she would make a good secretary of state. He depicts the effort to oust Boutros-Ghali as a pro-U.N. move, the only way left to build support for a discredited institution. He accuses the people around Boutros-Ghali of being so "arrogant and dull-witted" that they were incapable of separating the interests of their boss from the interests of the organization they served.

Boutros-Ghali hoped for a reprieve until the very end. A resilient politician, he had been through much worse before. As deputy Egyptian foreign minister, he had been denounced as "a traitor" by much of the Arab world for helping to negotiate the Camp David peace accords with Israel. On this occasion, he appeared to have the backing of the entire world, with the exception of the United States. He felt sure Clinton would change his mind under pressure from other heads of state once the U.S. presidential election was out of the way. "It's all politics," he kept on assuring his aides.

On November 19, two weeks after the Clinton reelection victory, Madeleine vetoed a second term for Boutros-Ghali in a 14–1 Security

Council vote. Even Britain voted against the United States. Contrary to Boutros-Ghali's expectations, however, it soon become clear that the administration would not yield.

The following month, Clinton named Madeleine Korbel Albright the first woman secretary of state in American history.

Albright was sworn in as secretary of state by Vice President Gore in January 1997, in the presence of President Clinton and her daughters. *The Washington Post.*

Madam Secretary

Madeleine had dreamed of becoming secretary of state from the time she started becoming a serious player on the Washington foreign policy circuit. Serving as foreign policy adviser to Democratic candidates—first Geraldine Ferraro, then Michael Dukakis—served as a spark for her own ambitions. If Ferraro could break through the glass barrier so spectacularly and generate so much excitement around the country, why not she? When she arrived in New York in 1993 as U.N. ambassador, many of her colleagues assumed that she had her sights set on even higher office.

Fantasizing about a job once held by Thomas Jefferson and John Quincy Adams and actually achieving that ambition were two very different matters, of course. Although she allowed herself to daydream, Madeleine had recurring doubts about whether the position would ever be offered to her. "The boys will never let it happen," she joked to her women friends. It had been an uphill struggle for her to be accepted as an equal by male colleagues, some of whom had made their reputations while she was concentrating her energy on raising children. In embarking on a career late in life as a fund-raiser rather than as an acknowledged expert on some area of the world, she had had to work doubly hard just to be taken seriously. She needed constant reassurance about her prospects and abilities.

One person to whom Madeleine confided her anxieties was Doug Bennet, a friend from her Beauvoir days and fellow Democratic Party activist. In many conversations over the years, she kept returning to the same questions. Has our generation lost its chance to influence public policy? If our candidate is elected, will anybody pay attention to you and me? If I am chosen for an important post, am I up to it? Bennet's answers were invariably the same. Politics is such an uncertain profession that it is impossible to predict the future. There will always be a large element of political calculation in making senior appointments. And yes, you can do anything you set your mind to.

The last such conversation took place in February 1995, as Bennet was leaving his job as assistant secretary of state for international organizations to become president of Wesleyan University. They met for lunch in the State Department cafeteria. By this time, Madeleine was being talked about in the press as a possible candidate to succeed Warren Christopher as secretary of state. "She wondered if it could happen," Bennet recalled. "My answer was yes, but don't plan on it, because these are things you can't control. Finally, the big question always from Madeleine. 'Do you think I can do this?' " His answer, once again, was "Yes."

Madeleine was testing the waters with other influential people around Washington. Steven Rosenfeld, deputy editorial page editor for *The Washington Post*, recalls an invitation to Madeleine's Virginia farm for Sunday brunch in the summer of 1996. The usual crowd was there. Barbra Streisand was in a corner of the living room, engaged in intense political discussion with other Democrats. Lolling about on the porch were General Neil Sheehan, of the U.S. Marine Corps, and Susan Eisenhower, granddaughter of the former president, with her husband Roald Sagdeev, former head of the Russian space program. At one point in the afternoon, Rosenfeld found himself in a little hallway with Madeleine. The conversation soon turned to the secretary of state sweepstakes. Madeleine recited her credentials for the job. She told Rosenfeld she was "the most powerful woman ever to hold a foreign policy position" in a U.S. administration. Jeane Kirkpatrick had been ambassador to the United Nations under Reagan but was never a member of the policy-making Principals' Committee. At the end of the conversation, Madeleine asked Rosenfeld who else he thought was in contention. He mentioned the usual suspects: former senator George Mitchell, who was negotiating a peace settlement in Northern Ireland, and Bosnia peace negotiator Richard Holbrooke. She listened attentively.

"Why shouldn't she be ambitious?" Rosenfeld asked his wife on the way home. "Everybody else in Washington is ambitious."

Madeleine and her supporters understood the conventions of high cabinet appointments very well. Signaling an interest in a position such as secretary of state—via trusted third parties—was acceptable. Open campaigning was not. Any overt lobbying effort would probably be counterproductive, because it would make it appear that the president could be pushed around by political interest groups. This had to be a non-campaign campaign. Madeleine had some influential allies. The most important was Hillary Rodham Clinton, a fellow Wellesley alumna. Although they represented different generations of Wellesley women—Hillary graduated in 1969, ten years after Madeleine—the connection gave them something to talk about. They had got to know each other when Madeleine accompanied the First Lady on a trip to Beijing for the International Women's Conference in September 1995. The following year, Madeleine played tour guide to Hillary in Prague, introducing her to Václav Havel. As their Chevrolet Suburban pulled into Wenceslas Square, the two Americans joined the Czech president in a hilarious rendition of "Good King Wenceslas." In some administration quarters, the Prague trip became known as "the Audition."

Madeleine also had the enthusiastic support of the old girls' network of which she had been an integral part since the Ferraro campaign. Friends like Barbara Mikulski, Barbara Kennelly, and Ann Wexler were now in key positions in the Democratic Party. The much-touted gender gap, which had not been strong enough to influence the outcome of the 1984 or 1988 campaign, was a decisive factor in the presidential elections of 1992 and 1996. Democratic women wanted their reward for helping send Bill Clinton to the White House and were more than willing to make their voices heard.

It was not just the women. During her four years as U.S. ambassador to the United Nations, Madeleine had succeeded in capturing the public's imagination as few cabinet members before her had done. Her political appeal became particularly evident in February 1996 after she denounced the shooting down by Cuba of two small civilian planes flown by anti-Castro pilots. "This is not *cojones*, this is cowardice," she thundered, echoing the Spanish vulgarity used by the Cuban fighter pilots as they boasted about their attack. The remark transformed her overnight into a heroine for the Cuban-American community. When she traveled to Miami a few days later for a memorial service in the Orange Bowl for the dead pilots, she was greeted with thunderous chants of "Madeleine, *Libertad*." "The only way I can describe it was that it was like being at a rock concert with Mick Jagger," said her aide, Elaine Shocas, who walked into the stadium with her through a tunnel normally used by the Miami Dolphins. As Madeleine's name was announced from the loudspeakers, a mighty roar erupted from the 60,000-strong crowd, continuing for many minutes as she walked the entire length of the stadium. Clinton, who had always had trouble wooing traditionally conservative Cuban-American voters, was impressed.

Helped by her press spokesman, Jamie Rubin, Albright had succeeded in getting her name "in play" among the candidates to succeed Warren Christopher, who had made clear that he would step down as secretary of state if Clinton were reelected. The front-runner was widely believed to be George Mitchell, who had helped prepare Clinton for his televised debates with Bob Dole. The former Senate majority leader lacked charisma but was trusted by the president's senior foreign policy advisers, particularly Christopher and Lake, the outgoing national security adviser. "I was very much for George," said Lake. "Most white men probably were for George." Word quickly spread, however, that Mitchell might have difficulty getting confirmed by the Senate, now under Republican control. In normal circumstances, senators usually rally around one of their own, even if he is from the other side of the aisle. On this occasion, however, aides to Foreign Relations Committee Chairman Jesse Helms began dumping on Mitchell as too "partisan" a figure to gain widespread support.

Initially, the Albright camp dared not lobby openly, for fear of harming her cause. "Madeleine was very, very cautious," recalled Ferraro. "She did not want to be seen to be lobbying." The restraint disappeared, however, after a story appeared in *The Washington Post* quoting an anonymous White House aide as saying that Madeleine was only in the "second tier" of candidates to succeed Christopher. The quote was tucked away in the twelfth paragraph of a story about new cabinet appointments. But the seemingly insignificant throwaway line served as the perfect pretext for mounting a real campaign on Madeleine's behalf. Soon, telephone calls and faxes were pouring into the White House complaining that a deserving female candidate had been "snubbed" by the white male mafia surrounding the president.

"The day those guys at the White House said [Madeleine] was in the second tier was one of the luckiest days of her life," said Wendy Sherman, one of the organizers of the pro-Albright effort. "It started a cacophony. . . . My telephone just rang off the hook from women around town who were mortified that someone would dare take someone who was a really capable person, who had been our U.N. ambassador for four years and done a terrific job, and say she was a second-tier candidate. It was a really stupid thing to say."

The old girls' network swung into action. In her words, Mikulski "went volcanic" over the *Post* story. "It seemed to me there was a whole wingtip gang at the White House determined to elbow Dr. Albright out. . . . I was not going to have second-raters deciding that she was second tier." She telephoned the president to express her dissatisfaction in the strongest possible terms. Ferraro also got on the phone to the White House, with a double-barreled argument. First, Madeleine was the best candidate. Second, women had made the difference in the last election. How can you not pay attention to that? "If we had not let our views be heard, the guys would have succeeded," she concluded later. "I think the guys were doing what guys do. They were looking after themselves. Now we were doing the same thing."

In the end, the choice came down to Albright and Holbrooke. Both of them were likely to be more vigorous in projecting American power than the shy and withdrawn Christopher. The negotiator of the Bosnia peace accords was a controversial figure, immensely talented but with a reputation for being difficult to control. He was like a bull in a diplomatic china shop. Like Madeleine, he was good with Congress and comfortable in front of the television cameras. Unlike her, he was not regarded as "a team player." Although Holbrooke had the support of Vice President Al Gore and Deputy Secretary of State Strobe Talbott—one of Clinton's oldest friends—he was seen as a more risky choice than Albright. The Albright camp began promoting Madeleine as "Holbrooke without the neuroses."

As is often the case with personnel appointments, Clinton had difficulty making up his mind. According to his chief of staff, Leon Panetta, "He is constantly churning these things in his mind. It is difficult to bring him to closure." A lot depended on how the key national security officials—at State, the Pentagon, and the NSC—would meld together as a team. The president was moving toward naming a Republican, William Cohen, as secretary of defense, and a Hispanic, Bill Richardson, as ambassador to the U.N. The new national security adviser, Sandy Berger, was Jewish. A woman would add something else to the mix. "It had a nice presentational quality to it," recalled Panetta. "It was a great cross-section of the country."

In the end, even Gore, who had been Holbrooke's leading supporter, accepted these arguments. When Clinton met with his top advisers on December 4, Gore argued that an Albright-Cohen combination would be well received in the country. "That basically clinched it," said Panetta.

The president phoned Madeleine on the morning of December 5, 1996, to tell her he had made up his mind. Later that afternoon, he introduced her to the press as the sixty-third secretary of state of the United States. The decision, he said, was based on merit, but he had not been oblivious of her gender. "Am I proud that I got a chance to appoint the first woman secretary of state?" he asked rhetorically. "You bet I am. My mama's smiling down on me right now." In her acceptance remarks, Madeleine talked once again about her immigrant background. "We came to America after being driven twice from our home in Czechoslovakia—first by Hitler and then by Stalin. Because of this nation's kindness, we were granted political asylum and I have had the opportunity to live my life among the most generous and courageous people on earth."

The confirmation process was a breeze. Jesse Helms, who had tormented the Clinton administration during the first term, went out of his way to be gallant and charming. Other senators saluted the nominee as a "role model" and "champion of democracy." Without much debate, the senators later voted 99–0 to confirm Madeleine as secretary of state. The appointment was greeted with widespread enthusiasm. Women's groups were ecstatic. Pundits and editorial writers competed with one another to heap praise on the new secretary. When she appeared in public, people rushed up to shake her hand and congratulate her. At the State Department, hurt by years of criticism and budget cuts, morale soared. No one, it seemed, had a bad word to say about her, at least for publication. "Washington is in love with hawkish, charming Madeleine Albright," wrote *Newsweek* in a gushing cover story entitled "Mad About Madeleine." *Time* talked about the "Star Is Born debut" of the new secretary.

In return for her confirmation, Madeleine promised the senators "to tell it like it is," both at home and abroad. "Telling it like it is" quickly became her mantra, boosting her image as a no-nonsense, plainspoken woman willing to stand up to supine bureaucrats and brutal dictators alike. Within days of assuming her new office, however, she found herself embroiled in controversy over whether she had told her own family history "like it was."

Dasha Šima, left, and Olga Gellner (former wife of Jan Korbel and Madeleine and Dasha's aunt) with a family friend in London in 1989. *Courtesy of the Albright Family.*

Out of the Past

When President Clinton nominated Madeleine Albright for the position of secretary of state, I had been covering the State Department for eighteen months for *The Washington Post*. I had spent a lot of time traveling around the world with the outgoing secretary, Warren Christopher, a self-effacing lawyer who was Madeleine's opposite in almost every respect. He was born in a small town in the Midwest, whereas she had emigrated to America from Europe. His public communication skills were lamentable; hers were superb. His approach to diplomacy was that of an attorney representing his client through long and dogged negotiations. She was a politician with a penchant for staking out firm moral positions and seeing the world in black and white. He once confessed to me that it took him several years as America's top diplomat to appreciate the need for "American leadership." She had been brought up to view America as the world's "indispensable nation" that had ridden to the rescue in two world wars.

In order to understand the worldview of the new secretary of state, I needed to understand the forces that had shaped her. She frequently made mention of her family history in her speeches, but the details were almost cliché-like in their sketchiness. I wanted to flesh out the story and explain the evolution in her political philosophy. My editors readily agreed that I should write a magazine article focusing on her family's escape from Nazism and communism, the twin totalitarian forces of the twentieth century. The editor of *The Washington Post* magazine, Steve Coll, wanted the story to run as soon as possible after Madeleine formally took office.

At this time, I had never met Madeleine and knew very little about her, other than what I had read in the press. I outlined my idea to her press spokesman, Jamie Rubin. A few days later, Madeleine herself phoned. She explained that she could not talk to me on the record until confirmed by the Senate—an understandable concern—but was intrigued by my project and was willing to help. We chatted for some fifteen minutes about her childhood. At one point, I asked if she had any relatives still living in Prague. She mentioned a long-lost cousin, who had somehow been trapped in Czechoslovakia after the Communist coup of February 1948. This immediately whetted my interest: I thought it would be fascinating to see how their lives had taken different directions during the Cold War. But Madeleine seemed reluctant to give me further details about the cousin, saying she had lost touch with her. She was similarly vague when I asked for names of family friends in Belgrade, where her father had served as Czechoslovak ambassador. It was clear to me that if I wanted to track these people down, I would have to do so on my own.

By chance, just as I was beginning to research Madeleine's family background, the *Post* asked me to go to Belgrade to report on street demonstrations against the regime of Slobodan Milošević. I had lived in Yugoslavia for four years as a journalist during the Tito era and spoke Serbo-Croat. I agreed with my editors that I would combine the two assignments, stopping over in Prague on my way back to Washington.

The anti-Milošević rallies were the Serbian equivalent of a Washington cocktail party for the political opposition. Every afternoon, under the watchful eye of riot police, thousands of disillusioned Serb intellectuals and journalists would gather to socialize with one another while occasionally chanting "Down with the dictatorship." It was an ideal place to exchange information. I was soon put in touch with the Janković family, who had been exceptionally close to the Korbels. Josef Korbel's Serb journalist friend, Pavle Janković, had died two years before, but his son Milan was still alive. He and his brother had played with Madeleine as young children in the courtyard of the Czechoslovak embassy. Milan gave me pictures from the family album and copies of letters between the Janković family and the Korbels. He also gave me clippings from Belgrade news-papers describing the friendship between the two families. The stories mentioned in passing that Madeleine's parents were both Czech Jews who had lost many of their relatives in Nazi concentration camps. This was the first I had heard about any connection between Madeleine Albright and the Holocaust. I was a little skeptical of the information but decided to follow it up when I got to Prague.

My first stop in Prague was the library of Radio Free Europe, a U.S.-funded radio station broadcasting to the former Soviet bloc. I asked for any newspaper clippings dealing with Madeleine Albright. There were not very many, but one, dated January 22, 1994, gave a potted version of the family history. It reported that Madeleine's grandfather, Arnošt, had lived in a little Bohemian town called Letohrad. The story mentioned, again in passing, that Arnošt and his wife, Olga, had died "in the gas chambers." Armed with this information, I called on the offices of the Prague Jewish community, which keeps records on all 77,297 Czech Jews who died in the Holocaust. They were quickly able to confirm that Arnošt and Olga Körbel had been taken to Terezín in July 1942. Arnošt had died in Terezín, and Olga was transported to Auschwitz in October 1944.

The Czech newspaper story also contained a reference to Madeleine's cousin Dasha, who had married a certain "Engineer Šima" and was still living in Prague. Unfortunately, the story did not give his first name. There were more than two full pages of Šimas in the Prague telephone directory. My Czech interpreter gamely began ringing the Šimas one by one, but no one acknowledged any connection with Madeleine Albright. The task of locating the correct Šima seemed beyond us. I left several mes-sages with Jamie Rubin in Washington in the hope that he could per-suade Madeleine to help, but he did not return the calls. With time running out, I decided to take a trip up to Letohrad to see the town where Madeleine's father was born.

The mayor of Letohrad was a friendly bear of a man named Petr Šilar. He was delighted to see me. Apart from its match factory, which Arnošt Körbel had helped to found, Letohrad was not famous for much of any-thing. The mayor had been trying since early 1994 to use the connection to a well-known American politician to put his town on the map, but had gotten nowhere. He had a little folder of letters and newspaper clippings that he had sent to Madeleine, describing her ties with Letohrad and mentioning her Jewish origins and the deaths of her relatives. He was disappointed that Albright had failed to reply to any of his letters but conceded that she was probably "busy" with other matters. (Rubin later said that Albright cannot remember receiving any letters from Šilar.)

The people in Letohrad knew all about Dasha Šima, as she had inherited the little row house that had previously belonged to Arnošt Körbel. They told me how I could get in touch with her. I called her that evening, as soon as I got to Prague, and she readily agreed to meet me the following day at my hotel.

I had no trouble recognizing Dasha. She was about five feet three inches tall, the same height as Madeleine, with the same stocky build and hawk-like facial features. Indeed, she looked like a less chic Eastern European version of her American cousin. She had a strong, forthright manner and was obviously a woman of keen intelligence. Her voice was deep and gravelly. She spoke almost perfect English, but the accent was British rather than American, the result of the war years spent in Britain. I was struck by her pale blue, almost translucent, eyes. Later, I came to recognize those eyes as distinguishing features of the extended Körbel clan, from Israel to America.

Dasha was eager to tell me her story—partly, I suspected, because I was the first person to really want to hear it. She seemed upset that Madeleine kept on coming to Prague without visiting her or even calling. "It's not so difficult to get hold of me," she told me. "I'm certain that she is busy, but also certain that she has a hotel room with a telephone in it. She could find the time to give me a ring. It would be quite enough." The two cousins had met, briefly, a couple of times since 1989. Dasha told me that she had attempted to get in touch with Madeleine in January 1994 after reading in the newspapers that her cousin was visiting Prague as U.S. ambassador to the United Nations. Since she had just changed apartments, she feared that Madeleine would not be able to get in touch, so she attended a press conference given by the ambassador. At the end of the press conference, she tried to hand her cousin a letter with her new address, but it was intercepted by a bodyguard. She had no idea if Madeleine ever received the note.

One of the reasons Dasha was so keen on maintaining ties with her relatives was that she had no immediate family of her own. Her father, mother, and younger sister had all perished in the concentration camps.

She had little contact with the outside world in the four decades during which Czechoslovakia was part of the Soviet bloc. She had kept in touch with her English cousins, George and Alena, and had visited them in England. It pained her that her contacts with her American cousins remained so sporadic even after the fall of the Berlin Wall. She had spent much of her adolescence with them and still felt much affection for them. Apart from her husband and children, they were the closest thing she had to family.

Like many Americans of Czech descent, Madeleine rejoiced at the end of the Cold War. When communism collapsed in 1989, she rushed back to Czechoslovakia and was among the first to seize the new political opportunities. It seemed strange that she should so enthusiastically embrace the removal of ideological barriers between East and West, but do very little about the wall within her own family.

As I flew back to Washington, I thought about what to do next. Clearly, I needed to get Madeleine's side of the story. She still had not been sworn in as secretary of state, and it might take some time to arrange an interview. Should I attempt to delicately explore how much she knew about her family background and the deaths of her relatives in the Holocaust, or should I tell her straight out what I had discovered? If I chose the latter course, should I wait until I was able to see her personally, or should I give her a heads-up first via her aide, Jamie Rubin? In the end, I decided that the most straightforward approach was also the best. The fairest thing to do would be to give Rubin a broad outline of the results of my research and ask to meet with Albright as soon as possible. Since I was under some pressure from my editors to get my story into the magazine, this was also the best way of securing an early interview with the new secretary.

I returned to Washington on a Sunday. The next day was a federal holiday in honor of Martin Luther King. The following day, Tuesday, January 21, I telephoned Rubin at the State Department. Since I did not want to put the emphasis on my discovery of Madeleine's Jewish origins, which seemed a secondary issue to me, I talked instead about the deaths of her relatives in the concentration camps. There was silence at the other end of the line as he digested this information. He then asked me whether they were killed "as Jews" or as Czechoslovak patriots. "As Jews," I replied. I asked for an early meeting with Madeleine and said I would also like to talk to her siblings and to her children. I repeated this last request to the State Department press office without telling them what I had found out.

I did not hear back from the State Department for two days. This did not worry me unduly, as I was busy writing my magazine story, which would take me until the end of the week. I also realized that nothing was likely to happen before Thursday, when Madeleine was due to be sworn in as secretary of state. On Thursday, David Leavy of the State Department press office rang to provide me with the telephone numbers of Madeleine's daughter Anne, her sister, Kathy, and her brother, John. Since Leavy worked closely with Rubin, I took his call as a green light to approach other members of the family. In view of subsequent events, it is conceivable that one arm of the State Department bureaucracy was unaware of what the other arm was doing.

I needed to get some kind of reaction from the family to include in my story. No date had been set for my requested interview with Madeleine. Since I did not want to interfere with the happy atmosphere surrounding her swearing-in, I waited until the following day, Friday, before calling Anne Albright, a thirty-five-year-old lawyer in Maryland. Once again, I debated with myself the best way of handling such a painful subject. Again, I decided to be as straightforward as possible, putting the emphasis on the tragic deaths of her ancestors rather than on their Jewish background. What I discovered is that it is very difficult, if not impossible, to gently break the news to someone over the telephone that three of her great-grandparents were murdered by the Nazis. In hindsight, it may have been wrong to try.

When I asked Anne if she had known anything about the family tragedy, she replied rather stiffly, "No comment." We then moved on to other matters, such as her memories of her grandparents. The conversation lasted for less than fifteen minutes. After Anne put down the phone with me, she rang her mother on a private line. Madeleine has subsequently claimed that this is how she learned about her family's connection to the Holocaust. She quickly made her anger known, describing my telephone call to her daughter as "unconscionable."

"Madeleine was upset that Dobbs called Anne first," her college friend Emily MacFarquhar told Ann Blackman, author of a 1998 biography of Albright. "He was very abrupt, throwing it in her face. Madeleine saw it as an underhanded assault on her daughter. She was angry about what she considered a sneak attack." As I saw it, my telephone call to Anne Albright might have lacked tact but was certainly not "a sneak attack." Indeed, quite the opposite. The information I gave Anne Albright on January 24 was almost identical to what I told Rubin on January 21. Since Rubin is so close to Madeleine, I assumed that he passed the information on to her immediately, but I have no way of knowing whether this happened. (Rubin concedes that I called him on January 21 but maintains that I waited until January 24 to inform him about the deaths of family members in the Holocaust.)

The State Department finally scheduled my interview with Albright for five P.M. on Thursday, January 30. My story for *The Washington Post* magazine was already set in type. The magazine has an exceptionally long lead time—in normal circumstances, at least three weeks—which we had managed to compress down to ten days. The final deadline was midnight Thursday, just a few hours away. Since I anticipated having to rewrite significant portions of the story, depending on what Madeleine had to say, I asked Steve Coll to accompany me to the interview. After the interview, we planned to work on the story together. While we had the option of running the story in the regular newspaper, thereby avoiding these logistical difficulties, we both very much wanted to break the news of Madeleine's family tragedy in the magazine. It was a story that screamed out for context and explanation, and for that I needed space. I also thought that a more nuanced magazine-type approach would ultimately be fairer to Madeleine than big headlines on the front page.

We met the secretary in her seventh-floor cherry-paneled office in the State Department. She was flanked by Rubin and several other aides. Later, Madeleine would complain bitterly about the allegedly "confrontational style" in which I presented my findings to her. "You would think we were in court," she told Ann Blackman. My own impression of the meeting—which is shared by Coll—was very different. It was certainly strained and awkward. The transcript reveals an unusually large number of disjointed sentences on both my part and Madeleine's. She was obviously upset by the whole business; I was somewhat nervous. While I handed her some documents and asked her some obvious questions, such as whether her parents had given her any explanation for the wartime deaths of their parents, I was hardly prosecutorial. In fact, I was trying so hard to be sympathetic that I failed to explore several apparent inconsistencies in Madeleine's story, including when exactly she found out about her Jewish origins. It is true that we devoted most of the one-hour interview to questions about the war and its immediate aftermath, but this is understandable given the circumstances. Both Coll and I were anxious to get Albright's side of an extraordinary story.

The secretary thanked me for showing her the results of my research, which she described as "fairly compelling." She said the information about the deaths of her relatives in Nazi concentration camps was completely new to her. On the question of her Jewish ancestry, she was less categorical. She said she had received "an occasional letter" since the opening up of Czechoslovakia saying "something about the fact that my family was of Jewish origin." The letters had "increased in intensity" following her nomination as secretary of state. She added, however, that some of the information in the letters was obviously wrong, such as the detail that she was born in Belgrade when in fact she had been born in Prague. She never bothered to look into the matter, partly because she was extremely busy and partly because the details were so confusing.

To bolster her assertion that her parents had kept her in the dark, Madeleine gave me a Xerox copy of a family history written by her mother and discovered in her papers after her death in 1987. The narrative breaks off abruptly at the end of World War II, just as her parents are on the point of leaving London and returning to Prague, where they finally discovered what had happened to their parents. The papers provided to me by Madeleine contain several cryptic references to the family tragedy. Describing their escape from Prague in March 1939, Mandula Korbel writes, for example, "That was the last time we saw our parents alive." A few pages farther on, she notes that "the horrible news about suffering of so many people in Czechoslovakia reached us much, much later." On the other hand, there is no explicit reference to the family's involvement in the Holocaust. Rubin pointed out that the word "Jewish" did not appear in the ten-page document.

(Albright aides have pointed to this document as strong evidence that Mandula Korbel never told her family about the deaths of family members in Nazi concentration camps. At the time, I largely accepted this argument. After examining the document more closely, I believe that it neither supports nor refutes such a conclusion. In particular, I am unable to tell whether the document provided by Albright's office is a complete copy of the original, or only a partial version, up until 1945.)

At the end of the interview, we had a brief discussion about when my article would be published. I explained why I wanted the story to appear in the magazine rather than the newspaper. Given the fact that the Korbel tragedy had remained undisclosed for half a century, it seemed to me that it would do no harm to keep it secret for another week and a half.

The State Department had other ideas. As I learned later, Madeleine was extremely concerned that my story would accuse her of concealing her Jewish origins and her family's connection to the Holocaust. Such a story would have been politically damaging to her, particularly with the Jewish community. As it happened, I had no intention of writing the story in the way that Madeleine feared. Lacking hard evidence either way, I had not at that time reached any conclusion about whether or not she had deliberately kept quiet about her Jewish background. I tended to believe her when she said that her parents had never discussed the matter with her, although I was struck by her lack of curiosity about her own past. Still, Albright and her advisers could not be sure how my story would turn out.

Fearing the worst, they decided on a preemptive strike. Getting your own version of a controversial story out first is a standard news management technique in Washington. The CBS program *60 Minutes* had already scheduled an interview with Madeleine for the Sunday after our meeting. She told reporter Ed Bradley that she had just learned that her parents were Jewish and her grandparents had died in the Holocaust. Rubin also arranged an interview for Barry Schweid of the Associated Press, making clear in advance that the secretary would be ready to answer questions about her family history. In the meantime, I received calls from both Rubin and State Department spokesman Nicholas Burns warning me that my world exclusive was "leaking" all over town and they were powerless to stem the flood. I was amused by their use of the passive voice. As I found out later, not only were they doing nothing to plug the leaks, they were actively manning the pumps. That evening, they even called other papers, including the *Post*'s archrival *The New York Times*, to alert them to the AP story.

The result of all this activity was the opposite of what the news managers intended. The *Post* rushed into print with a boiled-down version of my magazine story, stripped across the front page the next day. Newspapers and magazines competed against each other for new angles on the story. The question that I had deliberately avoided addressing—did Albright know?—became fodder for op-ed columns, dinner table conversations, and stand-up comedy shows across the country.

Writing a biography of a famous person is a little like assembling a vast and very complex jigsaw puzzle. First, you collect thousands of little chunks of information from a wide variety of sources: interviews, documents, letters, old high school yearbooks, archival records, newspaper clips, oral histories. Then you try to put them together in a pattern that makes sense. Sometimes the pieces refuse to fit in the way you expected, so you have to go back and reconstruct the puzzle in a slightly different way. Gradually, over time, a meaningful picture begins to emerge.

The part of the jigsaw puzzle dealing with how Madeleine learned about her Jewish ancestry proved to be particularly difficult to assemble in a logical, coherent fashion. She and her aides have an explanation for every unread letter and missed piece of evidence that might have caused her to stumble onto the family secret: The evidence was contradictory; she was incredibly busy; some of the people who were writing to her, particularly from Serbia, obviously "hated my guts"; there was so much mail that she "simply stopped reading" it. As for missing the overall picture, there is an explanation for that too. "Hindsight clarifies everything," Madeleine told Lally Weymouth of *Newsweek*. "It's a little bit like seeing a lot of dots on a piece of paper and when you finally draw the lines you've got a picture. But if you're not looking for a picture, then you don't see it."

Taken separately, each of these explanations seems plausible. Pieced together, they stretch the bounds of credibility.

Take the six-month period at the end of 1996 before Albright was named secretary of state by President Clinton. In July, Madeleine visited Prague with Hillary Clinton. While she was in Prague, the Czechoslovak Foreign Ministry presented her with the personnel records of her father, Josef Korbel. After the presentation, Madeleine told journalists she was "looking forward" to going through the file "to see if what my father told me about himself really is true." At the insistence of the Korbel family, the Czechoslovak Foreign Ministry has refused to release Josef's personnel file. However, I was able to see parts of the file during my visit to Prague in January 1997, when it was still available to researchers at the Institute for Contemporary History. I have also been briefed on the rest of the file by Czechoslovak researchers who have examined it closely.

Although the Foreign Ministry file contains several documents filed by Josef Korbel stating that he and his family are "without confession" (*"bez vyznání"* in Czech), it also provides conclusive proof of his Jewish origins. The proof comes in the form of a birth certificate from a Jewish registrar in the town of Žamberk describing Josef as "Jewish and legitimate." The certificate is dated March 1941, a time when Czechoslovakia's Nazi occupiers required Jewish authorities to provide records of all past Jewish births. Also in the file is a letter written by the Czechoslovak Ministry of Defense in October 1938—when the Prague government was under heavy pressure to purge Jews from public life—demanding Josef's recall from Belgrade. The letter includes the sentence "Dr. Körbel and his wife are Jews."

While it is impossible to prove that the file I was shown is the same as that handed over to Madeleine six months previously, the available evidence strongly suggests that it was. In December 1996—well *before* my visit to Prague—the Czechoslovak ambassador to Washington told the journalist Christopher Hitchens that his government had discovered documents showing that "nasty people" had sought to make an issue out of Josef Korbel's Jewish background "around the time of Munich." According to Hitchens, the ambassador went on to say that the Czechoslovak authorities had "made a present" of these documents to Madeleine.

Madeleine's own accounts of how she heard about her Jewish origins have been vague and somewhat confusing. She says she received a letter around November 1996 (four months after receiving her father's Foreign Ministry file) that for the first time made her seriously consider the possibility that she might be of Jewish origin. The letter caused her to mention the possibility of a Jewish background to White House investigators when she was vetted for the post of secretary of state later that month. But she no longer knows where the letter is, or who sent it. Clearly, the Czechoslovak Foreign Ministry documents could have provided more definitive proof of her Jewish origins than a letter from an anonymous person. As of January 1999, however, Madeleine said she had still not managed to "look through it all. . . ." "When I first opened it up, it had a bunch of stuff about expense accounts," she says. "I probably didn't dig into it deeply enough."

On at least one occasion, Madeleine still felt it necessary to deny her Jewish background even at a time when, by her own account, things were finally beginning to "make sense." On December 18, she had a farewell dinner with U.N. Secretary-General Boutros-Ghali. According to him, the fact of Madeleine's Jewish origins was "not a secret" at the United Nations, even though he cannot remember exactly how he himself learned about it. (Israeli ambassador to the U.N. Gad Yaacobi has also said that he had been aware of Madeleine's Jewish ancestry since 1994.) Boutros-Ghali had never bothered to raise the subject with the American envoy in the past. But this occasion was different. He was leaving office, a new foreign policy team was taking over in Washington, and nasty articles were appearing in the Arab press accusing the U.S. administration of being "completely in the hands of the Jews."

As Boutros-Ghali remembers the conversation, he ran down the list of new Clinton appointments. Incoming National Security Adviser Samuel Berger was a Jew. Incoming Secretary of Defense William Cohen was not himself Jewish, but he had a Jewish father and a Jewish name. "And then there's you," Boutros-Ghali blundered on, oblivious to the diplomatic faux pas he was making. "This is going to complicate your job of running U.S. foreign policy."

"I'm not a Jew," Madeleine interrupted, explaining that she had been raised a Roman Catholic.

While Albright acknowledges that she may have had a conversation with Boutros-Ghali similar to the one he describes, she says she certainly had no desire to get into a debate about her family ancestry with the outgoing secretary-general. She points out that she still had not discussed the subject with her daughters. "I don't believe that I had such a close relationship with Boutros that the first person I would tell that I thought I was Jewish would be Boutros-Ghali."

By the time Boutros-Ghali met with Madeleine, the gossip in the Arab press about Madeleine's Jewish ancestry had become sufficiently persistent for American reporters to make inquiries at the State Department. On December 11, the Jewish rumor even made the front page of the *Los Angeles Times*, only to be knocked down by a State Department spokesman. Five days later, the Associated Press reported, "The rumor races through the streets of the Arab world: Madeleine Albright is Jewish. It is accepted regardless of the fact that President Bill Clinton's choice for secretary of state was born a Catholic and is now an Episcopalian."

Madeleine's claim that she needed time to do her own research into her family background is disingenuous. Had she wanted to verify or disprove the rumors that were swirling around her by the fall of 1996, she could have done so with a couple of telephone calls. There were any number of people who could have told her the true story, including her own first cousins in Prague and London. But she made no attempt to contact them.

While it is easy enough to demonstrate that Madeleine has not been fully candid about her Jewish origins, pinpointing the moment when she first began to suspect that something was wrong with the story told by her parents is more difficult. The first opportunity, of course, was when the family returned to Prague from London after World War II, to be confronted with the tragic news of their murdered relatives. Living with the Korbels in their Prague apartment was Madeleine's seventeen-year-old cousin Dasha, who had lost her parents and her sister in the concentration camps. Another relative, Petr Novák, who had been sent to Auschwitz and had survived a mass execution, also lived with the Korbels during the three-month period before their departure for Belgrade in late September 1945. (An accomplished cellist before the war, Petr was the first cousin of Madeleine's mother, Mandula.)

Although there was considerable discussion of the family tragedy in the apartment, it is perfectly plausible to imagine that it was confined to the grown-ups and Dasha. In 1945, Madeleine was just eight years old. Her siblings were even younger. Madeleine's parents were intent on creating as normal a family life as possible for their children. Dasha says that she would not have talked about her search for her parents in front of Madeleine or the younger children. "It was not a subject for an eight-year-old." While it must have been difficult for Madeleine's parents to hide the truth from their children, the position they took was not at all unusual. Madeleine's English cousins, George and Alena, were also kept in the dark about the family connection to the Holocaust for many years.

As she looks back at her relationship with her parents, Madeleine is struck by the way they succeeded in creating a "sense of security and calmness" in the midst of turmoil. "I think that was their great talent, insulating us from whatever they were going through. . . . They focused everything on their children, trying to create a life that seemed like a semi-normal life." She says that the only time in her childhood when she felt that something was really amiss was after the Communist coup in Prague in 1948, when her parents showed up at her Swiss boarding school with the rest of the family and announced that they would not be going back to Czechoslovakia.

A more likely time for Madeleine to have suspected flaws in her parents' story was as a young woman when she began to take a serious interest in contemporary Czechoslovak history. Her graduating thesis at Wellesley was devoted to the subject of Zdeněk Fierlinger, the leader of the Czechoslovak Social Democrats who helped the Communists come to power in 1948. Madeleine's research put her in touch with several former Czechoslovak officials in London who were well aware of the Korbel family background.

Another occasion when Madeleine might have found out about what happened to her family during the war was in the summer of 1967, when she returned to Czechoslovakia for the first time since the 1948 Communist takeover. While in Prague, she met Petr Novák, who had kept in touch with the Korbel family. As a survivor of Terezín and Auschwitz, Novák was obviously exceptionally well placed to tell her the family story in great detail. In order to accept her account that she knew nothing about her family's connection to the Holocaust, you have to assume either that Novák did not think it was worth mentioning or that he was deliberately keeping the truth away from her. (Novák died of stomach cancer in 1968, so it is impossible to know for sure what took place at this meeting.)

Madeleine's memories of her meeting with Novák are vague, even though, according to her traveling companion Marcia Burick, she was extremely distraught by the encounter. She told Burick that Novák was a "friend" whose family were sent to the concentration camps in retaliation for hiding the Korbels in Prague after the Nazi takeover in March 1939. She maintains that she did not know of her family relationship to Petr until she went back to Prague in January 1994 with President Clinton and met a man who described himself as Novák's illegitimate son. "We started this weird conversation," she recalled. "He said 'Petr Novák is somehow your cousin.' " (Petr was the first cousin of Madeleine's mother.)

The person whom Madeleine met in Prague was Vladimir Ditmar, a close aide to President Havel. She had seen him in Havel's entourage on several previous occasions, beginning in 1990, during Havel's first trip to the United States as the newly inaugurated president of Czechoslovakia. But it was only in 1994, Albright says, that he finally approached her and mentioned the possible family connection. There was "a crowd of people" around and it was difficult to have a proper conversation. Independent genealogical research in Prague establishes that Vladimir was born out of wedlock in 1948 to Petr Novák and Michaela Nechvátal, the daughter of a well-known Czech poet. (Michaela later married a man called Ditmar and gave his name to her son.) Vladimir Ditmar refuses to discuss his conversation with Madeleine, describing it as a "private" family matter.

By Madeleine's own account, therefore, she knew by 1994 at the very latest that she was related to a man who had lost his entire family in the concentration camps. She might also have had a reason to suspect that her mother's branch of the family was Jewish, in view of the fact that she described Novák to her friends in 1967 as a "Zionist" who had taken part in pro-Israel demonstrations following the Six-Day War. She says, however, that in the rush of various events she failed to connect the various pieces of evidence.

"When I write my own book, I will make it very clear that I failed to put all these pieces together, and that hindsight is a wonderful thing [but] there are things in life you just miss. I missed this."

In the late sixties and early seventies, Madeleine's parents appear to have become less inhibited about discussing their Jewishness. While they certainly did not go out of their way to talk about it, neither did they go out of their way to hide it, as they had when they first arrived in America. It became an acceptable subject of conversation, particularly with close friends who had shared similar experiences.

After initially avoiding the company of other Czech Jews, Madeleine's parents began seeing old Jewish friends again. The most obvious example is Otto Kauders, one of Josef's oldest friends and a devout Jew. Josef and Mandula encouraged Otto and his wife Rita to move to Denver from

Buenos Aires so that they could spend their "golden years" together. The Korbels' willingness to help Czech Jewish friends soon set tongues wagging in Denver. Mandula asked her neighbor, Jack Newman-Clark, to help fix some welfare papers for Otto and Rita. He was unable to do much, but the incident stuck in his mind. "There go the Jews," he told his wife. "They help one another all the way through." The resumption of old friendships suggests that Josef and Mandula were becoming less concerned about concealing their Jewishness by the early seventies. Alena Korbel, Madeleine's English cousin, says that her mother resumed contact with many of her old Jewish friends after the family secret came into the open.

Although Madeleine saw relatively little of Otto and Rita, since she was living in Washington by the seventies, she knew all about them. After my story broke, Madeleine rang Rita in Denver late one night to ask for more information about her family. Kauders says she "believes" Madeleine's version, even though her Jewish friends are uniformly skeptical about it. Asked why she believes Madeleine, she shrugs: "Out of friendship."

Another person whom Madeleine called after the publication of my story was Kati Marton, whose husband Richard Holbrooke had been considered for the secretary of state position. Superficially at least, Kati's story was remarkably similar to Madeleine's. Her family had fled Hungary in 1956 following the abortive anti-Communist uprising. Like Madeleine, she had been raised a Roman Catholic. It was only when she went back to Hungary for the first time in the early eighties that she found out the real story of what had happened to her grandparents. Instead of being killed in the siege of Budapest at the end of the war, as she had been told by her parents, they had been taken to Auschwitz by the Nazis and gassed.

On one level, Kati identified with Madeleine. On another level, however, their stories were entirely different. She had discovered the truth about her family's past as soon as she began to ask questions, whereas Madeleine had taken years to reach this point. Even though there was only twelve years' difference in age between them, Kati came to feel that Madeleine had more in common with her parents' generation than hers. "I represent the postwar generation that wants the truth, the whole truth," Marton told Ann Blackman. "My parents' generation represents fear of the truth. The truth can hurt, and they have been hurt by it." She was struck by the fact that Madeleine was "using some of the same language that my parents had" in explaining why it is virtually impossible to understand "what they went through."

If one assumes that Madeleine belongs to the generation that felt it was better to conceal the trauma of the Holocaust rather than relive it, then much that is otherwise puzzling falls into place. It becomes clear why she avoided contacts with her cousin Dasha, why she never replied to the persistent letters from Czechoslovakia, why she failed to follow up the numerous clues about her Jewish heritage, why she was so protective of her daughters.

In fact—and this is the drama of her life—it is more accurate to say that Madeleine represents a transitional generation. One of the pernicious legacies of the Holocaust is the way it can reappear in the lives of successor generations in new and unexpected ways. The constant pressure Madeleine was under to fulfill the exceptionally high expectations of her parents, particularly her father, is typical of the children of Holocaust survivors. She grew up with the feeling that her parents had saved her from some terrible disaster. This explains why she adored them and bitterly resents any criticism of them. At the same time, like her parents, she is a survivor. In this, she is different from her younger siblings and from her own children, whose early life experiences were entirely different.

In the last resort, you don't survive by being sweet or loving or compassionate, although Madeleine has displayed all these qualities. You survive by being tough.

The reaction of the American Jewish community to Madeleine's version of events was one of skepticism tinged with outrage that she would want to hide her Jewish roots. The vehemence of the Jewish reaction can be explained, at least in part, by changing attitudes within the American Jewish community about questions of assimilation and identity, plus a lingering sense of guilt over the suppression of inconvenient truths. After the war, when Madeleine's family arrived in America, the goal of many Jews was to become full-blooded Americans as quickly as possible. As Frank Rich pointed out in *The New York Times*, "Even the Holocaust was not talked about too loudly among American Jews in the 1950s. However unintentionally, Madeleine Albright actually lived the darkest fantasy of the most assimilationist American Jews of that time."

Clearly, Madeleine had to do something to acknowledge her origins publicly and mend fences with the American Jewish community. The week after my story broke, she asked her brother and sister to go to Prague on a "fact-finding trip." John Korbel and Kathy Silva did much the same things I had done a few weeks earlier. They went up to Letohrad to visit their father's birthplace, called on the offices of the Jewish community in Prague, and had long talks with their cousin Dasha. They also visited the old Jewish cemetery in Prague and the adjacent Pinkas Synagogue where the names of all 77,297 Czech Jewish victims of the Holocaust have been painstakingly inscribed upon the walls. As they stopped in front of their grandparents' names, the significance of their parents' escape from Czechoslovakia in March 1939 became painfully clear. "John," Kathy murmured to her brother, "do you realize if [our parents] had not done what they did, their names and Madeleine's would be up here and we wouldn't be looking at it?"

Madeleine made her own pilgrimage back to Prague in July at the end of a trip intended to welcome the Czech Republic, Poland, and Hungary into the North Atlantic Treaty Organization. She arrived in the Czech capital after a hectic day that began at 4 A.M. in St. Petersburg, Russia, and included a stop in Lithuania. As usual, she had her own government plane, accompanied by a huge entourage of officials, bodyguards, and a dozen journalists. (As it happened, I was also on board the plane, making my last trip as State Department reporter for *The Washington Post*.) Particularly when traveling abroad, a secretary of state's movements are planned with choreographic precision, and this occasion was no exception.

As dusk began to gather over Prague, Madeleine walked into the Jewish cemetery, pausing to stop at the densely packed tombstones of noted rabbis and scholars. Accompanied by officials from the local Jewish community, she then entered the Pinkas Synagogue. There, on a side wall in front of the synagogue, just to the left of the Torah, she found the names of her murdered grandparents, Arnošt and Olga Körbel, meticulously painted in red and black. Other names filled the walls of the synagogue, from floor to ceiling, written reminders of a once-flourishing community that had been wiped out. After studying the names, Madeleine went to the nearby Jewish Town Hall, where she was shown copies of Nazi transportation records detailing the fate of her relatives.

Emerging from the Town Hall, Madeleine read a prepared statement to waiting journalists in a halting voice. On previous visits to the synagogue, she said, it had never occurred to her to look for the names of her own family members. "Tonight, I knew to look for those names—and their image will forever be seared into my heart." As she looked at the names, she thought about her parents and "the choice they made." "They clearly confronted the most excruciating decision a human being can face when they left members of their family behind even as they saved me from certain death. . . . That most painful of decisions gave me life a second time. . . . I have always felt that my life story is also the story of the evil of totalitarianism and the turbulence of twentieth-century Europe. To the many values and many facets that make up who I am, I now add the knowledge that my grandparents and members of my family perished in the worst catastrophe in human history."

After reading her statement, Madeleine took off her glasses and walked off into the gloom of the Prague night. The bodyguards trailed a respectful distance behind. To those of us who were watching her, it seemed that she wanted nothing more than to be left alone, completely alone, away from the din and fury of the media onslaught.

The next day, she was back in her element, receiving a high award from President Havel and lecturing her Czech compatriots about the obligations of democracy. Late that afternoon, we all climbed into the immaculately polished U.S. Air Force jet, with "United States of America" emblazoned along the side, and headed back across the ocean. As usual, at the end of a long trip, Madeleine came back to chat with journalists. She was in a genial mood. The standing ovation that she had received from leading Czech politicians and cultural figures still seemed to be ringing in her ears. She reminisced about a previous trip to Prague, shortly after the 1989 Velvet Revolution, when she walked across the Charles Bridge and dreamed of becoming an adviser to Václav Havel. That incident seemed funny now. That particular dream "didn't last long," she told a reporter. "I don't want people to think I'm Shirley MacLaine."

There was no doubt about it. Maria Jana Körbelova had become an American.

Madeleine and two former national security advisers, Henry Kissinger and Zbigniew Brzezinski, at the dedication of the Ford Library. *State Department.*

Against the Current

Rarely has a secretary of state come to office with as much support and goodwill as Madeleine Albright. When she moved into her seventh-floor office suite at Foggy Bottom in January 1997, she was applauded by liberals and conservatives alike. There was huge media interest in the highest-ranking female official in American history. Her popularity and high visibility made her a political force in her own right. The fact that she appeared to possess her own political power base—one that was broader in many respects than that occupied by the president—put her in a unique position in the new Clinton cabinet.

Part of the Albright appeal derived from the contrast with her immediate predecessor. Warren Christopher was widely regarded as decent and competent but unimaginative and hopeless at communicating policies to a broader audience. Under his leadership, power and resources had continued to drift away from the Department of State to other government departments, such as the Pentagon, the Treasury, and the National Security Council. When Madeleine became the nation's chief diplomat, she signaled that she intended to reverse this trend. She used her femininity to distance herself from her predecessor in subtle and unsubtle ways. Addressing a town hall meeting of State Department employees on her first full day in her new job, she did a little pirouette and joked, "You may have noticed I do not look like Warren Christopher." Loud laughter and applause greeted this remark. Everybody in the room understood that she was not just talking about her sex.

The euphoria spilled over into her first few months as secretary of state. More than three dozen media organizations competed for the twelve places reserved for journalists on the secretary's plane for her first ten-cities-in-eleven-days round-the-world trip to get to know foreign leaders. As one of the chosen few, I felt I was witnessing the birth of a new international celebrity. The image that danced before me as Madeleine made her triumphant progress from Rome to Bonn to Paris to Brussels to London to Moscow to Seoul to Tokyo to Beijing was that of Argentina's Evita Perón taking Europe by storm in 1947. Jet-lagged and sleep-deprived, we all survived on adrenaline. As I filed my reports to Washington describing how she had wowed the Italians with her Stetson, charmed the French by speaking to them in French, and melted the ice-cold heart of Russian foreign minister Yevgeny Primakov, I kept thinking of scenes from the hit musical *Evita*:

> Let's hear it for the Rainbow Tour
> It's been an incredible success
> We weren't quite sure, we had a few doubts . . .
> Will Evita win through?
> The answer is "Yes!"

Evidently the same thought occurred to Madeleine and her official handlers. On a trip later that year to the ASEAN economic conference in Malaysia, she played the part of Evita for the traditional final-night skits. Wearing a shimmering black and red dress and a flower behind her ear, lips painted blood red, she entertained her colleagues with a bawdy rendition of "Don't Cry for Me, ASEANies." The revised version of the Andrew Lloyd Webber hit alluded to the poor human-rights record of many Asian governments and the Asian finance scandal then rocking American politics. After referring to her fellow ministers as Asia's "sexiest" men and jokingly threatening to expand NATO to include Mongolia, she made fun of her own hard-line image:

I was told I should roar like a lion
And wake the bad men from their sleep.
But I'd much rather
Shop, flirt, and curtsy.
At heart I'm really
Little Bo Peep.

The performance was a hit with Asian leaders, even if it led to some grumbling back home about the "personality cult" being created around the new secretary of state.

Madeleine and her aides were able to point to some real accomplishments to justify at least some of the early hype. A photograph of her walking hand in hand with Jesse Helms suggested she had succeeded in repairing the badly strained relationship between the State Department and the Republican-controlled Congress. A few weeks later, she persuaded the Senate to ratify the stalled Chemical Weapons Treaty over the objections of conservatives. She brokered a deal with Helms intended to pave the way for the payment of nearly $1 billion in dues owed by the United States to the United Nations. She helped breathe new life into the floundering Dayton peace agreement in Bosnia, winning an argument with the Pentagon over the need to keep American troops in the country beyond the original mandate. She played an important role in consolidating democracy in former Soviet-bloc states, including her native Czech Republic, through the expansion of the North Atlantic Treaty Organization. Above all, she began talking about America's place in the world in terms that ordinary Americans could understand. Her goal, she made clear from the start, was to make foreign policy "less foreign."

And yet, as she settled into the job, elite opinion began to turn against Madeleine. Many of the same commentators and Washington insiders who had greeted her appointment so effusively took a more critical second look at her performance. They found fault in everything from an alleged thirst for personal publicity to a lack of clout within the administration to a penchant for making tough-sounding statements not always supported by subsequent action. The new mood was captured in an editorial published in August 1998 by the British weekly magazine *The Economist*, once one of her strongest supporters. "She had more star power than any secretary of state since Henry Kissinger, a fact especially noticeable because she succeeded the plodding Warren Christopher. Yet these days almost nobody speaks well of her." While Madeleine Albright was by no means a failure, it seemed unlikely that she would go down in the annals of outstanding secretaries of state.

Some of the criticism was as exaggerated as the earlier hype. Washington is a notoriously fickle town, where the political mood can swing almost overnight from elation to despair. At the same time, it was difficult to argue that the world had become a safer place on her watch. After a disastrous start, the Clinton administration was beginning to get its act together by the time Madeleine took over. The terrible four-and-a-half-year war in Bosnia had been brought to an end, thanks to a belated display of American leadership. China policy was back on track, after numerous U-turns. The strategy of expanding NATO to include the new democracies of Eastern Europe was being implemented without the dire negative impact on America's relations with Russia predicted by the critics. Both America and the world were prosperous and at peace.

By the middle of 1998, crises had reappeared on a number of fronts. Economic turmoil had spread from Asia to Russia and threatened to engulf the rest of the world. A brutal wave of ethnic cleansing had taken place in Kosovo, despite administration pledges not to permit "another Bosnia." Iraq was openly defying the United Nations and the United States over inspections of suspected weapons sites. A nuclear nonproliferation agreement with North Korea appeared to be unraveling. Both India and Pakistan had ignored repeated American entreaties not to test atomic weapons. The specter of global terrorism was again raising its head. The agreement to pay backlogged dues to the U.N. was held up by a squabble over the Clinton administration's support for abortion. While many of these crises were unrelated to each other, the overall result was a decline in the credibility of the world's sole remaining superpower.

It is unreasonable to blame the unraveling of so many foreign policy initiatives on a single individual, or even the Clinton administration as a whole. Part of the problem lay in the very complexity of the challenges facing America in the post–Cold War world. Part of the problem lay in the president's lack of attention to foreign policy and his preoccupation with domestic scandals, notably his affair with Monica Lewinsky. Beyond these factors, however, there was also the question of Madeleine's own personality, a personality molded in large measure by her past experience.

The challenges confronting Madeleine Albright when she became secretary of state in 1997 were comparable in some ways to those confronting her predecessors George Marshall and Dean Acheson in the immediate postwar period. America had won a war but was having a hard time adjusting to the peace. Just as victory in World War II left America saddled with foreign policy burdens that it had never assumed before, so too did victory in the Cold War vastly expand the sphere of American influence and responsibilities. The old international order had crumbled, almost overnight, and a new one had to be put in its place. The only country in a position to accomplish this task was the United States.

The postwar generation of American statesmen, led by Harry Truman, Marshall, and Acheson, put in place institutions and alliances that neutralized the military threat posed by the Soviet Union and brought unprecedented prosperity to the citizens of the so-called "Free World." The outcome of the Cold War was by no means obvious or guaranteed in advance. In order to wage it, American leaders had to do more than make fine speeches. They had to mobilize vast economic resources and educate public opinion to understand what was at stake. A couple of examples: Between 1948 and 1953, the U.S. army nearly tripled in size to counter the perceived threat from Soviet Russia; the Marshall plan for the economic reconstruction of Western Europe cost around $5 billion a year, the equivalent of 40 percent of the U.S. defense budget for 1948.

Albright openly aspired to follow in the footsteps of men like Marshall and Acheson. She hung their portraits in her private office, invoked their legacy in her speeches, and studied their biographies. Her influence over administration policies, however, can scarcely be compared to theirs. Acheson, for example, was the key figure in a series of epoch-making decisions, ranging from the dispatch of American warships to the Dardanelles in 1946 in response to Soviet threats, to the selling of the Marshall Plan, to the implementation of the containment doctrine after 1948. Albright, by contrast, has often appeared to wield less influence than National Security Adviser Sandy Berger, who sits a few yards down the hall from the Oval Office and meets with the president every day. In general, Berger has been noticeably less willing than Albright to resort to force, or threats of force, to back up diplomacy.

Since the end of the Cold War, diplomacy and military force have given way to economics and trade as the primary tools for exerting American influence around the world. While Albright moved to assert her authority over international economic policy by appointing a strong deputy to coordinate administration efforts, her role has been secondary to that of Treasury Secretary Robert Rubin. The big economic crises such as the meltdown in Indonesia and the turmoil in global markets have been handled largely out of Treasury or Commerce. The issues on which the State Department has clearly taken the lead have tended to be back-burner issues.

In the last resort, the authority of a secretary of state depends on the willingness of the president to back him or her up. Secretaries like Dean Acheson, Henry Kissinger, George Shultz, and Jim Baker had great influence because they acted in lockstep with their president, even if they had distinguishable views of their own. By contrast, Albright's brand of global activism has often been out of sync with Clinton's much more cautious approach. The disparity deepened as the president became enmeshed in the Lewinsky scandal and had to devote much of his time to fighting for his political survival. One result of the scandal was that Clinton became more than usually hostage to his relatively high public approval ratings, his first line of defense against impeachment. Foreign entanglements, particularly if U.S. troops were involved, carried political risks that Clinton was reluctant to run.

On occasion, the tough-sounding rhetoric of the secretary of state has failed to win support from the rest of the administration, creating a disparity between word and deed. Theodore Roosevelt liked to say that the United States should "speak softly but carry a big stick." Under the Clinton administration, the outcome was often the reverse. Albright or some other foreign policy spokesman would issue fire-breathing threats, but as often as not the "stick" turned out to be unimpressive.

The most obvious example of this phenomenon is the bloody crackdown by Serbian leader Slobodan Milošević in the largely Albanianinhabited province of Kosovo. In March 1998, as Milošević was preparing to send troops into Kosovo, Albright issued a very blunt warning: "We are not going to stand by and watch the Serbian authorities do in Kosovo what they can no longer get away with doing in Bosnia." And yet, for eight months, the United States did just that, watching from the sidelines as Serbian troops shelled and torched Albanian villages, killing hundreds of people and driving more than a quarter of a million ethnic Albanians from their homes. It was not until winter was beginning to set in, and the humanitarian catastrophe became compelling, that the administration finally backed up its diplomacy with a threat of real force. The belated American intervention led to an uneasy truce over the winter months, but fighting broke out again in early 1999.

There is no simple explanation for why it took so long for the Clinton administration to act in Kosovo. A variety of factors came into play. The European allies were reluctant to go along. The Pentagon was opposed. Clinton had his mind on other matters. The administration had reservations about providing air cover for a military campaign by Albanian secessionists to break away from Yugoslavia. But the bottom line was that Albright's voice counted for less than other people's in the administration, particularly Sandy Berger, who serves as the president's foreign policy filter. "You need to understand how the process works," she says. "You never get decisions [on military intervention] just like that, especially when you have . . . other people that are a part of it. I don't have the troops. This is a process which is consensual, incremental, [and] takes a while."

Subsequent events in Kosovo suggest that Madeleine's initial impulse to take some kind of preventative action was basically sound. Her family's experience in the wake of the 1938 Munich crisis and the 1948 Communist takeover of Czechoslovakia taught her to view America as the "indispensable nation." She was one of the first members of the Clinton administration to understand the threat posed to the new world order by the rise of nationalism in the geopolitical vacuum created by the collapse of communism. Her problem as secretary of state was essentially the same as it had been as U.S. ambassador to the United Nations: to translate these instincts into a coherent foreign policy strategy and a clear set of priorities, and cajole or maneuver the rest of the administration into implementing her ideas.

• • •

In some ways, of course, the challenges confronting Albright are much more complicated than those that confronted her predecessors. The single monolithic threat represented by the Soviet Union has been replaced by a multitude of different threats, including ethnic upheavals, global terrorism, nuclear proliferation, and economic chaos. Perhaps inevitably, it has proved much more difficult to mobilize resources to combat these hybrid menaces to global order than it was to fight a single, obvious enemy. The collapse of communism and the fall of the Soviet Union left Western governments and public opinion politically disoriented. The ideological certainties of the Cold War gave way to the practical problems of cleaning up the political and economic mess left behind by the failed experiment in utopia.

Marshall and Acheson had the advantage of facing an overwhelming and very obvious menace. The foreign policy bureaucracy, much smaller in those days, was galvanized into action by crises like the Communist coup in Czechoslovakia and the Berlin blockade in 1948, and the invasion of South Korea two years later. In the absence of such obvious threats to American interests, the law of bureaucratic inertia tends to take over. A former U.S. ambassador to Belgrade, Warren Zimmermann, complained that "it's rarely possible to win support for preventive action at a time when the circumstances that unambiguously justify such action have not yet arrived." Although the ambassador was referring to the Bush administration's failure to prevent Yugoslavia's descent into chaos in 1991, his words could equally well apply to the Clinton administration's handling of events in Kosovo. Put another way, inaction is usually preferable to action, up until the moment when the costs of inaction become impossible to defend.

The natural disinclination of bureaucracies to take new initiatives can be overcome only by extraordinary guile and persistence. Some of Madeleine's friends and supporters have been disappointed by her reluctance or inability to use her popularity to outmaneuver her bureaucratic rivals and impose her views within the administration. They complain that she travels too much, leaving "the boys" to run the show at home. It would be out of character for Albright to put on the kind of scenes staged by predecessors Henry Kissinger and George Shultz when they felt they were being overruled. Indeed, she is so intent on demonstrating her loyalty that she avoids doing anything that might suggest that she would be willing to break ranks with her colleagues. When a gossip columnist for *The New York Daily News* wrote that she was considering resigning because her influence was on the wane, the State Department went to considerable lengths to knock down the story.

Despite her strong feelings about adultery, which took a toll on her own marriage, Madeleine stood by Clinton through thick and thin during the Lewinsky scandal. When he denied allegations of an affair with Lewinsky at a cabinet meeting, she put her own credibility on the line by going out and publicly vouching for his truthfulness. She continued to show 100 percent support for the president even after he acknowledged having misled her and other members of the cabinet. Unlike her friend, Health and Social Services Secretary Donna Shalala, who criticized Clinton to his face at a cabinet meeting and was roundly accused of "disloyalty" in return, Madeleine never permitted the slightest hint of disapproval to cross her lips. When interviewers pressed her on the subject, she brushed their questions aside.

Such dogged displays of loyalty go to the heart of Madeleine's personality and upbringing. She got where she is today not by rebelling but by conforming. Her entire life—and the life of at least three generations of her ancestors—has been marked by a struggle for acceptance. As an immigrant and as a woman, she was in a doubly vulnerable position. She had to prove her loyalty and indispensability over and over again.

The public perception of Madeleine Albright is that of an outspoken woman who "tells it like it is," whatever the consequences. While it contains a kernel of truth, this image is ultimately misleading. In reality, her urge to tell it "like it is" has been tempered by a competing urge to please a succession of powerful, predominantly male, patrons. In recent years, what friends describe as "the lion in Madeleine" has become a key element in her public persona, and is particularly evident in her dealings with the outside world. When denouncing tin-pot dictators in small countries like Cuba, Burma, or Croatia, she allows full rein to this side of her character. She keeps the inner lion on a much tighter leash when addressing the failings of important countries like China or key U.S. allies such as Saudi Arabia. In internal administration debates, her loyalist instincts come to the fore.

Despite her best efforts, and despite her high position, Madeleine has yet to be fully accepted into the club of white males that has long exercised a grip over U.S. foreign policy. "Being a woman is a deficiency," says a woman friend who has worked with her in the government. "This is something you have to be female to understand. You are not one of the boys. If you insist on getting your way, they complain you are a pushy female. A man is never too pushy."

Paradoxically, Madeleine has been criticized for being both too tough *and* too conciliatory. She has gained a reputation within the administration for being too quick to advocate the deployment of U.S. military force, even in marginal situations like the civil war in Albania soon after she took the job of secretary. She tends to stake out strong moral positions but has difficulty coming up with a viable, step-by-step plan for achieving U.S. objectives that can gain general support. "Her strength is public articulation of clear positions," says another senior administration official. "Her weakness is making it happen bureaucratically." According to this source, who has seen Albright in action in Principals' Committee meetings, she rarely goes beyond her initial brief. The debate tends to swirl around her and she is reduced to reaffirming her basic position. As a result, she is less influential than she might otherwise be.

It is interesting to compare Madeleine to her rival for secretary of state, Richard Holbrooke. Their positions on many foreign policy issues are very similar—Holbrooke once boasted that they were "joined at the hip" on Bosnia—but their style is quite different. While he bulldozes his way through every conceivable obstacle, she prefers to work by consensus. Unlike Holbrooke, Albright is not a nimble tactical thinker who thrives on unexpected challenges. On the other hand, she has a much less abrasive personality. While he is willing to upset almost everyone to get his way, she tries to charm her opponents into agreeing with her.

Clinton's decision to nominate Holbrooke as ambassador to the United Nations in the summer of 1998 was generally viewed as a sign of Albright's waning influence in the administration. Madeleine put the best spin possible on the nomination by claiming that it was her idea, but few in Washington believed that. One Holbrooke ally went so far as to claim that she fought the appointment "with every fiber of her being," before eventually consenting when it became clear that this was what the White House wanted. Despite a common front in public, leaks from the two camps suggested a continuing rivalry between the secretary and the ambassador.

Given her family background and personal history, it is scarcely surprising that Madeleine's great strength as secretary of state should be in the area of public presentation. In their different ways, and in their different fields, both her grandfather and father were indefatigable salesmen. Her grandfather Arnošt found new markets for matches and building materials all over Bohemia. As the head of the broadcasting department of the Czechoslovak government-in-exile in World War II, her father Josef was a salesman of ideas. He went on to become an inspiring teacher. Madeleine, too, is a naturally gifted professor. In selling their products and their ideas, all three generations of the Korbel family were also selling themselves.

As the front person for a generally lackluster administration, Madeleine has done best when she has had time to prepare what she wants to say and can control the setting. Her most effective one-liners have all been carefully rehearsed. She performs superbly in front of a deferential audience and interviewer. When subjected to tough questioning or heckling, she can become testy or overdefensive. The first significant dent to her reputation resulted from her participation in February 1998 in a televised town hall meeting in Columbus, Ohio, designed to bolster the Clinton administration case for going to war with Iraq over its failure to grant free access to U.N. weapons inspectors. The meeting was disrupted by protesters and turned into a fiasco. Although she scored some rhetorical points along the lines of "I am willing to make a bet . . . that we care more about the Iraqi people than Saddam Hussein," she seemed at a loss over how to handle the hecklers. She acted as if she was shocked that anyone would challenge the word of a secretary of state.

Iraq policy came back to haunt Madeleine six months later following allegations that she had urged the U.N. inspectors to call off several intrusive inspections of suspected Iraqi weapons sites. The contrast with the administration position back in February—when it threatened to launch major bombing raids against Iraq in support of the principle of unfettered inspections—was stark. There was an explanation for the turn-around: The multinational coalition that had defeated Iraq in 1991 had largely disintegrated, and there was little support within the U.N. Security Council for an aggressive line against Saddam Hussein. The Clinton administration wanted to focus its energy on maintaining economic sanctions against Baghdad. The State Department, however, was slow to acknowledge that anything had changed. Instead, it retreated behind spurious arguments, such as noting that the secretary had been denounced as "a serpent" by the Iraqi regime, as if that made her immune from criticism.

As foreign policy adviser to Michael Dukakis in the 1988 presidential election, Madeleine observed that the candidate failed to cross "the threshold of machoism" to be taken seriously by the foreign policy establishment. His problem, in her eyes, was that he did not talk tough enough. As secretary of state, Madeleine has made sure that she passes the "macho test." She takes every opportunity both to talk tough and look tough, from being photographed in a Stetson to delivering speeches on warships. But this has led her into a different kind of trap, one in which people are constantly checking up to see if she is delivering on her rhetoric.

Her problems have been compounded, in the eyes of opponents and even some supporters, by the relentless attempts of her public relations team to shape the next day's news cycle. At times, she appears overdependent on a small circle of advisers, notably her chief spokesman, Jamie Rubin, who is in charge of her "image." Even the critics acknowledge that Rubin is extraordinarily adept at securing favorable media coverage for his boss by leaking flattering stories to favored journalists and arranging interesting photo ops. The rap is that Rubin is *too* successful and *too* influential. Sometimes it is better to lose the next day's news cycle than to act in ways that will return to haunt you later.

While some have sought to cast Rubin as the evil puppeteer pulling the strings behind the scenes, this image is almost certainly wrong. In my own dealings with him, I have had little doubt that he acts in accordance with Madeleine's wishes, under her direction. The simplest explanation for the fevered efforts to make the secretary look good is that this is what she wants. Madeleine has always been sensitive to what people say about her.

Madeleine's preoccupation with her own image has been reflected in an occasional tendency to lose her temper with subordinates, often on the pretext that they were somehow making her "look bad." The most public example of this phenomenon occurred at a press conference during the visit to Prague in July 1997, when she humiliated her official interpreter by repeatedly questioning his language ability. The poor man froze and was eventually unable to carry on. Although his work was undoubtedly inadequate, the spectacle of a relatively junior employee being dressed down so publicly by his boss shocked many people in the room. Such incidents have also taken place in private. "This is a woman who yells at the help," said a State Department official accused of being a "stupid idiot" by Albright for allegedly failing to deliver a piece of paper on time. "The shit flows downhill. Not a lot of buck stops at the top."

After the plaudits of her first few months in office, the sniping began to take its toll. In public, Madeleine reacted as if she was unconcerned. "There have been times when I've been queen of the May and times when I've been the ugly duckling," she told an interviewer. In private, however, she let it be known she was frustrated by her lack of influence. In September 1998, shortly after a trip to Washington, her friend Václav Havel dropped the tantalizing suggestion that Madeleine might succeed him as president of the Czech Republic. Since she was born in Prague and is wildly popular among Czechs, she would be both eligible for the position and a very strong candidate. It seemed unlikely that she would be seriously tempted—her ties are in America rather than Europe—but the vote of confidence was a boost for her morale.

At a roast for *The New York Times* columnist William Safire in October 1998, she neatly deflected the most wounding attacks on her performance as secretary of state by making light of them. She even made fun of her discovery of her Jewish ancestry, a particularly sensitive subject that she has rarely been inclined to joke about. The official State Department transcript demonstrated a comedian's flare for timing:

> Some say our foreign policy is hegemonic, that we're arrogant and seek to impose our views and values on others. But let's be honest. Who cares what they think? (Laughter.)
>
> Some say our foreign policy is all style and no substance, but they are just jealous of my hats and pins. (Laughter.)
>
> Some even say the secretary of state is thin-skinned and can't take criticism. I can't stand people who say that. (Laughter.)
>
> Finally, some in the press seem to hold America responsible for

everything that goes wrong anywhere in the world. This commentary never used to make me feel guilty, and then I found out I was Jewish. (Laughter.)

There is a circular quality to Washington reputations and bureaucratic battles. As George Shultz liked to remark, nothing ever gets finally decided in Washington, particularly in the national security field. By the beginning of 1999, the foreign policy landscape had changed yet again. An election campaign was under way in Israel that would have important consequences for the faltering Middle East peace process. After several rounds of brinkmanship, the United States had finally carried out its threat to bomb Iraq in retaliation for Saddam Hussein's refusal to cooperate with U.N. weapons inspectors. As NATO was gearing up to celebrate its fiftieth anniversary, it was confronted once again with a crisis in the Balkans that threatened to undermine its credibility. The wheel would undoubtedly turn a few more times before Madeleine stepped down as secretary of state.

For all the criticism, one lasting achievement was likely to remain. By virtue of her engaging personality—and the very fact that she *is* the first woman secretary of state—Madeleine succeeded in attracting new audiences for foreign policy at a time when America appeared to be in danger of turning inward. "I think she rewon a constituency for foreign policy," said Catherine Kelleher, head of the Aspen Institute in Berlin and a former Clinton administration colleague. "It hasn't been wonderful and she's made mistakes, but she's reconnected with the domestic popular base. That is very important. What might have been in the offing was a return to neo-isolationism. She has made that impossible."

It is tempting, as the twentieth century comes to an end, to see Madeleine Albright as the embodiment of its startling contradictions. No previous era in human history has witnessed such terrible atrocities, or such extraordinary social and economic progress, as the century that has just passed. The combination of modern technology and mass communication techniques made possible the tragedy of the Holocaust and the murders committed in the name of an unattainable Communist utopia, the genocide in Cambodia and Rwanda, and the mindless bloodletting of

countless wars. But they also made it possible for billions of people, particularly women, to lead freer, richer, and more productive lives than ever
before. Destruction and liberation have gone hand in hand in the twentieth century, touching the lives of vast numbers of people, including the
woman who was born Maria Jana Körbelova in the "faraway country" of
Czechoslovakia on the eve of World War II.

But Madeleine is more than just a symbol. She is also an individual
who has succeeded in taking maximum advantage of the hand that fate
has dealt her. There is a streak of the miraculous in the story of how she
and her family survived the Holocaust, escaped from the Communists,
and came to America. Once in America, Madeleine broke through traditional male barriers to rise to the highest position ever attained by a
woman through a mixture of persistence, personal charm, and dogged
hard work. The odds were stacked against her, as they had been stacked
against her ancestors, but she managed to overcome all the difficulties.
She not only survived; she triumphed.

There are so many different sides of Madeleine Albright that it is difficult to sum them up in a sentence. She can be both charming and ruthless. She can be extraordinarily kind and generous but also abrupt, even
vindictive. She campaigns passionately for causes that she believes in, but
she can also be excessively concerned with her own image. She is friendly
and spontaneous, but also very rehearsed. She is intelligent and exceptionally hardworking, a woman of enormous authority. But there are also
times when she appears vulnerable and insecure. In short, she is not a
saint. She is a human being.

America needs heroes and heroines. But since these are unheroic
times, and the Trumans and the Achesons are in short supply, there is
a tendency to create artificial heroes. The result, as often as not, is a succession of plasterboard role models who end up falling from grace in
one way or another. The media and the public relations industry build
public figures up and tear them down with bewildering frequency. As
Al Gore, Clinton's vice president, has observed, the media seem to have
only two categories: "Either you're a good guy in a white hat or you are a
hypocrite."

Madeleine Korbel Albright is a heroine, but a different kind of heroine from the two-dimensional cutout figure beloved of journalists and spin
doctors alike. She can be understood only in the context of where she came

from and the struggle to get to where she is. She represents a family that succeeded, in just four generations, in making the journey from a now nameless Galician ghetto to the pinnacle of American politics. In her own life, she has experienced triumph and tragedy, happiness and heartbreak. She has raised three children, known the pain of losing a baby, and overcome the trauma of divorce. By reaching one of the highest positions in the United States attainable by an immigrant, she has exceeded the expectations of her ancestors.

In some ways, Madeleine Albright's life reads like a work of fiction. It seems appropriate that the first place she ever lived in America should have been the real-life setting for *The Great Gatsby*, the greatest American novel of the twentieth century. When they first arrived in Long Island, the Korbel family were virtually penniless. By the time Madeleine returned in the sixties, she had married into the American aristocracy, a position that served as a springboard for scaling the highest levels of the American establishment.

There is a Gatsbyish quality to the Madeleine Albright story. Her friends and admirers will object that Gatsby reinvented himself cynically and unscrupulously while Madeleine's self-transformations have taken place honorably and naturally. Furthermore, wealth for Madeleine was a means to an end, rather than an end in itself as it was for Gatsby. That is no doubt true. Like Gatsby, however, Madeleine is a larger-than-life character who refuses to accept defeat. Like Gatsby, she has been single-minded in her pursuit of the American dream. Like Gatsby, she has sought to escape her past, or rather remold it to suit her convenience. It is fitting that the past should have caught up with her at the very moment she achieved her greatest ambition:

So we beat on, boats against the current, borne back ceaselessly into the past.

AFTERWORD
"Madeleine's War"

International peace monitors and journalists discovered the blood-spattered corpses of the Kosovo Albanian villagers the day after the massacre. In one house lay the body of an eighteen-year-old girl, Hanumshah Mehmeti, killed as she tried to protect her brother. In a nearby house, four bodies lay on the floor. Walking up a steep, ice-covered hill above the village, the monitors came across a headless corpse. The most gruesome sight of all was at the top of the ravine. A total of nineteen bullet-ridden bodies had been thrown down a gully. All were in civilian clothes, and all had been shot from what appeared to be close range.

The story of what happened in the village of Račak was pieced together later by war crimes investigators, who made the atrocity the first count of their indictment of Yugoslav president Slobodan Milošević for "crimes against humanity." Yugoslav security forces had mounted a full-scale assault on the village in retaliation for the murders of four Serbian policemen by Albanian guerrilla fighters a week earlier. As usual, in such cases, the attack began with shelling by the Yugoslav Army. Then, in the early morning hours of Friday, January 15, 1999, Serb police units entered the village to conduct house-to-house searches. Anyone who tried to flee was shot. Several dozen Albanian men attempting to hide in a building were discovered by Serb police. In the words of the indictment,

"They were beaten and then were removed to a nearby hill, where the policemen shot and killed them. Altogether, the [Serb security forces] killed approximately 45 Kosovo Albanians in and around Račak."

Madeleine Albright heard about the Račak massacre at her Georgetown home at 4:30 on Saturday morning, when her bedside clock radio snapped on with the news. For months, she and her Clinton administration colleagues had been arguing among themselves over how to react to the Serbian crackdown in Kosovo. Almost from the start, the secretary had favored a policy of threatening Milošević with the use of military force if he refused to back down. Other administration officials, notably National Security Adviser Sandy Berger, had been more cautious. The result was a series of confusing signals from Washington and renewed doubts about U.S. credibility. Negotiations between Milošević and U.S. special envoy Richard Holbrooke led to a temporary cease-fire in October 1998, and an agreement by Belgrade to accept thousands of international monitors in Kosovo. But few people expected the truce to hold. Soon, Western intelligence was picking up information about plans for a major spring offensive by the Yugoslav Army, codenamed "Operation Horseshoe."

As policy-makers in Washington woke up to news of the Račak massacre, the city was paralyzed by a severe winter ice-storm. Later that morning, when she got into the State Department, Albright called Berger at the White House. "Spring," she said dryly, "has come early to Kosovo."

Račak changed everything in Washington. Prior to the massacre, Clinton administration officials had struggled to agree on a policy that they could sell to the Pentagon, Congress, and America's NATO allies. The best they could come up with was a strategy known informally as "Status Quo Plus," which was approved at a meeting in the White House basement on January 15, the very day that Serb security forces entered Račak. Madeleine, who wanted the United States to broker a comprehensive peace settlement between Serbs and Albanians, could scarcely contain her frustration. "We're just gerbils running on a wheel," she fumed to her aides.

The next time that Clinton's national security team got together, on January 19, Albright found herself "pushing on an open door," in the phrase of a close associate. The terrible images of Račak—flashed across television screens and front pages around the world—had the effect of galvanizing the Clinton administration into action. It was not just the humanitarian catastrophe that grabbed everybody's attention. A public relations disaster also appeared to be looming on the horizon. On April 22, NATO would celebrate its fiftieth anniversary with a huge birthday party in Washington, attended by heads of government from nineteen countries. Since the end of the Cold War a decade earlier, the alliance that had successfully contained the Communist threat had been searching for a new role. To go ahead with an orgy of self-congratulation at the same time that massacres were occurring in the heart of Europe, just a half-hour plane ride from Rome or Athens, would expose the most powerful military organization in history to ridicule.

Prodded by Albright, the Clinton administration quickly came up with a new peace initiative for Kosovo. The warring parties—the Serbs and Albanians—would be summoned to a peace conference, loosely modeled on the Bosnia peace talks of October 1995 in Dayton, Ohio. On this occasion, however, they would not be given the chance to object or procrastinate. Instead, they would be presented with a detailed plan that would have the effect of turning Kosovo into an international protectorate. The Serbs would be required to pull most of their troops out of the province. The separatist Kosovo Liberation Army would disarm. If the Serbs rejected the plan, they would be bombed. If the Albanians refused to sign, they would lose international support, and risk seeing their arms supplies dry up.

The peace conference opened on February 6 at a former royal hunting lodge at Rambouillet, thirty miles south of Paris. The castle's architecture—full of winding staircases and long, drafty corridors—seemed to match the chaotic organization and tortuous, uncooperative mindset of the delegates. Despite the American ultimatum, nobody seemed pressed to find a solution to the Kosovo crisis. There were no real negotiations. Milošević did not even bother to attend the meeting, sending his deputies in his place. The Albanian delegation was deeply divided between moderates loyal to the pacifist Ibrahim Rugova, the unofficial "president" of Kosovo Albanians, and KLA leaders who were making their first appearance on the international stage.

The Europeans hoped that Rambouillet would be their answer to Dayton—a crowning diplomatic achievement that would bring peace to a troubled region of the Balkans. Perhaps predictably, it turned out that they had neither the political nor military muscle to ram through an agreement. On February 20, they effectively turned the conference over to

Albright, who arrived in Rambouillet in her trademark black Stetson, like a sheriff coming to impose order on unruly outlaws.

Although she was backed by the might of the United States, Albright did not fare much better than her European counterparts. Her strategy was to get the Albanians to sign the peace plan, which would set the stage for mounting international pressure against the Serbs. But the KLA delegates proved unexpectedly stubborn, despite increasingly desperate pleas from the Americans. The spectacle of a bunch of guerrilla fighters fresh out of the mountains and woods of Kosovo defying the world's sole remaining superpower was deeply embarrassing. For Albright, who desperately wanted a diplomatic triumph she could call her own, Rambouillet was a humiliating personal setback. She later told friends that it was "one of the worst experiences" of her life.

American diplomats managed to persuade the Albanians to "provisionally" agree to the peace plan by holding out the prospect of a referendum within three years on future independence for Kosovo. But even with this concession, they still insisted on consulting their supporters. The conference went into recess for two weeks. The obduracy of the Albanians took the pressure off Milošević at a crucial moment, enabling him to portray himself as the defender of national sovereignty. Many Serbs regarded Kosovo as the cradle of their country's medieval empire, a holy land sanctified by the blood of Serb martyrs in battles against the Turks. It was not difficult to convince Serb public opinion that Western diplomacy was hopelessly tilted in favor of the Albanians. Even more important, the two weeks' delay permitted Milošević to complete the military preparations for a final settling of accounts with Albanian "terrorists." He ended up rejecting the NATO ultimatum out of hand.

It is difficult to tell whether a more flexible American approach to the Rambouillet peace talks would have resulted in a different outcome. Some Serb officials who were present at Rambouillet are convinced that Milošević was on the point of agreeing to the American peace plan, with minor modifications. According to this account, the tough line taken by the Albanian side and Albright's determined wooing of KLA delegates, together with the two-week delay, only made Milošević harden his position. U.S. officials portray Milošević as "detached from reality"; they say he never intended to negotiate seriously, and had already settled on a military option.

The point, however, is that Milošević's readiness to negotiate was never really put to the test at Rambouillet. The Serbs were presented with a *fait accompli* that they could either accept or reject. With hindsight, the American peace plan reads like a remarkably hubristic document. Not only did it demand the stationing of NATO peacekeeping troops in Kosovo, it also insisted on unfettered access to the rest of Yugoslavia. The military annex to the draft Rambouillet peace agreement includes a clause stating that "NATO personnel shall enjoy, together with their vehicles, vessels, aircraft, and equipment, free and unrestricted passage and unimpeded access throughout the [Federal Republic of Yugoslavia] including associated airspace and territorial waters. This shall include, but not be limited to, the right of bivouac, maneuver, billet, and utilization of any areas or facilities as required for support, training and operations. It was scarcely surprising that the Serbs would regard such demands as an intolerable infringement on their sovereignty.

There seems little doubt that Albright and her advisers seriously misjudged Serbian intentions in the weeks leading up to the war. They believed that the mere threat of bombing, or at most a few days of bombing, would probably be sufficient to get Milošević to back down. They based this analysis on what had happened three and a half years previously in Bosnia, when a week of NATO bombing forced the Bosnian Serbs to agree to a cease-fire that they had long been resisting. But the Bosnia analogy was misleading for several reasons. First, Kosovo was part of Serbia proper, and much more central to the Serbian national myth than Bosnia. Second, in 1995, Milošević had aligned himself with the Americans in their attempt to impose peace on Bosnia. The NATO bombing raids helped him impose his will on his recalcitrant Bosnian Serb allies. Third, and perhaps most important, the NATO bombing campaign against the Bosnian Serbs was accompanied by a ground invasion by the well-equipped Croatian army, a much more effective fighting force than the KLA. In 1999, the Americans were essentially relying on airpower alone to kick the Serbs out of Kosovo.

If Madeleine had any doubts about the correctness of the strategy for bringing peace to Kosovo, she did not betray them. She seemed confident of success, even at a time when people around her were having second thoughts. "I don't see this as a long-term operation," she told a television interviewer on the opening night of air war. "I think that this is something . . . that is achievable within a relatively short period of time."

Shortly after midnight, just hours after the first NATO bombs began to fall on Kosovo, the telephone rang in Madeleine's Georgetown home. It was the president. He wanted to talk the day's events over with his secretary of state, and reassure himself about the correctness of the decision to go to war. "This is not going to be over quickly, and we're all in this. I feel we've explored every option, that we're doing the right thing," she later quoted him as saying.

Albright had already gone to bed, but she was never averse to stiffening Clinton's resolve. "I feel the same way," she replied. "Nobody should ever think we have got into this without our eyes wide open."

The Kosovo crisis was Madeleine's first really big test as secretary of state, and the one that is likely to have most impact on how she is judged by history. In other parts of the world, her influence frequently appeared to be limited, but she had made the Balkans a personal obsession. She had lived in Belgrade as a child and had followed developments in the region closely. More than any other senior member of the Clinton administration, she was keenly aware of the danger of communism transforming itself into nationalism. In a sense, the Yugoslav crisis had come full circle. Kosovo was the place where Milošević had launched his political career in 1988, shedding his former identity as a stodgy communist apparatchik in favor of that of a nationalist leader determined to protect the rights of the province's beleaguered Serb minority. After the breakup of the old Communist Yugoslavia in 1991, Milošević had waged war in Slovenia, Croatia, and Bosnia. There was every reason to believe that Kosovo represented the final battleground for Serbian nationalism.

But Madeleine's interest in the Balkans was not just academic. It was personal, even visceral. She reacted to events in Bosnia and Kosovo in an entirely different way from her administration colleagues. It was almost as if she saw shades of her own family tragedy in the lines of refugees streaming out of towns like Priština and Sarajevo and the massacres of civilians in places like Račak and Srebrenica. For a person who saw her own life as an expression of the upheavals of the twentieth century, it was hard not to be struck by the way in which the evils that afflicted her own family were returning to haunt Europe at century's end. In the words of the Roger Cohen, who covered the Balkans for *The New York Times*,

Milošević seemed to "fuse the dark forces in Madeleine Albright's dis-jointed life. . . . As a Communist, [he] represents the forces that drove her beloved father from his country. As the man who hounded the Muslims of Bosnia into concentration camps, and seven years later revived his trademark brutality for the Kosovar Albanians, he represents the forces that took three of her grandparents to their deaths in Terezín and Auschwitz." As a Communist and nationalist rolled into one, Milošević is the symbol of everything that Albright despises.

This brings us to one of the central mysteries of Madeleine Albright's life. She was brought up in ignorance of her roots, and her family's con-nection to the Holocaust, even though the "lessons of Munich" formed a key part of her political education. But, if my reconstruction of events is correct, she discovered the essential details about the family tragedy long before I stumbled on the story in early 1997. It seems likely that she knew she was related to Holocaust victims by the time she was a young adult and made her first trip back to her native Czechoslovakia in 1967. So why should she simultaneously refuse to acknowledge the facts of her own family's ethnic cleansing by Hitler, but identify so strongly with the victims of Milošević's ethnic cleansing campaigns?

In the absence of a satisfying explanation from Madeleine herself, one enters the realm of speculation. Several theories can quickly be dismissed. One is that she and her parents were "self-hating Jews," that their rejec-tion of their Jewish origins is indicative of latent anti-Semitic prejudice. There is no evidence of anti-Semitism in the Korbel family. At Wellesley College and in later life, Madeleine was naturally drawn to assimilated American-Jewish women like herself. Her parents had many Jewish friends. Another theory is that Albright suppressed talk about her Jewish background because she feared it might interfere with her political ambi-tions. There have been suggestions, for example, that Clinton might have been reluctant in 1996 to chose an "all-Jewish" national security team (Albright, Cohen, Berger. But this line of reasoning is illogical if one ass-umes Madeleine found out about her Jewish background in the sixties, at a time when the idea of becoming secretary of state seemed beyond the realm of possibility.

The truth, I suspect, is both simpler and more complex. Josef and Mandula Korbel converted to Catholicism for essentially utilitarian rea-sons, because they did not want to expose their children to discrimination and persecution. Their way of dealing with the horrors that had befallen their relatives in the Holocaust was to draw an unsentimental line under the past and move on. In this, they were no different from countless other immigrants to America over the years. As the oldest child, Madeleine was particularly close to her parents, and felt she had somehow owed her very survival to the choices they had made in life. Their choices became her choices. She felt she had no moral right to question their decisions. When I went to see her in January 1997 to talk about her hidden Jewish background, I was struck by the vehemence with which she defended the memory of her parents. She repeated several times, almost out of the blue, that she could not "question" the motivation of her parents. "I can't, I can't. I don't know how else to put it." It was as if she was defending not only their motivations, but her own.

Over time, of course, the reasons for the Korbels' denial of their Jewish roots became less valid, but they stuck to their original decision. It became too complicated to explain themselves. Once you have presented yourself to the outside world in a certain way, it is difficult to acknowledge that you are not who everybody thinks you are. In Madeleine's case, there also may have been social pressures from her husband's Waspish family. She had already converted from Catholicism to Episcopalianism to please Joe's mother. What would they and their friends think if she suddenly announced that she was Jewish? There was also the matter of how to explain herself to her own children who appear to have had little knowledge of the true family history. For all these reasons, she probably thought it better to remain silent. In order to protect herself from charges that she had hidden the truth, her story became increasingly convoluted. In the words of the poet Sir Walter Scott, "Oh what a tangled web we weave / When first we practice to deceive."

But denying her origins was not the same as denying her convictions. Indeed, over time, Albright has become increasingly outspoken on issues such as the Holocaust and ethnic cleansing. As she told me in January 1977, "All you have to do is read my speeches or talk to my friends or assess anything about my public life to know that I have always believed the Holocaust to be one of the great horrors of history. . . . I have comported myself in a way that is very much in line with somebody who has known repression and what it's like to be a victim of totalitarianism." It is tempting to conclude that Albright's preoccupation with the Holocaust and the horrors in the Balkans, and her insistence that the world remember its promise of "Never Again," is her way of keeping faith with her murdered ancestors. If she was unable to honor them through her religion and her personal identity, she would honor them through her deeds and her political beliefs.

With hindsight, there is a symmetry to Albright's life and the great events of the twentieth century. As a refugee from both Nazism and communism, she had direct experience of the twin totalitarian evils that made this century the "bloodiest century" in history. As long as the Cold War was going on, communism seemed a larger threat than nationalism. After the collapse of communism and the disintegration of the Soviet Union, nationalism again became the number one menace to the democratic community led by the United States. By coincidence, this geopolitical shift took place at the precise moment that Madeleine—up until then the "perfect staffer"—was transforming herself into a public figure. Her family's experience under the Nazis suddenly acquired a new relevance.

It is interesting to compare Albright's personality and political outlook with that of Henry Kissinger, the first person of Jewish origin to occupy the office of the secretary of state. Like the Korbel family, the Kissingers suffered grievously at the hand of the Nazis, losing at least thirteen close relatives during the Holocaust. As Kissinger's biographer, Walter Isaacson, has observed, there are two ways of reacting to such experiences. Kissinger reacted by adopting a realist, realpolitik view of the world that emphasized subtle shifts in the balance of power and the behind-the-scenes manipulation of political forces. Albright's approach, by contrast, has been idealistic and moralistic, with an emphasis on battling evil dictators and fighting for the rights of oppressed peoples.

Nowhere has Albright's almost Manichean, black-and-white view of the world been more evident than in the Balkans.

Had the war in Kosovo turned out badly, there seems little doubt that Madeleine would have received much of the blame. The finger-pointing began not long after the beginning of the bombing campaign, as soon as it became clear that Milošević had no intention of surrendering without a fight. As the orchestrator of the failed Rambouillet peace talks, which led directly to the war, Albright was in a very exposed position. In

Washington, there were rumblings about "Madeleine's war" and the alleged incompetence of President Clinton's national security team.

Perhaps the most wounding attack came from Peter Krogh, the former dean of the Georgetown School of Foreign Service and Albright's former mentor. Previously, he had had only good things to say about Madeleine, describing her as an inspired choice for secretary of state. But now, in an opinion-page article for *The Wall Street Journal*, he attacked "a foreign policy of sermons and sanctimony accompanied by the brandishing of Tomahawks." Depicting the Albright approach as "Do what we say or be bombed," he went on scathingly, "I can recall no time in the past thirty years when American foreign policy was in worse shape. This is not surprising because I cannot recall a time when our foreign policy was in less competent hands."

Albright brushed aside the talk about "Madeleine's war" by joking that she never expected to have a war named after her. She depicted the war as a crusade against a modern-day evil comparable to fascism and communism, and placed it in the context of her own experiences with totalitarian regimes, alluding once again to the failure of the Western democracies to stand up to Hitler in Czechoslovakia in 1938. "The great lesson of this century is that when aggression and brutality go unopposed, like a cancer, they spread. And what begins as a treatable sickness in one part of the body can rapidly endanger the whole." She told audiences she would much prefer to be answering questions about why it was taking so long to defeat Milošević than about why the United States was failing to take action in the face of atrocities in the Balkans.

The beginning of the war went badly for NATO and the United States. Far from hauling up the white flag, Milošević used the bombing campaign as a pretext for launching a "final offensive" against the KLA. Serb security forces imposed a reign of terror on Kosovo, forcing hundreds of thousands of Albanians to flee their homes and take refuge in Albania or Macedonia. Thousands of innocent people were brutally executed. Entire villages were looted and burned to the ground. The scale of the destruction caught Western leaders by surprise. While NATO pilots were able to destroy fixed targets such as military airfields, barracks, factories, and bridges across the River Danube with stunning efficiency, there was little they could do to prevent a Serb militiaman from machine-gunning groups of panicky Albanian refugees. Instead of stopping the Serb campaign of

ethnic cleansing in Kosovo, the NATO bombing campaign had the perverse effect of speeding it up. Unable to get even with their tormentors in
the sky, the Serbs vented their anger on their enemies on the ground.

It was a strange kind of war, fought with very unequal weapons. It
was almost as if two entirely different wars were taking place. At times,
the very high-tech war being waged by NATO in the air appeared to have
little to do with the low-tech war being fought on the ground. Even
though NATO enjoyed overwhelming military superiority, it was reluctant to do anything that would risk the lives of its soldiers and pilots.
"You are not willing to sacrifice lives to achieve our surrender," Milošević
taunted American leaders. "But we are willing to die to defend our
rights." There was an obvious disconnect between Albright's bellicose
rhetoric and the cautious half-war that NATO was actually waging.

What the critics failed to understand was that, in order to win the
war for Kosovo, American leaders first had to win the war for public opinion on both sides of the Atlantic. Had there been significant American
casualties, public support for military intervention in the Balkans would
have evaporated, as happened in Somalia in 1993. Had NATO been more
aggressive about going after civilian targets in downtown Belgrade during the early phase of the campaign, it would have been very difficult to
keep the Europeans on board. For political reasons, NATO was obliged to
wage war in a way that ran counter to all the military textbooks.

While Albright and her Clinton administration colleagues underestimated Serbia's staying power, Milošević also underestimated NATO's
staying power. The story of the war is largely the story of these twin mis-
calculations. In the end, Milošević's errors of judgment turned out to
be more serious than NATO's. Indeed, Serbian brutality proved to be a
major factor in keeping the alliance together. Without the daily television
images of terrified Albanian refugees crossing over into Macedonia and
Albania, it might have been very difficult to preserve a consensus within
NATO for bombing Serbian civilians. Once it became clear that NATO
would not fracture under the strain, and that Russia would not come to
Yugoslavia's assistance, Milošević had no reason to continue the war.

Even though America was fighting with one hand tied behind its
back, it eventually prevailed by reason of its overwhelming military superiority. But the costs of victory were huge. They included the deaths
of thousands of innocent people, Albanians and Serbs alike, billions of

dollars' worth of economic damage, and strained relations with Russia and China. By the time it was all over, the genie of Serbian nationalism had probably been vanquished, or at least weakened so severely that it is unlikely to pose a significant threat in the foreseeable future. But another equally uncompromising nationalism—inspired by a vision of a Greater Albania that would incorporate Kosovo and large parts of neighboring Macedonia—was beginning to raise its head. The mass exodus of Serbs from Kosovo suggests that the dream of a multiethnic society based on Western democratic principles is as far away as ever.

In political terms, America's victory in Kosovo was an ambivalent one. Despite talk of a new Clinton doctrine, under which America would come to the aid of oppressed peoples everywhere if it possessed the means to do so, it seemed unlikely that Kosovo would set a precedent for future military interventions by the United States. Future administrations, particularly Republican administrations, will think long and hard before embarking on the kind of war that the Clinton administration fought in Kosovo. Pragmatism—not moralism—will remain the guiding principle of American foreign policy in the post–Cold War era.

But for the woman who had escaped from almost certain death at the hands of the Nazis at the age of two, the defeat of ethnic cleansers in Kosovo was a personal vindication. Her stand earned her the hatred of many Serbs and the adoration of Albanians. "They called this Madeleine's war," German foreign minister Joschka Fischer told Albright on the day that Serbian forces began their retreat from Kosovo. "And you won it."

A few days after the end of the war, Madeleine visited a Macedonian refugee camp, and was besieged by people reaching out to hug her and shake her hand. Seven weeks later, she became the first senior American official to visit the Kosovo capital Priština, where she was greeted by rapturous crowds chanting "USA, USA." She had defied the critics, both at home and abroad, and withstood the ridicule. She had lived through what were likely to be the most difficult days of her secretary of stateship. She had seen smiles on the faces of people who—like herself six decades previously—had been rescued from terrible disaster by the force of American arms. She had reaffirmed her own history. And, in some deeply personal and perhaps indefinable way, she had restored her emotional links with her murdered—and almost forgotten—grandparents.

NOTE ON PRONUNCIATION

Although surnames are usually declined in Slavic languages, I have generally used the masculine form to denote both husbands and wives in order to avoid confusion. For example, in Czech, the name of Madeleine Albright's grandmother is Olga Körbelova, while her grandfather is named Arnošt Körbel. I have used the name Körbel for both of them.

Many towns in what is now the Czech Republic have both German and Czech names. If there is an English variant, e.g., Prague, I have used that. Otherwise, I have used the modern Czech name rather than the old German name. For example, I use Terezín rather than Theresienstadt to refer to the ghetto where Albright's grandparents were exiled, and Letohrad rather than Kysperk to refer to the town where her father was born. Similarly, when referring to people who have changed their names, I have used their most recent name throughout for the sake of consistency. This applies to many of Albright's college friends, who were known in college by their maiden names and are now known by their married names. The exception is the Körbel family. I switch between Körbel and Korbel, depending on the surname used by individual family members at any particular time.

Czech words are always stressed on the first syllable. Czech has some letters that do not occur in English. Č (as in Hradčany castle) is the equivalent of ch, š (as in Arnošt) is the equivalent of "sh," and ž (as in Nový Bydžov, where Albright's great-grandfather is buried) sounds like the "s" in "leisure." Adding the umlaut to a vowel is similar to adding an *e*. The name Körbel can also be written Koerbel. It rhymes with "jerbel," as opposed to Korbel, which rhymes with "doorbell," with the accent on the first syllable. The town Litoměřice (where Albright's grandfather was the stationmaster) is pronounced Litomerzhitse. A *c* in Czech is equivalent to the English sound *ts*. Vowels in Czech are short unless marked with an accent.

Serbian uses some of the same letters as Czech, e.g., š, č, and *c*. The final syllable *-ić* in Serbian is pronounced *-itch*. The surname of Serbian leader Slobodan Milošević is therefore pronounced Miloshevitch.

Polish has various additional letters, including ł (a soft *w*) and ę (a nasal sound). The surname of Solidarity leader Lech Wałęsa is pronounced Vahwehnsah.

ABBREVIATIONS

BBC	British Broadcasting Corporation
ČTK	Czech News Agency
DP	*Denver Post*
DU	Denver University
ESM	Edmund S. Muskie Archives, Bates College
HFG	Harry F. Guggenheim
ICRC	International Commission of the Red Cross
JCL	Jimmy Carter Library, Atlanta
LAT	*Los Angeles Times*
LC	Library of Congress, Washington
MKA	Madeleine Korbel Albright
NARA	National Archives and Record Administration, Washington
NYT	*The New York Times*
PRO	Public Records Office, London
RMN	*Rocky Mountain News,* Denver
WCN	*Wellesley College News*
WP	*The Washington Post*

NOTES

INTRODUCTION

6 "shaken and somehow violated": *Time,* February 17, 1997.

9 Frank Rich, *NYT,* February 19, 1997, op-ed page.

CHAPTER 1

14 Dates back to 1520: *Encyclopaedia Judaica,* Vol. 12, (1982), p. 1242. See also Hugo Gold (ed), *Die Juden und Judengemeinden Böhmens* (1934), pp. 416–19.

According to family tradition: Joža Pater Gruber, interview, November 1997.

16 got jobs with the railroads: *ibid.*

Joke about two coach-drivers: Quoted in Wilma Abeles Iggers, *The Jews of Bohemia and Moravia* (1992), pp. 231–32.

17 "we spoke German": Gruber, November 1997. Also Chaim Körbel, interview, November 1997.

Their first son: State archives of the Czech Republic.

18 "He was a humanitarian": Vera Ruprechtova, interview, January 1997.

"refused to have anything to do with Judaism": Alena Korbel, interview, July 1998.

19 "What kind of Judaism": quoted in Iggers, p. 290.

20 "I remained tied up": Dagmar Deiml Šima, interview, January 1997.

naming it Drollik: In September 1997 interview with author, MKA said "when we had a dog, [my father] had to name the dog Drollik, because my grandfather had a dog" with the same name. In a letter to her daughter Grete in July 1942, Olga Körbel appears to refer to the dog as "Trollo." Since the family tradition is that the dog was named Drollo or Drollik, I have used that version throughout.

"a bit of a bully": Alèna Korbel, July 1998.

"loyalty to his family": Handwritten notes to family by Mandula Korbel, provided to author by MKA.

operated the pub: Josef Korbel personal file, Czechoslovak foreign ministry, seen by author January 1997.

"a place of weddings and other celebrations": Helen Epstein, *Where She Came From* (1997), p. 28.

21 "municipal employees went around with accordions": Jan Koloc, interview, January 1997.

22 "You are a Czechoslovak": MKA, interview, January 1997.

"an intellectual and ethical giant": Josef Korbel, *Twentieth Century Czechoslovakia* (1977), pp. 12, 27, 157.

23 "the brains behind the business": Zdenek Beneš, interview, March 1998.

"anything to do with food": Avigdor Dagan, interview, November 1997.

24 "I can imagine all of you": letter dated July 3, 1967, printed in Kostelec High school yearbook.

Recall the song: Josef Marek, interview, March 1998.

25 "I disagree with absolutely everything": Rita Kauders, interview, February 1998.

The nickname Mandula: Kauders, February 1998.

26 "a very capricious woman": Gruber, November 1997.

"We are calm, well-organized": Chaim Körbel, November 1997.

28 Asked to state his religion: see, for example, Josef Korbel Foreign Ministry file.

"The only sense in which we were Jews": *NYT,* February 7, 1997.

29 "The secret of Jewish energy": quoted in Iggers, pp. 339–340.

CHAPTER 2

31 "a born leader": Dagmar Šima, February 1997.

32 "we were young and happy": Mandula Korbel notes to family.

33 "I stood like a statue": Josef Korbel, *Tito's Communism* (1951), p. 5.

"Belgrade was like a village": Jara Ribnikar, interview, January 1997.

34 "wiped off the map": William L. Shirer, *The Rise and Fall of the Third Reich* (1989), p. 496.

"My mind-set is Munich": *NYT Magazine,* September 22, 1996, p. 67.

35 talk with American journalists: Shirer, p. 510.

36 "crowds filled the streets": Nancy Bosanquet collection, Imperial War Museum, London.

The Czechs and the French outnumbered the Germans: Shirer, p. 542.

37   "We are alone": Korbel (1977), p. 141.

"Prague could never have been more beautiful": George F. Kennan, *From Prague After Munich* (1968), pp. 3–4.

38   "without firing a shot": Korbel (1977), p. 149.

"a real leader": *ibid.,* pp. 129, 147.

"we weren't scared": Jiři Weiss, interview, March 1997.

39   "hopelessly and irretrievably discredited": Kennan, p. 7.

"ready to report": Lidia Stefan Novaček, interview, November 1998. In her notes to her family, Mandula Korbel writes that Josef left Belgrade and reported to his regiment. She may be referring to an earlier partial mobilization, in March 1938.

40   "rather marry a street sweeper": Josef Korbel Foreign Ministry file.

"did not like my contacts": Korbel (1951), p. 2.

"a man of Beneš": CV, Korbel file, DU Archives.

42   "A full blizard was blowing": Kennan, p. 87.

"he haunted the house": Kennan, p. 86.

43   "told us we were Jewish": Irena Neumann Kirkland, interview, October 1997.

"my overwhelming impression is fear:" Eva Schick Beckmann, interview, October 1997.

"There was complete chaos in Prague": Mandula Korbel notes to family.

CHAPTER 3

45   "the Gestapo arrested people": *ibid.*

46   "Bribery became almost a national duty": Bondy, p. 125.

"When my country was occupied": Korbel (1951), p. 3; see also his official CV, Korbel file, DU.

finally granted exit visas: Mandula Korbel notes; Wanda Abrahammson, interview, February 1998.

47   "It was dangerous": Ribnikar, January 1997.

"a terrible time was coming": Alena Korbel, July 1998.

keep the family afloat: Dagmar Šima, February 1997.

included on a list: *Dokumenty z Historie Československé Politiky 1939–1943* (1966), p. 17.

48   "smell of cold bacon": George Weidenfeld, *Remembering My Good Friends,* (1995), pp. 82, 84.

50   "It was frightening": Chaim Körbel, November 1997.

51   "remembers the journey well": letter from Pedro Mahler to author, February 1998.

53   "If you prefer dead Jews": Nicholas Winton, interview, November 1997.

54   still unclear to Dasha: Dagmar Šima, November 1998.

changed her mind: Joe Schlesinger, *Time Zones* (1990), p. 23.

"Where is my home?": Schlesinger, p. 28.

55   "Policemen kept a gangway": Archives of Nicholas Winton.

"Madlenka is lovely": letter from Dagmar Šima to parents, July 2, 1939.

entry permits to the United States: Dagmar Šima, February 1997.

56   "the German army marched into Prague": Joža Gruber, November 1997.

CHAPTER 4

61   "I am prohibited": quoted in Iggers, p. 361. See also article by John G. Lexa, on "Anti-Jewish Laws and Regulations" in *The Jews of Czechoslovakia,* volume 3 (1984), p. 75.

63   "it will be very hard on father": letter from Olga Körbel to Grete Deiml, deposited by Dagmar Šima in the central Jewish museum, Prague.

65   "a reenactment of the Flood": Helen Lewis, *A Time to Speak* (1994), p. 39.

straw mattresses: interview with Eva Rocek, AAv survivor. Basic information on transports is taken from *Terezínská Pamětní Kniha* (Terezín Memorial Book) (1995), volumes 1 and 2. An invaluable reference source, the Memorial Book records the names of all Czech Jews transported to Terezín, together with details of their fate. There is a guide/annex in English: see below. For details of the fate of the Körbel and Spiegel families, I relied on the transport card index files held by Beit Theresienstadt, Israel, and the Terezín transport lists held by Yad Vashem, Jerusalem, Record Group 064 (Herman Weisz collection).

66   "finding a place for new arrivals": Gonda Redlich, *Terezín Diary* (1992), p. 57.

assigned to house number L304: Yad Vashem, Terezín records, 064/22, folder I.

67   "more human than in the barracks": Věra Hájkova, interview, March 1998.

"People arrive by the thousands": Redlich, p. 61.

68   "the clock ticks well": Lederer, p. 49.

highest number of deaths: *Terezín Memorial Book, A guide to the Czech original* (1996), p. 52.

"a typical family doctor": Hana Malka, Terezín survivor from Strakonice, interview, January 1998.

70   "Typhoid among children": Redlich, pp. 101–3. Redlich uses the generic German and Hebrew word "typhus," which can be translated as either typhus or typhoid fever. Descriptions of the disease make clear that he is referring to typhoid.

71   "His wife died of typhoid": note from Redlich to Dr. Paul Epstein, August 19, 1943, Yad Vashem records 064/18, folder I.

"we would wake up in the morning": "The Girls Home in Terezín," *Review of the Society for the History of Czech Jews,* volume 2, 1988–89, p. 13.

72   naturally happy disposition: Alena Korbel, July 1998.

three girls on top of a bunk: this painting has been on public exhibit at the Jewish Museum, Prague. Milena's other paintings are in the museum's private collection, which numbers some 4,000 works by Terezín children.

"we must not die!": *I Have Not Seen a Butterfly* (1993), p. 37.

73   "Frau Körbel has lost her husband": Yad Vashem Terezín archive, 064/22, file I.

74   "The Germans are going to make a film": extract from diary *Terezín* (1965), p. 111.

The chairman was favorably impressed: Report by ICRC commission, Terezín file at Holocaust Museum, Washington.

CHAPTER 5

77   "Ten Green Bottles": *Time,* February 17, 1997.

78   "Madlenka is very cute": letter from Dagmar Deiml Šima, deposited with Jewish Museum, Prague.

"the charming four-year-old": Prokop Drtina, *Československo Můj Osud* (1991), p. 566.

"sleeping in a bunk": MKA, September 1998.

79   "threw ourselves down": Drtina, pp. 573–74.

a seaside resort: Mandula told friends in Denver that she and Madeleine had been evacuated to the town of Paignton in Devon. Jack and Hilda Newman-Clark, interview, February 1998.

stayed with Jan's family: Alena Korbel, July 1998; MKA, interview, September 12, 1998.

"did not get on well": MKA, September 1998.

80   "the beds were kept in cupboards": Dagmar Šima, interview, March 1998. The London telephone directory shows that Josef Körbel lived at 35 Princes House, Kensington Park Road, from around September 1941 to May 1943. Czechoslovak government records confirm that the family was living at 35 Princes House in September 1941. In his memoirs, Drtina says he lived at adjacent Princess House, a detail confirmed by Czechoslovak government records. He says the Körbels lived in the same building as he. It is conceivable that Drtina confused the two buildings. It is also possible that the Körbel family lived at Princess House in 1940 and then moved to Princes House in 1941. MKA remembers only that her family lived on Kensington Park Road.

"I was a movie star": MKA, September 1998.

"The barrage was again terrific": diary of Vere Hodgson, Imperial War Museum archives, London.

"very good progress": Kensington High School report, December 17, 1942, quoted in London *Observer,* February 9, 1997.

81   "a lively member of her class": *The New York Times Magazine,* February 22, 1997, p. 9. See also *Esher News and Mail,* February 19, 1997, "America's First Female Secretary of State Grew up in Walton."

walked into a brick pillar: MKA, September 1998.

82   "I have to laugh": Eduard Goldstücker, interview, March 1998.

"some kind of steel table": *Time,* February 17, 1997.

beneath the V-1 flight path: Stephen Flower, *Raiders Overhead* (1994), pp. 147–53, 165. I also consulted local newspapers provided by John Pulford, of the Walton and Weybridge Local History Society.

83 "the intimacy is cold": Robert Bruce Lockhart diary, February 10, 1940, in archives of House of Lords, London.

84 "good journalistic instincts," Ota Orneš t, interview, January 1997.

"an outstanding success": minutes of BBC Czechoslovak service meeting, September 24, 1941, BBC Written Archives, Caversham Park.

"the ambience was unspoken Jewish": Pavel Tigrid, interview, March 1998.

inside the radio: MKA, September 1998.

85 "a heap of crimes": Körbel broadcast to Czechoslovakia May 27, 1942, in BBC Written Archives, Caversham Park. The archive has a separate file on Josef's wartime work for the BBC.

"hide his Jewishness": Dagan, November 1997.

"an inferiority complex": diary of Jaromír Smutný, chief of staff to President Beneš, June 5, 1941, quoted in *The Jews of Czechoslovakia*, volume 3, p. 490.

86 "just a poor old Jew": Goldstücker, March 1998.

all baptized at the same time: baptismal certificates, Sacred Heart Church, Berkhamsted, May 31, 1941; Ann Blackman, *Seasons of Her Life* (1998), p. 153.

celebrating with a couple of bottles: Jan M. Stránský, interview, October 1998; see also interview with Anna Sonnek, Ann Blackman, *Seasons of Her Life* (1998), pp. 53–54.

"That is our history": Marek, January 1997.

87 "not a churchgoer": remarks by Russell Porter, memorial service for Josef Korbel, July 20, 1977, in DU archives, Korbel biographical file.

"Körbel shared that": Lord Weidenfeld, interview, November 1997.

88 "Körbel was most contrite": memo from J. B. Clark, controller of BBC European services, to Ministry of Information, April 6, 1945, Körbel file, BBC Written Archives, Caversham Park.

89 "Hitler is deporting the Jews": letter to U.S. Ambassador to London Anthony Drexel Biddle, June 30, 1942, NARA, Washington.

"wholesale extermination": *The Jews of Czechoslovakia,* volume 3, p. 466.

90 "millions of Jews will be slaughtered": Jan Masaryk, *Speaking to My Country* (1944), p. 120.

"I am unable to believe you": E. Thomas Wood, *Karski: How One Man Tried to Stop the Holocaust* (1994), p. 188. See also: Jan Karski, *Story of a Secret State* (1944).

The reports reached London: the Vrba-Wetzler report was transmitted by the Czech government to the U.S. embassy in London, on August 14, 1944; the Rosin-Mordowicz report on July 4, NARA.

"dealing with these wailing Jews": comments of Foreign Office official A.R.

Dew quoted in Martin Gilbert, *Auschwitz and the Allies* (1981), p. 312. See
also p. 328 for reaction of U.S. war department.

CHAPTER 6

93   no longer had a mother: Dagmar Šima, February 1997.
"It was very rough": MKA, September 1998.
94   invited into the cockpit: Dagmar Šima, October 1998.
hiding under haystacks: Katalina Romero, interview, February 1998.
95   died in the course of the war: MKA, February 1997; Alena Korbel, July 1998.
"these pictures of Hell": unpublished memoir loaned to author by Alena Korbel.
"shot in a forest": Except where otherwise noted, I have relied on Zdenek
Lederer, *Ghetto Theresienstadt* (1953), pp. 199–242, for details on the fate of
all transports from Terezín to the East.
a similar fate: Marta Mahler was sent to Treblinka from Terezín in October
1942. Her son, Max, died in Majdanek in September 1942. See *Terezín
Memorial Book, op. cit.*
killing more than 23,000 people: Bondy, p. 285.
no survivors from transport AAk: Jakov Tsur, interview, December 1997. See
also Richard Rashke, *Escape from Sobibor,* Houghton Mifflin, 1982, p. 47,
Martin Gilbert, *The Holocaust* (1987), pp. 341–44, and Azriel Eisenberg,
Witness to Holocaust (1981), p. 252.
97   "another transport is being prepared": original document on display at Beit
Theresienstadt, Israel.
a drawing by Bedřich Fritta: reproduced in Gerald Green, *The Artists of Terezín*
(1969), p. 127.
98   Alisah Shek kept a diary: Extracts from diary have been published in *Theresien-
städter Studien und Dokumente* (1994), pp. 171–72. Alisah Shek now works at
Beit Theresienstadt in Israel.
99   Haindl "often snatched a walking stick": Lederer, p. 156.
"tears streaming down my cheeks": unpublished memoir loaned to author
by Eva Bloch Benda. For another account of a journey from Terezín to
Auschwitz, see *The Jews of Czechoslovakia*, volume 3, pp. 291–93.
"the refuse pail was in the middle": Eva Schick Beckmann, interview, October
1997.
100   "mayhem, complete mayhem": Beckmann, October 1997.
101   the infamous Auschwitz doctor Josef Mengele: Beckmann, October 1997;
also Helga Pollak Kinsky in the film *Terezín Diary*, The Terezin Foundation,
1992.
"a talent for laughter": Green, pp. 129–38.
102   "Never mind, my son": Redlich, p. 161.
"there are people who need those crutches": Kinsky, *Terezín Diary.*

103 "Cyclon B caused death": *Auschwitz Seen by the SS* (1978), p. 132.

"The gas rose": Interview with Filip Müller, *Shoah,* a film by Claude Lanzmann; see also, Filip Müller, *Eyewitness Auschwitz* (1979).

104 "iron will to succeed": letter to author from Jiři Deiml, Tel Aviv, January 30, 1998.

married to a fellow Zionist: Malka, interview, May 1998.

105 died just days: Chaim Körbel, November 1997.

CHAPTER 7

107 "watches up their arm": MKA, September 1998.

108 "The Russian army was master": Josef Korbel, "Free Czechoslovakia Fell Two Years Ago," *DP,* February 26, 1950.

change of name: Josef Korbel biography supplied to author by Czech Republic Foreign Ministry, January 1997.

some confusion about the job: DU archives, Josef Korbel file; Goldstücker, March 1998.

worked for both Masaryk and Clementis: MKA, interview, November 3, 1998. Albright was disturbed by the portrayal of her father in Blackman, *op. cit.,* particularly passages suggesting that Korbel overemphasized his anti-Communism for essentially opportunistic reasons. She said Blackman "did not understand the context of a coalition government, how it worked, and the short period of time involved."

109 The Nebrich side of the story: interview with Doris Nebrich Renner, Ruth Nebrich Harmer, and Philipp Harmer, March 1998.

110 "no credible basis": letter from Michael Jaffe of Arent Fox to Philipp Harmer, October 28, 1997, provided to author by Philipp Harmer.

111 in his possession: John Korbel, interview, January 1999.

"Josef was a man of character": Marek, March 1998.

112 "it was very dangerous": *Intervju,* Belgrade, January 27, 1995, pp. 9–11. Janković died in June 1995.

113 "Keep your eyes open": Korbel (1951), p. 18.

enjoyed an enviable degree of access: Korbel (1951), p. 72.

114 "for me, you are still a Czech": Ribnikar, January 1997; see also Josef's account of the incident in Korbel (1951), p. 23.

so frightened of airplanes: MKA, October 1998.

"a self-important guy": Blackman, pp. 74–75.

"a balanced, professional position": Jacques Reinstein, interview, October 1997.

115 the one room that stuck in her memory: comments to Czechoslovak ambassador to Belgrade, May 31, 1997.

"How can you do this?": MKA, September 1998.

116 "Madlenka is a real lady": "Beogradski Dani Madlen Olbrajt" (The Belgrade days of Madeleine Albright), *Politika,* March 6, 1994, p. 13.

"always in the forefront": Marek, March 1998.

"doesn't want to shake hands": MKA, September 1998.

"in order to eat": MKA, September 1998.

"communism cannot succeed": Memorandum on conversation with Clementis, November 26, 1948, Josef Korbel papers, Bakhmeteff archive, Columbia University.

117 "the army is fully behind me": Josef Korbel, *The Communist Subversion of Czechoslovakia* (1959), p. 199.

118 "the way Hitler talked": cable from U.S. ambassador Laurence Steinhardt to State Department, February 26, 1948.

appeal for political asylum: for exchange of telegrams between Foreign Office and British ambassador to Belgrade Charles Peake on Korbel case, PRO, file number FO/371/71321.

119 "very pessimistic and depressed": "Scholarly DU Dean Korbel Sees Optimistic Signs," *RMN,* July 28, 1968. See also *DP,* February 26, 1950.

"in memory of my best friend": Langus interview with Belgrade journalist Momir Ilić.

identical black cocker spaniels: MKA, September 1998.

120 *before* the February coup: See, for example, Korbel file, DU archives; *RMN,* July 28, 1968, *op. cit.; DP,* August 3, 1949, *op. cit.*

the archival evidence strongly suggests: cables from British embassy in Belgrade, February 27, 1948, and April 3, 1948, PRO, FO/371/71321; Josef Korbel biography, Czechoslovak foreign ministry. The British cables suggest that the initial suggestion came from Gottwald and Clementis. However, Lidia Novaček, a former embassy administrator, says that Jan Masaryk proposed Josef for the post well "before the coup."

increasingly unambiguous: see letter from Josef Korbel, February 12, 1949, NARA, US-UN files, IO: Delegations-Czechoslovakia; Josef Korbel, *Danger in Kashmir* (1954), p. 118; DU archives, Josef Korbel biography.

"we were very lucky in having Korbel": Foreign Office minute June 9, 1948, PRO, FO 1371/69719. See also Foreign Office cable to Belgrade, April 9, 1948, PRO, FO/371/71321.

"saw it as a challenge": MKA, November 1998.

121 "more sanguine and civilized": Cable from British embassy in Belgrade, February 27, 1948, *op. cit.*

"He was afraid of the Communists": Dagan, November 1997.

"very ambitious and very intelligent": Dagmar Šima, February 1997. MKA says she was not aware that her father was Dasha's guardian.

122 "really, really surprised": MKA, interview, February 1997.

not sure whether they could trust: Alena Korbel, July 1998.

"where is your guardian?": Dagmar Šima, February 1997.

CHAPTER 8

125   summoned back for consultations: cable from U.S. embassy Prague to State
       Department, March 2, 1948, NARA, RG-84, Yugoslav Desk files.

126   "whole family in detention": cable from U.S. embassy Belgrade to State
       Department, May 12, 1948, NARA, Yugoslav Desk files. In his book *Tito's
       Yugoslavia,* (p. 289), Korbel gives a slightly different account of this inci-
       dent. He says the Hebrangs' cook came crying to the cook of the Czechoslo-
       vak embassy.

       getting a new job: MKA, September 12, 1998.

       "the children slept endlessly": Goldstücker, March 1998. MKA is unsure
       whether her father accompanied Mandula and the other children to London.
       However, Goldstücker insists he did, and his memory is supported by For-
       eign Office documents, which show that Josef was in London at the end of
       May and beginning of June. He appears to have returned to Geneva by
       June 15, for a meeting of the U.N. commission on Kashmir, and traveled
       from there to India.

       "the single hardest school": MKA, September 12, 1998.

       "pitchforked in media relations": PRO, FO 371/71278.

127   "a good augury": letter dated August 25, 1948, Korbel file, PRO, FO
       371/69722.

       "a Democrat, no question": MKA, October 1998; the U.S. election took place
       on November 2, and the results came in on November 3.

       "I had to take care of everything": MKA, October 1998.

       the arrival of Marie Korbelova: SS *America* passenger list, November 11, 1948,
       NARA.

128   a philosophical discussion: Korbel memorandum on conversation with
       Clementis, Columbia University, Bakhmeteff archive.

       Clementis was himself purged: Clementis was hanged along with ten others on
       December 3, 1952. (Facts on File.)

       "perhaps three months": memorandum of conversation with Willard L. Thorp,
       November 25, 1948, NARA, RG-84, Records of Central Europe Desk.

       discuss his case: memorandum from Thomas F. Power, January 3, 1949,
       NARA, RG-84, Records of U.S. mission to U.N. See also memorandum
       from Thomas Power, March 14, 1949, NARA, RG-84, US-UN records.

129   "Off to America!": quoted in Iggers, pp. 148–49.

       "as to being Jewish": quoted in Barry Rubin, *Assimilation and Its Discontents*
       (1995), p. 66.

130   "we must be better Jews": Rubin, pp. 71–73.

"When I lived in France": "For a smiling nation–gratitude," *RMN,* December 5, 1954, p. 26.

131 "Don't say that I am Jewish": Arnošt Lustig, interview, October 1997.

132 "very sad memories": letter provided by Carol Zsolnay. New name of writer withheld.

133 "Somehow I had been saved": *Vogue,* September 1997; *Newsweek,* February 24, 1997, p. 31.

"didn't want to be left out": unpublished memoir of Alena Korbel; Alena Korbel, July 1998.

134 one passing reference: Korbel (1977), p. 157.

"he wanted to fit in": Arthur Gilbert, interview, February 1997.

"a very great deal": Sigmund Freud, Introduction to Hebrew edition of *Totem and Taboo,* quoted by Rubin, p. 32.

136 "a lot of stomach problems": Winnie Shore Freund, interview, September 1997.

quickly realized: MKA, September 1998.

"not necessary to drag in the Russians": memorandum from Thomas Power, February 2, 1949, NARA, US-UN records, *op. cit.*

137 called in a reporter: *NYT,* February 14, 1949.

"I would be arrested": letter from Josef Korbel, February 12, 1949, NARA, US-UN records, *op. cit.*

It took four months: Memorandum from Thomas Power, June 7, 1949, NARA, US-UN records, *op. cit.*

"remained longer than necessary": Tigrid, March 1998. See also Thomas Power memorandum quoting Jan Papánek (March 14, 1949, *op. cit.*) that there were some people with "a very strong opinion against Korbel."

refused to see him: see, for example, interview with Zdeněk Mastník, quoted in Blackman, p. 88.

urged Korbel to remain at his post: State Department memorandum, March 14, 1949, NARA, Central Europe department file.

"a friend of the West": memorandum from H. C. Vedeler, March 24, 1949, NARA, Central Europe department file.

A wave of persecutions: Antonin Sum, interview, February 1997; Korbel Foreign Ministry file.

138 sentenced him to death: see, for example, *WP* profile, January 6, 1991, p. F1.

split Josef's $5,000 salary: Korbel file, DU archives.

"Where's Denver?": Joe Szylowicz, interview, February 1998; MKA, September 1998.

"drove and drove and drove": MKA, September 1998.

139 "took off his hat": reminiscences by Robert C. Good, Dean GSIS, Korbel file, DU archives; MKA speech to Kent-Denver school, May 13, 1997.

CHAPTER 9

141   "constantly going somewhere else": *Time,* February 17, 1997.

"tried to pattern myself": *LAT,* February 8, 1995, p. E1; *Time,* February 17, 1997.

142   "a special relationship": *People,* December 23, 1996, p. 47; *NYT Magazine* profile, September 22, 1996.

"antithesis of stuffiness": David Bailey, interview, February 1997.

"amazed by the difference": Marion Gottesfeld, interview, February 1998.

143   "worrying about us": MKA, February 1997.

"scared to death": Jack Newman-Clark, February 1997.

"they all work too hard": Rita Kauders, interview, February 1997.

high parental expectations: quoted in Helen Epstein, *Children of the Holocaust* (1979), pp. 207–10.

144   "very special to that family": Dr. Robert DuPont, interview, October 1997.

"I wanted very much to be an American," *Vogue,* September 1997.

"I wanted very much to belong": MKA, November 1998.

145   "much more socialistic": Ruth Spensley, interview, February 1998.

"terrified" Madeleine: MKA, September 1998.

"screaming fights": MKA, September 1998.

146   "I will never find them again": Marie Valance, interview, February 1998.

The school ethos: interviews with Stephanie Allen, Melanie Grant, Kyle Hicks Reno, Julika Ambrose, February 1998.

147   "made myself president": speech at Kent-Denver school, May 13, 1997.

"this just proves it": *The Kentian,* 1955, Kent-Denver school archives.

148   "arguably the poorest": MKA, September 1998.

"such a couple": DuPont, October 1997.

"work ten times harder": DuPont, September 1998.

"a smothering type": Charles D. Vail, interview, February 1998.

149   met Elston at a friend's house: MKA, September 1998.

150   "these Kent women": written comment by Jack La Follette in 1954 *Angelus,* provided to author by Robert DuPont.

"for noblest usefulness": quoted in *Wellesley College 1875–1975: A Century of Women* (1975), p. 1.

151   as American as her friends: interviews with Emily Cohen MacFarquhar, January 1997 and May 1998, Winnie Shore Freund, January 1997 and September 1997.

152   "good body alignment": Wellesley physical education curriculum, 1955, Wellesley College Archives.

"sit up straight": *The Wellesley Townsman,* December 12, 1996, p. 3; see also *NYT Magazine,* January 15, 1995.

"it really bothered me": Shirlee Taylor Haizlip, interview, September 1997.

"We may be poor": Blackman, p. 117.

153   dressed in black: Susan Dubinsky Terris, interview, October 1997.

"more goal-oriented than the rest of us": Nada Rosenthal Westerman, interview, October 1997.

154   an original piece of work: Madeleine Jana Korbel, *Zdeněk Fierlinger's Role in the Communization of Czechoslovakia: The Profile of a Fellow Traveller* (1959), Wellesley College archives.

"a very serious Catholic": *NYT,* February 4, 1997, p 1; MKA, September 1998.

the perspective of "outsiders": Terris, October 1997.

155   "Madeleine's best friends were Jewish": Haizlip, September 1997; see also Haizlip, *The Sweeter the Juice* (1994), pp. 187–91.

the number of Jews was restricted: *Commentary,* August 1983, p 11; sermon by Rabbi Avis D. Miller, Adas Israel Synagogue, Washington D.C., March 11, 1994.

156   "they created cliques": Alice Arsham Moskowitz, interview, October 1997.

first article: *WCN,* November 5, 1956, p. 9.

157   "handsome candidate": *WCN,* October 16, 1958, pp. 1, 5.

"all in awe of James Reston": Ann Einhorn, interview, October 1997.

"underhanded, unpleasant tactics": Emily Cohen MacFarquhar, interview, May 1998.

158   "ninety percent Republican": Freund, January 1997.

"showed *esprit de corps*": letter to *The New Yorker* from Sara Lippincott, August 21, 1965; interview with Lippincott, October 1997.

threatened with arrest: Class of '59, 1984 yearbook, Wellesley College archives.

159   one of fifty Wellesley students: *WCN,* November 5, 1956, pp. 1, 6; Lucy Leinbach Robb, interview, October 1997.

160   "a desperation move": Lippincott, October 1997; see also Porter McKeever, *Adlai Stevenson: His Life and Legacy* (1989), pp. 385–89.

"Adlai had a real persona": Robb, October 1997.

beat his Republican opponent: *WCN,* November 13, 1958.

161   request for U.S. citizenship: Denver court records; DU Press release, March 26, 1957.

CHAPTER 10

163   marriage mania: *WCN,* October 13, 1955.

"a mixed message": MacFarquhar, May 1998.

164   "I will not have any knitting": Pamela Koehler Daniels, interview, October 1997.

"Ministers' wives": MKA, November 1998.

more than 80 percent: 1964 class yearbook, Wellesley College Archives.

"Wellesley Girls Take Any Date": *Harvard Crimson,* November 5, 1955.

165   "Elston was shy": Richard Seabass, interview, March 1998.

Elston's friends speculate: DuPont, October 1997; Vail, March 1998.

"not the winner": DuPont, September 1998.

166   "willing to do anything": Pat Collins Smedley, interview, April 1998; also
interviews with Lee Olson and Craig Gilborn, March 1998.

167   inviting his fellow intern: MKA, September 1998; see also Stan Peckham
interview with Bernie Bookbinder, September 1984, *Newsday* archives.

"obviously an idiot": MKA, September 1998.

"my uncle *is* Harry Guggenheim": MKA, September 1998. Josef Korbel
started his Guggenheim fellowship in March 1957. (DU press release,
March 26, 1957)

"I was blamed for Madeleine": Peckham interview with Bookbinder, *Newsday*
archives.

168   "married for love": Danielle Gardner, interview, March 1998.

"lost grandeur": DuPont, October 1997.

"not starry-eyed": DuPont, September 1998.

"very boring": MKA, September 1998.

169   "feet off my desk": Robert F. Keeler, *Newsday: A Candid History of the Respectable
Tabloid* (1990), p. 8. For history of Medill family, see also John Tebbel, *An
American Dynasty* (1947).

171   "his concubines": Josephine Albright interview with Keeler, March 1987,
Newsday archives.

"a pleasure and a hell": *Newsday,* April 12, 1952.

"the little cowboy": Alice Albright Arlen interview with Keeler, *Newsday*
archives; see also Keeler, p. 277.

172   most romantic house: Dorothea Straus, *Showcases,* pp. 94–95. Because of family
sensitivities, Straus disguises Falaise behind the fictional name "Finistère"
and calls Harry Guggenheim "Rupert" and Alicia "Candace."

173   master of Falaise: see Keeler, *op. cit.;* John H. Davis, *The Guggenheims, An American Epic* (1978); Noel Dean, chauffeur at Falaise, interview, September 1997.

174   "the first real people": letter to Elinor Patterson, October 1946, *Newsday*
archives, Alicia Patterson papers.

the "heir-apparent": *Saturday Evening Post,* May 12, 1951.

work hard "to prove": *Saturday Evening Post,* February 21, 1959, p. 51, quoted
in Keeler, p. 275.

175   "dress for dinner": MKA, September 1998.

first formal dinner party: Stephen Hess, interview, September 1997.

"a great idea": Jackie Gebhard, interview, September 1997.

"freeze anybody out": Alice Albright Arlen, interview with Keeler, *Newsday*
archives.

176   "so much poise": Einhorn, October 1997.

"the servant problem": MKA, September 1998.

announcement of her engagement: *WCN,* October 2, 1958; *NYT,* December 30, 1958. Dedication "to Madeleine": unpublished undergraduate thesis by Joseph M. Albright: "Joseph Medill Patterson: Right or Wrong, American," Williams College, 1958, *Newsday* archives.

177 "Marriage or Career?": *WCN,* May 21, 1959, p. 6.

"No responsible person": Address by Neil McElroy, June 8, 1959, Wellesley College Archives; see also *WCN,* June 8, 1959, p. 1.

"one of ours": Muriel Rosenblum Fleischmann, interview, October 1958.

178 "no better vocation": commencement address to Smith College, quoted in Betty Friedan, *The Feminine Mystique,* W.W. Norton, 1983, pp. 60–61.

the Tunicata: Harvard *Crimson,* May 8, 1959, reprinted *WCN,* May 14, 1959.

"easier if you were a Jew": MKA, September 1998; Geraldine Ferraro, interview, October 1997.

179 the divorce was illegal: MKA, September 1998.

"Bloody Mary": Keeler, p. 104.

"a gown of peau de soie": *RMN,* June 12, 1969.

180 ripped it into pieces: Blackman, p. 127.

181 "I lost courage": Friedan, p. 155.

CHAPTER 11

183 says she wrote obituaries: Blackman, p. 129.

any bylines: Steve Sowers, former publisher, *Rolla Daily News,* interview, June 1998.

"out of the question": *Chicago Sun-Times,* June 16, 1959.

184 "a very intense news town": Jim Hoge, interview, December 1997.

185 "Exclusive Story": Chicago *Sun-Times*, July 29, 1960, p. 1.

"another career": CBS News *60 Minutes,* February 9, 1997; *WP* profile, January 6, 1991, *Vogue,* September 1997; interview with author, November 1998.

a "career with a Capital C": Freund, September 1998.

"do something more": MKA, November 1998.

186 "I compose in motion": *Ivan Albright,* The Art Institute of Chicago (1997), p. 43.

a "tough" time with Josephine: MKA, September 1998.

187 both had collapsed lungs: Blackman, p. 131.

Russian-language class: *LAT,* February 8, 1995, p. E1; *Vogue,* September 1997.

"the best route to sanity": Class of '59 1969 yearbook, Wellesley College Archives.

"Get the check first": Keeler, p. 279.

188 "I really liked her": MKA, November 1998.

"formal-hilarious": Gebhard, September 1997; Katharine Graham, October 1997; Hoge, December 1997.

189 "the Babbitts were swept out": Ward Just, interview, January 1998.

190 "tried very much to Americanize ourselves": Danielle Gardner, March 1998.

191 "no hesitation in saying what she thought": Hoge, December 1997.

192 "mashed potatoes and skimmed milk": Keeler, p. 312.

"that same chance": quoted in letter from HFG to Joe Albright, January 11, 1967, LC-HFG collection. See also Keeler interview with Alice Arlen.

"That son of a bitch Harry": Keeler interview with Stan Peckham.

193 buried the ashes in a box: MKA, November 1998.

"A beautiful and spirited lady": author trip to Kingsland, November 1997.

Alicia's will: *Newsday* archives; Keeler, pp. 106–107, 492.

194 Snob Hollow Real Estate: Nassau County Real Estate Records, deed 745, page 243.

195 "we are highly grateful": letters from MKA and Joe Albright to HFG, Albright/Christmas files, Guggenheim collection, LC-HFG.

196 very un-Gatsby-like lives: Freund, January 1997; Martin Schram, interview, June 1997.

197 Brzezinski's graduate seminar: Steven Goldstein, interview, March 1998; Zbigniew Brzezinski, interview, July 1997.

198 "openly supported Kennedy": Marcia Burick, December 1997.

"licking stamps": *New Republic,* August 22, 1994, p. 20.

"the worst time in my life": Blackman, p. 139; MKA, November 1998.

CHAPTER 12

201 "slaving away at the job": Wellesley College Archives, Class of '59, 1969 class notes.

some exotic destination: Albright file, LC-HFG collection.

202 "all the synagogues": Burick, December 1997.

"Young Couple Stops in Castle": Burick, October 1998.

204 knocked on the door: MKA, November 1998.

"museum to a dead race": Goldstein, March 1998.

The conversations were depressing: MKA, November 1998.

205 "popped in and out": Dagmar Šima, October 1998.

survived the massacre: Dagmar Šima, March 1998.

reappeared, very distraught: apart from material otherwise attributed, these details come from Burick, December 1997 and October 1998.

Czechs were also "fodder": MKA, interview, January 1999.

206 "about their suffering": MKA, November 1998.

could not remember: Blackman, pp. 145–46.

207 tried to contact Josef: Joža Gruber and Chaim Körbel, November 1997.

208 a close physical resemblance: Alena Korbel, July 1998.

"a big deal": MKA, September 1998.

chance remarks by Mandula: Ruth Spensley, Hilda and Jack Newman-Clark, February 1998.

"a gut feeling": George Barany, interview, February 1998.

209   "better off not being Jewish": Gottesfeld, February 1998.

"didn't seem to be hiding anything": interviews with Vernon and Susan Aspaturian, December 1997.

"You must know Joe Korbel": interviews with Bernard and Vanda Abrahammson, February 1998.

210   "a little indignant": Kauders, February 1998.

211   "in this I envy them": letter to author, February 13, 1997.

CHAPTER 13

214   "very motivated to work": MKA, November 1998.

"distant from it all": Goldstein, March 1998.

"Up against the wall": *Columbia College Today,* Spring 1968 issue, pp. 4–14.

215   "most of the time we love it": Wellesley College archives, Class of '59, 1969 class notes.

"a barrier against Communism": Istvan Deak, interview, December 1997.

"a pig, for professor Zbig": Brzezinski, July 1997.

"fanatically pro-American": Christine Dodson, interview, January 1998.

216   air strikes against North Vietnam: Josef Korbel interviews with *RMN*, August 6, 1964, April 9, 1967.

217   "Imagine how embarrassing": Barany, February 1998.

"Joe was a control freak": Vince Davis, February 1998.

"a great and fierce lover of America": Gilbert, February 1998.

"a matter of style": Catherine Kelleher, interview, August 1997.

218   "a victim of the Tet offensive": interview with *RMN*, July 28, 1968.

"from hard-line to less hard-line": Bernard Abrahammson, February 1998.

an almost identical evolution: press conference en route to Hanoi, June 26, 1997.

Tet was a key turning point: MKA, November 1998.

219   "advance liberal causes": *The Social Science Foundation of the University of Denver,* monograph in local history section, Denver Public Library; Chester Alter, interview, February 1998.

220   a great champion of talented women students: interviews with Karen Feste, February 1998, and Condoleeza Rice, March 1998.

shaded the truth: Davis, February 1998.

221   "had enough": Barany, February 1998.

"My cockiness": Keeler, p. 381.

"a rough time at *Newsday*": Lou Schwartz, interview, July 1997; Keeler interview with Pat Byrne.

222   "you can't cease to glitter": letter from HFG to MKA, August 28, 1964, LC-HFG collection.

deeply disappointed: letter from HFG to Joe Albright, January 11, 1967; undated letter from HFG to Josephine Albright, LC-HFG collection.

223 "the impossible dream": letter from Joe Albright to HFG and Moyers, April 3, 1968, LC-HFG collection.

"Joe is in Washington": undated letter from MKA to HFG, LC-HFG collection.

"a little frustrated": Schram, June 1997.

"pathetically praying for the defeat of Richard Nixon": letter from HFG to Bill Moyers, November 6, 1968, *Newsday* archives.

224 "Your children are all New Left": Keeler, p. 473.

a second home in Georgetown: DC Real Estate division, deed number 12897, folio 055, July 5, 1968.

"a brick three-story rowhouse": undated letter from Joe Albright to HFG, LC-HFG collection.

"hope for a longer stay": 1969 yearbook, Class of '59, Wellesley College Archives.

225 "her instinct for strong behavior": Jiří Dienstbier, interview, January 1997.

226 "Pray for Joe": Keeler, p. 473.

"how to defeat the sale": Schram, June 1997.

"screwing up the cause": Joe Albright interview with Keeler, December 1986.

"You created a Frankenstein": memorandum of conversation between HFG and Bill Moyers, *Newsday* archives.

"a significantly better deal": Keeler, p. 492.

CHAPTER 14

230 Goodbody asked her: MKA, November 1998.

"how the whole thing started": *Vogue,* September 1997, p. 642.

"quintessential American politician": MKA, November 1998.

232 "chatting about each other's lives": interviews with Pie Friendly, October 1997, and Julie Finley, January 1998.

"a lot of work": James Goodbody, interview, February 1998.

contributed a total of $3,250: ESM Archives, Campaign Finance Files 1971–72, Box 436, Folder 04.

233 "What the hell is going on?": Berl Bernhard, interview, March 1998.

234 Strange things: see, for example, statement by Donald Segretti, ESM Archives, Box CA385, Folder 10, and Bernhard memorandum, September 25, 1973, ESM archives, Box CA385, Folder 12.

235 attacked the Nixon administration: *Portland Press Herald,* April 18, 1972.

"sabotaged by Segretti": "She survived Segretti 'Prank,' " *DP,* May 3, 1976.

236 "introduction to American politics": Barry Carter, interview, October 1997. In addition to those quoted elsewhere, I also interviewed former Beauvoir board members Michael Durr and Pat Meyers, both in January 1998.

237 caused a scandal: Pie Friendly, October 1997.

"supposed to read Piaget's works": Finley, January 1998.

238 "a great political lesson": Harry McPherson, interview, December 1997.

"Beauvoir was wishy-washy": Bitsy Folger, interview, January 1998.

239 "a strong sense of social justice": Lois Rice, interview, January 1998.

"He did not see anything peculiar": Sherri Migdail, interview, January 1998.

"truth speaking to power": Frances Borders, interview, January 1998.

"character assassination": Doug Bennet, interview, December 1997.

dipped into tuition money: Walter Haynes, interview, January 1998.

240 "She is like a sponge": Gardner, March 1998.

A woman's required talent: address to Bronx High School, Bronx, New York, October 1, 1997.

241 "zigzag all over the place": *Time,* February 17, 1997.

"little old people there": Blackman, p. 166.

"the hardest thing I ever did": *NR,* August 22, 1994, p. 20.

"an embarrassingly long time": Wellesley College Archives, Class of '59, 1979 Class Record.

242 "a dictionary of punishments": MKA, September 12, 1998.

double their initial investment: Nassau County Real Estate Records, deed 8720, page 492.

245 "worked me over": Charles Gati, interview, November 1997.

"Madeleine Albright, little housewife," *WP,* p. F01, January 1, 1991.

CHAPTER 15

248 the initial suggestion: Charles Micoleau, interview, August 1997.

the post of campaign finance director: former Mondale aide Mike Birman, interview, July 1997.

"You don't understand": Micoleau, August 1997. For MKA salary and budget, see ESM archives, 1976 Muskie campaign budget, Box CA 562, Folder 05.

249 Muskie activists in Maine: interviews with Phil Merrill, September 1997, and Charlie Jacobs, August 1997.

250 "this loyal band of merry men": ESM archives, 1976 campaign, Box MWH 01, Folder 06.

"not a happy occasion": Al From, interview, October 1997. Also Merrill, September 1997, and John McEvoy, July 1997.

second-in-charge of the office: ESM archives, Administration 1976 file, Box SE 3169, Folder 06.

251 "great surprise": Bennet, December 1997.

"the changeover generation": Folger, January 1998.

"you did not have to work": Anita Jensen, interview, July 1997.

252 "some sex in this office": Bernhard, March 1998.

almost debilitating shyness: *Boston Sunday Globe,* September 1, 1968, p. 1.

"a real sonofabitch": Leon Billings, interview, August 1997.

253 "Do you cry easily?" John McEvoy, interview, July 1997.

"entitled to my thoughts": Bernhard, March 1998.

"never yelled at me": MKA, November 1998.

"an equal opportunity disaster": Jensen, July 1997.

254 "keep it cool": ESM archives, Madeleine Albright files, Box CA 553, Folder 01, Box CA 555, Folder 09.

working conditions were so cramped: Jensen, July 1997; and Jacobs, August 1997.

256 "the world's perfect staffer": Bennet, December 1997; see also *NYT Magazine*, September 22, 1996, p. 66.

257 a list of deserving candidates: ESM archives, Micoleau memorandum to Frank Moore, January 11, 1977, Box SE 3168, Folder 13.

258 surprised some of the more experienced: From, October 1997.

"he is zbig": Estelle Lavoie, interview, August 1997.

259 "not a churchgoer": DU Archives, Josef Korbel file, transcript of memorial service, July 20, 1977; Rita Kauders, interview, February 1998.

"not father figures": Dodson, January 1998.

260 "superior social intelligence": Jensen, July 1997.

"played out the charade": Alena Korbel, July 1998.

"abdicated my social responsibilities": Bernard Abrahammson, February 1998.

261 "no longer an argument between gentlemen": Korbel file, *DP* article, August 3, 1949, DU archives.

"the ones to suffer": Jana Friesová, *Review of the Society for the History of Czechoslovak Jews,* volume 2, p. 16.

262 thick East European accent: Karen Feste, interview, February 1998.

"What made Madeleine tick": Al Friendly Jr., interview, September 1997.

CHAPTER 16

265 stop squabbling: Bob Beckel, interview, February 1998.

266 "the importance of proximity": Miller Center, Carter Presidency Project, interview with Brzezinski, MKA, Leslie Denend, and William Odom, February 18, 1982; also Christine Dodson, interview, January 1998.

"drives people crazy": Karl (Rick) Inderfurth, former staff assistant to Brzezinski, interview, February 1988.

"Working for Zbig was great": Robert Pastor, interview, January 1998.

267 "creative destruction": Miller Center, interview with Odom, *op. cit.*

"good at people-handling": Brzezinski, July 1997.

"his understanding of the Hill": Miller Center, Carter Presidency Project, Interview with Bob Beckel, November 13, 1981.

268 "She is fine, man": Beckel, February 1998.

"asked me to help": JCL, Albright files, Evening memo to Brzezinski, August 18, 1978.

first week on the job: JCL, Albright files, Evening memo to Brzezinski, March 17, 1978.

"always bad news": Miller center, interview with MKA, *op. cit.*

269   "not easily awed": JCL, MKA files, memo to Brzezinski, April 12, 1978.
      "I didn't want to be wiped out": Brzezinski, March 1998.
270   "She was right": Brzezinski, July 1997.
      opened his fly buttons: *WP,* December 19, 1979, p. C1.
      "vociferously unhappy": Al Friendly Jr., September 1997.
271   "kept better informed": JCL, Albright files, Memo to Brzezinski, February 22,
      1979.
      "the world's most important thing": Miller Center, interview with MKA, *op. cit.*
      "heightened tension": Al Friendly Jr., September 1997.
      "charming and helpful": JCL, MKA files, memo to Brzezinski, July 23, 1980.
      "facilitator": Miller center, interview with MKA, *op. cit.*
272   "hailed as a great idea": *WP,* June 1, 1991, p. F01.
      "a rotten time": Jessica Tuchman Mathews, interview, February 1998.
273   "I know Greeks": Beckel, December 1997.
274   "most unpredictable": JCL, MKA files, memo to Brzezinski, April 11, 1979.
      "a clever self-promoter": JCL, MKA files, memo to Brzezinski, March 15, 1979.
      "pleased to be called": JCL, MKA files, memo to Brzezinski, May 9, 1979.
      "most uncomfortable chairs": Miller Center, interview with Beckel, *op. cit.*
275   "did not lay a glove on us": JCL, MKA files, memo to Brzezinski, July 19, 1979.
      "the general mood is optimistic": JCL, MKA files, memo to Brzezinski,
      August 4, 1979.
      "we did not have 67 votes": JCL, MKA files, memo to Brzezinski, February 27,
      1980.
      "blindly optimistic about SALT'": Beckel, February 1998.
276   "a Maine Yankee": Billings, August 1997.
      Muskie/Packwood impressions of China: ESM archives, Box SE 2747, Folder 1.
277   "no time for jetlag": JCL, MKA files, memo to Brzezinski, November 20, 1978.
      "how useful I was": JCL, MKA files, memo to Brzezinski, February 22, 1979.
      trip to Europe: JCL, MKA files, memo from Brzezinski to MKA, April 23,
      1979.
278   a presidential drop-by: JCL, Frank Moore memo to President, March 28, 1979.
      "making mistakes together": *WP,* May 9, 1980; Miller center, interview with
      Albright, *op. cit.,* May 9, 1980.
      "Poles apart": Al Friendly Jr., September 1997.
279   power-grabbing move: Billings, August 1997; see also memorandum from
      Muskie to Lloyd Cutler, August 27, 1980, in ESM archives, U.S. Senate
      Office series, Box 1, ESM personal notes.
      caught in the middle: Les Denend, interview, January 1998; Billings, August
      1997.
280   "smooth ruffled feathers": Brzezinski, July 1997 and March 1998.
      rarely stay to gossip: Jensen, August 1997.
      not at home until 11 P.M.: Dodson, January 1998.

281   "a little nervous": From, October 1997.

"considerable personal sacrifice": JCL, memo from Robert J. Lipshutz, March 22, 1978.

282   "on the fast track": Pie Friendly, October 1997.

totally unaware: see, for example, MKA profile, *NYT Magazine*, September 22, 1996.

283   "knock on wood!": Wellesley College Archives, Class of '59, Record Book for 1979.

CHAPTER 17

285   "It's over": interviews with Inderfurth, February 1998, and Brzezinski, July 1997.

a shattering repudiation: Al Friendly Jr., September 1997; Jessica Mathews, February 1998.

286   "always partisan": Dodson, January 1998.

"who were the good guys": DuPont, October 1997.

"The only thing I'm sorry about": Blackman, p. 181.

287   the role of the press: the research resulted in a monograph, Madeleine K. Albright, *Poland: The Role of the Press in Political Change* (1983).

"packed shoulder to shoulder": Madeleine Albright, op-ed piece, *WP*, December 20, 1981.

"He couldn't keep his hands off her": Blackman, p. 184.

288   "a man who is so proud of his wife": Burick, December 1997.

request for a divorce: Superior Court of District of Columbia, *Joseph M.P. Albright v Madeleine K. Albright*, February 2, 1983. According to the divorce proceedings, they had "lived apart" since June 13, 1982.

"This marriage is dead": *NYT Magazine* profile, September 22, 1996, p. 104.

289   "always a winner": Gardner, March 1998.

"part of her world": Folger, October 1998.

"one of her thin phases": Blackman, p. 186.

290   "a woman scorned": Lavoie, August 1997.

a generous financial settlement: Executive Branch Public Financial Disclosure Reports filed by MKA, 1993–1996.

kept several canvases: *WP*, June 26, 1988, p C01.

assessed market value: District of Columbia and Loudoun County, VA, property records.

291   "the decision is final": ESM archives, letter from Joe Albright, Post Public Office series, Box 1, Correspondence 1983–1985.

the divorce came through: Superior Court of District of Columbia, *Joseph M.P. Albright v. Madeleine K. Albright*, February 2, 1983. According to the divorce proceedings, they had "lived apart" since June 13, 1982.

"I would not be sitting here": MKA, November 1998.

Her friends agree: e.g., Abramowitz, September 1997; Gardner, February
1998; Mathews, February 1998; Dodson, January 1998.

292   half the students were women: Peter Krogh, interview, January 1997.

"Madeleine was perfect": Putnam Ebinger, interview, December 1997.

time "to move on": Brzezinski, July 1997.

293   "how vulnerable she was": Bennet, December 1997.

294   the weather was blazingly hot: Daniels, October 1997.

working for a living: Wellesley College Archives, Class of '59, 1984 Year-
book; for a statistical study on the Class of '59, see also Emily MacFarquhar,
"Changing Times," *U.S. News and World Report,* June 6, 1994, p. 75, and
Wellesley Alumnae magazine, Summer 1994, p. 4.

295   "an unhappy time": Moskowitz, interview, October 1997.

"Divorce and Ronald Reagan": Wellesley Class of '59, 1984 Yearbook, *op. cit.*

CHAPTER 18

297   "either Kissinger or Vietnam": Carter, October 1997.

298   "a good match": Toby Gati, interview, December 1997.

dinner at Nora's: Blackman, p. 194.

the second contributor: FEC report 83FEC/218/0025 shows a $750 contribu-
tion from MKA to Mondale on November 22, 1982.

299   By the spring of 1983: Blackman, p. 194.

"paralyzed with fear": Blackman, p. 191.

white-water canoe trip: Blackman, p. 194.

300   "nasty op-ed pieces": Janne Nolan, interview, December 1997.

"My people aren't academics": Carter, November 1997.

301   from the floor of the convention center: Blackman, p. 199.

"The mood was so electric": Dowd, "Reassessing Women's Political Role,"
NYT Magazine, December 30, 1984, p. 19.

in-depth briefings: John Sasso, interview, September 1997.

"very informal": Carter, October 1997.

"Madeleine was very good": Geraldine A. Ferraro, interview, October 1997.

302   "just Barry Carter": Geraldine Ferraro, *My Story* (1985), p. 118.

"happy campers": Carter, October 1997.

303   "take to the hills": Sasso, September 1997.

"rise or fall": Francis O'Brien, interview, August 1997.

304   "doing a number": Ferraro, (1985), pp. 274–75.

"Goddam that X": Peter Goldman et al., *Quest for the Presidency* (1984), p. 362.

"talked the gender gap": Beckel, December 1997.

305   net benefit: Dowd, *NYT Magazine, op. cit.*

"No First Strike": Nancy Soderberg, interview, December 1997.

"Women will shoot higher": *WP* Ferraro stories, November 7, 1984, and
November 8, 1984.

306   "tie herself down": Pie Friendly, September 1997.

    "a nice person": MKA, November 1998.

    "nicest hotel in Moscow": Ferraro, October 1997.

    "It was surreal": Adi Guttag, interview, October 1997.

307   "acted like teenagers": Blackman, p. 204.

309   "sunshine soldiers": Barbara Mikulski, interview, January 1998.

    "from kids to diets": Wendy Sherman, interview, January 1998.

310   "I started watching her": Putnam Ebinger, interview, December 1997.

CHAPTER 19

313   a nationwide competition: advertisement in *The Economist*, February 25, 1984, p. 97.

314   split down the middle: interviews with Karl Cerny, January 1998; Robert Lieber, October 1997; Angela Stent, February 1998; Peter Krogh, January 1998; Putnam Ebinger, December 1997; Andre Marton, December 1997; Charles Gati, November 1997; and Jan Karski, January 1998. Gati collected two votes from the government department (Cerny, Stent) and one from the foreign policy school (Marton). Albright collected one vote from the government department (Lieber) and three from the foreign policy school (Ebinger, Goodman, and Stan Wasofsky). The two graduate student representatives on the committee voted in favor of other candidates from the shortlist.

315   "an equally strong letter": Charles Gati, November 1997.

316   "out of central casting": Krogh, January 1998.

    "She did not fill the position": Cerny, January 1998.

    Learning to speak out: *WP,* June 1, 1991, p. B1; *The Georgetown Voice,* September 17, 1992.

317   "wanted people to argue": Mike Sheehan, interview, January 1998.

    "Everybody liked her": Alex Gershanik, interview, August 1997.

    "I had to please myself": MKA, November 1998.

318   "what I thought of it": Schram, July 1997.

319   "my name began with A": Blackman, p. 196.

    "bothered by it": Nancy Bernhopf Tucker, interview, December 1997.

322   "Waiting in the Wings": *WP,* June 26, 1988, p. C01.

    "used many talents": Sally Bedell Smith, *Reflected Glory* (1996), p. 16.

323   "inadequacy as baggage": Katharine Graham, *Personal History* (1997), pp. 416–20.

    "you have to get along": MKA, November 1998.

    "lectured her way to the top": Toby Gati, December 1997.

    "totally self-made": Sally Quinn, interview, December 1997.

324   "the real agenda": Quinn, October 1998.

325   no illusions: Blackman, p. 12.

326 Dukakis was impressed: Michael Dukakis, interview, September 1997.

"seemed to make fun": James Woolsey, interview, December 1997.

"Are you serious?": Dukakis, September 1997.

CHAPTER 20

329 "hit it off immediately": Sasso, September 1997. See also Center for American History, University of Texas, MKA interview, April 20, 1989.

"interesting and appealing": MKA, April 1989.

330 "No important Democrat" [will say anything bad]: *WP,* June 26, 1988, p. C01.

331 "one of the grunts": MKA, April 1989.

"my kinda person": Dukakis, September 1997.

her political loyalty: David Broder, interview, October 1997.

332 "threshold of machoism": MKA, April 1989.

"a helluva lot more arrogant": Blackman, p. 214. Estrich became the campaign manager after Sasso's resignation in September 1987.

"before I was weaned": Dukakis, September 1997.

Swedish planning document: MKA, April 1989.

"hurt and angry": Brzezinski, July 1997.

wanted to "make up": Charles Gati, November 1997.

333 "never a fan of his": Dukakis, September 1997.

"what they care about is the picture": MKA, April 1989.

"a very funny event": *ibid.*

334 "can't afford that risk": Christine M. Black and Thomas Oliphant, *All By Myself* (1989), pp. 233–34.

"search for scapegoats": O'Brien, August 1997; MKA, April 1989; Dukakis, September 1997.

"a big-gun type": Tom Donilon, interview, October 1997. Also, Sasso, September 1997; Dukakis, September 1997.

335 "Madam Secretary": Anne Albright, quoted in *Boston Globe,* May 13, 1988, p. 47.

ambassador to the United Nations: Dukakis, September 1997.

"a strong national security figure": MKA, April 1989.

336 immediate credibility: Sherman, January 1998.

"She is not a Brzezinski": Charles Gati, November 1997.

Estrich began wondering: Blackman, p. 218.

"extremely smart": MKA, November 1998.

"hit it off right away": MKA letter to Council of Foreign Relations, February 26, 1989.

337 "a terrible nostalgia": letter supplied to author by Milan Janković.

"a knock-down, drag-out fight": Jack Newman-Clark, February 1998.

338 frequently grumbled: Kauders, February 1998.

"did everything she could": Ferraro, October 1997.

"sirtee-sree souzand dollars": Kauders, February 1998.

339 "I'm going to die now": Feste, February 1998.

"slap my face": Kauders, February 1998.

"on TV as Madeleine Albright": Mikulski, January 1998.

"enthusiastically accepts": ESM archives, Post Public Office Series, Box 3, Folder 4, Van Dyk memorandum to Muskie, June 12, 1985.

340 "How about you?": Richard Moe, interview, October 1997.

"an agonizing process": Blackman, p. 221.

"wanted her to succeed": Maureen Steinbruner, interview, June 1997.

"That made me mad": MKA, November 1998.

341 "more to prove": Billings, August 1997.

a $40,000 pay cut: ESM archives, Post Public Office Series, Box 19, Folder 4, Albright/Steinbruner memo, September 23, 1991. See also Executive Branch Public Financial Disclosure filed January 11, 1993.

342 "an out-of-body experience": MKA, talking to reporters on her plane, June 14, 1998, see *Vogue*, September 1997.

" 'Havel advance' ": *WP,* January 6, 1991, p. F01.

343 "a running joke": Don Kellerman, interview, September 1997.

getting themselves mistresses: Stan Meisler, interview, August 1997.

"Which would you prefer?": Andrew Kohut, interview, September 1997.

"raised very deliberately": MKA op-ed piece, *WP,* July 22, 1992, p A19.

344 "never have plugs": Robert Toth, interview, October 1997; see also, *LAT,* December 23, 1992, p. A18.

"not interested":ČTK report from Prague, February 11, 1998.

"not a lot to talk about": Blackman, p. 299.

345 "our little secret": Dagmar Šima, interview, January 1997.

346 "think through the fight scenario": *WP,* January 6, 1991, p. F01.

"a chameleon": Barry Rubin, interview, November 1997.

"we were wrong": Jacob Heilbrunn, "The Unquiet American Ambassador," *New Republic,* August 22, 1994, p. 19.

347 "They sat and talked": MKA, November 1998.

jotted down "good": Soderberg, December 1997.

an office in the West Wing: Inderfurth, February 1998.

almost the last to find out: Anne Wexler, interview, August 1997.

she learned officially: James P. Rubin, interview, May 1998.

CHAPTER 21

349 unpack a framed photograph: Inderfurth, February 1998.

350 "Broad-based coalitions": MKA speech, "Strategic Vision for the 1990s," reprinted in *Great Teachers of the Georgetown School of Foreign Service.*

rooms repainted cream: Geraldine Baum, *LAT,* p. E1, February 8, 1995.

"What I really need is a wife": Doreen Crawford Dun, interview, October 1997.

"She was a beginner": Boutros Boutros-Ghali, interview, July 1998.

351 "Fourteen Suits and a Skirt": *Time,* February 17, 1997.

"plugged into Washington": *Time,* October 31, 1994, p. 31.

352 "fly fast": Elaine Shocas, interview, May 1998.

"Et tu, Brute?": Meisler, August 1997.

353 "extraordinary vision": Jacob Heilbrunn, *The New Republic,* August 22, 1994; Barbara Crossette, *NYT,* December 6, 1996, p. 1.

a 100-room mansion: for family background, see Stanley Meisler, *United Nations: The First Fifty Years* (1995), pp. 280–86.

"arrogance" . . . inexperienced: interviews with MKA spokesman James Rubin, June 1998; Boutros-Ghali speechwriter Charles Hill, December 1997.

354 patronizing and ingratiating: Inderfurth, February 1998; Sheehan, January 1998.

"out of her league": Hill, December 1997.

"a beginner in diplomacy": Boutros-Ghali, July 1998.

"an incredible entourage": James Rubin, interview, June 1998.

355 "I should also be a general": Boutros-Ghali, July 1998.

Clinton even claimed: *NYT,* October 18, 1993, p. A1.

"we must perservere": MKA, "Yes, There Is a Reason to Be in Somalia," *NYT,* August 10, 1993.

356 "a whipping boy": Bennet, December 1997.

"I just let it go": *NYT Magazine,* September 22, 1996.

357 vetoed by Albright: *NYT,* May 17, 1994, p. A1; May 18, 1994, p. A1.

"100 percent American responsibility": Boutros-Ghali, July 1998.

"untenable politically": Sheehan, January 1998.

"unfairly tarred": Susan Rice interview, February 1998.

358 "the size of my little grandson": MKA, Statement to Senate Foreign Relations Committee, January 8, 1997. For regrets on Rwanda, see *WP,* December 10, 1997, p. A28.

now understood: James Rubin, May 1998.

359 "This happened before": Edward W. Gnehn, interview, February 1998.

"We have to do more": Toby Gati, December 1997.

"It wasn't easy": *NYT Magazine,* September 22, 1996.

"intimidated by the generals": Bennet, December 1997.

360 "an aneurysm": Colin Powell, *My American Journey* (1995), pp. 576–77.

"because you can bomb": Colin Powell, interview, December 1997.

sided with Powell: Anthony Lake, interview, December 1997.

"the earth is flat": *The New Yorker,* October 2, 1995, p. 46.

the "Vietnam syndrome": MKA, November 1998.

362 "I got stoned": Sheehan, January 1998; *Newsday,* March 22, 1996, p. A7.

"the anti-Serb faction": see, for example, *Intervju,* January 27, 1995.

"the subject of harsh criticism": letter supplied to author by Janković family.

"not very happy": Toby Gati, December 1997.

363   "makes the president look weak": secret MKA memorandum to Clinton, "Elements of a New Strategy," July 1995.

"without really understanding": Richard Holbrooke, *To End a War* (1998), pp. 65–68.

"highly ritualistic": Ivo Daalder, interview, January 1998.

"Her weakness": Lake, December 1997.

364   infuriated Albright: Rubin, June 1998.

"a symbol of U.N. arrogance": Rubin, June 1998.

365   "go to the movies?": Rubin, interview, *NYT,* January 10, 1998.

"We called him J.R.": Sylvana Foa, interview, January 1998.

"more times": Meisler, August 1997.

working out a plan: for detailed account, see *WP*, July 1, 1997, p. A1.

366   "head on a silver platter": Foa, January 1998.

"arrogant and dull-witted": Rubin, June 1998.

"It's all politics": Foa, January 1998.

CHAPTER 22

369   "never let it happen": Wexler, August 1997.

370   confided her anxieties: Bennet, December 1997.

recited her credentials: Steven Rosenfeld, interview, October 1997.

371   "the Audition": Sciolino, *NYT Magazine,* September 22, 1996.

372   "not *cojones* . . . cowardice": *NYT,* February 28, 1996, p. A1.

"a rock concert with Mick Jagger": Shocas, May 1998.

"Most white men": Lake, December 1997.

"very, very cautious": Ferraro, October 1997.

372   "second tier": John F. Harris, *WP,* November 8, 1996, p. A01.

373   "one of the luckiest days": Sherman, January 1998.

374   "a nice presentational quality": Leon Panetta, interview, September 1998.

"My mama's smiling down": *WP*, December 6, 1996, pp. A1, A25.

"champion of democracy": *WP,* January 9, 1997, p. A10.

375   "Mad About Madeleine": *Newsweek,* February 10, 1997; see also *Time*, February 17, 1997.

CHAPTER 23

377   the need for "American leadership": Warren Christopher, interview, October 1996.

378   on my own: Blackman, p. 273, quotes MKA as saying that she gave Dobbs "the names of her father's friends, as well as that of her sixty-year-old Czech cousin." This is inaccurate. Had this been the case, there would have been no need for me to find these people independently, without initially knowing their names.

379   both Czech Jews: see, for example, *Politika,* March 6, 1994; *Intervju,* January 27, 1995.

379   the family history: *Zemědělské Noviny,* January 22, 1994.

380   little row house: Dasha had inherited the shares of her mother, Margareta, and uncle, Jan. The portion belonging to MKA's father, Josef, was confiscated by the Czechoslovak state after his arrival in America in December 1948.

       no idea: MKA later told Dasha that she had not received the letter.

382   "Madeleine was upset": Blackman, p. 275. Blackman also writes that I was "confrontational" with Anne Albright, and "peppered [her] with difficult questions, reducing her to tears." While it is possible for two people to remember a conversation differently, this gives a false impression of what took place. Blackman's reconstruction of the conversation appears to depend on third parties.

383   almost identical: Rubin, who has consulted State Department phone records, concedes that I called him on January 21, two days after my return from Prague, and that I may have mentioned Albright's Jewish ancestry at that time. However, he maintains that I did not discuss Albright's Holocaust connection during this telephone call. He says that call came around the time I phoned Anne Albright. (See, for example, Blackman, p. 274.)

       "You would think we were in court": Blackman, p. 276.

385   extremely concerned: MKA called Katharine Graham, whose family owns *The Washington Post,* to express her concerns and request an advance copy of the story. Graham gave her a sympathetic hearing but made clear that she did not want to interfere with editorial decisions.

       ready to answer: Blackman, p. 277.

386   "simply stopped reading": Frank Rich, "Albright Comes Home," *NYT,* February 26, 1997.

       "Hindsight clarifies everything": *Newsweek,* February 24, 1997, p. 30.

       "really is true": Reuter dispatch from Prague, July 5, 1996.

387   "nasty people": Christopher Hitchens, "Minority Report," *The Nation,* March 3, 1997. The ambassador, Michael Zantovsky (*The Nation,* April 21, 1997), denied he had used the words attributed to him by Hitchens. Given the essential accuracy of the details reported by Hitchens, the ambassador's denial is unconvincing. At the time he wrote his story, Hitchens could only have got these details from Zantovsky.

       received a letter: MKA, January 1999; see also Blackman, p. 280; in *Newsweek,* February 17, 1997, p. 4, Rubin referred to "some communications" received by MKA in November 1996.

388   Gad Yaacobi: *WP,* February 13, 1997, p. A27.

       "I'm not a Jew": Boutros-Ghali, July 1998; MKA, January 1999.

389   "Albright is Jewish": AP dispatch from Washington, December 16, 1996; see also *LAT*, December 11, 1996, p. A1.

390   "sense of security and calmness": MKA, September 1998.

391   "weird conversation": MKA, November 1998. She says she later confirmed the relationship by looking at genealogical charts.

he finally approached her: MKA, January 1999; Vladmir Ditmar, December 1998; genealogical research by Eugen and Ira Stein.

392   "There go the Jews": Newman-Clark, February 1998.

"Out of friendship": Kauders, February 1998.

"the whole truth": Blackman, p. 285.

393   typical of the children: see, for example, Helen Epstein, *Children of the Holocaust* (1979), p. 207.

"Even the Holocaust": *NYT,* February 19, 1997, op-ed page.

394   "their names . . . would be up here": Silva interview, *Vogue,* September 1997, p. 645.

395   "the choice they made": MKA statement, Jewish Museum, Prague, July 13, 1997.

"don't want people to think": *Vogue,* September 1997, p. 726.

CHAPTER 24

398   "Don't Cry for Me": State Department press release, July 28, 1997.

399   "less foreign": MKA, interview, June 3, 1997.

400 · "almost nobody speaks well": *The Economist,* August 15, 1998, p. 25.

403   "We are not going to stand by": "Albright Warns Serbs on Kosovo Violence," *NYT,* March 8, 1998, p. 6.

"how the process works": MKA, November 1998.

404   "rarely possible to win support": Warren Zimmermann, *Origins of a Catastrophe* (1996), p. 140.

407   "I am willing to make a bet": Town Hall Meeting, Ohio State University, February 18, 1998.

408   "threshold of machoism": Center for American History, University of Texas, MKA interview, April 20, 1989.

409   "the ugly duckling": *WP,* August 30, 1998, p. A1.

410   "I found out I was Jewish": Remarks at William Safire Roast, October 1, 1998.

"rewon a constituency": Kelleher, October 1998.

411   only two categories: *The New Yorker,* December 8, 1997, p. 58.

AFTERWORD

413   In the words of the indictment: indictment against Slobodan Milošević, International Criminal Tribunal for the former Yugoslavia, May 22, 1999; see also *The Observer,* p. 13, July 18, 1999; WP, January 23, 1999, p. A15.

414   heard about the Račak massacre: interview with Bart Gelman, WP, April 18, 1999, p. A1.

      "Spring has come early": *ibid.*

416   "one of the worst experiences": NYT, April 18, 1999, p. A1.

      Some Serb officials: for example, former Yugoslav deputy prime minister Vuk Drasković, interview with author, May 1999.

417   "NATO personnel shall enjoy": Annex B, Interim Agreement for Peace and Self-Government in Kosovo, Rambouillet, February 23, 1999.

      "a relatively short period": interview with Jim Lehrer, *PBS Newshour*, March 24, 1999.

418   "doing the right thing": NYT, April 18, 1999, *op cit.*

419   "fuse the dark forces": Roger Cohen, "Memory Goes to War," *The New Republic*, July 12, 1999, pp. 29–35.

      Clinton might have been reluctant: see, for example, Christopher Hitchens, *The Nation*, March 3, 1997.

420   "a victim of totalitarianism": WP magazine, February 9, 1997.

421   two ways of reacting: Walter Isaacson, Kissinger: *A Biography*, Simon and Schuster, 1992, p. 31.

422   "a foreign policy of sermons and sanctimony": Peter F. Krogh, *The Wall Street Journal*, April 28, 1999, p. A18.

      never expected to have a war: interview with Jim Lehrer, *PBS Newshour*, June 10, 1999. See also Commencement address at Georgetown University, School of Foreign Service, May 29, 1999.

423   "we are willing to die": *Washington Times*, May 1, 1999, p. A8.

424   "you won it": Press conference, G-8 meeting, Cologne, Germany, June 11, 1999.

BIBLIOGRAPHY

Albright, Joseph M.P. *Joseph Medill Patterson: Right or Wrong, American.* Williams College, undergraduate thesis, 1958.

Albright, Madeleine Korbel. *The Role of the Press in Political Change: Czechoslovakia 1968.* New York: Columbia University Ph.D. dissertation, 1976.

————. *Poland: The Role of the Press in Political Change.* New York: Praeger, 1983.

Asbell, Bernard. *The Senate Nobody Knows.* Garden City, N.Y.: Doubleday, 1978.

Bergmann, Martin S., and Milton E. Jucovy, eds. *Generations of the Holocaust.* New York: Basic Books, 1982.

Berkley, George E. *Hitler's Gift: The Story of Theresienstadt.* Boston: Branden Books, 1993.

Bezwinska, Jadwiga, ed. *KL Auschwitz Seen by the SS.* Krakow: Drukarnia Narodowa, 1978.

Black, Christine M., and Thomas Oliphant. *All By Myself.* Chester, Conn.: Globe Pequot Press, 1989.

Blackman, Ann. *Seasons of Her Life.* New York: Scribner, 1998.

Bondy, Ruth. *Elder of the Jews: Jacob Edelstein of Theresienstadt.* New York: Grove Press, 1989.

Chace, James. *Acheson: The Secretary of State Who Changed the American World.* New York: Simon and Schuster, 1998.

Cramer, Richard Ben. *What It Takes.* New York: Vintage, 1993.

Czech, Danuta. *Auschwitz Chronicle.* New York: Henry Holt and Co., 1990.

Davis, Flora. *Moving the Mountain: The Women's Movement in America Since 1960.* New York: Touchstone, 1991.

Davis, John H. *The Guggenheims: An American Epic.* New York: William Morrow, 1978.

Dokumenty z Historie Československé Politiky 1939–1943. Prague: Academia, 1966.

Drew, Elizabeth. *On the Edge: The Clinton Presidency.* New York: Simon and Schuster, 1994.

Drtina, Prokop. *Československo Můj Osud.* Prague: Melantrich, 1991.

Epstein, Helen. *Where She Came From.* New York: Little, Brown and Co., 1997.

———. *Children of the Holocaust.* New York: Penguin, 1979.

Ferraro, Geraldine. *My Story.* New York: Bantam Books, 1985.

Friedan, Betty. *The Feminine Mystique.* New York: Touchstone, 1991.

Gilbert, Martin. *Auschwitz and the Allies.* New York: Holt, Rinehart, and Winston, 1981.

———. *Holocaust Journey.* New York: Columbia University Press, 1997.

———. *The Holocaust.* New York: Henry Holt and Co., 1987.

Glasscock, Jean, ed. *Wellesley College, 1875–1975: A Century of Women.* Wellesley, Mass.: Wellesley College, 1975.

Gold, Hugo, ed. *Die Juden und judengemeinden Böhmens in vergangenheit und gegenwart.* Prague: 1934.

Goldman, Peter Louis, and Tony Fuller. *The Quest for the Presidency, 1984.* New York: Bantam Books, 1985.

Graham, Katharine. *Personal History.* New York: Alfred A. Knopf, 1997.

Green, Gerald. *The Artists of Terezín.* New York: Hawthorn Books, 1978.

Haizlip, Shirlee Taylor. *The Sweeter the Juice.* New York: Simon and Schuster, 1994.

Hoge, Alice Albright. *Cissy Patterson.* New York: Random House, 1977.

I Have Not Seen a Butterfly Around Here. Prague Jewish Museum, 1993.

Iggers, Wilma Abeles. *The Jews of Bohemia and Moravia.* Detroit: Wayne State University Press, 1992.

Jacobson, Kenneth. *Embattled Selves.* New York: Atlantic Monthly Press, 1994.

Jewish Publication Society of America. *The Jews of Czechoslovakia.* 3 vols. Philadelphia: Jewish Publication Society of America, 1968–83.

Karski, Jan. *Story of a Secret State.* Boston: Houghton Mifflin, 1944.

Keeler, Robert F. *Newsday: A Candid History of the Respectable Tabloid.* New York: William Morrow, 1990.

Kennan, George F. *From Prague After Munich.* Princeton, N.J.: Princeton University Press, 1968.

Korbel, Josef. *The Communist Subversion of Czechoslovakia, 1938–1948.* Princeton, N.J.: Princeton University Press, 1948.

———. *Danger in Kashmir.* Princeton, N.J.: Princeton University Press, 1954.

———. *Poland Between East and West: Soviet and German Diplomacy Toward Poland.* Princeton, N.J.: Princeton University Press, 1963.

———. *Détente in Europe: Real or Imaginary?* Princeton, N.J.: Princeton University Press, 1972.

———. *Tito's Communism.* Denver, Colo.: University of Denver Press, 1951.

———. *Twentieth Century Czechoslovakia: The Meaning of Its History.* New York: Columbia University Press, 1977.

Korbel, Madeleine Jana. *Zdenek Fierlinger's Role in the Communization of Czechoslovakia.* Wellesley, Mass.: Wellesley College, 1959.

———. *The Soviet Diplomatic Service: Profile of an Elite.* New York: Columbia University, master's thesis, 1968.

Korman, Gerd, ed. *Hunter and Hunted: Human History of the Holocaust.* New York: Viking, 1973.

Lederer, Zdenek. *Ghetto Theresienstadt.* London: Edward Goldston, 1953.

Lewis, Helen A. *Time to Speak.* New York: Carroll and Graf, 1994.

Lustig, Arnošt. *Night and Hope.* Washington: Inscape, 1996.

McKeever, Porter. *Adlai Stevenson: His Life and Legacy.* New York: William Morrow, 1989.

Maraniss, David. *First in His Class.* New York: Simon and Schuster, 1995.

Martin, Ralph G. *Cissy.* New York: Simon and Schuster, 1979.

Masaryk, Jan. *Speaking to My Country.* London: Lincolns-Prager, 1944.

Meisler, Stanley. *United Nations: The First Fifty Years.* New York: Atlantic Monthly Press, 1995.

Müller, Filip. *Eyewitness Auschwitz.* New York: Stein and Day, 1979.

Powell, Colin. *My American Journey.* New York: Random House, 1995.

Randall, Monica. *The Mansions of Long Island's Gold Coast.* New York: Rizzoli, 1987.

Rashke, Richard. *Escape from Sobibor.* New York: Houghton Mifflin, 1982.

Redlich, Gonda. *Terezín Diary.* Editor, Saul S. Friedman. Lexington: University Press of Kentucky, 1992.

Rossen, Susan F., ed. *Ivan Albright.* Chicago: Art Institute of Chicago, 1997.

Rubin, Barry. *Assimilation and Its Discontents.* New York: Times Books, 1995.

Schlesinger, Joe. *Time Zones.* Toronto: Random House, 1990.

Shirer, William L. *The Rise and Fall of the Third Reich.* New York: Fawcett Crest, 1989.

Smith, Sally Bedell. *Reflected Glory.* New York: Simon and Schuster, 1996.

Tebbel, John. *An American Dynasty: The Story of the McCormicks, Medills, and Pattersons.* New York: Greenwood Press, 1968.

Terezín Initiative. *Terezín Memorial Book: A Guide to the Czech Original.* Prague: Melantrich, 1996.

Terezínská Iniciativa. *Terezínská Pamětní Kniha* [Terezín Memorial Book]. Vols. 1 and 2. Prague: Melantrich, 1995.

Verešová, Charlotte. *Terezín Diary.* Prague: Council of Jewish Communities, 1965.

Weidenfeld, George. *Remembering My Good Friends.* London: HarperCollins, 1995.

Wheeler-Bennett, J. W. *Munich: Prologue to Tragedy.* London: Macmillan, 1948.

Witt, Linda, et al. *Running as a Woman: Gender and Power in American Politics.* New York: The Free Press, 1995.

Wood, E. Thomas. *Karski: How One Man Tried to Stop the Holocaust.* New York: John Wiley, 1994.

Ziegler, Philip. *London at War: 1939–1945.* New York: Alfred A. Knopf, 1995.

Zimmermann, Warren. *Origins of a Catastrophe.* New York: Times Books, 1996.

ACKNOWLEDGMENTS

The idea for this book arose out of reporting for *The Washington Post*, my professional home for the last eighteen years. I therefore have primarily the editors at *The Post* to thank for getting me started on researching Madeleine Albright's life and for granting me a year's leave of absence from the paper to work on this biography. I am particularly grateful for the friendship and encouragement of Steve Coll, now managing editor of *The Post*, who sent me to Prague in January 1997 for a magazine article on the Albright family's background. Coll accompanied me to my first interview with the new secretary of state and supervised publication of my initial stories on Madeleine's hitherto undiscovered past.

I have benefited greatly from the traditionally generous and liberal policy of *The Post* toward reporters with book projects. For this and many other kindnesses over the years, I owe a huge debt to the publisher of the newspaper, Don Graham, whose solicitude for his employees is surely unmatched in the industry. I want to thank Len Downie, Bob Kaiser, Karen DeYoung, Bob McCartney, Rick Atkinson, and other editors who have helped make *The Post* such a special place to work. At *The Post*, I have also benefited from the invaluable assistance of researchers Robert Thomason, Margot Williams, Kim Klein, and Alice Crites.

During the research stage of this project, I traveled widely, in America, Europe, and Israel. The list of people who offered me friendship, hospitality, and assistance is too long to enumerate, but I would particularly like to mention my colleagues David Remnick and Jeff Frank of *The New Yorker*, Robert Keeler of *Newsday*, Johnny Apple of *The New York Times*, Ann Imse of the *Rocky Mountain News*, Lee Olson, formerly of the *Denver Post*, and Laurie Hays and Carla Robbins of *The Wall Street Journal*. In the Czech Republic, I owe a huge debt to Petr Lunak, a talented diplomatic historian and researcher, who opened many doors and accompanied me to numerous interviews. Eugen and Iva Stein helped with genealogical research in Prague, and Iva Drapalova helped me track down Madeleine's cousin Dagmar Šima in January 1997, when I almost despaired of finding her. In Israel, Ramit Plusnick was an able translator. Gretchen Hoff of the Paris bureau of *The Washington Post* was very helpful. In Yugoslavia, Ljiljana Smajlović, now foreign editor of the newsmagazine *Evropljanin*, helped me find old friends of Madeleine's father, Josef Korbel, in between covering a street uprising against President Slobodan Milošević. John Pulford, of the local history society in Walton-on-Thames, England, gave me a guided tour of Madeleine's childhood haunts. Here in Washington, Flavia Sekles helped me contact Madeleine's cousins in Brazil, and Daniela Kotcharova provided translating assistance from Czech. My thanks, too, to Dita Smith of *The Washington Post,* for help with translations from German.

One of the joys of researching a biography like this is the opportunity to reconstruct people's lives from the pieces of paper diligently collected long ago by largely unknown archivists. My research has taken me from Yad Vashem in Jerusalem, one of the foremost centers for Holocaust research, to the BBC Written Archives in Caversham, England, to the magnificent holdings of the Library of Congress and National Archives in Washington, D.C. I would particularly like to thank Chris Beam of the Edmund S. Muskie archive at Bates College, Maine, Wilma Slaight of the Wellesley College archives, Robert Pastor and Martin Elzy at the Carter Center and Library in Atlanta, Karen Franklin of the Leo Baeck Institute in New York, Robin Russel and Laura Dennison of Kent School, Denver, and the staff of the Holocaust Museum and Center for Responsive Politics in Washington, D.C.

I am most grateful to Secretary of State Madeleine Albright for finding the time to meet with me twice in the fall of 1998, and go over some final points by phone in January 1999. In all, we spoke for a total of about three hours for the purposes of this book. In addition, I met with her privately four times in 1997, when I was covering the State Department for *The Post*. She is a wonderfully engaging storyteller, who can fit more interesting and amusing anecdotes into a single hour of conversation than practically anyone I know. I think it is fair to say that she approached this project with a mixture of interest, suspicion, and nervousness. Eventually, she adopted a policy of "limited cooperation," in the words of her spokesman, Jamie Rubin. Her office helped me reach a number of friends and former colleagues who might otherwise have been reluctant to speak to me, and provided some of the photographs used in this book. Rubin and chief of staff Elaine Shocas, the two people closest to the secretary at the State Department, spent ample time with me. Susie George, of the secretary's personal office, was unfailingly efficient and courteous. John Korbel met with me to discuss the question of his father's art collection. To my regret, other members of Albright's family refused to see me. The question of the family's Jewish origins remains an exceptionally delicate subject. When I attempted to do my own genealogical research at the State Archives in Prague, the relevant files, normally accessible to researchers, were closed to me at "the request of the Korbel family." In fairness, I must add that neither Albright nor her staff made any attempt to set conditions for their cooperation. Inevitably, there are passages in this book with which she and they will strongly disagree.

Numerous people have made helpful comments on the manuscript. Both David Ensor of CNN and Bart Gelman of *The Post* read the entire manuscript before publication and made many useful suggestions, saving me from a number of embarrassing errors. My agent, Rafe Sagalyn, and editor, Tracy Brown, were pillars of support from beginning to end. Jen Charat of Henry Holt helped pull the manuscript together in a very professional way. Jackie Aher did wonderful work on the family trees. At the Sagalyn agency, Amy Pastan provided a valuable critique of an early draft of the book. As usual, my most attentive reader and perceptive critic has been my wife, Lisa, who has an uncanny eye for the dull and the nonsensical. As with my last book, my parents, Joseph and Marie Dobbs, were an unstinting source of encouragement and constructive criticism. For that, and so much else, I dedicate this book to them.

MICHAEL DOBBS
Washington, January 1999

Index